Combining Mediation and Arbitration in International Commercial Dispute Resolution

Securing fast, inexpensive, and enforceable redress is vital for the development of international commerce. In a changing international commercial dispute resolution landscape, the combined use of mediation and arbitration has emerged as a dispute resolution approach which offers these benefits. However, to date there has been little agreement on several aspects of the combined use of processes, which the literature often explains by referring to the practitioner's legal culture, and there is debate as to how appropriate it is for the same neutral to conduct both mediation and arbitration.

Identifying the main ways of addressing concerns associated with the same neutral conducting both mediation and arbitration (same neutral (arb)-med-arb), this book examines how effectively these methods achieve the goal of fast, inexpensive, and enforceable dispute resolution, evaluating to what extent the perception and use of the same neutral (arb)-med-arb depends on the practitioner's legal culture, arguing that this is not a 'one-size-fits-all' process.

Presenting an empirical study of the combined use of mediation and arbitration in international commercial dispute resolution, this book synthesises existing ways of addressing concerns associated with the same neutral (arb)-med-arb to provide recommendations on how to enhance the use of combinations in the future.

Dilyara Nigmatullina is an Arbitration and Mediation Consultant and an affiliated member of Academic Staff at the University of Antwerp Faculty of Law. She holds an LLM in International Commercial Arbitration Law from Stockholm University and a PhD in Law from the University of Western Australia.

Routledge Research in International Commercial Law

Available titles in this series include:

International Commercial and Marine Arbitration
Georgios I. Zekos

International Commercial Arbitration and the Arbitrator's Contract
Emilia Onyema

Jurisdiction and Arbitration Agreements in International Commercial Law
Zheng Sophia Tang

Progressive Commercialization of Airline Governance Culture
Jan Walulik

Economic and Environmental Regulation of International Aviation
From Inter-National to Global Governance
Steven Truxal

International Dispute Resolution and the Public Policy Exception
Farshad Ghodoosi

Combining Mediation and Arbitration in International Commercial Dispute Resolution
Dilyara Nigmatullina

Combining Mediation and Arbitration in International Commercial Dispute Resolution

Dilyara Nigmatullina

Routledge
Taylor & Francis Group
LONDON AND NEW YORK

First published 2019 by Routledge

2 Park Square, Milton Park, Abingdon, Oxfordshire OX14 4RN
52 Vanderbilt Avenue, New York, NY 10017

Routledge is an imprint of the Taylor & Francis Group, an informa business

First issued in paperback 2020

British Library Cataloguing-in-Publication Data
A catalogue record for this book is available from the British Library

Library of Congress Cataloging-in-Publication Data
Names: Nigmatullina, Dilyara, author.
Title: Combining mediation and arbitration in international commercial dispute resolution / by Dilyara Nigmatullina.
Description: New York, NY : Routledge, 2018. | Series: Routledge research in international commercial law
Identifiers: LCCN 2018006612 | ISBN 9781138478404 (hardback)
Subjects: LCSH: International commercial arbitration. | Mediation. | Dispute resolution (Law)
Classification: LCC K2400 .N547 2018 | DDC 341.5/22–dc23
LC record available at https://lccn.loc.gov/2018006612

ISBN: 978-1-138-47840-4 (hbk)
ISBN: 978-0-367-58911-0 (pbk)

Typeset in Galliard
by Swales & Willis Ltd, Exeter, Devon, UK

Contents

Figures

Tables

Acknowledgements

I am immensely grateful to everyone who contributed to this book. Without your support and guidance this work would not have been possible.

I owe my greatest debt of gratitude to my supervisor Professor Robyn Carroll from the University of Western Australia (UWA) for her knowledgeable advice, insightful comments, and unwavering mentorship. My special thanks must go to my co-supervisors from UWA: Associate Professor Jill Howieson, whose expertise in empirical research assisted me greatly in designing and conducting my empirical study and reporting its results, and Adjunct Professor Kanaga Dharmananda SC, for his constructive and comprehensive comments at the key stages of the project. Sincere thanks are due to Professor Stacie Strong from the University of Missouri, Professor Luke Nottage from the University of Sydney, and Associate Professor Bobette Wolski from Bond University for extremely helpful comments on an earlier version of the manuscript when they acted as examiners of my PhD thesis. I would also like to thank Professor Thalia Kruger from the University of Antwerp and anonymous reviewers of my book proposal for their useful comments.

I wish to record my gratitude to the International Court of Arbitration of the International Chamber of Commerce, the Organising Committee of the 2014 Asia Pacific Regional Arbitration Group Conference, and the Arbitration Institute of the Stockholm Chamber of Commerce for assistance in collecting the questionnaire data. In particular, thank you to Angela Herberholz, Ron Salter, and Natalia Petrik. Collection of the questionnaire data would not have been possible without the funding of Graduate Women (WA) Inc, for which I am most grateful.

To those dispute resolution practitioners who found the time to complete the questionnaire and participate in an interview, a special thank you. In particular, I would like to thank Professor Bernardo Cremades, Professor Bernard Hanotiau, Professor Thomas J. Stipanowich, Professor Doug Jones, and Mr Christopher To.

I extend my thanks to the faculty and staff of the UWA Faculty of Law, particularly to Professor Holly Cullen and Professor Camilla Baasch Andersen for their kind assistance during my time at UWA. I would like to thank my former colleagues Madeleine Hartley, Peta-Jane Hogg, and Fiona McGaughey for their encouragement and support.

I am thankful to Professor Patricia Shaughnessy, Dr Dmitry Davydenko, and Mr Johan Billiet for inspiring me to undertake this research.

Many thanks also go to UWA and the Australian Government for funding my research and the grant of an International Postgraduate Research Scholarship. I am truly grateful for the opportunity to gain this invaluable research and life experience in Australia.

Finally, I am greatly indebted to my parents, my partner and my sister for all their optimism, loving support, endless care, patience, and understanding throughout this journey. I dedicate this book to them.

Part I

Introduction

1 Introduction

Everything changes and nothing stands still.[1] The dispute resolution landscape is no exception.[2] While initially, the international commercial arbitration community praised arbitration for its flexibility and expedition, this process has recently drawn criticism for becoming as slow and expensive as judicial proceedings, if not more so.[3]

A number of empirical studies provide evidence of the discontent of users with the international arbitration process due to the escalated costs and protracted proceedings. For example, in a 2006 survey conducted by the School of International Arbitration (SIA), Queen Mary University of

1 Heraclitus, a Greek philosopher, quoted in Plato, *Cratylus*, in IV *Plato in Twelve Volumes* 383, 401d (Harold N. Fowler trans., Cambridge, MA: Harvard University Press, 1921).

2 The focus of this book is international (cross-border) commercial dispute resolution.

3 *See, e.g.*, Joerg Risse, *Ten Drastic Proposals for Saving Time and Costs in Arbitral Proceedings*, 29(3) Arb. Int'l. 453, 453 (2013); Lucy Greenwood, *A Window of Opportunity? Building a Short Period of Time into Arbitral Rules in order for Parties to Explore Settlement*, 27(2) Arb. Int'l. 199, 199–200 (2011); Bobette Wolski, *Arb-Med-Arb (and MSAs): A Whole Which Is Less than, not Greater than, the Sum of Its Parts?* 6(2) Contemp. Asia Arb. J. 249, 255 (2013); Tai-Heng Cheng, *International Mediation, Arbitration, and Innovation*, in *Contemporary Issues in International Arbitration and Mediation: The Fordham Papers 2010*, 434 (Arthur W. Rovine ed., Brill 2011); S. I. Strong, *Beyond International Commercial Arbitration? The Promise of International Commercial Mediation*, 45 Wash. U. J. L. & Pol'y 10, 26 (2014); Luke Nottage, *Drafting Arbitration Clauses to Minimise Costs and Delays in International Commercial Arbitration: An Asia-Pacific Perspective*, Japanese Law and the Asia-Pacific (16 May 2011), available at <http://blogs.usyd.edu.au/japaneselaw/2011/05/> (accessed 27 Mar. 2018); Sundaresh Menon, Keynote Address, *International Arbitration: The Coming of a New Age for Asia (and Elsewhere)*, ICCA ¶¶ 30, 35 (ICCA 2012 Congress, Jun. 2012), available at <www.arbitration-icca.org/AV_Library/AV_Library_textformat/ICCA_2012_Singapore_Keynote_Menon.html> (accessed 27 Mar. 2018); Fan Kun, *The Risks of Apparent Bias When an Arbitrator Acts as a Mediator: Remarks on Hong Kong Court's Decision in Gao Haiyan*, 13 Y. B. Private Int'l. L. 535, 549 (2011); *but see* Remy Gerbay, *Is the End Nigh Again: An Empirical Assessment of the 'Judicialization' of International Arbitration*, 25(2) Am. Rev. Int'l Arb. 223, 239 n. 76 (2014) (observing that the concerns about arbitration's judicialisation (that is believed to be a cause of increased costs and delay in arbitration) are not a recent phenomenon).

London, expense and the length of time to resolve disputes were the two most commonly cited disadvantages of international arbitration.[4] Participants of a 2010 study of the Corporate Counsel International Arbitration Group reiterated concerns over costs and delays in arbitration proceedings.[5] A more recent 2015 SIA survey similarly found that cost is seen as arbitration's worst feature, followed by, among others, lack of speed.[6]

Many factors have contributed to the growing concerns over the costs and delays of arbitration proceedings. These factors include counsel fees,[7] fees of arbitrators and institutions,[8] the procedures and methods employed,[9] the limited possibility of appeal and minimal curial intervention,[10] and parties' fixation with involving the best arbitrators and lawyers in the process.[11]

Despite concerns over costs and delays, arbitration seems to still be the preferred means for resolving international commercial disputes,[12] mostly because it is better adapted to the special environment of international commercial disputes than litigation.[13] Neutrality and enforceability, rather

4 School of International Arbitration (Queen Mary, University of London), *2006 International Arbitration Study: Corporate Attitudes and Practices*, available at <www.arbitration.qmul.ac.uk/research/2006/> (accessed 14 Jan. 2018).

5 Andreas Respondek, *Five Proposals to Further Increase the Efficiency of International Arbitration Proceedings*, 31(4) J. Int'l. Arb. 507, 507–508 (2014) (reporting results of a 2010 study of the Corporate Counsel International Arbitration Group).

6 School of International Arbitration (Queen Mary, University of London), *2015 International Arbitration Survey: Improvements and Innovations in International Arbitration*, available at <www.arbitration.qmul.ac.uk/research/2015/index.html> (accessed 14 Jan. 2018).

7 Menon, *supra* n. 3, at ¶ 35; Cheng, *supra* n. 3, at 438; Arthur Marriott, *Litigate, Arbitrate, Mediate – Frustrate? Breaking the Dispute Deadlock*, Clayton Utz, available at <www.claytonutz.com/ialecture/2005/transcript_2005.html> (accessed 14 Jan. 2018); *Q&A with Professor Pierre Lalive*, 3(5) Global Arb. Rev. 1, 3 (2008) (reporting results of an empirical study).

8 Examples from case law show parties' discontent with fees of arbitrators and institutions. Two cases dealt with challenges of arbitrator and institutional fees for their excessiveness: *Coffee Beanery v. WW, LLC*, No. 07-1830, 2008 U.S. App. LEXIS 23645 (6th Cir. 14 Nov. 2008) and *Soyak Int'l Constr. & Investment Inc. v. Hobér, Kraus & Melis*, No. Ö 4227-06 (3 Dec. 2008) (Swedish Supreme Court) cited in Menon, *supra* n. 3, at ¶ 35. In one Singaporean case a party attempted, though unsuccessfully, to challenge the costs awarded by a tribunal as being disproportionate and contrary to public policy. *VV and anor v. VW* [2008] 2 SLR(R) 929 cited in Menon, *supra* n. 3, at ¶ 35.

9 Marriott, *supra* n. 7; Greenwood, *supra* n. 3, at 200.

10 Menon, *supra* n. 3, at ¶ 25.

11 *Ibid*, at ¶ 35.

12 Gary B. Born, *International Commercial Arbitration*, 93–97 (2d ed., Kluwer Law International 2014); *2006 International Arbitration Study: Corporate Attitudes and Practices, supra* n. 4; *2015 International Arbitration Survey: Improvements and Innovations in International Arbitration, supra* n. 6.

13 Cheng, *supra* n. 3, at 434–435.

than high speed and low cost, emerge as the true drivers behind the use of arbitration for international disputes.[14] The selection of arbitrators with specialist competencies and the privacy afforded by the process might be others.[15]

As concerns over the effectiveness of international arbitration remain, the time is right for reforms in the field of international commercial arbitration.[16] Reforms could focus on improving efficiency within the arbitration process and creating better conditions for settlement.[17]

It appears that, so far, the international arbitration community has concentrated on the former, rather than the latter.[18] In recent years, arbitration institutions have introduced, for example, fast-track proceedings and emergency arbitration. There is probably no international arbitration institution that has not revised its rules to speed up the arbitration process.[19] Despite these and other measures, there has been little visible improvement in recent years in the management of arbitrations,[20] while delays seem to be on the rise.[21] The common call is to use stand-alone mediation and a combination

14 Gerbay, *supra* n. 3, at 246–247; Greenwood, *supra* n. 3, at 204; Strong *supra* n. 3, at 27–28; Final Report of the CEDR Commission on Settlement in International Arbitration (Nov. 2009), ¶ 1.1, available at <www.cedr.com/about_us/arbitration_commission/> (accessed 27 Mar. 2018) [hereinafter, CEDR Final Report]. The reasons why parties choose arbitration over litigation for international disputes differ from those for domestic disputes. *See, e.g.*, Christopher R. Drahozal & Stephen J. Ware, *Why Do Businesses Use (or Not Use) Arbitration Clauses?* 25 Ohio St. J. on Disp. Res. 433, 451–452 (2010).

15 Cheng, *supra* n. 3, at 435; Menon, *supra* n. 3, at ¶ 8.

16 *See, e.g.*, Bernd Ehle, *The Arbitrator as a Settlement Facilitator* in *Walking A Thin Line – What an Arbitrator Can Do, Must Do or Must Not Do, Recent Developments and Trends* 77, 94 (Bruylant 2010); Menon, *supra* n. 3, at ¶¶ 42–50; Respondek, *supra* n. 5, at 508; Thomas J. Stipanowich & Zachary P. Ulrich, *Commercial Arbitration and Settlement: Empirical Insights into the Roles Arbitrators Play*, 6 Y.B. On Arb. Mediation 1, 5–6 (2014); Nottage, *supra* n. 3.

17 Greenwood, *supra* n. 3, at 200–201, 205; Stipanowich & Ulrich, *supra* n. 16, at 6.

18 Greenwood, *supra* n. 3, at 205.

19 *See, e.g.*, International Court of Arbitration of the International Chamber of Commerce (ICC) Rules of Arbitration, arts. 22(1), 25(1), 30 (effective 1 Mar. 2017), available at <https://iccwbo.org/dispute-resolution-services/arbitration/rules-of-arbitration/> (accessed 27 Mar. 2018) [hereinafter, ICC Rules of Arbitration]; London Court of International Arbitration (LCIA) Arbitration Rules, art. 14.4(ii) (effective 1 Oct. 2014), available at <www.lcia.org/Dispute_Resolution_Services/lcia-arbitration-rules-2014.aspx> (accessed 27 Mar. 2018) [hereinafter, LCIA Arbitration Rules].

20 Greenwood, *supra* n. 3, at 204.

21 Respondek, *supra* n. 5, at 509.

of mediation and arbitration.[22] This call is supported by recent empirical findings.[23]

Increasingly disenchanted with lengthy and costly international arbitration, parties are choosing mediation as an alternative.[24] While arbitration is often referred to as the 'new litigation', mediation has now been coined the 'new arbitration'.[25] Although the extent to which mediation is practised is not yet comparable to that of arbitration, it appears to be constantly growing.[26]

22 Greenwood, *supra* n. 3, at 200–201 (referring to a solution proposed by a team of in-house counsel at the round table discussion on the issue of increased time and cost of international arbitration organised by Global Arbitration Review); Gabrielle Kaufmann-Kohler, *When Arbitrators Facilitate Settlement: Towards a Transnational Standard*, Clayton Utz, available at <www.claytonutz.com/ialecture/2007/transcript_2007.html> (accessed 14 Jan. 2018) (expecting that arbitration will develop new less formal ways of resolving disputes: resorting to (separate) mediation may be one, having an arbitrator act as mediator may be another); Kun, *supra* n. 3, at 549 (observing that because arbitration is now being criticized for becoming 'judicialized', due to the slowness and expensiveness of the procedure, practitioners are beginning to see the merits of integrating mediation and other alternative dispute resolution (ADR) means into arbitration); Nottage, *supra* n. 3 (suggesting that costs and delays be managed by, among other measures, using Arb-Med – authorising tribunal (in writing) to facilitate settlement during proceedings); Ehle, *supra* n. 16, at 94 (observing that although no established transnational consensus exists on how the international arbitrator may meet users' expectations of more efficient process, the trend clearly favours the arbitrator as a more active settlement facilitator); Stipanowich & Ulrich, *supra* n. 16, at 6 (noting that while early settlement of a dispute can be a uniquely effective way of minimising cost and length of a dispute resolution process, the role of arbitrators in promoting informal settlement has not been sufficiently looked into, at least in places like the US).

23 The participants of the Global Pound Conference Series 2016–2017 survey ranked combining adjudicative and non-adjudicative processes (*e.g.*, arbitration/litigation with mediation/conciliation) and non-adjudicative dispute resolution methods (mediation or conciliation) as top second (45%) and third (43%) processes respectively that should be prioritised to improve the future of commercial dispute resolution. Pre-dispute or pre-escalation processes to prevent disputes were ranked as priority number one (51%). Greater emphasis on collaborative instead of adversarial processes was ranked first in response to the question about trends with the most significant influence on the future of commercial dispute resolution (57%) *Global Pound Conference Series 2016–17 Cumulated Data Results March 2016–September 2017*, Global Pound, available at <http://globalpound.org/wp-content/uploads/2017/11/2017-09-18-Final-GPC-Series-Results-Cumulated-Votes-from-the-GPC-App-Mar.-2016-Sep.-2017.pdf> (accessed 14 Jan. 2018) [hereinafter, GPC Cumulated Data Results]. *See* further discussion of GPC survey and its limitations in Section 3.2.1 *infra*.

24 Donna Ross, *Med-Arb/Arb-Med: A More Efficient ADR Process or an Invitation to a Potential Ethical Disaster?* in *Contemporary Issues in International Arbitration and Mediation: The Fordham Papers 2012* 352, 353 (Arthur W. Rovine ed., Martinus Nijhoff 2013).

25 *Ibid.*

26 Ximena Bustamante Vasconez, *The Mediated Settlement Agreement*, 28(3) J. Int'l. Arb. 283, 283 (2011); UNCITRAL, *Planned and Possible Future Work – Part III, Proposal by the Government of the United States of America: Future Work for Working Group II (A/CN.9/822)* (47th Session, 7–18 Jul. 2014, New York), 2, available at <www.uncitral.org/uncitral/en/commission/sessions/47th.html> (accessed 27 Mar. 2018) [hereinafter, *Future Work for Working Group II*]. The extent of the use of mediation, however, varies greatly from jurisdiction to jurisdiction. For example, in the European Union (EU) one study showed that while in one country a reported number of

Legislation on mediation has been enacted in an increasing number of jurisdictions.[27] Mediation institutes and training for mediators have proliferated.[28] Bustamante Vasconez even argues that mediation is becoming the best alternative to international litigation.[29]

Parties benefit from mediation because it offers them the ability to control the process and tailor their own solution in a setting that helps preserve their relationship.[30] Mediation is also praised for outstanding settlement rates.[31]

Nevertheless, it appears that the mediation of many international commercial disputes does not constitute the quick, easy and inexpensive dispute resolution process that many commercial actors envision.[32] Contributing to this is the increasing complexity of international commercial disputes and the involvement of many participants, which presents some additional challenges, non-existent in a two-party process.[33] Cheng even contends that there may be little or no difference in costs involved in international mediation and international arbitration.[34] According to Cheng, this is because the most expensive items in a dispute resolution

mediation cases exceeded 200,000 annually, in the next three countries that number exceeded 10,000, and in many EU Member States a reported number of mediation cases per year was fewer than 500. *See* European Parliament, Directorate-General for Internal Policies, Policy Department, Citizen's Rights and Constitutional Affairs, *Rebooting the Mediation Directive: Assessing the Limited Impact of its Implementation and Proposing Measures to Increase the Number of Mediations in the EU* (2014), available at <www.adrcenterinternational.com/wp-content/uploads/2015/07/IPOL-JURI_ET2014493042_EN.pdf> (accessed 27 Mar. 2018) [hereinafter, *Rebooting the Mediation Directive Study*].

27 UNCITRAL, *Settlement of Commercial Disputes. International Commercial Conciliation: Enforceability of Settlement Agreements. Note by the Secretariat (A/CN.9/WG.II/WP.190)*, ¶ 10 (13 Jul. 2015), available at <www.uncitral.org/uncitral/en/commission/working_groups/2Arbitration.html> (accessed 27 Mar. 2018) [hereinafter, *2015 Note by the Secretariat*]; Sophie Pouget, *Arbitrating and Mediating Disputes, Benchmarking Arbitration and Mediation Regimes for Commercial Disputes Related to Foreign Direct Investment*, 9 (The World Bank, Policy Research Working Paper 6632, October 2013).

28 UNCITRAL, *Settlement of Commercial Disputes: Enforceability of Settlement Agreements Resulting from International Commercial Conciliation/Mediation. Note by the Secretariat (A/CN.9/WG.II/WP.187)*, paras 16–17, Annex 1 (27 Nov. 2014), available at <www.uncitral.org/uncitral/en/commission/working_groups/2Arbitration.html> (accessed 27 Mar. 2018) [hereinafter, *2014 Note by the Secretariat*].

29 *See, e.g.*, Bustamante Vasconez, *supra* n. 26, at 283.

30 *See, e.g.*, Edna Sussman, *Combinations and Permutations of Arbitration and Mediation: Issues and Solutions*, in *ADR in Business: Practice and Issues across Countries and Cultures* vol II 381, 381–382 (Arnold Ingen-Housz ed., Kluwer Law International 2011); Wolski, *supra* n. 3, at 255; *Model Law on International Commercial Conciliation of the United Nations Commission on International Trade Law*, G. A. Res. 57/18, A/RES/57/18 (2002), 1, available at <www.uncitral.org/uncitral/en/GA/resolutions.html> (accessed 14 Jan. 2018).

31 *See, e.g.*, Bustamante Vasconez, *supra* n. 26, at 283.

32 Strong, *supra* n. 3, at 18–24.

33 *Ibid.*

34 Cheng, *supra* n. 3, at 438.

budget are the fees of counsel and experts that are similar in international mediation and arbitration.[35]

Researchers and practitioners in some countries argue that mediation is not a viable mechanism on its own and its likely future lies with integration in other dispute resolution mechanisms.[36] One of the most frequently cited impediments for more widespread use of mediation as a stand-alone method of international commercial dispute resolution is the lack of a coherent enforcement mechanism for international mediated settlement agreements.[37] As explained in the next paragraph, the combined use of mediation and arbitration offers parties a chance to remove this impediment.

The use of mediation and arbitration in combination is not new,[38] and its practice has ancient roots.[39] The combined use of mediation and arbitration (combinations), and particularly the combination where the same neutral[40] acts as a mediator and an arbitrator (same neutral (arb)-med-arb), may provide parties with a process that is faster and less expensive, as compared to arbitration used on its own.[41] In addition, it allows parties to convert their mediated settlement agreement into a consent arbitral award that is, arguably, enforceable worldwide pursuant to the New York Convention.[42]

Despite these and other advantages, dispute resolution practitioners around the world express different, and sometimes conflicting, views about a number of

35 *Ibid.*

36 Barbara Baarsma and Maurits Barendrecht, *Mediation 2.0*, Hiil Innovating Justice, available at <www.hiil.org/project/mediation-2-0?goback=%2Egmp_1863991%2Egde_1863991_member_123727192> (accessed 14 Jan. 2018).

37 Geoff Sharp, *The Handbrake on Global Mediation*, Kluwer Mediation Blog (31 Aug. 2012), available at <http://mediationblog.kluwerarbitration.com/2012/08/31/the-handbrake-on-global-mediation/> (accessed 27 Mar. 2018); *Future Work for Working Group II, supra* n. 26, at 2–3; Wolski, *supra* n. 3, at 255; *Rebooting the Mediation Directive Study, supra* n. 26, at 160. To address this impediment, UNCITRAL started in 2014 considering the feasibility of the preparation of a convention on enforcement of settlement agreements resulting from international commercial mediation. For further discussion of this issue, *see* section 3.2.2 *infra.*

38 Wolski, *supra* n. 3, at 257; Mercedes Tarrazon, *Arb-Med: A Reflection a Propos of a Bolivian Experience*, 2(1) NYSBA New York Disp. Res. Law. 87, 87 (2009) (noting that a combination of mediation and arbitration has been the customary practice in many jurisdictions throughout the world, including Latin America).

39 Derek Roebuck, *The Myth of Modern Mediation*, 73(1) Arb. 105, 106 (2007) (observing that everywhere in the Ancient Greek world, including Ptolemaic Egypt, arbitration was normal, and in arbitration the mediation element was primary; mediation was attempted first and a mediated settlement was preferred).

40 For the purposes of this book, 'a neutral' means a neutral third party requested to resolve or assist in resolving a dispute in which the third party has no financial, official, or personal interest.

41 *See* discussion in Section 3.2.1 *infra.*

42 Convention on the Recognition and Enforcement of Foreign Arbitral Awards, 10 Jun. 1958, E/CONF.26/8/Rev.1. At the moment of writing 159countries are parties to this Convention, according to the UNCITRAL website <www.uncitral.org/uncitral/en/uncitral_texts/arbitration/NYConvention_status.html> (accessed 10 Apr. 2018).

aspects of the combined use of processes. Commentators often explain this divide in views by reference to the practitioners' legal culture.[43] In particular, no agreement exists on whether it is appropriate for the same neutral to act as both a mediator and an arbitrator in the same dispute.[44] In the same neutral (arb)-med-arb, caucuses become the most problematic issue. This is largely due to the danger that an arbitrator will appear to or actually lack impartiality and the risk that the process may offend the principles of due process.[45] As a consequence, the arbitrator and the award resulting from the same neutral (arb)-med-arb may be challenged. The pitfalls of enforcing international arbitral awards resulting from the same neutral (arb)-med-arb are illustrated by *Gao Haiyan*, a case to which some commentators attribute the recent emergence of the same neutral (arb)-med-arb as a 'hot topic' among practitioners.[46]

This book investigates the value of combinations in international commercial dispute resolution. The current demands of international business for more efficient dispute resolution solutions and yet-untapped potential[47] of combinations justify this investigation.

Moreover, even though academic debate is ongoing about acceptable ways of combining mediation and arbitration, there is little evidence to suggest that practitioners actually use any combinations. The author has found no empirical research focused on the combined use of processes in an international commercial dispute resolution context. Existing empirical studies either explore how particular questions related to the combined use of processes are dealt with in certain jurisdictions[48] or constitute part of broad-based inquiries into the practice of

43 For the purposes of this book, 'a practitioner' means a dispute resolution practitioner with or without a legal qualification. *See* discussion of the influence of the practitioners' legal culture on their perception of the same neutral (arb)-med-arb in Chapter 4 *infra*.

44 *See, e.g.*, Ross, *supra* n. 24, at 352; *see also* Michael E. Schneider, *Combining Arbitration with Conciliation*, in *International Dispute Resolution: Towards an International Arbitration Culture*, 8 ICCA Congress Series 57, 77 (Albert Jan van den Berg ed., Kluwer Law International 1998).

45 *See* discussion in Section 3.3 *infra*.

46 *See* discussion of this case in Sections 8.2.2.3.1.2 and 9.5.2 *infra*.

47 Haig Oghigian, *Perspectives from Japan: A New Concept in Dispute Resolution – the Mediation – Arbitration Hybrid*, 2(1) NYSBA New York Disp. Res. Law. 110, 112 (2009) (noting that 'the suggestions put forward … are meant to stimulate dialogue and attract comments from other practitioners and academics who may have innovative suggestions on how to better make the med-arb hybrid an effective tool for alternative dispute resolution'); Pierre Tercier, *Foreword*, in *ADR in Business: Practice and Issues across Countries and Cultures* vol I xxi, xxiii (J. C. Goldsmith et al. eds, Kluwer Law International 2006) (observing that '[a]rbitration and ADR are … complementary … [t]he problem is how to combine them so as to benefit from the synergy they are capable of offering').

48 *See, e.g.*, Donald E. Conlon et al., *Putting the Cart Before the Horse: The Benefits of Arbitrating Before Mediating*, 87(5) J. Applied Psychol. 978 (2002) (where the authors examine the impact of mediation-arbitration and arbitration-mediation and three disputant dyadic structures (individual vs. individual, individual vs. team, and team vs. team) on various dispute outcomes; participants were undergraduate students from a large mid-western US university);

international dispute resolution.[49] These do not provide significant insight into the dynamics of the combined use of processes as a discrete dispute resolution approach.[50] Commentators expressly recognise the lack of empirical research related to the combined use of processes[51] and specifically invite researchers to conduct studies to remedy this deficit.[52] Taking up these invitations, the author conducted an empirical study investigating the use of combinations in international commercial dispute resolution for the purposes of this book. Its results are presented in Part III.

The same neutral (arb)-med-arb is the central combination for this book for two reasons. First, as noted in Section 3.2, the same neutral (arb)-med-arb appears to be a combination with the most potential for the increased time and cost efficiency of dispute resolution, as compared to arbitration and other

Neil B. McGillicuddy et al., *Third-Party Intervention: a Field Experiment Comparing Three Different Models*, 53(1) J. Personality & Soc. Psychol. 104 (1987) (where the authors conducted a field experiment at a community mediation centre to test the impact on behaviour in mediation of three models of third-party intervention; third parties and disputants were randomly assigned to one of three conditions: (a) straight mediation; (b) mediation-arbitration (same); or (c) mediation-arbitration (different); the data was collected at the Dispute Settlement Center of Western New York); Gerald F. Phillips, *The Survey Says: Practitioners Cautiously Move Toward Accepting Same-Neutral Med-Arb, But Party Sophistication Is Mandatory*, 26(5) Alternatives 101 (2008) (where the author surveyed US commercial arbitrators and mediators; the survey questions addressed mostly practitioners' perceptions of the same neutral med-arb).

49 *See, e.g.*, Christian Bühring-Uhle et al., *Arbitration and Mediation in International Business*, 105 (2d ed., Kluwer Law International 2006) (where the authors surveyed in-house counsel, advocates and arbitrators/mediators globally on the practice of international business dispute resolution; the survey included questions about the explicit integration of elements of mediation in arbitral proceedings); empirical studies conducted by the School of International Arbitration (Queen Mary, University of London) in 2006, 2008, 2010, 2012, 2013, 2015, 2016 and 2018 available at <www.arbitration.qmul.ac.uk/research/index.html> (accessed 14 Jan. 2018); Thomas J. Stipanowich & J. Ryan Lamare, *Living with ADR: Evolving Perceptions and Use of Mediation, Arbitration and Conflict Management in Fortune 1000 Corporations*, 19 Harv. Negot. L. Rev. 1 (2014) (where the survey aimed to obtain information regarding the use of mediation, arbitration, and other ADR approaches by major US corporations).

50 Stipanowich & Lamare, *supra* n. 49, at 67.

51 *See, e.g.*, Richard P. Flake, *MED/ARB – A Viable ADR Vehicle? Nuances of Med/Arb—A Neutral's Perspective*, CEDIRES 2, available at <www.cedires.com/index_bestanden/FLAKE_http-www.cbylaw.com-filebin_files_flake_rpf-AAA_Med-Arb.pdf> (accessed 14 Jan. 2018) (observing that '[w]hile there is more recent literature on the med-arb process, mostly from the theoretical perspective, field studies are still largely anecdotal').

52 Stipanowich & Lamare, *supra* n. 49, at 67 (concluding that broad-based surveys offer a springboard for research on the performance and effectiveness of multi-step dispute resolution approaches, among other areas of interest); International Institute for Conflict Prevention and Resolution, *Attitudes Toward ADR in the Asia-Pacific Region: A CPR Survey*, available at <www.cpradr.org/strategy/international-initiatives/asia/asia/_res/id=Attachments/index=0/asia-pacific-survey.pdf> (accessed 14 Jan. 2018) (recognising the need to develop and deploy a survey to achieve more detailed measurement of forms of mediation, including a combination of mediation and arbitration, in use, because the actual use of mediation appeared to lag behind positive attitudes toward mediation).

combinations. Second, as discussed in Section 3.3, the same neutral (arb)-med-arb is a combination that raises numerous concerns, particularly in some jurisdictions. The book aims to explore ways to address concerns associated with the same neutral (arb)-med-arb, which should allow parties to benefit from the time and cost efficiency of the process and an internationally enforceable result. In addition, the book sets out to examine whether the perception and use of the same neutral (arb)-med-arb varies depending on the practitioners' legal culture. In particular, the book is going to address the following five questions:

1 What are the advantages and concerns associated with the same neutral (arb)-med-arb?
2 What is the influence of the practitioners' legal culture on their perception and use of the same neutral (arb)-med-arb?
3 What is the current state of use of combinations, including the same neutral (arb)-med-arb, in international commercial dispute resolution, and how are they perceived?
4 How can the concerns associated with the same neutral (arb)-med-arb be addressed?
5 How can the use of the same neutral (arb)-med-arb and other combinations in international commercial dispute resolution be enhanced?

In terms of methodology, the book involved an analysis of primary and secondary legal sources complemented by empirical research. A review of legal sources provided the theoretical foundation for the design of the empirical study that comprised two phases.

The first phase employed a questionnaire to investigate the current use of mediation in combination with arbitration in international commercial dispute resolution and how combinations are perceived. It was conducted between February and June 2014 and involved 81 participants. The analysis of the questionnaire data in the context of legal sources assisted in defining the scope of the second phase of the empirical study undertaken through semi-structured interviews.

The second phase involved interviews with six highly experienced international commercial dispute resolution practitioners.[53] The interviews were conducted in March and April 2015 and aimed to elicit views about the most significant questionnaire results and explore ways to enhance the use of the combined processes in international commercial dispute resolution.

The methodology of each phase is described in more detail in Sections 5.2.1 and 5.3.1, respectively.

The book is divided into five parts. This chapter comprises Part I and provides an introduction to the book.

53 As explained in section 5.3.1.1 *infra*, although 13 professionals were invited to participate in an interview, only six of them accepted the invitation.

Part II consists of three chapters (Chapters 2, 3, and 4). It lays out the theoretical foundation for this work, in general and for the design of the empirical study in Part III, in particular. Chapter 2 synthesises the existing approaches to defining terms denoting various combinations, and formulates definitions of the terms used to denote the key combinations in this book. This is necessary because of the lack of clarity that surrounds the use of terms denoting various combinations. Chapter 3 examines advantages and concerns associated with the same neutral (arb)-med-arb. It also analyses a challenge posed by the same neutral (arb)-med-arb to dual role neutrals. Chapter 4 explores the influence of the practitioners' legal culture on their perception and use of the same neutral (arb)-med-arb in different jurisdictions in the world and analyses the ongoing changes and adaptations in this field.

Part III comprises Chapter 5 that presents and discusses the key results of the two-phase empirical study carried out for the purposes of this book.

Part IV consists of three chapters (Chapters 6, 7, and 8) that investigate ways to address concerns associated with the same neutral (arb)-med-arb discussed in Chapter 3. It identifies three major ways to address these concerns: first, by involving different neutrals in each, mediation and arbitration, phase of combinations; second, by modifying the same neutral (arb)-med-arb procedure; and third, by implementing safeguards for using the same neutral (arb)-med-arb. These three ways are examined in Chapters 6, 7, and 8, respectively.

Part V comprises the final Chapter 9 that investigates initiatives directed to enhance the use of the same neutral (arb)-med-arb and other combinations in international commercial dispute resolution.

Part II
Theoretical foundations

Part II comprises three chapters and lays out the theoretical foundation for this work. Chapter 2 synthesises the existing approaches to defining terms denoting various combinations and formulates definitions of the terms denoting the key combinations described in this book. Importantly, Chapter 2 coins the term 'the same neutral (arb)-med-arb' to denote the central combination for this book. Chapter 3 draws on the extensive literature to examine advantages and concerns associated with the same neutral (arb)-med-arb. Chapter 4 reviews the literature, including a number of empirical studies, to investigate the influence of the practitioners' legal culture on their perception and use of the same neutral (arb)-med-arb in different jurisdictions in the world. On the basis of the theoretical foundation laid out in Part II, the two-phase empirical study was designed and conducted for the purposes of this book. Its results are presented and discussed in Part III.

2 Key combinations, terms, and definitions

2.1 Introduction

This chapter demonstrates the lack of clarity surrounding the use of terms denoting various combinations and proposes remedies to this situation by formulating definitions of the terms denoting the key combinations in this book.

Clarity in the terminology is paramount to parties and neutrals intending to use combinations. This is because mediation and arbitration can be combined in different ways and every combination has its specific characteristics, advantages and concerns associated with its use. Prior to embarking on any combination, it is necessary to make sure that all participants of a dispute resolution process know exactly what combination they are about to use, what advantages and concerns are associated with its use, and what safeguards, if any, they need to implement. This course of action will allow parties to maximise advantages of any combination and minimise concerns associated with its use.

Before examining the terminology used to denote various combinations, it is important to define the terms 'mediation', 'arbitration', and 'the combined use of mediation and arbitration'.

For the purposes of this book, **'mediation'** means an assisted decision-making process in which the mediator assists parties in making decisions about the issues in dispute between them.[1] This book uses the term mediation interchangeably with conciliation in a broad sense, which encompasses different models of mediation practice, including facilitative and evaluative.[2]

Throughout the book, the term **'arbitration'** is used to refer to a means by which disputes can be definitively resolved, pursuant to the parties' agreement, by

1 This definition is based on the discussion of mediation in Nadja Alexander, *International Comparative Mediation: Legal Perspectives (Global Trends in Dispute Resolution)*, 12–17 (Kluwer Law International 2009). On key differences between the processes of mediation and arbitration, *see* Section 3.3 *infra*. On differences between the roles of a mediator and an arbitrator, *see* Section 5.2.3.2.4 *infra*.

2 Evaluative and facilitative models of mediation practice are defined in Section 5.2.1.3 *infra*.

independent, non-governmental decision-makers, selected by or for the parties, applying neutral judicial procedures that provide the parties with an opportunity to be heard.[3]

The term **'the combined use of mediation and arbitration'**, or simply **'combinations'**, is used to denote the actual use of the discrete processes of mediation and arbitration in combination. It includes any combination of processes in whatever order and whether conducted by the same or different neutrals. This definition is intentionally broad to encompass all combinations. This, however, calls for the use of more specific terms to denote particular combinations.

Mediation and arbitration can be combined in sequence, in parallel and otherwise.[4] Commentators employ different terms to denote various combinations, often attributing different meanings to the same term, while using the same term to denote different combinations. For example, Sawada notes that the expressions 'hybrid', 'arb-med', and 'med-arb' are sometimes used synonymously to refer to any process involving some interrelation of arbitration and mediation, whereas on other occasions these terms are used to refer to distinct processes.[5] To avoid the confusion that can result, this chapter synthesises approaches to defining terms used to denote various combinations and formulates definitions of the terms denoting the key combinations in this book. For ease of understanding, the definitions presented in this chapter are summarised in Appendix 1.

This chapter comprises two sections. 'Med-arb', the most common term used to denote the combined use of mediation and arbitration, is the focus of Section 2.2. This section suggests the use of the term 'the same neutral med-arb' rather than 'med-arb' to denote a combination where the same neutral acts first as a mediator and then as an arbitrator. To justify this suggestion, Section 2.2 explores differing interpretations of med-arb. This section concludes by specifying the meaning of med-arb and its two main variations, the same neutral med-arb and diff neutral med-arb for the purposes of the book.

Section 2.3 provides an overview of combinations other than med-arb, examines terms used to denote them, and defines the terms denoting the key combinations for the purposes of the book. Importantly, this section coins the term the same neutral (arb)-med-arb to denote the central combination for this book. Key combinations introduced in Section 2.3 are explored further in Chapters 6 and 7 in the context of addressing concerns associated with the same neutral (arb)-med-arb discussed in Section 3.3.

3 Gary B. Born, *International Commercial Arbitration*, 70 (2d ed., Kluwer Law International 2014).

4 Jeremy Lack, *Appropriate Dispute Resolution (ADR): The Spectrum of Hybrid Techniques Available to the Parties*, in *ADR in Business: Practice and Issues across Countries and Cultures* vol. II 339, 357–372 (Arnold Ingen-Housz ed., Kluwer Law International 2011).

5 Toshio Sawada, *Hybrid Arb-Med: Will West and East Never Meet?* 14(2) ICC Int'l Ct. Arb. Bull. 29, 29 (Fall 2003).

All combinations introduced in this chapter are valuable flexible process design options that parties might find useful depending on the particular circumstances of their case. Training of dispute resolution practitioners in flexible process design is one of the initiatives to enhance the use of combinations that will be discussed in Section 9.5.3.

2.2 Med-arb, the same neutral med-arb, and diff neutral med-arb

This book uses the term 'the same neutral med-arb' to refer to the sequential use of mediation and arbitration, with the mediation phase taking place first, where the same neutral acts as the mediator and the arbitrator. As explained further, the book uses this term instead of a more common 'med-arb' to distinguish it from the process where mediation is followed by arbitration using a different neutral.

2.2.1 Lack of clarity surrounding the term 'med-arb'

Med-arb appears to be the most common term used in the literature to refer to the combined use of mediation and arbitration.[6] Another frequently used term is arb-med; however, often arb-med is perceived as merely a variation of the original med-arb.[7] For this reason, arb-med will be discussed in Section 2.3.1.

Despite its common use, the term med-arb lacks a generally accepted definition.[8] Approaches to defining this term vary. The major point of difference in definitions is whether med-arb is understood only as a process where both mediation and arbitration stages are conducted by the same neutral, or whether the term encompasses situations where different neutrals are involved in each stage.[9]

2.2.1.1 Med-arb as a process conducted by a dual role neutral

De Vera defines med-arb as a process in which the same neutral serves both as the mediator and the arbitrator if the matter is not settled in

6 Harold I. Abramson, *Protocols for International Arbitrators Who Dare to Settle Cases*, 10 Am. Rev. Int'l Arb. 1, 2 n. 1 (1999).

7 *See, e.g.*, Richard Fullerton, *The Ethics of Mediation-Arbitration*, 38(5) Colorado Law. 31, 36 (2009); James T. Peter, *Note & Comment: Med-Arb in International Arbitration*, 8 Am. Rev. Int'l Arb. 83, 100 (1997).

8 Richard Hill, *MED-ARB: New Coke or Swatch?* 13(1) Arb. Int'l. 105, 105 (1997); Fullerton, *supra* n. 7, at 33; John T. Blankenship, *Developing Your ADR Attitude: Med-Arb, a Template for Adaptive ADR*, 42(11) Tennessee Bar J. 28, 29–30 (2006).

9 Other criteria may be employed to differentiate between the existing approaches to defining med-arb. *See, e.g.*, Peter, *supra* n. 7, at 89 (speaking about two ways to define med-arb: the first way is to describe the med-arb process; the second way concentrates on the goals and the elements of the process, and is broader); Blankenship, *supra* n. 8, at 30.

mediation.[10] Similar meaning is attributed to med-arb by Mironi,[11] Deekshitha and Saha,[12] Fullerton,[13] Burr,[14] Baizeau and Loong,[15] Leathes,[16] Giaretta and McMenamin,[17] Ross,[18] Blankley,[19] and Med-Arbitration Rules of Colorado Mediators & Arbitrators (COMA Med-Arbitration Rules).[20]

In defining med-arb, Greenbaum underlines the importance of the parties' agreement in advance that the same neutral will act as a mediator and, if mediation is not successful or if only a few issues remain unresolved, as an arbitrator.[21] Hill, however, criticises this approach on the basis that it does not appear to correspond to actual practice since it is more common not to specify in advance that the mediator will definitely act as arbitrator.[22]

The Alternative Dispute Resolution Practice Guide (ADR Guide) takes a strict approach and emphasises that if separate people serve as the mediator and the arbitrator, the process is not med-arb.[23] The essence of med-arb is that a single

10 Carlos De Vera, *Arbitrating Harmony: 'Med-Arb' and the Confluence of Culture and Rule of Law in the Resolution of International Commercial Disputes in China*, 18 Colum. J. Asian L. 149, 156 (2004).

11 Mordehai Mironi, *From Mediation to Settlement and from Settlement to Final Offer Arbitration: An Analysis of Transnational Business Dispute Mediation*, 73(1) Arb. 52, 56 (2007).

12 Srikant Deekshitha & Arka Saha, *Amalgamating the Conciliatory and the Adjudicative: Hybrid Processes and Asian Arbitral Institutions*, III(1) Indian J. Arb. L. 76, 77–78 (Jodhpur 2014).

13 Fullerton, *supra* n. 7, at 31–32 (drawing his definition of med-arb from the Colorado Bar Association website).

14 Andrew Burr, *Med-Arb: A Viable Hybrid Solution?* 8 Les Arbitres Internationaux 57, 61 (2005).

15 Domitille Baizeau & Anne-Marie Loong, *Multi-tiered and Hybrid Arbitration Clauses*, in *Arbitration in Switzerland: The Practitioner's Guide* 1451, 1451-1452 (Manuel Arroyo ed., Kluwer Law International 2013) (regarding med-arb as a kind of multi-tiered clause).

16 Michael Leathes, *Dispute Resolution Mules – Preventing the Process from Being Part of the Problem*, International Mediation Institute 2 (14 Mar. 2012), available at <www.imimediation.org/wp-content/uploads/2017/09/dispute-resolution-mules-final-.pdf> (accessed 27 Mar. 2018) (referring to med-arb as the process that is the reverse of arb-med and that is also known as binding mediation).

17 Ben Giaretta & Katherine McMenamin, *The Singapore International Mediation Centre*, Singapore International Mediation Centre (2 Nov. 2014), available at <http://simc.com.sg/resources-2/page/3/> (accessed 27 Mar. 2018).

18 Donna Ross, *Med-Arb/Arb-Med: A More Efficient ADR Process or an Invitation to a Potential Ethical Disaster?* in *Contemporary Issues in International Arbitration and Mediation: The Fordham Papers 2012* 352, 359 (Arthur W. Rovine ed., Martinus Nijhoff 2013).

19 Kristen M. Blankley, *Keeping a Secret from Yourself? Confidentiality When the Same Neutral Serves Both as Mediator and as Arbitrator in the Same Case*, 63 Baylor L. Rev. 317, 318 (Spring 2011).

20 Colorado Mediators & Arbitrators Med-Arbitration Rules of Procedure, Rule MA-1 (effective 1 Nov. 2013), available at <http://coma.com/rules/med-arbitration#Rule MA-1. Purpose of Med-Arbitration Proceedings> (accessed 27 Mar. 2018) [hereinafter, COMA Med-Arbitration Rules].

21 Marcia L. Greenbaum, *Process and the Professional Practitioner*, 2(3) Negotiation J. 225, 227 (Jul. 1986).

22 Hill, *supra* n. 8, at 105.

23 Sam Kagel & Bette J. Roth, *MED-ARB (Mediation-Arbitration)*, in *Alternative Dispute Resolution Practice Guide* § 37:8 (Sep. 2014).

individual conducts both mediation and arbitration. The ADR Guide defines med-arb as a two-step process, where the first step involves mediation of the issues, and the second step uses formal arbitration (by the same neutral) to decide the issues not settled in mediation. The final result is a binding decision that includes the agreement achieved during mediation together with the decisions resulting from arbitration. The final decision is enforceable as an ordinary arbitration award.

Bartel, similarly to the ADR Guide, argues that it is misleading to call med-arb the process in which different people perform the mediation and arbitration functions.[24] Only where the same person performs both functions is the process properly called med-arb. Where different people perform these two functions, it is more accurately called mediation and arbitration as distinct processes.

Stipanowich and Ulrich define med-arb as a process in which a single third party serves, or agrees to serve, as the mediator and arbitrator. However, one significant point distinguishes their definition of med-arb from those already mentioned in this section.[25] This point relates to the sequence of processes. According to Stipanowich and Ulrich, dual role arrangements include situations when neutrals engaged in mediating a dispute are asked to shift to an arbitral role and adjudicate the dispute as well as situations when arbitrators are invited to assume the role of mediators. Thus, this definition of med-arb encompasses situations when the process starts with either mediation or arbitration, whereas other definitions presume that med-arb starts with mediation only.

Lew attributes an even broader meaning to med-arb.[26] In his view, med-arb can begin as an arbitration where, after appointment, the arbitrator acts as a mediator and assists parties to settle. If mediation is unsuccessful, the mediator resumes as the arbitrator. Equally, parties can begin mediation and then arbitrate specific issues before returning to mediation. Or, it can be a fully hybrid process whereby the parties go backwards and forwards between mediation and arbitration.

2.2.1.2 Med-arb as a process conducted by a dual role neutral or different neutrals

Onyema defines med-arb as two separate dispute resolution processes combined to form one process.[27] If parties fail to settle in mediation, the mediator

24 Barry C. Bartel, *Med-Arb as a Distinct Method of Dispute Resolution: History, Analysis, and Potential*, 27 Willamette L. Rev. 661, 681 n. 103 (1991).

25 Thomas J. Stipanowich & Zachary P. Ulrich, *Commercial Arbitration and Settlement: Empirical Insights into the Roles Arbitrators Play*, 6 Y.B. On Arb. & Mediation 1, 10 (2014); *see also* Royden Hindle, *Mixing it up: Medarb Re-visited*, ¶¶ 6, 8 (unpublished paper prepared for the AMINZ Seminar 'Current issues in Arbitration', Mar. 2014).

26 Julian D. M. Lew, *Multi-Institutional Conciliation and the Reconciliation of Different Legal Cultures*, in *New Horizons in International Commercial Arbitration and Beyond*, 12 ICCA Congress Series 421, 422 (Albert Jan van den Berg ed., Kluwer Law International 2005).

27 Emilia Onyema, *The Use of Med-Arb in International Commercial Dispute Resolution*, 12 Am. Rev. Int'l Arb. 411, 412 (2001).

can continue by transforming from mediator into arbitrator. The parties, however, can equally decide to nominate a different tribunal when the dispute reaches the arbitration stage.[28] Mason[29] and Wolski[30] refer to the term med-arb along the same lines – as a sequential process where mediation precedes arbitration and the same or different neutrals act as a mediator and an arbitrator. So does Hill, adding that the mediation phase should be facilitative.[31]

The Singapore International Mediation Centre (SIMC) also defines med-arb as a process commencing with mediation, and, if mediation does not result in a settlement, followed by arbitration.[32] While not mentioning anything about the neutrals, and, thus, presumably encompassing both options (dual role neutral or different neutrals), it specifies that the reference to mediation is done by 'the parties to an arbitration agreement'.

Some commentators in this group do not specify the exact sequence, although one might assume from what they say, that arbitration is expected to follow mediation. For example, Mills and Brewer use the term med-arb for any ADR procedure combining mediation and arbitration in sequence.[33] Some commentators do not refer to any sequence at all. For instance, for Pappas, med-arb is a dispute resolution process that combines mediation and arbitration,[34] while Blankenship emphasises that in med-arb, mediation and arbitration can 'be combined and operate effectively free of the "in sequence" mandate'.[35]

Most commentators who define med-arb broadly, as a process where the same or different neutrals act as the mediator and the arbitrator, tend to either identify the original/typical med-arb or distinguish variations within med-arb.

28 *Ibid*, at 414.

29 Paul E. Mason, *The Arbitrator as Mediator, and Mediator as Arbitrator*, 28(6) J. Int'l. Arb. 541, 544–545 (2011) (using the unusual term 'medi-arb' instead of the common 'med-arb').

30 Bobette Wolski, *Arb-Med-Arb (and MSAs): A Whole Which Is Less than, not Greater than, the Sum of Its Parts?* 6(2) Contemp. Asia Arb. J. 249, 258 (2013).

31 Hill, *supra* n. 8, at 105–106 (adopting this definition from Arnold, a well-known US practitioner).

32 Singapore International Mediation Centre, *What is Arb-Med-Arb?* available at <http://simc.com.sg/arb-med-arb/> (accessed 14 Jan. 2018).

33 Thomas J. Brewer & Lawrence R. Mills, *Combining Mediation & Arbitration*, 54(4) Disp. Res. J. 32, 34 (1999).

34 Brian A. Pappas, *Med-Arb and the Legalisation of Alternative Dispute Resolution*, 20 Harv. Negot. L. Rev. 157, 159 (Spring 2015).

35 Blankenship, *supra* n. 8, at 30.

2.2.1.2.1 IDENTIFYING ORIGINAL/TYPICAL MED-ARB

There are many of those who identify a 'typical',[36] 'original',[37] or 'traditional'[38] med-arb, or single out its 'pure form',[39] or describe its 'usual case'[40] or 'most common variety'.[41]

Oghigian points out the difficulty of coming up with a single acceptable definition of a 'typical' med-arb process.[42] While this might be true, almost all commentators who speak about 'original', 'traditional', 'typical' etc. med-arb conceptualise it as a process that starts with mediation and if mediation does not resolve the dispute, the same neutral becomes the arbitrator.[43] Newmark and Hill disagree. For them, the usual case of med-arb involves one person being appointed as a mediator and, if mediation fails, either the mediator or another person subsequently arbitrates the dispute.[44]

2.2.1.2.2 DISTINGUISHING VARIATIONS WITHIN MED-ARB: THE SAME NEUTRAL MED-ARB AND DIFF NEUTRAL MED-ARB

Those scholars who do not identify any original or pure form of med-arb tend to distinguish different variations within med-arb. For example, Wolski observes that different models of med-arb have emerged over time, the most popular of which are med-arb (diff) and med-arb (same).[45] In med-arb (diff), mediation and arbitration phases are conducted by different neutrals. In med-arb (same), the same neutral first acts as a mediator and then, if necessary, decides on any unresolved issues. Similarly, Blankenship distinguishes between the same neutral med-arb and med-arb-diff.[46] Phillips uses the term the 'same-neutral med-arb', explaining that this term is used in lieu of a more common 'med-arb' to distinguish it from the process whereby mediation is followed by arbitration using a different neutral.[47]

36 Haig Oghigian, *The Meditation/Arbitration Hybrid*, 20(1) J. Int'l. Arb. 75, 76 (2003); David C. Elliott, *Med/Arb: Fraught with Danger or Ripe with Opportunity*, 34 Alta. L. Rev. 163, 163 (1995–1996).
37 James T. Peter, *Med-Arb in International Arbitration*, 4 Revista de Arbitragem e Mediação 155, 159 (2005).
38 Sawada, *supra* n. 5, at 29; Claude Thomson, *Med-Arb: A Fresh Look*, 2–3 (2006) (on file with the ICC Documentation & Research Centre).
39 Blankenship, *supra* n. 8, at 28; Bartel, *supra* n. 24, at 665.
40 Christopher Newmark & Richard Hill, *Can a Mediated Settlement Become an Enforceable Arbitration Award?* 16(1) Arb. Int'l. 81, 81 (2000).
41 Pappas, *supra* n. 34, at 159.
42 Oghigian, *supra* n. 36, at 76.
43 *See, e.g.*, Thomson, *supra* n. 38, at 2–3; Sawada, *supra* n. 5, at 29; Peter, *supra* n. 37, at 159; Peter, *supra* n. 7, at 91–92; Bartel, *supra* n. 24, at 665; Blankenship, *supra* n. 8, at 28; Elliott, *supra* n. 36, at 163; Pappas, *supra* n. 34, at 159.
44 Newmark & Hill, *supra* n. 40, at 81.
45 Wolski, *supra* n. 30, at 258–259.
46 Blankenship, *supra* n. 8, at 30–31.
47 Gerald F. Phillips, *Same-Neutral Med-Arb: What Does the Future Hold?* 2(1) NYSBA New York Disp. Res. Law. 75, 75 n. 3 (2009).

Given the fact that med-arb may have many different meanings, parties wishing to use this dispute resolution mechanism need to specify in detail, preferably in a written protocol, exactly what process they wish to follow before the proceedings begin.[48]

2.2.2 Definition of med-arb, the same neutral med-arb, and diff neutral med-arb for the purposes of this book

Throughout this book, the term **'med-arb'** is used to refer to the sequential use of mediation and arbitration, with the mediation phase taking place first. Similarly to Wolski and Blankenship, the book distinguishes two main variations of med-arb, **'the same neutral med-arb'** and **'diff neutral med-arb'**, depending on whether the mediation and arbitration phases of the process are conducted by the same or different neutrals. In view of differing approaches to defining the term med-arb and importance of delineating med-arb conducted by the same and different neutrals, the book uses the terms 'the same neutral med-arb' and 'diff neutral med-arb' that leave no ground for doubt and ensure clarity as to exactly what process is meant whenever any of these terms is used.

2.3 Combinations other than med-arb and their definitions

Med-arb and its two variations, the same neutral med-arb and diff neutral med-arb, are some of many ways mediation and arbitration can be used in combination. Arguably, many combinations have emerged in response to concerns associated with the use of the same neutral med-arb[49] that will be discussed in the next chapter. This section provides an overview of combinations other than med-arb, examines terms used to denote them, and defines the terms denoting the key combinations in this book. A review of the literature identified four valuable combinations that will be in the focus of this section and Chapters 6 and 7. These are arb-med, arb-med-arb, MEDALOA, and co-med-arb.

2.3.1 Arb-med

Similarly to the case with med-arb, there is no unanimity of opinion in the literature as to what the term arb-med stands for.

Nevertheless, the majority of commentators who address arb-med describe it as a process that begins with the arbitration phase resulting in a binding award that

48 Brewer & Mills, *supra* n. 33, at 34.

49 *See, e.g.*, Peter, *supra* n. 7, at 99 (speaking about formats alternative to the 'original med-arb'); Bartel, *supra* n. 24, at 666–669 (discussing variations of med-arb in its 'pure form'); Fullerton, *supra* n. 7, at 34–36 (referring to several variations of med-arb); Kagel & Roth, *supra* n. 23, at § 37:8 (noting that in response to criticism directed at 'pure' med-arb, there are now many variations on the med-arb process).

is sealed and kept confidential while parties proceed with the same neutral to the mediation phase. If parties settle in mediation, the neutral never discloses the arbitral award. Otherwise, the award is revealed and becomes binding.[50] Some commentators refer to this process differently. For example, Lawday refers to it as post-arbitration mediation.[51]

The definition of arb-med of Lack and Leathes differs from the above in one point. According to these two commentators, the mediation phase may be conducted by the same or a different neutral.[52]

Contrary to all the commentators above, the ADR Guide conceptualises arb-med as a variation of med-arb, where the dual role neutral conducts an arbitration proceeding concerning all issues first and, before issuing a decision, conducts mediation.[53] Thus, according to the guide, mediation in arb-med takes place before the neutral renders the award.

Blankenship, and Baizeau and Loong identify two variations of arb-med. While all these commentators regard the sealed award and the dual role neutral as the first variation,[54] their views differ on what they understand as the second variation. For Blankenship, the second variation is similar to the first, except the mediator is a different person from the arbitrator. This variation seems to require an additional decision to be made on whether the mediator is present throughout arbitration.[55] The second arb-med variation for Baizeau and Loong is when an attempt to mediate is made within the arbitration proceedings. Usually a member of the tribunal acts as the mediator. If the dispute is not resolved in mediation, arbitration resumes with the same tribunal.[56]

Some commentators, for example Mason[57] and Wolski,[58] define arb-med solely as the second variation of Baizeau and Loong. While it appears that Mason and Wolski speak about one mediation attempt in the course of arbitration proceedings, Sawada seems to have a slightly different understanding of arb-

50 Fullerton, *supra* n. 7, at 36; Deekshitha & Saha, *supra* n. 12, at 80; Peter, *supra* n. 37, at 165; Ross, *supra* n. 18, at 359; Alan L. Limbury, *Hybrid Dispute Resolution Processes – Getting the Best While Avoiding the Worst of Both Worlds?* in *CIArb's Mediation Compendium* 6 (A. Hudson-Tyreman et al. eds, London 2009); Martin C. Weisman, *Med/Arb – A Time and Cost Effective Hybrid for Dispute Resolution*, Weisman, Young & Ruemenapp, P.C. 2, available at <www.wysr-law.com/articles.html> (accessed 14 Jan. 2018).

51 Geoff Lawday, *Hybrid Dispute Resolution Processes* 22 (unpublished paper presented at 'Mediation in a Global Village – Cross-cultural and International Aspects of Mediation and Negotiation', Germany 2009).

52 Lack, *supra* n. 4, at 358 n. 19; Leathes, *supra* n. 16, at 2.

53 Kagel & Roth, *supra* n. 23, at § 37:9.

54 Blankenship, *supra* n. 8, at 31; Baizeau & Loong, *supra* n. 15, at 1452 (noting, however, that unless another neutral is appointed, it is the arbitrator who conducts mediation in arb-med).

55 Blankenship, *supra* n. 8, at 31.

56 Baizeau & Loong, *supra* n. 15, at 1452.

57 Paul E. Mason, *Follow-Up Note to 'The Arbitrator as Mediator, and Mediator as Arbitrator' (2011), J. Int. Arb. 6, 541 et seq.*, 29(2) J. Int'l. Arb. 225, 225 n. 1 (2012).

58 Wolski, *supra* n. 30, at 260.

med. According to Sawada, arb-med is a process whereby subject to the parties' agreement, an arbitrator will try mediation *on one or more occasions*[59] within the course of the same proceedings so that those proceedings can end successfully either with a settlement agreement or other constructive agreement, or with an arbitral award.[60]

Wolski observes that in practice, most such processes are more likely to be in the nature of arb-med-arb, because if parties settle in mediation they would still want to resume arbitration in order to formalise their agreement as a consent award. If parties do not settle in mediation, the arbitration will be resumed and the arbitrator will render an award.[61] Hindle addresses the same point and notes that despite the fact that much of the literature uses the term 'arb/med' that ends with 'med',[62] in many cases the processes being discussed finish with an award not a settlement agreement.[63]

2.3.2 Arb-med-arb

Recognising the nature of the process, many commentators employ the terms arb-med-arb[64] or mediation window,[65] or both terms synonymously[66] instead of arb-med for the use of mediation within an already-existing arbitration. Abramson suggests a term with a broader meaning, 'arb-settlement-arb' for settlement efforts, including mediation, attempted after the formal arbitration has been commenced.[67]

However, there is no clear and shared understanding among the commentators addressing arb-med-arb on how many times mediation can be attempted throughout arbitration and whether the arbitrator or a different neutral acts as the mediator.

For Peter, mediation may take place at any time, and on more than one occasion. It may be conducted either by the arbitrator, or a separate mediator.[68]

59 Emphasis added.

60 Sawada, *supra* n. 5, at 29 (using the terms 'arb-med', 'hybrid', and 'hybrid arb-med' synonymously).

61 Wolski, *supra* n. 30, at 260.

62 Hindle, *supra* n. 25, at 3 n. 11 (referring to Luke Nottage's article as an example of this approach: Nottage, *Arb-Med and New International Commercial Mediation Rules in Japan*, Japanese Law and the Asia-Pacific (21 Jul. 2009), available at <http://blogs.usyd.edu.au/japaneselaw/2009/07/arbmed_and_new_international_c_1.html> (accessed 27 Mar. 2018).

63 Hindle, *supra* n. 25, at 3 n. 11.

64 Ross, *supra* n. 18, at 361; *What is Arb-Med-Arb? supra* n. 32.

65 Peter, *supra* n. 7, at 103; Peter, *supra* n. 37, at 167; Blankenship, *supra* n. 8, at 32.

66 Lack, *supra* n. 4, at 360.

67 Abramson, *supra* n. 6, at 2 n. 1, 3 n. 3.

68 Peter, *supra* n. 7, at 103; Peter, *supra* n. 37, at 167 referring to Christian Bühring-Uhle, *Arbitration and Mediation in International Business: Designing Procedures for Effective Conflict Management* 370 (Kluwer Law International 1996); *see also* Blankenship, *supra* n. 8, at 32 (adding that parties are not required to mediate but are merely encouraged to do so).

While SIMC's general definition of arb-med-arb focuses on the sequence of the processes – a dispute is referred to arbitration before mediation is attempted – it specifies that under a combined process jointly develped by SIMC and the Singapore International Arbitration Centre (SIAC), the SIAC-SIMC Arb-Med-Arb Protocol, the arbitrators and the mediators will generally be different persons, unless parties agree otherwise.[69] According to the SIAC-SIMC Arb-Med-Arb Protocol, the dispute is referred to mediation once.

Similarly to the SIAC-SIMC Arb-Med-Arb Protocol, Ross conceptualises arb-med-arb as a three-stage process that involves one attempt to resolve the dispute by mediation. In Ross' view, all three stages in arb-med-arb are conducted by the same neutral.[70] She observes that the initial arbitration stage may be conducted in a condensed and fast-track manner. The arbitrator may open mediation windows to dispose of issues as they are raised, thereby, helping parties to streamline the process. If mediation is not completely successful, the arbitration stage is resumed.

For Lack, in arb-med-arb the arbitral tribunal suspends arbitration at some stage to allow parties to meet with another (non-evaluative) neutral to mediate. Mediation can be limited to only certain aspects of the dispute.[71] At the same time, Lack distinguishes arb-med-arb from arb-con-arb (conciliation window). This is due to the fact that, contrary to many other commentators, Lack does not use the terms conciliation and mediation interchangeably. By mediation he means a subjective and non-evaluative process that focuses on the parties' needs and interests. Conciliation, in Lack's view, is a process that focuses on objective norms and is an evaluative process, in which the conciliator is expected to make proposals to the parties as to possible settlement solutions based on these norms.[72] According to Lack, in the arb-con-arb, parties start with arbitration and later on open a window for conciliation. Arbitrators become conciliators, but they do not caucus with the parties and their role remains evaluative at all times.[73] Lack identifies even one more variation – the arb-con-med-con-arb process – where parties move from arbitration to conciliation to mediation and, after trying to conciliate once more, back to arbitration.

To avoid any confusion, this book uses the term arb-med-arb for any attempt to resolve the dispute by mediation within an ongoing arbitration. Depending on whether the same or different neutrals conduct mediation and arbitration, this book suggests distinguishing between the same neutral arb-med-arb and diff neutral arb-med-arb.

69 *What is Arb-Med-Arb? supra* n. 32.
70 Ross, *supra* n. 18, at 361.
71 Lack, *supra* n. 4, at 360.
72 *Ibid*, at 350 n.9.
73 *Ibid*, at 359.

2.3.3 MEDALOA

MEDALOA stands for mediation and last offer arbitration.[74] This process is very similar to med-arb[75] and is often referred to as its variation.[76] The difference lies in the arbitration stage. If parties do not reach a settlement in the mediation stage, each party submits a 'last offer' to the neutral who must choose between one of them.

Similarly to the situation with med-arb, the main point of difference among commentators who conceptualise MEDALOA is whether the same or different neutrals act as the mediator and the arbitrator. According to the majority, it is the same neutral.[77] However, Borris speaks about the involvement of different neutrals in the mediation and the arbitration stage of MEDALOA,[78] whereas Lawday does not specify in his description of MEDALOA whether the same or different neutrals conduct both phases of the process.[79]

Borris suggests another way of combining last offer arbitration with mediation. This uses mediated negotiation rounds between offers in multi-round last offer arbitration.[80] This variation provides for several rounds of offers, with mediated negotiation rounds in between, which gives parties an opportunity for strategic manoeuvres. Mediator's tasks include not only keeping parties' manoeuvres in check, but also fostering a settlement in the negotiation rounds between submissions of offers.

2.3.4 Co-med-arb

Co-med-arb is commonly conceptualised as a process that involves two different people who perform the roles of a mediator and an arbitrator.[81] Both neutrals preside over an information exchange between parties, after which the mediator works with parties, including in private sessions, in the absence of the arbitrator. If mediation fails to achieve a settlement, the dispute is then submitted to the

74 *Ibid*, at 366–368; Blankenship, *supra* n. 8, at 31; Peter, *supra* n. 37, at 165–166; Ross, *supra* n. 18, at 361; Lawday, *supra* n. 51, at 21; Christian Borris, *Final Offer Arbitration from a Civil Law Perspective*, 24(3) J. Int'l. Arb. 307, 311 (2007) (attributing the invention in the early 1990s of the term MEDALOA to Robert Coulson, a former President of the American Arbitration Association).

75 Blankenship, *supra* n. 8, at 31.

76 *See, e.g.*, Peter, *supra* n. 37, at 165; Ross, *supra* n. 18, at 361.

77 Lack, *supra* n. 4, at 367 (specifying that the dual role neutral may engage in caucuses); Peter, *supra* n. 37, at 165; Ross, *supra* n. 18, at 361–362; Elliott, *supra* n. 36, at 164 (describing the process of MEDALOA, but calling it a variation of the med-arb process, instead of MEDALOA).

78 Borris, *supra* n. 74, at 311 n. 12.

79 Lawday, *supra* n. 51, at 21.

80 Borris, *supra* n. 74, at 311.

81 Wolski, *supra* n. 30, at 269; Peter, *supra* n. 7, at 102; Burr, *supra* n. 14, at 70; Blankenship, *supra* n. 8, at 31; Kagel & Roth, *supra* n. 23, at § 37:12.

arbitrator for a binding decision.[82] The ADR Guide adds that if the dispute moves to the arbitration phase, the arbitrator conducts it alone, although there may be a continuing role for the mediator either to conduct a later planned mediation, or spontaneously to mediate any issues that may arise in arbitration.[83]

As with other combinations, some commentators attribute a different meaning to co-med-arb. For example, Lawday, and Newmark and Hill understand co-med-arb as a sequential use of mediation and arbitration with a different person becoming the arbitrator in the event of a failed mediation (a combination that is referred to as diff neutral med-arb in this book).[84]

2.3.5 Other combinations

Med-arb, arb-med, arb-med-arb, MEDALOA, and co-med-arb are the most frequently discussed combinations. Many other possibilities of using mediation and arbitration in combination exist.[85] These include combinations like med-arb opt-out and shadow mediation. In med-arb opt-out, parties need to agree after the mediation phase whether the same neutral will continue as an arbitrator.[86] In shadow mediation a separate mediator 'shadows' the arbitration process.[87] Parties may resort to the shadow mediator at any time to mediate any particular issue. Med-arb opt-out and shadow mediation will be explored further in Chapter 6.

2.3.6 Definition of arb-med, arb-med-arb, MEDALOA, co-med-arb, and the same neutral (arb)-med-arb for the purposes of this book

Throughout this book, the term **'arb-med'** is used to refer to a process beginning with arbitration resulting in an award that is placed in a sealed envelope and kept confidential. Then the former arbitrator becomes a mediator. If parties do not settle in mediation, the award is revealed and becomes binding. Otherwise, the neutral never discloses the award.

The book uses the term **'arb-med-arb'** for a separate mediation process in the course of arbitration. Depending on whether the same or a different neutral

82 Peter, *supra* n. 7, at 102; Burr, *supra* n. 14, at 70; Blankenship, *supra* n. 8, at 31; Wolski, *supra* n. 30, at 269.

83 Kagel & Roth, *supra* n. 23, at § 37:12.

84 Lawday, *supra* n. 51, at 21; Newmark & Hill, *supra* n. 40, at 87.

85 *See* combinations discussed in, *e.g.*, Bartel, *supra* n. 24, at 665–668; Kagel & Roth, *supra* n. 23, at §§ 37:10, 13–14; Fullerton, *supra* n. 7, at 34–36; Elliott, *supra* n. 36, at 164; Ross, *supra* n. 18, at 358; Leathes, *supra* n. 16; Lawday, *supra* n. 51, at 21–22; Lack, *supra* n. 4, at 357–372.

86 Peter, *supra* n. 37, at 164; Peter, *supra* n. 7, at 99; Bartel, *supra* n. 24, at 666 (referring to this combination as a contingent form of the same neutral med-arb); Blankenship, *supra* n. 8, at 31 (noting that med-arb opt-out is basically the same as the contingent form of the same neutral med-arb).

87 Kagel & Roth, *supra* n. 23, at § 37:11.

conducts mediation in the course of arbitration, the book will distinguish **'the same neutral arb-med-arb'** and **'diff neutral arb-med-arb'**.

The book uses the term **'MEDALOA'** to refer to a process that starts with mediation and if parties do not settle in the mediation stage, each party submits a 'last offer' to the dual role neutral who chooses between one of them.

The book uses the term **'co-med-arb'** to refer to a process where the arbitrator attends joint sessions in mediation (but does not participate in caucusing) and if no settlement is reached in mediation, renders an award.

The term **'the same neutral (arb)-med-arb'** is used to refer jointly to the same neutral med-arb and the same neutral arb-med-arb.

2.4 Conclusion

Mediation and arbitration can be combined in many different ways. The terms used to denote various combinations can cause misunderstanding. Med-arb – the most common term used in the literature to denote the combined use of mediation and arbitration – lacks a universally accepted definition. Usually, though not always, it means a sequential process, where mediation precedes arbitration. Commentators, however, disagree as to whether it is a process where both mediation and arbitration stages are conducted by the same neutral only or whether the term encompasses situations where different neutrals are involved in each stage. Similarly, the inconsistent use of terms to denote other combinations, such as arb-med, arb-med-arb, MEDALOA, and co-med-arb may be a source of confusion. To avoid any uncertainty, the book has defined the terms denoting the key combinations for the purposes of the book. The main approaches to defining terms denoting the key combinations and definitions used in this book are summarised in Appendix 1.

The book uses the term **'the same neutral (arb)-med-arb'** to denote the central combination for this book. This term refers jointly to the same neutral med-arb and the same neutral arb-med-arb. In both combinations the same neutral acts as a mediator and an arbitrator. The processes differ in that the same neutral med-arb starts with mediation, whereas the same neutral arb-med-arb starts with arbitration.

The next chapter will discuss the controversy surrounding the use of the same neutral (arb)-med-arb as well as the advantages and concerns associated with the process. Other key combinations defined in this chapter will be revisited in Chapters 6 and 7, where they will be analysed in the context of addressing concerns associated with the same neutral (arb)-med-arb. All combinations introduced in this chapter will serve as an illustration of how practitioners could adopt a flexible approach to process design. Training of practitioners in flexible process design is an initiative to enhance the use of combinations in international commercial dispute resolution that is discussed in Section 9.5.3.

3 Controversy surrounding the use of the same neutral (arb)-med-arb

Advantages and concerns associated with the process

3.1 Introduction

The issue of whether it is appropriate and admissible for the same neutral to act as a mediator and arbitrator in the same dispute has been a controversial and much-disputed subject within the field of the combined use of mediation and arbitration for two decades or more. Ross vividly depicts the controversy surrounding this issue:

> The practice of combining arbitration and mediation into a single, hybrid process when the role of mediator and arbitrator is assumed by the same neutral raises a tidal wave of controversy. Certain detractors of Med-Arb/Arb-Med oppose it so fervently they consider it not only an ethical disaster, but heretical – a process that should be burned at the stake. On the other side of the spectrum, some of its devotees believe it is not only more efficient, but a panacea, encompassing the best of both worlds. [1]

The literature provides numerous examples of the divide of opinions among commentators regarding the issue of the same neutral acting as a mediator and an arbitrator. Some commentators disapprove of the process involving a dual role neutral and insist on keeping the functions of a mediator and an arbitrator separate by having different neutrals for each stage.[2] Others recognize that in

1 Donna Ross, *Med-Arb/Arb-Med: A More Efficient ADR Process or an Invitation to a Potential Ethical Disaster?* in *Contemporary Issues in International Arbitration and Mediation: The Fordham Papers 2012* 352, 352 (Arthur W. Rovine ed., Martinus Nijhoff 2013).

2 *See, e.g.*, Eric W. Fiechter, *Mediation – Casting Issues: Can or Should the Same Person be Mediator, or Conciliator and Arbitrator?* 15 Croatian Arb. Y.B. 255, 261 (2008); Ahmed Masood, *Settlement in International Arbitration: Comments on the CEDR Settlement Rules*, 76 (2) Arb. 269, 276 (2010); Jon Lang, *Med-Arb – An English Perspective*, 2(1) NYSBA New York Disp. Res. Law. 98, 102 (2009); Pedro Alberto Costa Braga de Oliveira, *Designing Effective Med-Arb and Arb-Med Processes in Brazil*, 2(1) NYSBA New York Disp. Res. Law. 89, 89 (2009).

certain circumstances (where parties are fully informed of the pros and cons, and safeguards are put in place) the same neutral (arb)-med-arb is a viable option.[3] Yet others believe that the process involving a dual role neutral is the most flexible of all the ADR and combined processes, more efficient and less costly.[4] This divide in views is often explained by reference to the practitioner's legal culture, which will be examined in Chapter 4.

The advantages and concerns will be discussed in the context of both the same neutral med-arb and the same neutral arb-med-arb, because, subject to a limited number of exceptions that will be pointed out throughout Sections 3.2 and 3.3, the advantages and concerns raised in respect of these two combinations appear to be the same. The concerns seem to arise whenever arbitration follows mediation and the same neutral performs the functions of a mediator and an arbitrator.[5] The literature often discusses the advantages and concerns in reference to both combinations.[6]

Notably, the review of the literature reveals that the discussion of advantages and concerns associated with the same neutral (arb)-med-arb is mostly theoretical, having very little empirical support. Where possible, the book refers to the empirical evidence. In cases where it does not, empirical data is yet to be collected. Where available, the book illustrates the way advantages and concerns materialise in practice through cases anecdotally reported by dispute resolution practitioners. It is important to note that unless commentators expressing their

3 *See, e.g.*, Christopher Newmark, *Controlling Time and Costs in Arbitration*, in *Leading Arbitrators' Guide to International Arbitration* 81, 89 (Lawrence W. Newman & Richard D. Hill eds, 2d ed., Juris Publishing, Inc. 2008).

4 *See, e.g.*, Gerald F. Phillips, *Same-Neutral Med-Arb: What Does the Future Hold?* 2(1) NYSBA New York Disp. Res. Law. 75, 77 (2009).

5 Bobette Wolski, *Arb-Med-Arb (and MSAs): A Whole Which Is Less than, not Greater than, the Sum of Its Parts?* 6(2) Contemp. Asia Arb. J. 249, 265 (2013); James T. Peter, *Note & Comment: Med-Arb in International Arbitration*, 8 Am. Rev. Int'l Arb. 83, 103 (1997); *see generally* Section 3.3 on concerns associated with the same neutral (arb)-med-arb. In the same neutral arb-med-arb, concerns are raised not when the arbitrator takes on the role of a mediator, but when mediation does not result in a settlement and the mediator has to resume as the arbitrator.

6 *See, e.g.*, Geoff Lawday, *Hybrid Dispute Resolution Processes* 4–10 (unpublished paper presented at 'Mediation in a Global Village – Cross-cultural and International Aspects of Mediation and Negotiation', Germany 2009); Domitille Baizeau & Anne-Marie Loong, *Multi-tiered and Hybrid Arbitration Clauses*, in *Arbitration in Switzerland: The Practitioner's Guide* 1451, 1453–1455 (Manuel Arroyo ed., Kluwer Law International 2013); Thomas J. Stipanowich & Zachary P. Ulrich, *Commercial Arbitration and Settlement: Empirical Insights into the Roles Arbitrators Play*, 6 Y.B. on Arb. & Mediation 1, 25–26 (2014); Jacob Rosoff, *Hybrid Efficiency in Arbitration: Waiving Potential Conflicts for Dual Role Arbitrators in Med-Arb and Arb-Med Proceedings*, 26(1) J. Int'l. Arb. 89, 89–100 (2009); Srikant Deekshitha & Arka Saha, *Amalgamating the Conciliatory and the Adjudicative: Hybrid Processes and Asian Arbitral Institutions*, III(1) Indian J. Arb. L. 76, 88 (Jodhpur 2014); Ross, *supra* n. 1, at 358–362 (observing that the same neutral arb-med-arb is a form related to the same neutral med-arb); J. Brian Casey, *Arbitration Law of Canada: Practice and Procedure*, 16 (JurisNet 2005).

views on different aspects of the same neutral (arb)-med-arb specifically indicate, it is not clear whether they have actual experience in the process.

The discussion of the advantages and concerns raised in respect of the same neutral (arb)-med-arb is important because it will help shape the type of activity in which dual role neutrals may engage.[7] This will be addressed in Chapter 8.

This chapter comprises three sections. The focus of Sections 3.2 and 3.3 is the advantages and concerns associated with the same neutral (arb)-med-arb. Section 3.4 analyses the challenge posed by the same neutral (arb)-med-arb for practitioners acting as dual role neutrals. These practitioners need to be skilled to function effectively as mediators and arbitrators while switching from one role to another.

3.2 Advantages associated with the same neutral (arb)-med-arb

Supporters of the same neutral (arb)-med-arb see it as a process that attempts to capture the independent strengths of both mediation and arbitration while limiting their perceived weaknesses.[8]

The key advantages commonly attributed to mediation are the opportunity for parties to create solutions that uphold convergent interests and reconcile divergent ones, and parties' maximum control over the outcome.[9] Mediation, however, does not guarantee reaching a settlement[10] or a final resolution.[11] A mediator cannot render a binding decision if mediation does not result in a settlement.[12] Contrary to mediation used on its own, the same neutral (arb)-med-arb ensures that a final resolution of the dispute will be achieved.[13]

One of the main benefits of arbitration is a final and binding outcome.[14] At the same time, arbitration can be slow and expensive, and in the end a decision may be imposed upon the parties that is not desired by any of them.[15] Arbitration has limited capacity to restructure the parties' relationships because it usually produces a win or lose outcome.[16] Also, the formality of the arbitration process may

7 Gabrielle Kaufmann-Kohler, *When Arbitrators Facilitate Settlement: Towards a Transnational Standard*, Clayton Utz, available at <www.claytonutz.com/ialecture/2007/transcript_2007.html> (accessed 14 Jan. 2018).

8 *See, e.g.*, Claude Thomson, *Med-Arb: A Fresh Look*, 2 (2006) (on file with the ICC Documentation & Research Centre); Wolski, *supra* n. 5, at 258; Barry C. Bartel, *Med-Arb as a Distinct Method of Dispute Resolution: History, Analysis, and Potential*, 27 Willamette L. Rev. 661, 665 (1991); Royden Hindle, *Mixing it up: Medarb Re-visited*, ¶ 1 (unpublished paper prepared for the AMINZ Seminar 'Current issues in Arbitration', Mar. 2014).

9 Wolski, *supra* n. 5, at 258.

10 *Ibid.*

11 Bartel, *supra* n. 8, at 665.

12 Thomson, *supra* n. 8, at 2.

13 Bartel, *supra* n. 8, at 665.

14 Wolski, *supra* n. 5, at 258.

15 Thomson, *supra* n. 8, at 2.

16 Wolski, *supra* n. 5, at 258.

prevent parties from providing information that would allow an arbitrator to address their underlying interests in an arbitral award.[17] In the same neutral (arb)-med-arb, which is less formal than arbitration, a neutral can play an active role and easily address underlying interests.[18]

The most zealous advocates of the process contend that the same neutral (arb)-med-arb offers benefits that neither mediation nor arbitration offers alone.[19]

The literature review shows that six advantages are commonly attributed to the same neutral (arb)-med-arb: efficiency, finality and legal enforceability, quality of the outcome, flexibility, incentive to settle, and more honest behaviour of parties (as compared to mediation only). Some advantages, for example, finality and legal enforceability, are not unique to the same neutral (arb)-med-arb, but are common to other combinations. This chapter will turn now to examining these advantages.

3.2.1 Efficiency

Efficiency in terms of cost and time appears to be the most commonly cited advantage of the same neutral (arb)-med-arb.[20] Some authors even regard efficiency as the key advantage of the process[21] and the most compelling reason to engage in it.[22]

17 Bartel, *supra* n. 8, at 665.

18 *Ibid.*

19 *See, e.g.*, Phillips *supra* n. 4, at 77; Bartel, *supra* n. 8, at 665; Richard H. McLaren & John P. Sanderson, *Innovative Dispute Resolution: The Alternative*, 6–1 (Carswell 1994) cited in David C. Elliott, *Med/Arb: Fraught with Danger or Ripe with Opportunity*, 34 Alta. L. Rev. 163, 165 (1995–1996) and Michael E. Schneider, *Combining Arbitration with Conciliation*, in *International Dispute Resolution: Towards an International Arbitration Culture*, 8 ICCA Congress Series 57, 97 (Albert Jan van den Berg ed., Kluwer Law International 1998); Barry Leon & Alexandra Peterson, *Med-Arb in Ontario: Enforceability of Med-Arb Agreement Confirmed by Court of Appeal*, 2(1) NYSBA New York Disp. Res. Law. 92, 92 (2009).

20 *See, e.g.*, Toshio Sawada, *Hybrid Arb-Med: Will West and East Never Meet?* 14(2) ICC Int'l Ct. Arb. Bull. 29, 33 (Fall 2003); Houzhi Tang, *Combination of Arbitration with Conciliation – Arb-Med*, in *New Horizons in International Commercial Arbitration and Beyond*, 12 ICCA Congress Series 547, 555 (Albert Jan van den Berg ed., Kluwer Law International 2005); Thomas J. Brewer & Lawrence R. Mills, *Combining Mediation & Arbitration*, 54(4) Disp. Res. J. 32, 34 (1999); Edna Sussman, *Developing an Effective Med-Arb/ Arb-Med Process*, 2(1) NYSBA New York Disp. Res. Law. 71, 73 (2009); Bartel, *supra* n. 8, at 665; Leon & Peterson, *supra* n. 19, at 92; Victor Lau & Vanja Bulut, *Resolution of Disputes in China – What It Means for Australia*, Clayton Utz (15 Mar. 2012), available at <www.claytonutz.com/publications/edition/15_march_2012/20120315/resolution_of_disputes_in_china-what_it_means_for_australia.page> (accessed 28 Mar. 2018); Ross, *supra* n. 1, at 360; Harold I. Abramson, *Protocols for International Arbitrators Who Dare to Settle Cases*, 10 Am. Rev. Int'l Arb. 1, 4 (1999).

21 *See, e.g.*, John T. Blankenship, *Developing Your ADR Attitude: Med-Arb, a Template for Adaptive ADR*, 42(11) Tennessee Bar J. 28, 34 (2006); Kaufmann-Kohler, *supra* n. 7.

22 Thomson, *supra* n. 8, at 2; Richard P. Flake, *MED/ARB – A Viable ADR Vehicle? Nuances of Med/Arb—A Neutral's Perspective*, CEDIRES 8, available at <www.cedires.com/index_bestanden/FLAKE_http-www.cbylaw.com-filebin_files_flake_rpf-AAA_Med-Arb.pdf> (accessed

Parties can save considerable time by having the mediator as an arbitrator or an arbitrator as a mediator. First, they do not need to review the qualifications of potential arbitrators if they move to the arbitration phase, eliminating, thereby, a time-consuming task of selecting a new arbitrator.[23] Second, parties can save the time necessary to prepare for arbitration or mediation before a separate neutral.[24] Third, parties can proceed to the arbitration phase with almost no delay.[25] Very little time might be needed at the end of mediation that has not brought a complete settlement to commence or resume the arbitration phase of the same neutral (arb)-med-arb.[26] Fourth, if the dispute goes or returns to the arbitration phase, the arbitrator already knows the case and there is no need to educate another neutral.[27]

The arbitration phase has the potential to be truncated or presented in a summary fashion, which is not possible in a separate arbitration conducted by a different neutral.[28] There may not even be a need for a hearing.[29] If parties agree, the arbitrator can render an award based on the facts presented in mediation. The savings can be magnified in international arbitrations where scheduling of sessions is more difficult among neutrals, parties, and attorneys coming from different jurisdictions.[30]

Blankley suggests that parties could introduce a financial disincentive for the mediator to arbitrate by arranging to pay the neutral a premium if the case settles in mediation.[31] Another financial arrangement could provide a discounted rate for neutrals if they must render both mediation and arbitration services.

14 Jan. 2018); Bernd Ehle, *The Arbitrator as a Settlement Facilitator* in *Walking A Thin Line – What an Arbitrator Can Do, Must Do or Must Not Do, Recent Developments and Trends* 77, 85 (Bruylant 2010).

23 Phillips, *supra* n. 4, at 76.

24 Blankenship, *supra* n. 21, at 34.

25 *Ibid.*

26 Phillips, *supra* n. 4, at 76.

27 Gabrielle Kaufmann-Kohler & Fan Kun, *Integrating Mediation into Arbitration: Why It Works in China*, 25(4) J. Int'l. Arb. 479, 490 (2008); Kaufmann-Kohler, *supra* n. 7; Roman Rewald & Kimberly Jachimek Weil, *Expanding ADR in Poland: Mediation and Arbitration Together*, Lexology 2 n. 16, available at <http://documents.lexology.com/63de58ab-0582-410b-97aa-1c6f490e7f67.pdf> (accessed 14 Jan. 2018) (citing Brian Pappas); Leon & Peterson, *supra* n. 19, at 92; Blankenship, *supra* n. 21, at 34; Fan Kun, *The Risks of Apparent Bias When an Arbitrator Acts as a Mediator: Remarks on Hong Kong Court's Decision in Gao Haiyan*, 13 Y.B. Private Int'l. L. 535, 537 (2011); Abramson, *supra* n. 20, at 4.

28 Blankenship, *supra* n. 21, at 34.

29 Phillips, *supra* n. 4, at 77.

30 Abramson, *supra* n. 20, at 4.

31 Kristen M. Blankley, *Keeping a Secret from Yourself? Confidentiality When the Same Neutral Serves Both as Mediator and as Arbitrator in the Same Case*, 63 Baylor L. Rev. 317, 329 (Spring 2011); *but see* Brian A. Pappas, *Med-Arb and the Legalisation of Alternative Dispute Resolution*, 20 Harv. Negot. L. Rev. 157, 202 (Spring 2015) (criticising this suggestion because, while it might save parties money, it would put an extraordinary amount of pressure on settlement and potentially damage the neutral's impartiality and the parties' self-determination).

Two empirical studies support the perception of the same neutral (arb)-med-arb as a cost- and time-efficient process. The first study is the Global Pound Conference Series 2016–17 survey (GPC survey) that collected data from more than 2,800 participants from all over the world.[32] Although the GPC study has a number of limitations,[33] it provides an insight into general perceptions of current dispute resolution practices and their future evolution. When participants were asked what the most effective commercial dispute resolution processes presently usually involve, a combination of adjudicative and non-adjudicative processes (e.g. arbitration with mediation) emerged as the participants' top choice. The GPC survey does not define the word 'effective'. This word, however, is generally understood as successful in producing a desired result,[34] which brings us to the question of what parties want from a dispute resolution process. Answers to another GPC survey question revealed that parties want efficiency – their choice of a dispute resolution process is influenced first and foremost by its time and cost efficiency. Thereby, it appears that combined processes are perceived as the most effective processes because parties consider that such combined processes are cost and time efficient. The second empirical study to support the perception of the same neutral (arb)-med-arb as a cost- and time-efficient process is the study conducted for the purposes of this book. As reported in Section 5.2.3.3, faster resolution of the dispute and its lower cost (as compared to arbitration only) were rated as two of the top three benefits of the combined use of process. It should be noted, however, that this result relates to all combinations rather than the same neutral (arb)-med-arb only. The result of the GPC survey applies to an even broader category of dispute resolution processes – combinations of adjudicative and non-adjudicative processes.

32 *Global Pound Conference Series 2016–17 Cumulated Data Results March 2016 – September 2017*, Global Pound, available at <http://globalpound.org/wp-content/uploads/2017/11/2017-09-18-Final-GPC-Series-Results-Cumulated-Votes-from-the-GPC-App-Mar.-2016-Sep.-2017.pdf> (accessed 14 Jan. 2018) [hereinafter, GPC Cumulated Data Results]. The participants included in-house counsel and clients, external lawyers and consultants, providers of dispute resolution services, researchers, educators, and government representatives. The data was collected during conferences at 28 venues and via online voting.

33 These limitations include the way the GPC survey organisers divided the participants into groups. For example, a group of adjudicative providers comprised very diverse categories of participants such as judges, arbitrators, and representatives of provider organisations. Another limitation is a very broad wording of some questions and answer options, opening a way to their multiple interpretations. Yet another limitation relates to the way the participants were to rank their choices: they had to do it in order of priority without being given a possibility to give equal rank to selected answers. Thomas J. Stipanowich, *What Have We Learned From The Global Pound Conferences?* Kluwer Arbitration Blog (27 Nov. 2017), available at <http://mediationblog.kluwerarbitration.com/2017/11/27/learned-global-pound-conferences/> (accessed 28 Mar. 2018).

34 *See, e.g.*, Oxford Dictionaries, available at <https://en.oxforddictionaries.com> (accessed 9 Jan. 2018).

3.2.1.1 Same neutral med-arb v. same neutral arb-med-arb

Comparing the same neutral med-arb and the same neutral arb-med-arb, it appears that the former can potentially save more time and money than the latter. This is because in the same neutral med-arb, if a dispute is settled in the mediation stage, parties will not incur any costs related to arbitration; however, the situation is different in the same neutral arb-med-arb where, regardless of whether a dispute is settled in the mediation stage, parties have to invest time and financial resources into the initial arbitration stage.

3.2.2 Finality and legal enforceability

Apart from allowing resolution of a dispute in a time- and cost-efficient manner, the same neutral (arb)-med-arb appears to ensure that a final resolution of a dispute is achieved within a reasonable time.[35] Parties either settle in the mediation stage or, if they do not, the dual role neutral renders an award in the arbitration stage. Thereby, the same neutral (arb)-med-arb seems to overcome the non-binding element of mediation and commit parties to engage in the process that achieves final resolution.[36] Moreover, a mediated settlement agreement reached in the course of arbitration can be recorded as a consent award and thus, arguably, become enforceable internationally pursuant to the New York Convention.[37] For some authors, the finality and legal enforceability of the outcome of the same neutral (arb)-med-arb is the most appealing attribute of the process,[38] and a reason why other advantages, such as savings of time and money, exist.[39]

Although mediation offers many advantages, the absence of a unified enforcement mechanism for international mediated settlement agreements is often seen as an obstacle to its greater use as a stand-alone method of international commercial dispute resolution.[40] Steele observes that while in a perfect world, no enforcement mechanism might be required for mediation because a voluntary

35 Blankenship, *supra* n. 21, at 34–35; Brewer & Mills, *supra* n. 20, at 34; Lawday, *supra* n. 6, at 9.

36 Lawday, *supra* n. 6, at 9; Bartel, *supra* n. 8, at 665; Ross, *supra* n. 1, at 362; *but see*; Pappas, *supra* n. 31, at 171 (observing that mediation inherently does not suffer due to the lack of a guaranteed, final, and binding settlement).

37 Kaufmann-Kohler & Kun, *supra* n. 27, at 490–491; Lau & Bulut, *supra* n. 20; Kun, *supra* n. 27, at 537; Ross, *supra* n. 1, at 362.

38 Flake, *supra* n. 22, at 5; Blankenship, *supra* n. 21, at 35; Rewald & Jachimek Weil, *supra* n. 27, at 2.

39 Blankenship, *supra* n. 21, at 35.

40 *See, e.g.*, Geoff Sharp, *The Handbrake on Global Mediation*, Kluwer Mediation Blog (31 Aug. 2012), available at <http://kluwermediationblog.com/2012/08/31/the-handbrake-on-global-mediation/> (accessed 28 Mar. 2018) Wolski, *supra* n. 5, at 249; Jean Francois Guillemin, *Reasons for Choosing Alternative Dispute Resolution*, in *ADR in Business: Practice and Issues across Countries and Cultures* vol II 13, 34 (Arnold Ingen-Housz ed., Kluwer Law International 2011).

agreement should yield voluntary compliance, in the world of international business, imperfect circumstances may affect the performance of mediation agreements.[41] For instance, human rights abuses could make investors balk, the commodity in question could be subject to embargo, or the currency designated for payment could suffer devaluation.[42]

3.2.2.1 UNCITRAL's consideration of instruments on enforcement of mediated settlement agreements

To address the abovementioned concerns, the United Nations Commission on International Trade Law (UNCITRAL) started in 2014 considering the feasibility of the preparation of a convention on enforcement of settlement agreements resulting from international commercial mediation.[43] Interestingly, the idea of this kind of convention is not new. In 1982, the International Bar Association (IBA) drafted a convention for the enforcement of foreign conciliation settlements. It was, however, never implemented.[44]

The 2014 proposal to develop a multilateral convention on the enforcement of mediated settlement agreements drew a mixed reaction. On the one hand, it was said that a convention providing a mechanism to enforce settlement agreements would encourage parties to consider investing resources in mediation by providing greater certainty that any resulting settlement agreements could be relied on and easily enforced.[45] Such a convention would also provide a clear and uniform framework for facilitating enforcement in different jurisdictions.[46]

41 Brette L. Steele, *Enforcing International Commercial Mediation Agreements as Arbitral Awards under the New York Convention*, 54 UCLA L. Rev. 1385, 1387 (2007).

42 *Ibid.*

43 UNCITRAL, *Report of Working Group II (Arbitration and Conciliation) on the Work of its Sixty-Second Session (New York, 2–6 February 2015) (A/CN.9/832)*, 4–11 (11 Feb. 2015), available at <www.uncitral.org/uncitral/en/commission/working_groups/2Arbitration.html> (accessed 28 Mar. 2018) [hereinafter, *2015 Report of Working Group II*].

44 Ottoarndt Glossner, *Enforcement of Conciliation Settlements*, 11 Int'l Bus. Law. 151, 151–153 (1983) (reporting that the draft followed closely the New York Convention of 1958).

45 *2015 Report of Working Group II*, at ¶ 18.

46 *Ibid.* Some empirical studies confirm the desirability of an enforcement mechanism for international mediated settlement agreements. *See, e.g.*, S. I. Strong, *Use and Perception of International Commercial Mediation and Conciliation: A Preliminary Report on Issues Relating to the Proposed UNCITRAL Convention on International Commercial Mediation and Conciliation*, Social Science Research Network 41–45 (17 Nov. 2014), available at <https://papers.ssrn.com/sol3/papers.cfm?abstract_id=2526302> (accessed 28 Mar. 2018); *How Users View the Proposal for a UN Convention on the Enforcement of Mediated Settlements*, International Mediation Institute, available at <www.fd.unl.pt/docentes_docs/ma/MFG_MA_23458.pdf> (accessed 14 Jan. 2018); GPC Cumulated Data Results, *supra* n. 32 (reporting that legislation or convention that promotes recognition and enforcement of settlements, including those reached in mediation, ranked first as the area that would most

On the other hand, it was underlined that preparing a convention might be a lengthy process.[47] It was said that, in some countries, there was a lack of experience in international mediation, particularly due to the diversity in mediation processes as well as different legal traditions.[48] The empirical data collected for this book and presented in Sections 5.2.3.2.8, 5.2.3.3.1 and 5.3.3.4 also casts doubt on the necessity of a convention providing for the enforceability of international mediated settlement agreements.

Taking into account a varying degree of countries' experience in mediation, in the course of the discussion within the Working Group II (Arbitration and Conciliation), it was suggested that a more gradual approach should be taken to harmonize the regime of enforcement of settlement agreements, possibly starting from the harmonization of domestic legislation.[49] In line with that suggestion, it was considered that model legislative provisions could be prepared, which would be proposed for enactment by countries in their domestic legislation.[50] In a spirit of compromise, it was agreed to work on preparing both a model legislative text complementing the UNCITRAL Model Law on International Commercial Conciliation 2002 (UNCITRAL ML on Conciliation) and a convention on enforcement of international commercial settlement agreements resulting from mediation.[51] It was further suggested that the resolutions of the General Assembly accompanying those two instruments do not express any preference on the instrument to be

improve commercial dispute resolution). The results of the second and third studies are indicative, despite their non-scholarly nature.

47 *2015 Report of Working Group II*, at ¶ 19.

48 *Ibid.* Similarly, differing views were expressed by commentators. For example, McIlwrath commended the proposed convention for its practical value and strong incentive to use mediation to resolve international commercial disputes. Michael McIlwrath, *UNCITRAL to Consider Proposal for Convention on Enforcement of Mediated Settlements*, Kluwer Arbitration Blog (7 Jul. 2014), available at <http://kluwerarbitrationblog.com/blog/2014/07/07/uncitral-to-consider-proposal-for-convention-on-enforcement-of-mediated-settlements/> (accessed 28 Mar. 2018). Alexander, however, warned against rushing its adoption because the narrative assuming the need for this kind of convention may fail to consider significant variables and issues relevant to the nature of cross-border mediation practice. Nadja Alexander, *The Race Towards a New York Convention for Cross-Border Mediated Settlement Agreements: The Fable of the Tortoise and the Hare Revisited?* Kluwer Mediation Blog (13 Jul. 2014), available at <http://kluwermediationblog.com/2014/07/13/the-race-towards-a-new-york-convention-for-cross-border-mediated-settlement-agreements-the-fable-of-the-tortoise-and-the-hare-revisited/> (accessed 28 Mar. 2018).

49 *2015 Report of Working Group II, supra* n. 43, at ¶ 19.

50 UNCITRAL, *Settlement of Commercial Disputes. International Commercial Conciliation: Enforceability of Settlement Agreements. Note by the Secretariat (A/CN.9/WG.II/WP.190)*, ¶ 54 (13 Jul. 2015), available at <www.uncitral.org/uncitral/en/commission/working_groups/2Arbitration.html> [hereinafter, *2015 Note by the Secretariat*].

51 UNCITRAL, *Settlement of Commercial Disputes. International Commercial Mediation: Preparation of Instruments on Enforcement of International Commercial Settlement Agreements Resulting from Mediation. Note by the Secretariat (A/CN.9/WG.II/WP.205/Add.1)*, ¶ 1 (23 Nov. 2017), available at <www.uncitral.org/uncitral/en/commission/working_groups/2Arbitration.html> (accessed 28 Mar. 2018).

adopted by countries.[52] At the moment of writing, the Working Group II has completed its work on the preparation of a draft convention and a draft amended Model Law on international settlement agreements resulting from mediation.[53]

3.2.2.2 Current situation with enforcement of mediated settlement agreements

In August 2014, the UNCITRAL Secretariat circulated to countries a questionnaire to collect information on the existing legislative framework and practices with respect to enforcement of international settlement agreements resulting from mediation.[54] Replies to the questionnaire illustrate that national legislation is diverse and no dominant trend can be identified in this respect.[55]

Some jurisdictions have no specific legislation on enforcement of settlement agreements that are treated as commercial contracts between private parties and enforced accordingly.[56] Consequently, a mediated settlement agreement can be the subject of a breach of contract or specific performance claim.[57] A breach of contract, however, is usually the reason why the parties decide to use mediation. It is unlikely that litigating a contract resulting from successful mediation is the outcome that the parties want.[58]

52 *Ibid.*

53 UNCITRAL, *New Instruments on Settlement Agreements from an UNCITRAL Working Group* (12 Feb. 2018), available at <http://uncitral.tumblr.com/post/170792413006/new-instruments-on-settlement-agreements-from-an> (accessed 10 Apr. 2018). Both draft instruments are to be considered for finalisation by the UNCITRAL at its upcoming session in New York on 25 Jun.–13 Jul. 2018.

54 Replies to the questionnaire were published in UNCITRAL, *Settlement of Commercial Disputes, Enforcement of Settlement Agreements Resulting from International Commercial Conciliation/Mediation. Compilation of Comments by Governments (A/CN.9/846)* (27 Mar. 2015), available at <www.uncitral.org/uncitral/en/commission/working_groups/2Arbitration.html> (accessed 28 Mar. 2018) [hereinafter, *Comments by Governments*] and its addenda. An overview of the legislative trends is contained in UNCITRAL, *Settlement of Commercial Disputes: Enforceability of Settlement Agreements Resulting from International Commercial Conciliation/Mediation. Note by the Secretariat (A/CN.9/WG.II/WP.187)*, ¶¶ 20–30, Annex 1 (27 Nov. 2014), available at <www.uncitral.org/uncitral/en/commission/working_groups/2Arbitration.html> (accessed 28 Mar. 2018) [hereinafter, *2014 Note by the Secretariat*]; *2015 Note by the Secretariat, supra* n. 50, at ¶¶ 12–16.

55 *2014 Note by the Secretariat, supra* n. 54, at ¶ 30.

56 *2015 Note by the Secretariat, supra* n. 50, at ¶ 13.

57 Sharp, *supra* n. 40; Edna Sussman, *Combinations and Permutations of Arbitration and Mediation: Issues and Solutions*, in *ADR in Business: Practice and Issues across Countries and Cultures* vol II 381, 392–393 (Arnold Ingen-Housz ed., Kluwer Law International 2011).

58 Sharp, *supra* n. 40; Sussman, *supra* n. 57, at 393; *but see* Mercedes Tarrazon, *Arb-Med: A Reflection a Propos of a Bolivian Experience*, 2(1) NYSBA New York Disp. Res. Law. 87, 88 (2009) (stating that '[t]he question of enforceability is not important here because when parties settle through a well-conducted mediation they voluntarily comply with the terms of the agreements').

Jurisdictions that have provided for a method of enforcing settlement agreements generally aim to ensure that settlement agreements benefit from some form of expedited recognition of their enforceability. In this respect, three main approaches can be identified.[59]

First, a mediated settlement agreement may be entered as a judgment.[60] Such procedure may include specific expedited enforcement mechanisms. For example, in some jurisdictions, a settlement agreement can be enforced in a summary fashion if it is signed by the mediator or by legal counsel representing the parties and contains a statement expressing the parties' intent to seek summary enforcement of the agreement.[61] Some jurisdictions make settlement agreements enforceable through their deposition or registration at the court.[62] Sussman, however, points out that even where it is possible to incorporate a mediated settlement agreement into a judgment, difficulties of enforcement in foreign jurisdictions often diminish the judgment's value.[63]

Second, a settlement agreement can be enforced once it has been notarized according to the regime applicable to notarized documents.[64]

Finally, a settlement agreement can be enforced through an arbitration procedure.[65] The same neutral (arb)-med-arb, similar to other combinations, offers parties the possibility of converting their settlement agreement into a consent arbitral award, which Wolski and Ross believe to be the reason why parties resort to combinations.[66] Almoguera contends that this possibility by itself

59 *2015 Note by the Secretariat, supra* n. 50, at ¶ 13. Notably, some jurisdictions have adopted more than one approach. *Ibid*, at ¶ 14.

60 *2014 Note by the Secretariat, supra* n. 54, at ¶¶ 22–25. Many EU states incorporated such provision into their national legislation further to Directive 2008/52/EC of the European Parliament and of the Council on Certain Aspects of Mediation in Civil and Commercial Matters art. 6(1–2), 21 May 2008, OJL 136/3:

> 1. Member States shall ensure that it is possible for the parties, or for one of them with the explicit consent of the others, to request that the content of a written agreement resulting from mediation be made enforceable. The content of such an agreement shall be made enforceable unless, in the case in question, either the content of that agreement is contrary to the law of the Member State where the request is made or the law of that Member State does not provide for its enforceability.
> 2. The content of the agreement may be made enforceable by a court or other competent authority in a judgment or decision or in an authentic instrument in accordance with the law of the Member State where the request is made.

61 *2014 Note by the Secretariat, supra* n. 54, at ¶ 22.

62 *Ibid.*

63 Sussman, *supra* n. 57, at 393.

64 *2015 Note by the Secretariat, supra* n. 50, at ¶ 14.

65 *Ibid.*

66 Wolski, *supra* n. 5, at 249; Ross, *supra* n. 1, at 362. Interestingly, the same reasoning was used as an argument in favour of a convention on enforcement of settlement agreements: the

should help dissipate any mistrust about a combination of mediation and arbitration.[67]

Arbitration laws of many countries equate the status and the effect of consent awards to any other award on the merits of the case.[68] This is a strong argument in support of enforceability of consent awards pursuant to the New York Convention, although the convention itself is silent in this respect. The *travaux préparatoires* of the convention show that the issue of the convention's application to consent awards was raised during its deliberations but no decision was made in this respect.[69] While this silence can be interpreted as raising the question of whether consent awards qualify as arbitral awards under the convention,[70] according to the prevailing view, consent awards can be enforced in the same way as any other awards.[71] The enforceability of consent awards has found support in some empirical studies. Kaufmann-Kohler's research could find no judgment from courts anywhere in the world where a consent award had been successfully challenged either at the seat or in the country of enforcement.[72] The United States (US) courts

convention would address the enforceability of settlement agreements directly, rather than relying on the legal fiction of deeming them to be arbitral awards. Thereby, the adoption of the convention will eliminate the need to initiate an arbitration process simply to incorporate a settlement agreement into an award. *2014 Note by the Secretariat, supra* n. 54, at ¶ 31.

67 Jesus Almoguera, *Arbitration and Mediation Combined. The Independence and Impartiality of Arbitrators*, in *Liber Amicorum Bernardo Cremades* 101, 130 (M. A. Fernandez-Ballesteros & David Arias eds, La Ley 2010).

68 *See, e.g.*, UNCITRAL Model Law on International Commercial Arbitration art. 30 (effective 7 Jul. 2006), available at <www.uncitral.org/pdf/english/texts/arbitration/ml-arb/07-86998_Ebook.pdf> (accessed 28 Mar. 2018) [hereinafter, ML on Arbitration]; Arbitration Act 1996, c. 23, s. 51(3) [hereinafter, UK Arbitration Act].

69 *Travaux préparatoires*, Recognition and Enforcement of Foreign Arbitral Awards, Report by the Secretary-General, Annex I, Comments by Governments, E/2822, 7 & 10; *Travaux préparatoires*, United Nations Conference on International Commercial Arbitration, Consideration of the Draft Convention on the Recognition and Enforcement of Foreign Arbitral Awards, E/CONF.26/L.26. *See also Travaux préparatoires*, United Nations Conference on International Commercial Arbitration, Activities of Inter-Governmental and Non-Governmental Organizations in the Field of International Commercial Arbitration, Consolidated Report by the Secretary-General, E/CONF.26/4, 26.

70 Steele, *supra* n. 41, at 1397–1398.

71 W. Laurence Craig et al., *International Chamber of Commerce Arbitration*, 358 (Oceana Publications Inc. 2001) cited in Yaraslau Kryvoi & Dmitry Davydenko, *Consent Awards in International Arbitration: From Settlement to Enforcement*, 40 Brook. J. Int'l L. 827, 852 n. 107 (2014–2015).

72 Reported in Luke Nottage, *Arb-Med in Australia: The Time has Come*, Japanese Law and the Asia-Pacific ¶ 3 (31 Oct. 2007), available at <http://blogs.usyd.edu.au/japaneselaw/ArbMed.pdf> (accessed 28 Mar. 2018); *see also* UNCITRAL Secretariat Guide on the New York Convention, Article I, ¶ 36, available at <http://newyorkconvention1958.org/index.php?lvl=cmspage&pageid=10&menu=617&opac_view=-1> (accessed 12 Jan. 2018) (observing that there is no reported case law on the issue of the application of the New York Convention to consent awards).

have recently confirmed that consent awards are enforceable in the US pursuant to the New York Convention.[73]

The New Jersey International Arbitration, Mediation, and Conciliation Act appears to be the first legislative instrument to expressly provide for the enforceability of consent awards as regular arbitral awards pursuant to the New York Convention. This Act defines an arbitral award as an award signed by an arbitrator that may be the result of a settlement in arbitration, mediation, conciliation, or other form of dispute resolution that involves the assistance of a neutral.[74] It further specifies that, as a general rule, arbitral awards issued pursuant to the Act shall be enforced as permitted by law and consistent with the Federal Arbitration Act (FAA), and the enforcement provisions of the New York Convention, as implemented by the FAA.[75]

The empirical data collected for this book and presented in Sections 5.2.3.2.8, 5.2.3.3.1 and 5.3.3.4 does not support the narrative in the literature that the reason why parties use a combination of mediation and arbitration is the possibility of incorporating a mediated settlement agreement into a consent award.

3.2.2.3 Same neutral med-arb v. same neutral arb-med-arb

While, as mentioned in Section 3.2.1, the same neutral med-arb has the potential to save more time and money than the same neutral arb-med-arb, in terms of enforceability the latter can be more attractive to parties than the former. It is worth considering formally beginning the process as arbitration,[76] namely same neutral arb-med-arb rather than the same neutral med-arb. If the process starts as mediation, which succeeds, one could argue that there is no more dispute capable of triggering arbitration and hence generating an enforceable consent award. This issue will be explored further in Section 5.2.3.2.8.

73 *See Transocean Offshore Gulf of Guinea Vii v. Erin Energy Corp.*, Case No. H-17-2623 (S.D. Tex. 12 Mar. 2018) and *Albtelecom SH.A v. UNIFI Communs., Inc.*, Case No. 16 Civ. 9001, 2017 U.S. Dist. LEXIS 82154 (S.D.N.Y. 30 May 2017) discussed in Ava Borrasso, *U.S. District Courts Rule Consent Awards Fall Within New York Convention*, Kluwer Arbitration Blog (6 Apr. 2018), available at <http://arbitrationblog.kluwerarbitration.com/2018/04/06/u-s-district-courts-rule-consent-awards-fall-within-new-york-convention/> (accessed 11 Apr. 2018).

74 New Jersey International Arbitration Mediation and Conciliation Act, Title 2A § 23E-3 (2017).

75 *Ibid*, at § 23E-8.

76 *See, e.g.*, Alan L. Limbury, *Hybrid Dispute Resolution Processes – Getting the Best While Avoiding the Worst of Both Worlds?* in *CIArb's Mediation Compendium* 5 (A. Hudson-Tyreman et al. eds, London 2009); Luke Nottage & Richard Garnett, *Top 20 Things to Change in or Around Australia's International Arbitration Act*, 6(1) Asian Int'l. Arb. J. 1, 35 n. 93 (2010); Christopher Newmark & Richard Hill, *Can a Mediated Settlement Become an Enforceable Arbitration Award?* 16(1) Arb. Int'l. 81, 85 (2000).

3.2.3 Quality of the outcome

The quality of the outcome is reported to be another strength of the same neutral (arb)-med-arb.[77] This process, arguably, allows parties to achieve an outcome of better quality than the outcome resulting from either stand-alone mediation or stand-alone arbitration.

The best-case scenario for parties in the same neutral (arb)-med-arb is to resolve the entire dispute in the mediation phase of the process. The quality of the outcome resulting from the mediation phase of the same neutral (arb)-med-arb may be even better than the outcome resulting from stand-alone mediation because the former may help parties achieve a fair outcome of mediation. This is because while the primary role of mediators in stand-alone mediation is to assist parties in their negotiation, mediators in the same neutral (arb)-med-arb are more likely to consider the fairness of the result, as they will be required to render a decision if mediation does not result in a settlement.[78]

Even if no settlement is reached in the mediation phase and the dispute proceeds to the arbitration phase, the ultimate award resulting from the same neutral (arb)-med-arb is likely to be more acceptable to the parties than the award resulting from stand-alone arbitration. This is because previous negotiations may have narrowed the issues and resulted in procedural measures (for example, a third-party evaluation on key findings of fact), that could lead to more predictable and acceptable solutions.[79] The enhanced knowledge that neutrals have from participating in the mediation phase may allow them to render a more informed decision, as compared to arbitration used on its own.[80]

The same neutral (arb)-med-arb allows parties to work out in the mediation phase remedies unavailable in arbitration alone.[81] Parties can agree to rewrite their business arrangement, terminate it and agree on a division of assets, or come up with any other mutually satisfactory solution, which is illustrated by the following two cases.

77 *See, e.g.*, Carlos De Vera, *Arbitrating Harmony: 'Med-Arb' and the Confluence of Culture and Rule of Law in the Resolution of International Commercial Disputes in China*, 18 Colum. J. Asian L. 149, 156–157 (2004); Elliott, *supra* n. 19, at 171 (citing Vince Ready, a leading British Columbia labour relations mediator and arbitrator).

78 Bartel, *supra* n. 8, at 682.

79 Kaufmann-Kohler & Kun, *supra* n. 27, at 491; Kun, *supra* n. 27, at 537; Ehle, *supra* n. 22, at 86.

80 Sawada, *supra* n. 20, at 33; Marcia L. Greenbaum, *Process and the Professional Practitioner*, 2(3) Negotiation J. 225, 227 (Jul. 1986); De Vera, *supra* n. 77, at 156–157; Bartel, *supra* n. 8, at 665.

81 Phillips, *supra* n. 4, at 76; *see also* Andrew Burr, *Med-Arb: A Viable Hybrid Solution?* 8 Les Arbitres Internationaux 57, 68 (2005) (noting that the same neutral med-arb covers more human elements such as politics, cultural differences, effective communication, as opposed to litigation-relevant selection of facts).

In one case, the neutral first acted as a mediator, but when it became clear that the dispute could not be settled in mediation, the neutral became the arbitrator and decided to award a permanent injunction to the claimant.[82] The parties expressed their wish to elaborate the terms of the injunction together and the arbitrator mediated these terms with counsel. According to the professional who participated in the process, the parties appeared to be very satisfied with the result. The claimant even waived its claim for damages, happy with the injunctive relief.

In another so-called 'Machinery Joint Venture' case, a dispute arose between an American and an Asian company and they commenced arbitration proceedings before a sole arbitrator.[83] At a certain point the parties agreed to let the arbitrator try mediation. The arbitrator tried to mediate twice, meeting separately with the parties. Those meetings, however, were not successful and he resumed his work as an arbitrator after each meeting. Nevertheless, this eventually enabled the parties to draft 'Heads of Agreement' to create a joint venture in a spirit of mutual trust and cooperation. The dispute thus ended with neither a formal settlement agreement nor a consent award, but with a 'constructive forward-looking agreement saying nothing about the past'.[84]

The questionnaire data collected for this book confirms that the quality of the outcome is perceived as a strength of the combinations. As reported in Section 5.2.3.3.1, about half of the participants considered that a high-quality outcome, i.e., the outcome of a dispute resolution process is more in line with parties' needs (as compared to arbitration only), is a benefit of combinations (50.6%). Similar to the situation with cost and time efficiency addressed in Section 3.2.1, this result relates not only to the same neutral (arb)-med-arb, but to all combinations.

3.2.4 Flexibility

Flexibility is another significant beneficial attribute of the same neutral (arb)-med-arb.[85] Phillips regards this process as the most flexible of all the ADR processes.[86] According to Schneider, the flexibility with which the dual role neutral may switch from one method to the other in the same neutral (arb)-

82 Blankenship, *supra* n. 21, at 33 (discussing a case from practice of Gerald Phillips, a full-time neutral in California who specializes in large complex commercial and entertainment disputes).

83 Discussed in Sawada, *supra* n. 20, at 31–32.

84 *Ibid.*

85 Blankenship, *supra* n. 21, at 33–34; *but see* Lawday, *supra* n. 6, at 6 (observing that the flexibility of the same neutral (arb)-med-arb is considered by some to be a major weakness: the ability to be versatile, shifting back and forth, is an anathema to many practitioners from Anglo-American based systems).

86 Gerald F. Phillips, *Same-Neutral Med-Arb: What Does The Future Hold?* 60 Disp. Res. J. 24, 30 (2005).

med-arb, makes this combination superior to each of the two methods taken alone.[87]

Although it is commonly expected that in the same neutral med-arb, mediation will be followed by arbitration, nothing prevents parties from taking breaks in mediation to negotiate a settlement or even in arbitration to head back to mediation.[88] The flexibility of the same neutral arb-med-arb lies in the fact that arbitration can be resumed at any moment and new attempts to mediate the dispute can be initiated at any moment.[89] Arbitrators are free to choose the most appropriate moment in the course of arbitration to offer their services as mediators.[90] Often this tends to happen after the exchange of written briefs and before the hearing.[91] It may also be after a partial award. It should not be too early or too late in the proceedings.[92] In fact, arbitrators are best placed to know when it is a good moment to facilitate settlement.[93] Experienced arbitrators will generally know when the time is ripe.[94] Since the timing of settlement efforts may be crucial for their success, the same neutral arb-med-arb appears to maximise the opportunity to settle.[95] Arbitrators' awareness of the case and the strengths and weaknesses of parties' positions makes arbitrators well placed to mediate.[96]

3.2.5 Incentive to settle

The same neutral (arb)-med-arb, arguably, makes parties work harder because they may want to avoid having to arbitrate.[97] Knowing that a binding decision will be imposed if parties do not settle in mediation may motivate them towards resolution.[98]

The pressure on parties to settle in mediation seems to be higher in the same neutral (arb)-med-arb than in stand-alone mediation[99] or in mediation within diff

87 Schneider, *supra* n. 19, at 77.
88 Blankley, *supra* n. 31, at 329–330.
89 Ehle, *supra* n. 22, at 86; Phillips, *supra* n. 4, at 76.
90 Kaufmann-Kohler & Kun, *supra* n. 27, at 490; Kaufmann-Kohler, *supra* n. 7; Kun, *supra* n. 27, at 537.
91 Kaufmann-Kohler, *supra* n. 7.
92 *Ibid.*
93 Ehle, *supra* n. 22, at 85.
94 Kaufmann-Kohler, *supra* n. 7; Lau & Bulut, *supra* n. 20.
95 Lau & Bulut, *supra* n. 20.
96 Schneider, *supra* n. 19, at 77.
97 Phillips, *supra* n. 4, at 77; Arthur Marriott, *Litigate, Arbitrate, Mediate – Frustrate? Breaking the Dispute Deadlock*, Clayton Utz, available at <www.claytonutz.com/ialecture/2005/transcript_2005.html> (accessed 14 Jan. 2018).
98 Phillips, *supra* n. 4, at 77 (citing James P. Groton of Sutherland, Asbill & Brennan in Atlanta, Georgia); Martin C. Weisman, *Med/Arb – A Time and Cost Effective Hybrid for Dispute Resolution*, Weisman, Young & Ruemenapp, P.C. 4, available at <www.wysr-law.com/articles.html> (accessed 14 Jan. 2018); Sawada, *supra* n. 20, at 33; Thomson, *supra* n. 8, at 3; Greenbaum, *supra* n. 79, at 227.
99 Blankenship, *supra* n. 21, at 34.

neutral (arb)-med-arb.[100] The possible explanation for this might be that, when the mediator is going to be the arbitrator, the imminence of a binding award seems closer whereas, when mediation is followed by arbitration with an unknown person, arbitration seems more remote.[101] The imminence of an imposed award might create a strong incentive for parties to successfully mediate their dispute.[102] Interestingly, some practitioners perceive this strong incentive as a coercion that makes parties feel they have no choice other than to settle to avoid upsetting the neutral; this will be discussed in Section 3.3.1.4. The irony of the divide between different members of the ADR community is that exactly the same circumstance is viewed as appropriate subtle pressure by some and as a loss of free will by others.[103]

Empirical data supports the argument that parties are more encouraged to reach an agreement in mediation conducted as part of the same neutral med-arb, than in stand-alone mediation or mediation conducted within diff neutral med-arb. McGillicuddy, Welton, and Pruitt conducted a field experiment at a community centre to test the impact on behaviour in mediation of stand-alone mediation, mediation within the same neutral med-arb process, and mediation within diff neutral med-arb.[104] Results showed that parties in the same neutral med-arb engaged in more problem solving and were less hostile and competitive than were parties in stand-alone mediation, with diff neutral med-arb intermediate on these dimensions.[105] Parties were also more conciliatory in mediation as part of the same neutral med-arb than in stand-alone mediation, making more proposals and exhibiting a trend towards more concession making.[106] McGillicuddy, Welton, and Pruitt explain this result by the twofold influence of the same neutral med-arb procedure on party motivation.[107] First, parties showed greater motivation to settle in the mediation part of the same neutral med-arb as opposed to stand-alone mediation because they feared losing control of the process if the dispute moved to the arbitration stage. Second, parties were more motivated to follow the mediator in the same neutral med-arb because of the respect that is naturally given to a person who has the power to ultimately decide on a dispute.

Mediators in diff neutral med-arb were less involved throughout mediation than were mediators in stand-alone mediation and mediation conducted as part of the same

100 Phillips, *supra* n. 4, at 77.
101 *Ibid.*
102 *Ibid*; Blankenship, *supra* n. 21, at 34.
103 Blankenship, *supra* n. 21, at 34.
104 Neil B. McGillicuddy et al., *Third-Party Intervention: A Field Experiment Comparing Three Different Models*, 53(1) J. Pers. Soc. Psychol. 104 (1987).
105 *Ibid*, at 104.
106 *Ibid*, at 110; *see also* Blankenship, *supra* n. 21, at 34 (suggesting that a process with more conciliatory, more creative, and less hostile parties logically should achieve a more satisfying result, and referring to a study where the same neutral med-arb emerged as a more satisfying process over either mediation or arbitration alone. Cynthia F. Cohen & Murray F. Cohen, *Relative Satisfaction with ADR: Some Empirical Evidence*, 57 Disp. Res. J. 37 (2002)).
107 McGillicuddy et al., *supra* n. 104, at 110.

neutral med-arb.[108] The researchers explained this result by three reasons. First, mediators in diff neutral med-arb may feel less responsible for the case because another person can take it over. Second, they may see themselves as low-power adjuncts to a process that may be dominated by a high-power figure at a later time. Third, parties may see the mediator as a weak figure in comparison to the arbitrator and, feeling this, the mediator may become disinterested in the case.

Mediation attempts by arbitrators may be even more persuasive than those by judges.[109] Arbitration laws usually provide limited grounds for having an award reviewed by the courts. Knowing about the ability to appeal adverse judgments, a party can disregard mediation attempts by judges. Nottage reports a situation when he advised a New Zealand defendant in a case before a Japanese court.[110] Although Japanese judges traditionally encourage settlement in civil proceedings, the Japanese plaintiff showed zero interest in engaging in mediation despite the proceedings unfolding in a manner unfavourable to him. Later on, the plaintiff appealed the adverse judgment. Nottage concludes that had the matter been arbitrated with no possibility of appeal for error of law, the plaintiff might have been more conciliatory.[111]

Sometimes just becoming aware of how long arbitration may take may be a sufficient incentive for parties to give mediation another try.[112] In one recorded case, at a certain point, it became clear that parties were unable to settle in mediation.[113] With the parties' written consent the mediator became the arbitrator in the same dispute; however, soon both counsel acknowledged that arbitration seemed to be long and costly and requested to resume mediation. Then the parties settled.

3.2.6 Parties' more honest behaviour

Parties to the same neutral (arb)-med-arb are likely to participate in the mediation phase in good faith and to approach the bargaining table with honest demands,[114] because if they hold back on a particular issue, they know that the dual role neutral is going to make a decision.[115] For Kagel, the power to keep parties honest is the key to the same neutral (arb)-med-arb.[116]

108 *Ibid*, at 111.

109 Luke Nottage, *Is (International Commercial) Arbitration ADR?* 21(1) Arbit. Mediat. 83, 89 (2002).

110 *Ibid*, at 89 n. 26.

111 *Ibid.*

112 Phillips, *supra* n. 4, at 76.

113 *Ibid* (referring to a case from his own practice).

114 Blankenship, *supra* n. 21, at 34.

115 Sam Kagel, *Combining Mediation and Arbitration*, 96 Monthly Lab. Rev. 62, 62 (1973) cited in Bartel, *supra* n. 8, at 685.

116 *Ibid; but see* Roselle L. Wissler, *Court-Connected Settlement Procedures: Mediation and Judicial Settlement Conferences*, 26 Ohio St. J. on Disp. Resol. 271, 295 (2011) (reporting the results of the 2008 survey of Ohio lawyers indicating that there is little difference between mediators (court staff and private) and judges (assigned or not to the case) in their ability to help counsel manage difficult parties and ensure their good behaviour in judicial settlement conferences).

Using the same neutral (arb)-med-arb might even assist a party who is in a weaker bargaining position in the mediation phase.[117] A weaker party may negotiate secure in the knowledge that if no mutually acceptable agreement is reached, the dual role neutral will render a decision.[118] This differs from stand-alone mediation, where a party may yield to what it regards an unfair result as the only way of putting an end to the dispute.[119] Also, a mediator in stand-alone mediation may be unable or simply unwilling to equalize bargaining skill or power.[120] Although the weaker party is not guaranteed a favourable result in the mediation phase of the same neutral (arb)-med-arb, the process appears to help ensure that weakness will not be a factor in and of itself.[121]

At the same time, the awareness that the mediator may ultimately decide the dispute may induce the stronger party to be reasonable and fair.[122] A contractual commitment to the same neutral (arb)-med-arb should prevent the stronger party from refusing to use this process because of this kind of discomfort.

3.3 Concerns associated with the same neutral (arb)-med-arb

While in the view of its supporters the same neutral (arb)-med-arb enables parties to have the best of mediation and arbitration,[123] many experienced and highly ethical practitioners remain convinced that mediation and arbitration by the same person are inherently incompatible and the process is fatally flawed.[124] Concerns regarding the same neutral (arb)-med-arb are so serious that some neutrals take the position that they would never agree to arbitrate a case in which they have previously served as the mediator.[125]

Critics of the same neutral (arb)-med-arb question whether the mediation and arbitration phases can both remain valid while conducted by the same neutral[126] because mediation and arbitration are radically,[127] inherently,[128] and fundamentally[129] different processes with different aims and even moralities.[130]

117 Lawday, *supra* n. 6, at 9.
118 Bartel, *supra* n. 8, at 682–683.
119 *Ibid*, at 682.
120 *Ibid.*
121 *Ibid*, at 683.
122 *Ibid.*
123 *See generally* Section 3.2.
124 Thomson, *supra* n. 8, at 3; Blankenship, *supra* n. 21, at 29; Lau & Bulut, *supra* n. 20; Stipanowich & Ulrich, *supra* n. 6, at 25; Brewer & Mills, *supra* n. 20, at 35. Ross, *supra* n. 1, at 352.
125 Brewer & Mills, *supra* n. 20, at 35–36.
126 Blankenship, *supra* n. 21, at 29; James T. Peter, *Med-Arb in International Arbitration*, 4 Revista de Arbitragem e Mediação 155, 159 (2005); Wolski, *supra* n. 5, at 267.
127 De Vera, *supra* n. 76, at 159.
128 Lawday, *supra* n. 6, at 8; Peter, *supra* n. 126, at 159.
129 Bartel, *supra* n. 8, at 663; Stipanowich & Ulrich, *supra* n. 6, at 25.
130 Bartel, *supra* n. 8, at 688; Blankenship, *supra* n. 21, at 34.

The key differences between mediation and arbitration are as follows. In the privatised legal process of arbitration, arbitrators render a decision that they usually base on their interpretation of the relevant law as applied to the facts of the case.[131] Mediation is not a legal process, but a communication and negotiation process, whereby a mediator helps parties negotiate a settlement.[132] An arbitrator's award is legally binding and enforceable in national courts if necessary.[133] Parties' agreement reached in mediation, in general, is only contractually binding. While arbitration is about what happened in the past (e.g., who was liable), mediation focuses on fixing problems in the present as well as preserving future relationship. Also, the arbitrator's award is usually limited in scope by what parties have asked for in their arbitration clause. A mediator, on the contrary, can help parties expand the scope of what terms can be considered. Perhaps, that it is the reason why arbitration is said to be more of a science and mediation more of an art.[134]

For critics, the same neutral (arb)-med-arb inevitably compromises the neutral's legal capacity to act in an adjudicative capacity, while at the same time undermining the efficacy of the prior mediation.[135] It appears that the single most problematic issue in the same neutral (arb)-med-arb and the cause of the majority of concerns associated with the process is caucuses.[136] Notably, objections to caucuses arise whenever a dual role neutral becomes an arbitrator after acting as a mediator in mediation that involved the use of caucuses.[137] If arbitration comes to an end and mediation is commenced, caucuses do not seem to raise any concerns.

The main concerns associated with the same neutral (arb)-med-arb can be divided into two groups: behavioural concerns that surface in the mediation stage, and procedural that arise in the arbitration stage.[138]

131 Julian D. M. Lew, *Multi-Institutional Conciliation and the Reconciliation of Different Legal Cultures*, in *New Horizons in International Commercial Arbitration and Beyond*, 12 ICCA Congress Series 421, 425 (Albert Jan van den Berg ed., Kluwer Law International 2005); Paul E. Mason, *The Arbitrator as Mediator, and Mediator as Arbitrator*, 28(6) J. Int'l. Arb. 541, 541 (2011). This, however, is not the case if parties authorise the arbitrator to decide *ex aequo et bono*.

132 Mason, *supra* n. 131, at 541; Bartel, *supra* n. 8, at 663.

133 Mason, *supra* n. 131, at 542.

134 *Ibid*, at 542–543.

135 Lawday, *supra* n. 6, at 4 (citing Newman); Peter, *supra* n. 126, at 164.

136 Ross, *supra* n. 1, at 360; Leon & Peterson, *supra* n. 19, at 93; Hindle, *supra* n. 8, at 15.

137 Hindle, *supra* n. 8, at 8 n. 11.

138 This division is made on the basis of discussion in Alan L. Limbury, *Making Med-Arb Work*, 9 (7) ADR Bulletin 1, 1–2 (2007); Wolski, *supra* n. 5, at 259–260. Other commentators enumerate concerns related to the same neutral (arb)-med-arb. These repeat and/or complement those that appear in two groups suggested by Limbury and Wolski. *See, e.g.*, Stipanowich & Ulrich, *supra* n. 6, at 25–26; Bartel, *supra* n. 8, at 678–689; Peter, *supra* n. 126, at 159–164; Peter, *supra* n. 5, at 92–99; Elliott, *supra* n. 19, at 166–168; Lawday, *supra* n. 6, at 4–8.

3.3.1 Behavioural concerns

Behavioural concerns[139] include the possible reluctance of parties to be open in their discussions with mediators knowing that at a certain point they might become arbitrators, the inhibited conduct of mediators, parties' use of mediation as a tactical tool, and the abuse of power by mediators resulting in the coercion of parties into a settlement.

3.3.1.1 Parties' reluctance to be open in mediation

Knowledge of parties' true intentions, underlying interests and preferences, and business background enables a mediator to guide parties in exploring areas of mutual gain.[140] Therefore, a mediator encourages parties to be candid. In arbitration, parties tend to focus on persuading the arbitrator that their side is right, which prevents them from revealing any weaknesses and letting the arbitrator explore the background of the case.

The same neutral (arb)-med-arb is often criticised for the risk of inhibiting parties' willingness to share information candidly with the neutral during the mediation phase of the process.[141] Marriott even considers that this is the main conceptual objection to the same neutral (arb)-med-arb.[142] A negative impact on the mediation phase may occur because of a party's knowledge that the mediator may eventually become the arbitrator. Fearing that their disclosure will prejudice arbitration, parties may become less forthcoming during caucusing and more reluctant to reveal their true settlement positions, as they would be in mediation followed by arbitration with another neutral.[143] There is a risk that one of the biggest advantages of mediation that is essential to its success, the safe exploration of mutual gain without the danger of conveying confidential information to the party's own detriment, is substantially weakened.[144] The available empirical

139 Limbury, *supra* n. 138, at 1–2; Wolski, *supra* n. 5, at 259. Most concerns in this group were suggested by Limbury and Wolski.

140 Peter, *supra* n. 126, at 163; Peter, *supra* n. 5, at 98.

141 *See e.g.*, Brewer & Mills, *supra* n. 20, at 35; Kaufmann-Kohler & Kun, *supra* n. 27, at 491; Thomson, *supra* n. 8, at 3; Phillips, *supra* n. 4, at 76; Kaufmann-Kohler, *supra* n. 7; Peter, *supra* n. 5, at 98; Sawada, *supra* n. 20, at 33; Blankenship, *supra* n. 21, at 36–37; Lang, *supra* n. 2, at 101; Limbury, *supra* n. 138, at 1; Stipanowich & Ulrich, *supra* n. 6, at 26; Flake, *supra* n. 22, at 6–7; Kun, *supra* n. 27, at 538; Abramson, *supra* n. 20, at 5; Safeguards for Arbitrators Who Use Private Meetings with Each Party as a Means of Facilitating Settlement (Final Report of the CEDR Commission on Settlement in International Arbitration, Appendix 2), ¶ 5, available at <www.cedr.com/about_us/arbitration_commission/> (accessed 14 Jan. 2018) [hereinafter, CEDR Appendix 2].

142 Arthur L. Marriott, *Arbitrators and Settlement*, in *New Horizons in International Commercial Arbitration and Beyond*, 12 ICCA Congress Series 533, 541 (Albert Jan van den Berg ed., Kluwer Law International 2005).

143 Ross, *supra* n. 1, at 360; Phillips, *supra* n. 4, at 76; Rewald & Jachimek Weil, *supra* n. 27, at 2 (citing Brian Pappas).

144 Peter, *supra* n. 5, at 98.

data supports the view that placing the decision maker in the room might be detrimental to parties' candour. Ohio lawyers who participated in 2008 in a survey about their experiences with mediation and settlement conferences in federal court, thought that parties could be much less candid with judges assigned to the case than with judges not assigned to the case, court staff mediators, volunteer mediators, and private mediators.[145]

At the same time, one may assume that this shortfall of information and frankness as compared to stand-alone mediation may be partly compensated in the same neutral arb-med-arb by dual role neutrals' thorough knowledge of the file resulting from their prior participation in the process as arbitrators.[146] Independent mediators usually spend only a few days on a case and are unable to gain an insight comparable to dual role neutrals who mediate after acting as arbitrators. No empirical data has been found to confirm this assumption.

Also, Lang expresses concerns that knowing that there is an easy and available alternative option of achieving finality (namely have the mediator (as arbitrator) make a decision for them), parties may not work as hard at the mediation phase as they otherwise might.[147] This is an example of a situation when the exact same circumstance, i.e., parties' knowledge that a binding decision will be imposed if parties do not settle in mediation, is perceived by some authors as creating a motivation for parties to work harder in mediation,[148] and as having directly the opposite effect by others. The empirical data discussed in Section 3.2.5 supports the view that parties in the same neutral med-arb work harder and engage in more problem solving than parties in stand-alone mediation and mediation conducted within diff neutral med-arb.[149]

3.3.1.2 *Inhibited conduct of a mediator*

Not only parties may become reluctant to be open in mediation, dual role neutrals' conduct of the mediation phase may also be inhibited.[150] Mediators' knowledge that they might become arbitrators, may prevent them from conducting the mediation phase with their usual vigour.[151] Speaking from his own professional experience as a dual role neutral, Flake suggests that neutrals should be less probative and opinionated in the mediation phase of the same neutral

145 Wissler, *supra* n. 116, at 286.
146 Schneider, *supra* n. 19, at 93.
147 Lang, *supra* n. 2, at 101.
148 This kind of perception has been discussed in Section 3.2.5 *supra*.
149 McGillicuddy et al., *supra* n. 104, at 110 discussed in Section 3.2.5 *supra*.
150 Brewer & Mills, *supra* n. 20, at 35; Abramson, *supra* n. 20, at 5, n. 9.
151 Brewer & Mills, *supra* n. 20, at 35; Pappas, *supra* n. 31, at 189; Ellen E. Deason, *Combinations of Mediation and Arbitration with the Same Neutral: A Framework for Judicial Review*, 5 Y.B. On Arb. & Mediation 219, 224 (2013).

(arb)-med-arb.[152] Flake expects a lower success rate of resolution in the mediation phase of the same neutral med-arb as compared to stand-alone mediation because of the 'chilling effect' on both parties and mediators.[153] Nevertheless, the available empirical data presented in Section 3.2.5 demonstrates the opposite: parties appear to be more encouraged to reach an agreement in mediation conducted as part of the same neutral med-arb than in stand-alone mediation or mediation conducted as part of diff neutral med-arb.

3.3.1.3 Tactical use of mediation

If parties know that the mediator will become the arbitrator, should mediation not result in a settlement, there is a fear that they may use mediation strategically, to introduce material strictly to influence the arbitrator's award, rather than to reach a settlement.[154] After receiving the mediator's assurances about confidentiality of discussions in caucuses, a party may embellish its story about the other side.[155] Then it may drive mediation to an impasse and move the dispute to arbitration.[156]

It may be less the parties than the counsel who misuse the mediation process in this way. For example, counsel may attempt to 'spin' the mediator towards the client's side in preparation for arbitration.[157] To be fair, it should be noted that counsel may do this even in stand-alone mediation, in an attempt to present the case to the advantage of their client so that the mediator facilitates a settlement more favourable to that party.[158] Thereby, it appears that neutrals in all types of processes need to distil the real facts of the case despite the posturing of counsel.

The perception that the same neutral (arb)-med-arb enables parties to abuse mediation by using it strategically contrasts with the perception referred to in Section 3.2.6 that parties to this process are likely to participate in the mediation phase in good faith and approach the bargaining table with honest demands. The available empirical data shows marginal difference between dual role and separate neutrals in their ability to ensure parties' good behaviour in settlement conferences.[159]

152 Flake, *supra* n. 22, at 7.

153 *Ibid*, at 8.

154 Elliott, *supra* n. 19, at 179; Thomson, *supra* n. 8, at 3; Lucy Greenwood, *A Window of Opportunity? Building a Short Period of Time into Arbitral Rules in order for Parties to Explore Settlement*, 27(2) Arb. Int'l. 199, 201 (2011).

155 Jeff Kichaven, *Med-Arb Should Be Dead*, 2(1) NYSBA New York Disp. Res. Law. 80, 80 (2009); Blankenship, *supra* n. 21, at 36.

156 Kichaven, *supra* n. 155, at 80; *see also* Blankenship, *supra* n. 21, at 36 (noting that later consideration of this embellished information by the neutral arguably has the effect of allowing 'perjury' to influence an award).

157 Phillips, *supra* n. 4, at 76; Ross, *supra* n. 1, at 360.

158 Ross, *supra* n. 1, at 360.

159 *See* n. 116 and Wissler, *supra* n. 116, at 295.

3.3.1.4 Power of a dual role neutral and a threat of coercion

Vesting the authority to render a binding decision in the same person who mediates the dispute creates enormous power in the neutral.[160] There is a fear that consciously or unconsciously the neutral may abuse this power and use the threat of an award to coerce parties into a settlement during the mediation stage.[161] Blankenship calls this power the 'muscle' of the process that, depending on the commentator's opinion, is either a source of abuse or the strength of the same neutral (arb)-med-arb. The latter view has been addressed in Section 3.2.5.

For some critics, coercion is the fatal flaw in the process.[162] Agreements reached in this process may be a result of strong-arm tactics.[163] The value of mediation is compromised when mediators, knowing they could later decide a dispute, coerce parties into a settlement.[164] A negotiated resolution may be perceived by parties as an imposed one, thus diminishing the degree of satisfaction and commitment.[165] By eliminating the ability of parties to withdraw from mediation voluntarily, the process deprives parties of a key mediation principle – the right to self-determination.[166]

Importantly, the focus of mediation in the same neutral (arb)-med-arb seems to shift from parties' interests and options to the neutral.[167] The frequent best alternative to a negotiated agreement (BATNA) question of 'What will happen if the dispute goes to court?' becomes irrelevant. What matters is how the mediator will decide the matter, if parties do not settle in mediation and the mediator becomes an arbitrator. Parties will closely examine the mediator's statements because the mediator informally controls their BATNA. Pappas concludes that the same neutral (arb)-med-arb incentivizes the neutral to impose a solution and essentially turn mediation into a judicial settlement conference.[168]

Some anecdotally reported cases demonstrate how the potential to abuse the power materialises in practice.

160 Bartel, *supra* n. 8, at 679.

161 *Ibid*; Phillips, *supra* n. 4, at 76; Kichaven, *supra* n. 155, at 82; Deekshitha & Saha, *supra* n. 6, at 93; Kaufmann-Kohler, *supra* n. 7; Ross, *supra* n. 1, at 360.

162 Blankenship, *supra* n. 21, at 36.

163 *Ibid;* Deekshitha & Saha, *supra* n. 6, at 93; Peter, *supra* n. 126, at 159.

164 De Vera, *supra* n. 77, at 159. One of the reasons why they might pressure settlement in mediation is to avoid impartiality issues in arbitration discussed in Section 3.3.2.1. Pappas, *supra* n. 31, at 181.

165 William Ury et al., *Getting Disputes Resolved: Designing Systems to Cut the Costs of Conflict*, 57 (San Francisco: Jossey-Bass 1988) cited in De Vera, *supra* n. 77, at 160 n. 38; Bartel, *supra* n. 8, at 679; Peter, *supra* n. 126, at 159.

166 Richard Fullerton, *The Ethics of Mediation-Arbitration*, 38(5) Colorado Law. 31, 34 (2009).

167 Pappas, *supra* n. 31, at 179.

168 *Ibid.*

In a Brazilian-US arbitration, the parties did not have a same neutral arb-med-arb clause in their contract and did not agree to mediate.[169] Nevertheless, the sole arbitrator, who was trained primarily as a mediator, threatened the parties with 'punishment' if they did not settle the case in mediation. Parties were not able to negotiate a settlement and the arbitrator 'carried out his threat through his award'.[170]

In another International Court of Arbitration of International Chamber of Commerce (ICC) arbitration case, an arbitrator from Zürich informed the parties at the Terms of Reference conference that both parties had a weak position and that they needed to settle.[171] He made some proposals. The French party was concerned that the arbitrator was prepared to rule against them. Thus, they accepted the proposals, but not because they thought that they were reasonable, but because they felt obliged to do so. The counsel who represented the French party in that case reported that he doubted the fairness of the settlement.

In yet another case the German Supreme Court annulled a settlement concluded before a lower court.[172] The ground for annulment was that the lower court had announced that its decision against the defendant had been prepared and that, if the defendant would not immediately accept the settlement offer, the court would render this decision. The Supreme Court regarded this conduct as the exercise of illegal pressure.

The risk that a dual role neutral may coerce parties into a settlement seems confirmed by empirical data. The field experiment introduced in Section 3.2.5 investigated whether the power available to the dual role neutral could elicit directive behaviour from neutrals in the mediation phase and encourage them to dictate terms.[173] There was a hint of these dangers in the study's data. Mediators used heavier tactics in the same neutral med-arb, more often threatening to terminate mediation or insisting on a particular proposal (as compared to stand-alone mediation). However, it appeared that mediators tended to use these tactics at the very end of mediation, in a last-ditch effort to save a failing mediation rather than a policy of forceful advocacy. The post-hearing questionnaire filled out by disputing parties showed that the parties saw themselves as more involved in working out the terms of the agreement and the mediator as less forceful in the same neutral med-arb than in stand-alone mediation or diff neutral med-arb.

169 Mason, *supra* n. 131, at 550 (reporting a case from his own experience that he was peripherally involved in).

170 *Ibid.*

171 Schneider, *supra* n. 19, at 82, n. 111 (citing Derains, a French counsel with extensive experience in international arbitration both as arbitrator and counsel, who represented a French party in that case).

172 *Ibid*, at 84–85, n. 122.

173 McGillicuddy et al., *supra* n. 104, at 110; Dean G. Pruitt, *Process and Outcome in Community Mediation*, 11(4) Negotiation Journal 365, 368 (Oct. 1995).

3.3.2 Procedural concerns

Procedural concerns[174] relate to the arbitration stage and are directed at the danger that arbitrators will appear or actually be biased, because of the information received in mediation and particularly in caucuses. Moreover, the inability of a party to hear and respond to the issues raised by the other party in caucuses with mediators who later become arbitrators, may lead to a breach of due process.

3.3.2.1 Bias of a dual role neutral

The literature often refers to the threat to arbitrator's impartiality as the main drawback of the same neutral (arb)-med-arb.[175] Events may occur during the mediation phase that could cause parties later to question the fairness of the arbitration part of the process.[176] For example, if dual role neutrals express in mediation a view as to the merits of the dispute, this might be seen as affecting their impartiality for the remaining arbitration part of the process.[177]

Another fear is that if settlement efforts fail and neutrals become or resume their role of arbitrators, they may lose their impartiality because of the information that they have become aware of in the mediation stage but that is not on the record.[178] Dual role neutrals might have difficulty remaining unaffected by private and perhaps intimate, emotional, and other legally irrelevant information or compromise positions revealed in mediation.[179] They may become consciously or unconsciously empathetic towards one of the parties or may become involved with the subject matter.[180] This may happen especially if dual role neutrals engage in caucuses and invite parties to discuss, for example, emotional issues that may be relevant for settlement purposes, though not strictly relevant for resolution purposes.[181] It might be challenging for neutrals to ignore

174 Limbury, *supra* n. 138, at 2; Wolski, *supra* n. 5, at 259–260.
175 *See, e.g.*, Kaufmann-Kohler, *supra* n. 7; Ehle, *supra* n. 22, at 86.
176 Brewer & Mills, *supra* n. 20, at 35.
177 Michael Hwang, *The Role of Arbitrators as Settlement Facilitators – Commentary*, in *New Horizons in International Commercial Arbitration and Beyond*, 12 ICCA Congress Series 571, 572 (Albert Jan van den Berg ed., Kluwer Law International 2005); Peter, *supra* n. 126, at 161; Peter, *supra* n. 5, at 94 n. 57 (citing J. Martin H. Hunter from Christian Bühring-Uhle, *Arbitration and Mediation in International Business: Designing Procedures for Effective Conflict Management* 204 (Kluwer Law International 1996)).
178 Kaufmann-Kohler, *supra* n. 7; Baizeau & Loong, *supra* n. 6, at 1455; Kaufmann-Kohler & Kun, *supra* n. 27, at 491; Blankenship, *supra* n. 21, at 35; Brewer & Mills, *supra* n. 20, at 35; Bartel, *supra* n. 8, at 679 & 685–686; Ross, *supra* n. 1, at 360; Lew, *supra* n. 131, at 426; Stipanowich & Ulrich, *supra* n. 6, at 26; Flake, *supra* n. 22, at 5–6; Kun, *supra* n. 27, at 538; CEDR Appendix 2, *supra* n. 141, at ¶ 4.
179 Peter, *supra* n. 5, at 92–93; Peter, *supra* n. 126, at 160; Lang, *supra* n. 2, at 100.
180 Peter, *supra* n. 5, at 92–93; Peter, *supra* n. 126, at 160 & n. 53 (citing Claude Reymond and Richard W. Hulbert from Bühring-Uhle, *supra* n. 177, at 205–206).
181 Peter, *supra* n. 126, at 160.

information disclosed in mediation when called on to decide as arbitrators.[182] This will allow the losing party to challenge the award on the ground of actual or apparent bias, which would bring to nought the time- and cost-saving advantages of the process.[183]

Even arbitrators in stand-alone arbitration may be influenced by what they see and hear. Nevertheless, dual role neutrals undoubtedly become privy to much more than arbitrators in stand-alone arbitration would.[184] This exposes dual role neutrals much more to the danger of bias than arbitrators.[185] Even if parties limit the decision-making to only certain facts, a dual role neutral might still struggle to block out information gained in mediation.

While it may be difficult for the dual role neutral to block out the information from mediation in the arbitration stage, it may be even more difficult for the losing party to believe that the neutral did so.[186] Counsel might fear that the mediator who has become the arbitrator has developed a skewed view of their client's position that is not possible to set right anymore.[187]

This situation might be a variation of the classic tautology: I can't tell you what you don't know because I don't know what you don't know. Counsel cannot correct a misrepresentation that may have been made to dual role neutrals in mediation because counsel do not know what may have been said nor can they gauge what evidentiary weight neutrals have already given it in their mind. It is not so much that neutrals are no longer impartial as that counsel have no effective method of determining whether a bias has been formed. Like most risk-averse people, counsel would rather not take a chance if they sense that they might lose.[188]

Some empirical data supports the view that neutrals with subsequent settlement authority are viewed as partial as compared to neutrals without such authority. In 2008 survey, 60% of Ohio lawyers strongly or somewhat disagreed with the statement that the judge assigned to the case is 'able to fully explore settlement without prejudice to ongoing litigation if the case is not settled'.[189] By contrast, lawyers strongly or somewhat disagreed with the same statement relating to judges not assigned to the case (16%), court staff mediators (5%), volunteer mediators (3%), or private mediators (1%).[190]

Another set of empirical data, however, indicates that the threat to arbitrator impartiality might be more a perception than a reality. The research conducted by Kaufmann-Kohler found no cases where arbitrators were challenged or removed,

182 *Ibid*; Elliott, *supra* n. 19, at 167.
183 Ross, *supra* n. 1, at 360; Deekshitha & Saha, *supra* n. 6, at 89.
184 De Vera, *supra* n. 77, at 159; Bartel, *supra* n. 8, at 685; Peter, *supra* n. 126, at 160.
185 De Vera, *supra* n. 77, at 159; Peter, *supra* n. 126, at 160.
186 Ury et al., *supra* n. 165, at 57 cited in Bartel, *supra* n. 8, at 686 n. 123.
187 Haig Oghigian, *The Meditation/Arbitration Hybrid*, 20(1) J. Int'l. Arb. 75, 77 (2003).
188 *Ibid.*
189 Wissler, *supra* n. 116, at 286–287.
190 *Ibid*, at 287.

or where awards were set aside or denied enforcement on the ground that an arbitrator facilitated settlement.[191] Instead, the research found some court cases that held exactly the opposite: the involvement of judges in settlement of their own cases is admissible. According to Kaufmann-Kohler, the same must necessarily apply to arbitrators.

3.3.2.2 Breach of due process

Arbitrators may only make decisions on the evidence presented in hearings at which each side has the opportunity to challenge the evidence.[192] Mediation differs from arbitration; a party does not have an inalienable right to defend all accusations in mediation, and the mediator is not ruling on the dispute.[193] The same neutral (arb)-med-arb becomes problematic when mediation fails and dual role neutrals take on or resume their role as arbitrators.[194]

The process may offend the principles of due process[195] because parties have no chance to hear and respond to the issues raised by each of them in caucuses with the mediator who later becomes an arbitrator.[196] An award resulting from the same neutral (arb)-med-arb may be unfairly influenced by evidence from caucuses.[197] Kun regards the risk of a breach of due process as the main argument against arbitrators serving as mediators.[198] Notably, concerns about due process seem to arise only in some countries but not in others. For example, the ICC Mediation Guidance Notes observe that the risk of offending the rules of due process is a common concern in jurisdictions where the same neutral arb-med-arb is used rarely, if at all.[199] The notes, however, do not specify what jurisdictions in particular, they mean. Lawday and Ross speak about the risk of offending principles of due process as understood in Anglo-American/common law system.[200]

191 Kaufmann-Kohler, *supra* n. 7.
192 Phillips, *supra* n. 4, at 76; Blankenship, *supra* n. 21, at 36.
193 Michael E. Schneider, *Combining Arbitration with Conciliation*, 1 Transnat'l Disp. Mgmt 9, 27 (2004).
194 Rosoff, *supra* n. 6, at 93.
195 Natural justice, procedural fairness, and due process are terms used to describe the same principle in different countries.
196 Rosoff, *supra* n. 6, at 92–93; Barney Jordaan, *Hybrid ADR Processes in South Africa*, 2(1) NYSBA New York Disp. Res. Law. 117, 117 (2009); Alan Limbury, *ADR in Australia*, in *ADR in Business: Practice and Issues across Countries and Cultures* vol II 429, 454 (Arnold Ingen-Housz ed., Kluwer Law International 2011); Kaufmann-Kohler & Kun, *supra* n. 27, at 491; Kaufmann-Kohler, *supra* n. 7; Blankenship, *supra* n. 21, at 36; Peter, *supra* n. 126, at 161; Thomson, *supra* n. 8, at 3; Elliott, *supra* n. 19, at 166–167.
197 Phillips, *supra* n. 4, at 76.
198 Kun, *supra* n. 27, at 537.
199 International Court of Arbitration of the International Chamber of Commerce (ICC), *Mediation Guidance Notes* ¶ 34 (International Chamber of Commerce 2013).
200 Lawday, *supra* n. 6, at 8; Ross, *supra* n. 1, at 361.

As discussed in detail in Part IV (Chapters 6, 7, and 8), this book identifies three major ways to address behavioural and procedural concerns associated with the same neutral (arb)-med-arb: the involvement of different neutrals in combinations, procedural modifications of the same neutral (arb)-med-arb, and the implementation of safeguards for using the same neutral (arb)-med-arb.

If parties choose the last option, as explained in Chapter 8, they can reduce behavioural and procedural concerns through the implementation of two key safeguards. These are party voluntary and informed consent to the process and one of the two safeguard options for reducing concerns related to the use of caucuses. Section 8.2.2 considers whether and, if so, to what extent parties can waive the impartiality requirement and their due process rights.

3.4 The challenging task of a dual role neutral in the same neutral (arb)-med-arb

The success of any dispute resolution method often depends on the quality of the neutral selected.[201] Proponents of the same neutral (arb)-med-arb argue that many criticisms of the process are dramatically overstated and much depends on finding a competent neutral,[202] which might, however, present a challenging task.[203] A competent neutral will be skilled to deal with information from caucuses, overcome the difficulties of information quality and exchange, and minimise the possibilities of bias and breach of due process.[204]

In the same neutral (arb)-med-arb, even assuming that neutrals are willing to make a transition from one process to another, they will not necessarily be capable of performing this task without proper training.[205] A significant concern with the process is the skill of dual role neutrals and their capacity to effectively handle both roles.[206] No matter in what sequence the processes are used, dual role neutrals need to possess qualifications for both mediation and arbitration and likely will have topic-specific expertise in the issues involved.[207]

Mediation focuses on finding an efficient and value-creating solution, which requires an exploration of parties' underlying interests.[208] Mediators, therefore, may ask parties for confidential information or engage in 'reality testing' – a

201 Bartel, *supra* n. 8, at 688.

202 *Ibid*, at 687–688; Lawday, *supra* n. 6, at 8; Blankenship, *supra* n. 21, at 36.

203 Blankley, *supra* n. 31, at 337 (observing that although time may be saved because parties have to select only one neutral, finding a neutral to serve as a mediator and an arbitrator may be more difficult than finding one of each).

204 Lawday, *supra* n. 6, at 8; Blankenship, *supra* n. 21, at 36; Bartel, *supra* n. 8, at 687–688.

205 Christian Bühring-Uhle et al., *Arbitration and Mediation in International Business*, 265 (2d ed., Kluwer Law International 2006).

206 *Ibid*; De Vera, *supra* n. 77, at 159; Leon & Peterson, *supra* n. 19, at 92; Bartel, *supra* n. 8, at 679, 688–689; Stipanowich & Ulrich, *supra* n. 6, at 26; Abramson, *supra* n. 20, at 4.

207 Weisman, *supra* n. 98, at 2.

208 Bühring-Uhle et al., *supra* n. 205, at 248; Lew, *supra* n. 131, at 425.

process where mediators confront and question parties' positions on the merits to narrow the difference between them and to deflate exaggerated demands and expectations. Both reality testing and exploring parties' real interests work particularly well in caucuses. Good mediators need to possess traits and skills oriented towards interpersonal awareness and dynamics, securing the trust of all parties to the dispute, understanding the psychology of negotiations, finding issues that may underlie the parties' dispute, and being creative in helping parties find a unique solution for themselves.[209] Effective mediation often relies on a well-developed personal relationship between a mediator and parties.[210]

Arbitration, on the contrary, requires a high level of detachment and emotional distance from the parties and their interests and positions.[211] In general, arbitrators should use the facts and law to resolve the issues in dispute.[212] They need to understand the commercial realities and blend these with the contractual and legal. They must also be capable of rendering difficult decisions.[213] Good arbitrators need to have traits and skills such as strict neutrality and impartiality, knowledge of the law, ability to evaluate documents and witnesses, and time-management, organisational, and decision-making skills.[214] An arbitrator must possess a judicial temperament in order to command parties' respect.

Given different natures of arbitration and mediation, these processes require different core competences from their respective neutrals.[215] The core competence of arbitrators is to make a binding decision on legal questions, whereas the core competence of mediators is to help parties negotiate an amicable settlement.[216] It appears that good mediators and good arbitrators employ a completely different set of tools; arbitrators use a wide range of legal tools, while mediators rely on an array of intangible attributes.[217] This may make it difficult for one person to perform both roles effectively.[218]

The training offered for mediation and arbitration appears to have little in common. Sussman observes that although in arbitration training a good deal of attention is devoted to how to manage the pre-hearing process efficiently, in mediation training significant attention is devoted to how to overcome impasse.[219]

209 Mason, *supra* n. 131, at 543.
210 Bühring-Uhle et al., *supra* n. 205, at 248.
211 *Ibid*, at 248–249.
212 This, however, is not the case if parties authorise the arbitrator to decide *ex aequo et bono*.
213 Lew, *supra* n. 131, at 425.
214 Mason, *supra* n. 131, at 543.
215 Matthias M. Pitkowitz & Marie-Therese Richter, *May a Neutral Third Person Serve as Arbitrator and Mediator in the Same Dispute?* 4 Schieds VZ 225, 226 (2009); De Vera, *supra* n. 77, at 159; Bartel, *supra* n. 8, at 688.
216 Pitkowitz & Richter, *supra* n. 215, at 226; Bartel, *supra* n. 8, at 688–689; Peter, *supra* n. 126, at 164.
217 Mason, *supra* n. 131, at 542.
218 Sussman, *supra* n. 20, at 73; Thomson, *supra* n. 8, at 3.
219 Sussman, *supra* n. 20, at 73.

Even if neutrals are skilled and able to function effectively as either mediators or arbitrators, they may face other challenges when taking up both roles. For example, dual role neutrals may have difficulty switching from being problem solvers to being decision makers.[220] Or, they may have difficulty giving their entire energy to mediating a dispute when in the back of their mind they realize that they may need to ultimately resolve the dispute.[221] Effective mediators may have difficulty keeping the arbitral role fully in mind, even if they are able to function well as arbitrators on a separate occasion.[222]

Dual role neutrals appear to face a dilemma between the effectiveness of a mediation attempt and the integrity of the arbitral procedure.[223] When dual role neutrals switch from the role of a mediator to the role of an arbitrator, they might experience difficulties in dealing with information from caucuses and trying to distance themselves from any views they have expressed in mediation, so that they can render an impartial decision.[224] Neutrals need to endeavour to view the facts of the case in a completely new light, as if they had previously known nothing about them. This is a difficult thing to do. It will be hard for them to hear arguments with an open mind. If they fail in this attempt, the integrity of arbitration is impaired.[225] Also, neutrals must remain capable of issuing a decision against one party, which requires a certain distance from the parties. Even in stand-alone arbitration, arbitrators may struggle with an 'urge to split the baby, to soften the results'.[226] Having acted as a mediator this might become much harder.[227]

Bühring-Uhle et al. argue that because the dual role is so demanding, many practitioners prefer to err on the side of caution.[228] Interestingly, it appears that even if practitioners do not doubt their own ability to juggle the roles of a mediator and arbitrator, they might feel sceptical about others' ability to do so.[229] Oghigian notes:

220 Phillips, *supra* n. 4, at 76; *see also* Mason, *supra* n. 131, at 545 (noting that apart from skills and experience in both processes, the dual role neutral needs to know how and when to put on and take off each hat); Bühring-Uhle et al., *supra* n. 205, at 250 (observing that to be able to jump back and forth requires a rare strength of character).

221 Bartel, *supra* n. 8, at 689.

222 *Ibid.*

223 Bühring-Uhle et al., *supra* n. 205, at 248.

224 *Ibid*, at 250.

225 Peter, *supra* n. 126, at 160 n. 51.

226 Bühring-Uhle et al., *supra* n. 205, at 250 n. 632 (quoting an American in-house counsel interviewed in Apr. 1992); *but see* Mason, *supra* n. 131, at 543 (noting that despite a common perception that arbitrators in stand-alone arbitration act more like mediators and 'split the baby' in their arbitral awards, his own experience as arbitrator and counsel in arbitrations has been the opposite – rarely, if ever, has arbitration been decided this way).

227 Bühring-Uhle et al., *supra* n. 205, at 250.

228 *Ibid. See also* Pappas, *supra* n. 31, at 201 (observing that the difficulty of locating neutrals who can adequately perform both functions is the reason why the same neutral (arb)-med-arb will not save time or expense for participants).

229 *Ibid;* Oghigian, *supra* n. 187, at 75.

> When acting as a mediator, I have no doubt about my own impartiality should I later find myself as the arbitrator in the same matter. However, if I am acting as counsel, I may well be concerned about the appropriateness of such a structure and may be sceptical about the mediator/adjudicator's ability to remain impartial. It is a bit like one of those irregular verbs: *I* am impartial, *you* are capable of being impartial; *he* is probably biased.[230]

Bairstow makes the following comment about the heavy responsibility of a dual role neutral:

> When you sit there with the parties, separately or together – listening, persuading, cajoling, looking dour or relieved – your responsibility is a heavy one. Every lift of your eyebrow can be interpreted as a signal to the parties as to how you might eventually decide an issue if agreement is not reached.[231]

In view of the above, the issue of a party's trust in dual role neutrals comes to the fore. It appears that for the same neutral (arb)-med-arb to work well, it is not sufficient for neutrals to be capable of performing both roles. Parties need to have confidence in neutrals' capacity to handle both roles as well.[232] Blankenship observes that the competence and reputation of the neutral and, particularly, the trust the parties and their counsel have in the neutral are even more essential to the success of the same neutral (arb)-med-arb than to traditional mediation and arbitration.[233]

3.5 Conclusion

The same neutral (arb)-med-arb is a combination that raises a tidal wave of controversy. For supporters, it as a process that attempts to capture the independent strengths of both mediation and arbitration while limiting their perceived weaknesses. In particular, the process is often praised for its cost and time efficiency, finality and legal enforceability, quality of the outcome, flexibility, incentive to settle, and more honest behaviour of parties in mediation (as compared to stand-alone mediation). Critics, however, remain convinced that mediation and arbitration by the same neutral are inherently incompatible and that the same neutral (arb)-med-arb is a fatally flawed process. Caucuses appear as the single most problematic issue in the process and the cause of the majority of concerns associated with it.

230 Oghigian, *supra* n. 187, at 75.

231 Bairstow, *The Canadian Experience*, in *Arbitration Issues for the 1980s: Proc. of the Thirty-Fourth Ann. Meeting of the Nat'l Acad. of Arb.* 92, 93 (J. Stern & B. Dennis eds, 1982) cited in Bartel, *supra* n. 8, at 688 n. 131.

232 Bühring-Uhle et al., *supra* n. 205, at 265.

233 Blankenship, *supra* n. 21, at 34.

The main concerns associated with the same neutral (arb)-med-arb may be divided into two groups: behavioural concerns that surface in the mediation stage, and procedural concerns that arise in the arbitration stage. Behavioural concerns include the possible reluctance of parties to be open in their discussions with mediators, knowing that at a certain point they might become arbitrators; the inhibited conduct of mediators; parties' use of mediation as a tactical tool; and the abuse of power by mediators resulting in the coercion of parties into a settlement. Procedural concerns are directed to the danger that arbitrators will appear or actually be biased because of the information received in mediation and particularly in caucuses. Moreover, the inability of parties to hear and respond to the issues raised by each of them in caucuses with mediators who later become arbitrators may lead to a breach of the rules of due process. As discussed in Chapters 6, 7, and 8, the book has identified three major ways to address concerns associated with the same neutral (arb)-med-arb. These are the involvement of different neutrals in combinations, procedural modifications of the same neutral (arb)-med-arb, and the implementation of safeguards for using the same neutral (arb)-med-arb.

The same neutral (arb)-med-arb also poses a significant challenge to dual role neutrals. Not only must dual role neutrals be skilled and experienced in both mediation and arbitration, but they also must be capable of effectively handling both roles while switching from one to another. Only this kind of neutral may earn parties' trust essential to the success of the same neutral (arb)-med-arb. The book suggests in Section 9.5 that this challenge may be met by making a concerted effort to build the capacity of dispute resolution practitioners, in particular, by training more legal practitioners in both mediation and arbitration.

Having discussed the advantages and concerns associated with the same neutral (arb)-med-arb and the challenges it poses to dual role neutrals, the book will turn now to examine the issue of the legal culture. As explained in the next chapter, the legal culture emerges from the analysis of the literature and available empirical data as the reason why practitioners around the world have different, if not conflicting, views on the same neutral (arb)-med-arb and perceive it either as essentially a beneficial or a flawed process.

4 Influence of practitioners' legal culture on their perception and use of the same neutral (arb)-med-arb

4.1 Introduction

The literature suggests that the reason for the divide in views of practitioners on whether the same neutral (arb)-med-arb is an appropriate and admissible process lies in the practitioners' legal culture.[1] Before examining the specific factors that appear to shape practitioners' perception of the same neutral (arb)-med-arb, some attention needs to be given to the explanation of the meaning of a 'legal culture' for the purposes of this book.

1 *See, e.g.*, Mark Goodrich, *Arb-med: Ideal Solution or Dangerous Heresy?* 15(1) Int'l Arb. L. Rev. 12, 15 (2012); Jesus Almoguera, *Arbitration and Mediation Combined. The Independence and Impartiality of Arbitrators*, in *Liber Amicorum Bernardo Cremades* 101, 112–113 (M. A. Fernandez-Ballesteros & David Arias eds, La Ley 2010); Bernardo M. Cremades, *Overcoming the Clash of Legal Cultures: The Role of Interactive Arbitration*, 14(2) Arb. Int'l. 156, 164 n. 10 (1998); Bernd Ehle, *The Arbitrator as a Settlement Facilitator* in *Walking A Thin Line – What an Arbitrator Can Do, Must Do or Must Not Do, Recent Developments and Trends* 77, 79 (Bruylant 2010); Michael E. Schneider, *Combining Arbitration with Conciliation*, in *International Dispute Resolution: Towards an International Arbitration Culture*, 8 ICCA Congress Series 57, 78 (Albert Jan van den Berg ed., Kluwer Law International 1998); Fan Kun, *The Risks of Apparent Bias When an Arbitrator Acts as a Mediator: Remarks on Hong Kong Court's Decision in Gao Haiyan*, 13 Y.B. Private Int'l. L. 535, 536 (2011). Some authors, however, refer to cultural differences in general (rather than differences in legal cultures). *See, e.g.*, Lucy Greenwood, *A Window of Opportunity? Building a Short Period of Time into Arbitral Rules in order for Parties to Explore Settlement*, 27(2) Arb. Int'l. 199, 207 (2011); Paul E. Mason, *The Arbitrator as Mediator, and Mediator as Arbitrator*, 28(6) J. Int'l. Arb. 541, 545 (2011); Harold I. Abramson, *Protocols for International Arbitrators Who Dare to Settle Cases*, 10 Am. Rev. Int'l Arb. 1, 5–6 (1999); Nabil N. Antaki, *Muslims' and Arabs' Practice of ADR*, 2(1) NYSBA New York Disp. Res. Law. 113, 113 (2009); *but see* Tai-Heng Cheng, *International Mediation, Arbitration, and Innovation*, in *Contemporary Issues in International Arbitration and Mediation: The Fordham Papers 2010*, 437 (Arthur W. Rovine ed., Brill 2011) (cautioning against making generalisations about culture and referring to a case where a party from the Middle East – the region that is believed to have a cultural preference against conflict – had zero interest in conciliation or avoiding conflict).

Interestingly, various authors referring to the legal culture in the context of the same neutral (arb)-med-arb do not explain, intentionally or not, what they mean by a legal culture. The only comment found addressing the meaning of a legal culture in this particular context belongs to Cremades who noted that it 'is difficult to state what is understood by a legal culture'.[2]

It appears, however, that defining a legal culture is a challenging task, and not only in the context of the combined use of mediation and arbitration. Little agreement seems to exist on how best to grasp the concept in the literature on legal culture, in general.[3] This term is understood as referring to multiple different ideas.[4] Nelken observes:

> For different purposes, and in line with competing approaches to social theory, legal culture will be seen as manifested through institutional behavior, or as a factor shaping and shaped by differences in individual legal consciousness, as a pattern of ideas that lie behind behavior, or as another name for politicolegal discourse itself.[5]

Friedman draws a distinction between internal and external legal culture.[6] While internal legal culture refers to the ideas and practices of legal professionals, external legal culture refers to public knowledge about law and the general population's attitude towards the legal system. This book uses the term 'legal culture' in the former sense.

Specifically, a 'legal culture' in this book means the shared values, attitudes, standards, and beliefs that characterise members of the legal profession practising in a particular jurisdiction or region.[7] In particular, the key factors that appear to shape one's attitude to the same neutral (arb)-med-arb are the practice of the judiciary and the way disputes are resolved in a particular jurisdiction.

This chapter comprises three sections. Section 4.2 examines how the practice of the judiciary in the cilvil-law and common-law countries of Continental Europe and those of Anglo-American law influences the perception and use by legal practitioners of the same neutral (arb)-med-arb. Section 4.3 analyses how the way that disputes are resolved in the Western world and in

2 Cremades, *supra* n. 1, at 160.

3 David Nelken, *Comparing Legal Cultures*, in *The Blackwell Companion to Law and Society* 3 (Austin Sarat ed., Blackwell Publishing 2004), available at <www.blackwellreference.com/subscriber/tocnode.html?id=g9780631228967_chunk_g97806312289679> (accessed 14 Jan. 2018).

4 Ralf Michaels, *Legal Culture*, Duke Law Scholarship Repository, available at <http://scholarship.law.duke.edu/cgi/viewcontent.cgi?article=3012&context=faculty_scholarship> (accessed 14 Jan. 2018).

5 Nelken, *supra* n. 3, at 3.

6 Lawrence M. Friedman, *The Legal System: A Social Science Perspective*, 223 (Russel Sage Foundation, New York 1975).

7 U.S. Legal Forms, Inc., *Legal Definitions and Legal Terms Dictionary*, available at <http://definitions.uslegal.com/l/legal-culture/> (accessed 14 Jan. 2018).

East Asia has an effect on the practitioners' perception and use of the same neutral (arb)-med-arb. Section 4.4 investigates whether different traditions and cultures are moving closer together and whether one can speak about a harmonisation trend favouring the same neutral (arb)-med-arb.

It is important to acknowledge that this chapter engages in generalisations that tend to disregard the complexities and vast differences that exist in any country, region, legal system, or culture. Nevertheless, generalisations appear necessary when comparing one legal or cultural system with another.[8]

4.2 The influence of the practice of the judiciary on the perception and use of the same neutral (arb)-med-arb

The literature often links the practitioner's attitude regarding the same neutral conducting both mediation and arbitration to the practice of the judiciary in the country of that practitioner.[9] Overall, commentators agree upon the existence of a divide between common-law and civil-law systems in the question of facilitation of settlement by a judge; while some civil-law systems have traditionally regarded promotion of settlement as the duty of judges, their common-law counterparts have not allowed judges to be actively involved in facilitation of settlement.[10] The typical common-law approach is explained by a fear that active involvement in settlement facilitation may suggest that judges have prejudged the case before hearing all the evidence and argument.[11]

In this context, one could contrast the inquisitorial legal traditions of Continental Europe with the adversarial approach of the Anglo-American legal

8 M. Scott Donahey, *Seeking Harmony: Is the Asian Concept of the Conciliator/Arbitrator Applicable in the West?* 50(2) Disp. Res. J. 74, 74 n. 1 (Apr.–Jun. 1995). In addition, it is necessary to recognise that this chapter is silent on the position in some regions, e.g., African continent or countries of Latin America. This is because the data that the author managed to collect on the topic, due to its scarcity, does not allow drawing conclusions regarding trends (even emerging) in these regions.

9 Goodrich, *supra* n. 1, at 15; Kun, *supra* n. 1, at 538–539 n. 16 referring to Gabrielle Kaufmann-Kohler & Victor Bonnin, *Arbitrators as Conciliators: A Statistical Study of the Relation between an Arbitrators' Role and Legal Background*, 18(2) ICC Int'l Ct. Arb. Bull. 79 (2007).

10 Ehle, *supra* n. 1, at 79–80; Schneider, *supra* n. 1, at 78; Andrew Burr, *Med-Arb: A Viable Hybrid Solution?* 8 Les Arbitres Internationaux 57, 63 (2005); Cremades, *supra* n. 1, at 164 n. 10; Luke Nottage & Richard Garnett, *Top 20 Things to Change in or Around Australia's International Arbitration Act*, 6(1) Asian Int'l. Arb. J. 1, 35–36 (2010); Julian D. M. Lew, *Multi-Institutional Conciliation and the Reconciliation of Different Legal Cultures*, in *New Horizons in International Commercial Arbitration and Beyond*, 12 ICCA Congress Series 421, 427 (Albert Jan van den Berg ed., Kluwer Law International 2005) (noting that the position of a judge differs in common- and civil-law countries from a distant, 'blind umpire' to what is effectively a case manager); *see generally* Schneider, *supra* n. 1, at 78–81 on attitudes to a combination of arbitration and conciliation in different jurisdictions.

11 Final Report of the CEDR Commission on Settlement in International Arbitration (Nov. 2009), ¶ 2.3, available at <www.cedr.com/about_us/arbitration_commission/> (accessed 29 Mar. 2018) [hereinafter, CEDR Final Report].

system.[12] While under the inquisitorial legal traditions of Continental Europe, facilitation of settlement is generally regarded as a desirable part of a judge's and an arbitrator's role,[13] common-law courts under the adversarial system traditionally were entrusted with adjudicating not settling disputes.[14]

At the same time, Cremades points out differences in Continental Europe between areas following the Germanic and Latin traditions.[15] Schneider contrasts the approach of common-law countries with that of countries following the Germanic tradition, observing that other countries of the civil-law tradition take a place somewhere in between.[16] While German judges systematically attempt to settle a dispute before them, French judges appear to be more reluctant to become involved in the settlement of their own cases, despite the fact that the French Code of Civil Procedure (French CCP) expressly regards conciliation as one of the functions of a judge.[17]

Empirical research confirms that arbitration practitioners often approach the role of the arbitrator by referring to the rules applicable in their home courts.[18] In one empirical study, Kaufmann-Kohler and Bonnin reviewed 63 consent awards rendered under the ICC Rules of Arbitration between 2002 and 2005.[19] In 13 of all examined consent awards an arbitrator actively participated in the settlement process. In all 13 cases, all arbitrators were from jurisdictions where courts facilitate settlement.[20] These cases involved seven German or Swiss co-arbitrators. Six cases were chaired by a German or Swiss arbitrator. Cases also included two tribunals composed exclusively of Argentinian nationals and one tribunal composed exclusively of Brazilian nationals.[21]

12 Ehle, *supra* n. 1, at 80–83; Almoguera, *supra* n. 1, at 120 (observing that differences separate the Anglo-Saxon and Continental European systems); Gabrielle Kaufmann-Kohler, *When Arbitrators Facilitate Settlement: Towards a Transnational Standard*, Clayton Utz, available at <www.claytonutz.com/ialecture/2007/transcript_2007.html> (accessed 14 Jan. 2018) (comparing the approach of common law courts with the approach of the courts in Romano-Germanic tradition, in which it is part of a judges' mission to attempt to settle a dispute brought before them).

13 Ehle, *supra* n. 1, at 80.

14 Kaufmann-Kohler, *supra* n. 12.

15 Cremades, *supra* n. 1, at 159.

16 Schneider, *supra* n. 1, at 80; *see also* Jason Fry et al., *The Secretariat's Guide to ICC Arbitration* 264 (International Chamber of Commerce 2012) (differentiating the Anglo-Saxon system where the initiative to settle is traditionally taken by the parties' legal counsel or the parties themselves and certain civil-law traditions, notably Germany, Austria, and parts of Switzerland, where arbitral tribunals may be very proactive in encouraging the parties to settle the case).

17 Arts. 21, 1464 C. pr. civ.; Kaufmann-Kohler, *supra* n. 12; Ehle, *supra* n. 1, at 82; Schneider, *supra* n. 1, at 78.

18 Kaufmann-Kohler, *supra* n. 12.

19 Gabrielle Kaufmann-Kohler and Victor Bonnin, *Arbitrators as Conciliators: A Statistical Study of the Relation between an Arbitrator's Role and Legal Background*, ICCA, available at <www.arbitration-icca.org/media/0/12319144605970/00950003.pdf> (accessed 14 Jan. 2018).

20 *Ibid*, at 4.

21 *Ibid*.

The findings of another empirical study demonstrated that practitioners with common-law and civil-law backgrounds were divided on the question of an arbitrator acting as a mediator.[22] Bühring-Uhle et al. surveyed in-house counsel, advocates, and arbitrators/mediators globally on the practice of international business dispute resolution. The participants, however, comprised mostly Americans and Germans. Very few participants were from Asia. That survey revealed that the German participants were familiar with the involvement of the arbitrator as mediator and had very few objections to it, which stood in stark contrast to the common-law respondents who had rarely encountered this practice and who by a two-thirds majority regarded it as inappropriate.[23]

Both above-mentioned studies confirm the narrative in the literature indicating that German practitioners are familiar with the practice of facilitation of settlement by judges and arbitrators. It seems worthwhile to have a closer look at the German approach to facilitating settlement.

4.2.1 The German approach to facilitating settlement

Jones observes that in the German civil tradition, judges have always performed a settlement role.[24] The requirement to attempt to settle a matter arises from law.[25] Similarly, German arbitrators appear to traditionally encourage settlement.[26] Section 3.2.1 of the German Institution of Arbitration (DIS) Arbitration Rules 1998 states that 'at every stage of the proceedings, the arbitral tribunal should seek to encourage an amicable settlement of the dispute or of individual issues in dispute'.[27] Ehle conceptualises the 'German approach' as the expectations of parties and their lawyers that an arbitrator will at some stage in the procedure – ex officio – express a preliminary but clear view on the merits of the case and explicitly encourage an amicable settlement.[28]

The German approach to facilitating settlement, however, does not seem to be mediation, but a sui generis method of proactive 'managerial judging'.[29] Four differences and limitations set German facilitation of settlement apart from what is generally understood as a mediation process.

22 Christian Bühring-Uhle et al., *Arbitration and Mediation in International Business*, 122 (2d ed., Kluwer Law International 2006).

23 *Ibid.*

24 Doug Jones, *Various Non-binding (ADR) Processes*, in *New Horizons in International Commercial Arbitration and Beyond*, 12 ICCA Congress Series 367, 406 (Albert Jan van den Berg ed., Kluwer Law International 2005).

25 Art. 278 Abs. 1-2 ZPO.

26 Ehle, *supra* n. 1, at 81.

27 German Institution of Arbitration (DIS) Arbitration Rules (effective 1 Jul. 1998), available at <www.dis-arb.de/scho/16/rules/dis-arbitration-rules-98-id10> (accessed 6 Apr. 2018) [hereinafter, DIS Arbitration Rules].

28 Ehle, *supra* n. 1, at 80.

29 *Ibid*, at 82; James T. Peter, *Note & Comment: Med-Arb in International Arbitration*, 8 Am. Rev. Int'l Arb. 83, 110 (1997).

1 The obligation to promote and facilitate a settlement in Germany does not appear to be the tribunal's main remit but merely its additional task.[30] Ehle and Peter emphasise that the main purpose of the tribunal is to decide, not to settle the case.[31] Rendering an enforceable award and ensuring impartiality of an arbitrator appear as key priorities, which leads to a rather low-intensity form of mediation.[32] This contrasts with the situation in the same neutral arb-med-arb, where a mediation part is as important as an arbitration part because the latter will only take place if the former does not lead to a settlement of the entire dispute.[33]
2 German judges and arbitrators tend to be very legalistic and interventionist in their approach.[34] In Peter's view, they do not try to depart from the level of the legal issues in order to reveal the underlying interests.[35]
3 German judges and arbitrators appear to intervene minimally, if at all, in the parties' negotiation process.[36] The purpose of any intervention is, arguably, to help parties evaluate their chances to prevail before the judge or arbitrator, rather than to facilitate negotiation.[37]
4 Caucuses do not appear to be common for German judges and arbitrators.[38]

Thereby, because the process is neither called nor understood as the same neutral arb-med-arb, the agreement of the parties to a formal same neutral arb-med-arb process might result in an increased emphasis on mediation.[39]

Notably, Schaefer points out minor differences between the approaches of German judges and arbitrators to facilitating settlement.[40] Contrary to judges, arbitrators propose to facilitate settlement only if both parties agree and they try to fully understand the commercial background before suggesting any number

30 Ehle, *supra* n. 1, at 81–82.
31 *Ibid*; James T. Peter, *Med-Arb in International Arbitration*, 4 Revista de Arbitragem e Mediação 155, 174 (2005); Peter, *supra* n. 29, at 113.
32 Peter, *supra* n. 29, at 113; Peter, *supra* n. 31, at 174.
33 Peter, *supra* n. 29, at 113; Peter, *supra* n. 31, at 174.
34 M. Damaska, *The Faces of Justice and State Authority: A Comparative Approach to the Legal Process* 360 (Yale University Press 1986) cited in Jones, *supra* n. 24, at 406 n. 120.
35 Peter, *supra* n. 29, at 113–114; Peter, *supra* n. 31, at 174.
36 Peter, *supra* n. 29, at 114; Peter, *supra* n. 31, at 174.
37 Peter, *supra* n. 29, at 115; Peter, *supra* n. 31, at 175.
38 Peter, *supra* n. 29, at 114; Christian Bühring-Uhle, *Arbitration and Mediation in International Business: Designing Procedures for Effective Conflict Management* 191, 195 (Kluwer Law International 1996); Christopher Newmark, *Controlling Time and Costs in Arbitration*, in *Leading Arbitrators' Guide to International Arbitration* 81, 88 (Lawrence W. Newman & Richard D. Hill eds, 2d ed., Juris Publishing, Inc. 2008); Peter, *supra* n. 31, at 173–174.
39 Peter, *supra* n. 29, at 110; Peter, *supra* n. 31, at 172–173.
40 *Summary Report of the First Meeting in September 23–24, 2016 of the International Task Force on Mixed Mode Dispute Resolution: Inaugural Summit at Pepperdine University, Malibu, CA, USA*, International Mediation Institute 26 (2017), available at <www.imimediation.org/about-imi/who-are-imi/mixed-mode-task-force/> (accessed 29 Mar. 2018) [hereinafter, First Summary Report of Mixed Mode Task Force].

for a settlement amount. However, similarly to judges, arbitrators do not wait for the examination of witnesses or experts (which increases costs) before they engage in facilitation of settlement.

According to Ehle, Austria and Switzerland follow the German approach.[41] Interestingly, similarities in approaches are found not only among countries of Germanic origin, but they can also be traced in countries that geographically and culturally are far from Germany.[42] The practice of arbitration in some East Asian countries resembles the German approach.[43] The reason for this might be that mediation is natural and closer to the mentality of East Asian jurists than litigation, which this chapter turns now to examine.

4.3 The influence of the way disputes are resolved on the perception and use of the same neutral (arb)-med-arb

Cremades observes that the Western world is traditionally characterised as a litigious culture (although with widely differing approaches to dispute resolution), whereas East Asian and Arab and Islamic societies are known for their emphasis on conciliation.[44]

A closer look at litigation in Western countries reveals differences in the perception of a judge's role. As we have seen in Section 4.2, Anglo-American law countries have traditionally entrusted judges with adjudicating not settling disputes; they disapproved of the involvement of judges in facilitating settlement. Countries in Continental Europe differ in their approach to the question of facilitation of settlement by judges. Germany and countries following its tradition regard facilitation of settlement as a part of a judge's role and favour this practice. Other countries in Continental Europe seem to be less open to it. Nevertheless, it appears that, overall, Continental European countries have fewer objections to facilitation of settlement by judges than their Anglo-American counterparts.

Jones believes that the success of mediation in some Anglo-American law countries and a lower level of success in Continental European countries is due to the fact that the legal culture in Europe has not created the demand for ADR processes to the same extent that the litigiousness in Anglo-American law countries has.[45] At the same time, Cairns links the slow development of

41 Ehle, *supra* n. 1, at 81; *see also* David J. A. Cairns, *Mediating International Commercial Disputes: Differences in U.S. and European Approaches*, 60(3) Disp. Res. J. 62, 67 (2005) (observing that in European countries of the Germanic tradition settlement initiatives are traditionally judge-led).

42 Schneider, *supra* n. 1, at 58.

43 Ehle, *supra* n. 1, at 82.

44 Cremades, *supra* n. 1, at 158–159; *see also* Fan Kun, *Arbitration in China: A Legal and Cultural Analysis* 137 (Hart Publishing 2013) (contrasting the Western world with the Oriental world).

45 Jones, *supra* n. 24, at 406.

mediation in Continental Europe to the reasonable costs of litigation there.[46] Litigation in Anglo-American law countries in general appears to be much more expensive and disruptive as compared to litigation in Continental Europe.[47] But these disadvantages of litigation in Anglo-American law countries seem to have inspired the acceptance of and enthusiasm for mediation.

In East Asia, mediation has an exceptionally long history, and in some senses it is the cornerstone of the region's legal tradition.[48] Similarly to East Asia, in Arab countries mediation is also preferred to court proceedings and arbitration.[49] Although there is no uniform legal system for all Arab countries, most of the Arab countries have adopted the codified civil-law system, based on the Egyptian Civil Code, rather than the English common-law system.[50]

Various authors observe that East Asian cultures in general do not share Western values of privacy, favouring instead to handle conflict diplomatically and within the community.[51] Donahey points out a profound societal and philosophical preference for agreed solutions in East Asian countries and a predisposition towards a natural hierarchy which governs conduct in interpersonal relations, rather than a cultural bias towards 'equality' in relationships.[52] In accordance with these preferences and predisposition, East Asian cultures frequently seek a 'harmonious' solution, one which tends to preserve the relationship, rather than one which, while arguably factually and legally correct, may severely damage the relationship of the parties involved.[53]

However, this does not mean that conflict is unknown. Kun notes that in East Asian cultures, especially those influenced by Confucianism, an outright conflict is perceived as a failure or an embarrassment.[54] Because of the deeply rooted

46 Cairns, *supra* n. 41, at 68.

47 *Ibid.* Comments of the Belgian practitioner interviewed for the empirical study carried out for the purposes of this book (discussed in Part III) were along the same lines. He noted:

> ... of course, in the United States there are lots of mediations ... anything else than going to court is a good solution, because it is so expensive. It is not a problem in Belgium, because the court proceedings are inexpensive.

Practitioner from Belgium, Interview 6.

48 Jones, *supra* n. 24, at 407.

49 Almoguera, *supra* n. 1, at 109; Cremades, *supra* n. 1, at 159 n. 3.

50 *See* Saleh Majid & Faris Lenzen, *Application of Islamic Law in The Middle East*, Mondaq (25 Mar. 2011), available at <www.mondaq.com/x/52976/international+trade+investment/Application+Of+Islamic+Law+In+The+Middle+East> (accessed 6 Apr. 2018) (adding that the Egyptian Civil Code of 1948 reconciled and harmonised the principles of Sharia and the provisions of European Civil Codes and in particular the French Civil Code).

51 Carlos De Vera, *Arbitrating Harmony: 'Med-Arb' and the Confluence of Culture and Rule of Law in the Resolution of International Commercial Disputes in China*, 18 Colum. J. Asian L. 149, 183 (2004); Srikant Deekshitha & Arka Saha, *Amalgamating the Conciliatory and the Adjudicative: Hybrid Processes and Asian Arbitral Institutions*, III(1) Indian J. Arb. L. 76, 84–85 (Jodhpur 2014).

52 Donahey, *supra* n. 8, at 74.

53 *Ibid.*

54 Fan Kun, *International Dispute Resolution Trends in Asia*, 10(4) Transnat'l Disp. Mgmt 1, 11 (2013) (observing that this is particularly relevant to China, Singapore, and Hong Kong).

tradition of conflict avoidance, East Asian arbitrators tend to play a very active role in assisting parties to settle their dispute.[55]

The active role of East Asian arbitrators in facilitating settlement has been confirmed by the findings of a survey, case statistics, case studies, and interviews that Ali conducted for her PhD project.[56] The findings demonstrate that participants in East Asian international arbitration proceedings exhibit a greater openness to exploring settlement options and a greater degree of support for arbitrator-initiated settlement discussions than in Western countries.[57]

In interviews that Ali conducted, East Asian practitioners noted that a good arbitrator is one who assists parties to reconcile their relationship and acts as a guardian of the best interests of the parties, which makes it advantageous for the arbitrator to act as mediator.[58] East Asian perceptions about the integration of mediation into the arbitration process contrasted with those commonly held in the West.[59] In particular, several Western arbitrators noted a widely held concern that the arbitrator would become biased on prior ex parte communications.[60] This concern has been examined in Section 3.3.2.1.

From the analysis of the literature and available empirical data, China and Japan emerge as East Asia's foremost proponents of the practice of the combined role of a mediator and an arbitrator, which will be discussed now in more detail.

4.3.1 Chinese practice of the combined role of a mediator and an arbitrator

The practice of combining mediation and arbitration seems to be one of the cornerstones of Chinese arbitration.[61] Following the practice of the Chinese judiciary, Chinese arbitrators systematically offer assistance to parties by facilitating settlement.[62] Article 51 of the Chinese Arbitration Law encourages promotion of settlement by arbitrators.[63] It states:

> The arbitration tribunal may carry out conciliation prior to giving an award. The arbitration tribunal shall conduct conciliation if both parties voluntarily seek conciliation. If conciliation is unsuccessful, an arbitration award shall be made promptly.

55 *Ibid*, at 12.

56 Shahla Ali, *International Arbitration and Mediation in East Asia: Examining the Role of Domestic Legal Culture and Globalization on Shaping East Asian Arbitration* (PhD thesis, University of California, 2007).

57 *Ibid*, at 99.

58 *Ibid*, at 201.

59 *Ibid*, at 202.

60 *Ibid.*

61 Sally A. Harpole, *The Combination of Conciliation with Arbitration in the People's Republic of China*, 24(6) J. Int'l. Arb. 623, 623 (2007).

62 Ehle, *supra* n. 1, at 82; Kun, *supra* n. 1, at 540.

63 Arbitration Law of the People's Republic of China, art. 51 (1994), Zhonghua Renmin Gongheguo Falu Huibian [hereinafter, Chinese Arbitration Law].

The Chinese Arbitration Law does not specify what procedures, methods, and techniques arbitrators may employ in mediation. Neither does it impose any limitation on the timing of mediation. Arbitrators might attempt to mediate the differences at any stage of the proceedings and, if their efforts fail, continue with arbitration, ready to mediate again once another opportunity arises.[64] No clear distinction is generally made between the mediation and arbitration phases.[65] The necessary condition for arbitrators' mediating activity is party consent. No other jurisdictions appear to offer a level of fluidity in the combined use of mediation and arbitration similar to the Chinese.[66] In other Asian countries, for example South Korea or Indonesia, an arbitrator attempts to mediate only at the outset of arbitral proceedings, or, if mediation takes place in the course of arbitral proceedings, an arbitrator usually suspends arbitration while parties are engaged in mediation.[67]

Rules of arbitration institutions that administer cases in China seem to support the flexible approach promoted by the Chinese Arbitration Law.[68] Since its establishment, the China International Economic and Trade Arbitration Commission (CIETAC) has promoted the integration of mediation into arbitration.[69] Apparently, even before enactment of the Arbitration Law and, with the first Arbitration Rules having no provision regarding mediation, CIETAC attempted to mediate its arbitration cases.[70] According to CIETAC's Secretary General Yu Jianlong, 20–30% of cases submitted for arbitration are resolved through mediation conducted within arbitration.[71]

A series of interviews carried out by Kaufmann-Kohler with Chinese arbitrators acting for CIETAC, the Beijing Arbitration Commission (BAC), and arbitration commissions in Shanghai and Wuhan confirmed that Chinese arbitrators systematically ask the parties at the beginning of the hearing whether they wish the tribunal to assist them in reaching a settlement.[72] Interview data showed that in about 50% of the cases, the response is affirmative. Most often, arbitrators then

64 Donahey, *supra* n. 8, at 76; Kun, *supra* n. 44, at 166.
65 Kun, *supra* n. 44, at 166.
66 Donahey, *supra* n. 8, at 76.
67 Kun, *supra* n. 44, at 166.
68 Harpole, *supra* n. 61, at 624.
69 Tai-Heng Cheng & Anthony Kohtio, *Some Limits to Applying Chinese Med-Arb Internationally*, 2(1) NYSBA New York Disp. Res. Law. 95, 95 (2009).
70 Gabrielle Kaufmann-Kohler & Fan Kun, *Integrating Mediation into Arbitration: Why It Works in China*, 25(4) J. Int'l. Arb. 479, 485 (2008).
71 Royden Hindle, *Mixing it up: Medarb Re-visited*, ¶ 3 n. 6 (unpublished paper prepared for the AMINZ Seminar 'Current issues in Arbitration', Mar. 2014); Clemmie Jepson-Turner, *The Problems of Med-Arb – Should Keeneye Open Our Eyes?* Global Arb. Rev. (22 Sep. 2011), available at <http://globalarbitrationreview.com/journal/article/29833/london-problems-med-arb-keeneye-open-eyes> (accessed 29 Mar. 2018); Herbert Smith Freehills LLP, *Going Global: CIETAC's New Arbitration Rules 2012*, Lexology (4 Jul. 2012), available at <www.lexology.com/library/detail.aspx?g=d7e31792-27c5-47f6-9815-859a8763f4ea> (accessed 29 Mar. 2018).
72 Kaufmann-Kohler, *supra* n. 12.

engage in caucuses with parties and in shuttle diplomacy.[73] During the caucus, arbitrators tend to ask each party for its bottom line.[74] If the difference between parties' bottom lines is considerable, arbitrators terminate mediation and render an award. Otherwise, arbitrators may try to narrow the gap to reach settlement.

Interestingly, Chinese arbitrators tend to refrain from assessing the merits of the case because they consider that it would be improper and may jeopardise their impartiality and independence.[75] This happens despite the fact that an element of evaluation appears to be always present when arbitrators engage in mediation.[76] This evaluation, however, is usually limited to the indication of possible deficiencies of the parties' positions and does not involve expressing any opinion on the merits of the case.[77]

4.3.2 Japanese practice of the combined role of a mediator and an arbitrator

Facilitation of settlement by both judges and arbitrators seems to be a long-established tradition of Japanese legal culture and one of its important features.[78] The legal basis for facilitation of settlement by arbitrators is established in Article 38(4) of the Japanese Arbitration Law, whereby an arbitral tribunal or one or more arbitrators designated by it may attempt to settle the civil dispute, subject to the arbitral proceedings, if consented to by the parties.[79]

Many cases are settled thanks to the active involvement of arbitrators. As reported by Ohara at the Chartered Institute of Arbitrators (CIArb) Centennial Conference 2015, parties settled in 52 out of 171 cases administered by the Japan Commercial Arbitration Association (JCAA) and terminated between 2005 and 2014 (30.4%).[80] In 30 of these 52 cases, arbitrators acted as mediators (57.7%). While it is not clear from the record how exactly arbitrators acted as mediators, Ohara assumed that arbitrators would disclose their impression on the outcome of the case on an ex parte basis, which would prompt parties to settle.

Another study on arbitrators acting as mediators in JCAA arbitration showed that arbitrators attempted to mediate in 48 out of 121 arbitration cases

73 Shuttle diplomacy usually means that the mediator moves from one party to another.
74 Kun, *supra* n. 44, at 167.
75 *Ibid*; Kaufmann-Kohler, *supra* n. 12.
76 Kun, *supra* n. 44, at 166.
77 *Ibid*, at 167. This feature makes the practice of Chinese arbitrators quite different from that of their German and Swiss colleagues, who do not hesitate to express their view on the merits of the case.
78 Peter Godwin, *Japanese Arbitration in the Wake of the 2004 Reforms: Time to Recognise the End of the Ragan Myth*, 21 JCAA Newsletter 1, 2 (Nov. 2008).
79 Chusai Ho [Arbitration Law] Law No. 138 of 2003 [hereinafter, Japanese Arbitration Law].
80 Yoshimi Ohara, *Mediation and Adjudication: Where Asia Stands Now (Japan)*, CIArb Centennial Conference (Hong Kong, 21 Mar. 2015) (recorded and transcribed by D. Nigmatullina).

administered by the JCAA over 1999–2008 (39.7%).[81] In 25 of these 48 cases, mediation efforts resulted in a settlement agreement (52%). The study also found a clear tendency for the same neutral arb-med-arb to be widely employed by arbitrators with the civil-law background, the majority of whom were Japanese.[82] Arbitrators with the common-law background, on the contrary, appeared to be unlikely to attempt to mediate their cases.

The approach of Chinese and Japanese judges and arbitrators, however, differs from that of their German colleagues in two primary respects.

4.3.3 Differences between the German approach and that of China and Japan

First, as noted in Section 4.2, in Germany, the main purpose of a judge and arbitrator is to decide on a case, not to settle it. Facilitation of settlement is merely an additional task. In China, on the contrary, it appears that the main purpose of a judge and arbitrator is to dissolve the dispute, persuade parties to cease it, rather than render a binding decision.[83] In Japan, similarly to China, in accordance with the culture of conflict avoidance that is deeply embedded in the people's mind,[84] harmony in interpersonal relationships appears to be paramount, and conflicts are dealt with indirectly.[85] Interestingly, Tateishi disagrees with the view that Japanese people prefer amicable settlement by nature and notes that Japanese people are more practical than sentimental in resolving their disputes.[86] It appears that, particularly where the prospects of recovering damages are limited, Japanese parties may see benefits from settling their case at minimal expense.

Second, while caucuses are uncommon for German judges and arbitrators,[87] they appear to be widely used by their colleagues in China and Japan.[88]

81 Tatsuya Nakamura, *Brief Empirical Study on Arb-Med in the JCAA Arbitration*, 22 JCAA Newsletter 10, 10 (Jun. 2009).

82 *Ibid*, at 12.

83 De Vera, *supra* n. 51, at 164.

84 Kun, *supra* n. 54, at 12; Donahey, *supra* n. 8, at 75.

85 Kun, *supra* n. 54, at 12.

86 Takao Tateishi, *The Role of the Two-tier 'Med/Arb' Scheme in Japanese Dispute Resolution*, 1 Asian Disp. Rev. 24, 25 (2000).

87 Peter, *supra* n. 29, at 111; Bühring-Uhle, *supra* n. 38, at 191, 195; Newmark, *supra* n. 38, at 88; Peter, *supra* n. 31, at 174; Arthur Marriott, *Litigate, Arbitrate, Mediate – Frustrate? Breaking the Dispute Deadlock*, Clayton Utz, available at <www.claytonutz.com/ialecture/2005/transcript_2005.html> (accessed 14 Jan. 2018).

88 Kaufmann-Kohler & Kun, *supra* n. 70, at 488; Luke Nottage, *Arb-Med and New International Commercial Mediation Rules in Japan*, Japanese Law and the Asia-Pacific (21 Jul. 2009), available at <http://blogs.usyd.edu.au/japaneselaw/2009/07/arbmed_and_new_international_c_1.html> (accessed 29 Mar. 2018) (referring to a conversation with Professor Nakamura regarding the use of caucuses in Japan); Albert Monichino, *Inquiry into Commercial Arbitration Bill 2011(WA) – Clause 27D Mediation Clause*, 3 (unpublished submission to Legislative Council of Western Australia, 17 Oct. 2011).

The overview provided in this section and Section 4.2 explains why Germany, Austria, Switzerland, Japan, and mainland China are frequently referred to as examples of civil-law countries where judges and arbitrators are eager to mediate cases that come before them.[89]

4.4 The emerging harmonisation trend

International arbitration is a field where arbitrators and counsel of different legal cultures meet and work together to resolve disputes. This confluence of legal cultures appears to have led to harmonisation of the arbitration procedure.[90] The differences between the arbitral procedures in the common-law and the civil-law traditions seem to be fading in today's international arbitration practice. Parties, their counsel, and tribunals often agree to apply a mixture of the evidence procedures of the common-law and civil-law traditions.[91]

Kaufmann-Kohler attributes harmonisation of law and practice of international arbitration to the effect of the New York Convention, UNCITRAL Arbitration Rules and the Model Law on International Commercial Arbitration (UNCITRAL ML on Arbitration), a series of national laws and institutional rules, as well as soft-law texts such as the IBA Rules on the Taking of Evidence.[92] It is notable that both common-law and civil-law countries have adopted the UNCITRAL ML on Arbitration, despite the fact that it contains

89 *See, e.g.*, Goodrich, *supra* n. 1, at 15; Karl-Heinz Böckstiegel, *Past, Present, and Future Perspectives of Arbitration*, 25(3) Arb. Int'l. 293, 299 (2009); Nottage & Garnett, *supra* n. 10, at 35–36; Kaufmann-Kohler, *supra* n. 12; Ehle, *supra* n. 1, at 80–83; Schneider, *supra* n. 1, at 80; J. Martin Hunter, *Commentary on Integrated Dispute Resolution Clauses*, in *New Horizons in International Commercial Arbitration and Beyond*, 12 ICCA Congress Series 470, 472 (Albert Jan van den Berg ed., Kluwer Law International 2005); Haig Oghigian, *The Meditation/Arbitration Hybrid*, 20(1) J. Int'l. Arb. 75, 76 (2003); Arthur L. Marriott, *Arbitrators and Settlement*, in *New Horizons in International Commercial Arbitration and Beyond*, 12 ICCA Congress Series 533, 537 (Albert Jan van den Berg ed., Kluwer Law International 2005); CEDR Final Report, *supra* n. 11, at ¶ 2.2.

90 Cremades, *supra* n. 1, at 159–160.

91 Karl-Heinz Böckstiegel, *Assumptions regarding Common Law versus Civil Law in the Practice of International Commercial Arbitration*, ICCA 2, available at <www.arbitration-icca.org/media/4/67308804210771/media113194214157020l-common_law_versus_civil_law_.pdf> (accessed 14 Jan. 2018); *but see Q&A with Professor Pierre Lalive*, 3(5) Global Arb. Rev. 1, 2 (2008) (referring to the Anglo-American conquest of the international arbitration market and the 'Americanisation' of arbitration; and expressing preference for the 'comparative approach' in international arbitration).

92 Kaufmann-Kohler, *supra* n. 12; *see also* Sundaresh Menon, Keynote Address, *International Arbitration: The Coming of a New Age for Asia (and Elsewhere)*, ICCA ¶ 12 (ICCA 2012 Congress, Jun. 2012), available at <www.arbitration-icca.org/AV_Library/AV_Library_text format/ICCA_2012_Singapore_Keynote_Menon.html> (accessed 29 Mar. 2018) (explaining unprecedented harmonisation of national laws governing international arbitration by the widespread adoption of the Model Law).

several principles, which correspond more with the civil-law rather than the common-law concept of arbitration.[93]

Despite the powerful wave of harmonisation, the role of the arbitrator as a mediator in international arbitration appears to be resistant to this convergence.[94] Kaufmann-Kohler observes that in domestic arbitration, particularly in areas where a weaker party needs protection, national legislation differs significantly.[95] However, divergences are not desirable in international arbitration, where the factual matrix giving rise to a dispute is transnational and the participants come from different national and legal cultures. With time, a transnational practice on the issue of an arbitrator acting as a mediator may be settled, as has already been done for many other issues, including separability of the arbitration agreement, Kompetenz-Kompetenz,[96] limited remedies against the award, and party autonomy.[97]

4.4.1 Increasing influence of East Asian cultures

In view of the rapidly growing economy of the East Asian region[98] and its increasing commercial influence worldwide,[99] dispute resolution approaches adopted in East Asia, in general, and in China, in particular, require attention.[100] These include the use of the same neutral arb-med-arb.

In the late 1990s, Tang pointed out an expanding culture favouring the same neutral arb-med-arb in international commercial dispute resolution spreading from the East to the West and elsewhere.[101] Other authors allude to changes in the traditional hostile common-law attitude to mediating efforts by a judge and arbitrator.[102] Several common-law jurisdictions, such as Canada,[103]

93 Cremades, *supra* n. 1, at n. 29.
94 Kaufmann-Kohler, *supra* n. 12.
95 *Ibid.*
96 That is, the competence of an arbitral tribunal to decide upon its own competence (sometimes referred to as 'competence-competence'). *See, e.g.*, Nigel Blackaby et al., *Redfern and Hunter on International Arbitration* (6th ed., Oxford University Press 2015).
97 Kaufmann-Kohler, *supra* n. 12.
98 Kun, *supra* n. 54, at 16.
99 Mason, *supra* n. 1, at 551.
100 *See, e.g., ibid*; Hindle, *supra* n.71, at ¶ 34; Kun, *supra* n. 54, at 16.
101 Houzhi Tang, *Is There an Expanding Culture that Favors Combining Arbitration with Conciliation or Other ADR Procedures?* in *International Dispute Resolution: Towards an International Arbitration Culture*, 8 ICCA Congress Series 101, 101 (Albert Jan van den Berg ed., Kluwer Law International 1998).
102 Cremades, *supra* n. 1, at 164 n. 10; Schneider, *supra* n. 1, at 80; Kaufmann-Kohler, *supra* n. 12; Nottage & Garnett, *supra* n. 10, at 36.
103 *See, e.g., British Columbia International Commercial Arbitration Act*, R.S.B.C. 1996, c. 233, s. 30(1) [hereinafter, *British Columbia ICAA*]. For the sake of accuracy, it should be noted that all provinces and territories in Canada, except for Quebec, are governed essentially by common law.

Hong Kong,[104] Singapore,[105] and Australia[106] have adopted legislation facilitating mediation by an arbitrator. It appears, however, that these legislative provisions are rarely used in practice.[107]

These changes in the traditional Western approach are, arguably, happening under the influence of East Asian cultures.[108] The eastern outposts of Western culture have the closest relationships with the East Asian cultures and the earliest opportunities to assimilate useful concepts. This might be the reason why the acceptance and facilitation of the concept of the same neutral arb-med-arb is occurring mostly in Western jurisdictions on the Pacific Rim.[109] Kaufmann-Kohler is convinced that the provisions in the Hong Kong and Singapore arbitration statutes are the result of the influence of the Chinese tradition.[110] The experience of Asian trading partners and citizens of Asian background could have influenced the drafting of the provisions of the British Columbia International Commercial Arbitration Act.[111] Vancouver, the capital of British Columbia, is a busy seaport city with a large Asian population.

4.4.2 *Inter-influence of Western and East Asian cultures*

Differences between the Western and East Asian cultures might be diminishing due to adaptations in both directions.[112] With the growth of international arbitration in China, Western arbitrators sitting on the tribunals with their Chinese colleagues are learning about the advantages of the combined approach. Developments in Western jurisdictions have triggered reforms in China. For instance, the CIETAC and BAC Arbitration Rules contain a provision that allows parties to appoint as a mediator a neutral other than their current arbitrator if they fear that the award may be influenced by their current

104 Arbitration Ordinance (Cap. 609, 1 Jun. 2011), L.N. 38 of 2011, ss. 32–33 [hereinafter, Hong Kong AO].

105 International Arbitration Act (Ch. 143A, 31 Dec. 2002), ss. 16–17 [hereinafter, Singapore IAA].

106 In Australia, a possibility for an arbitrator to act as a mediator is recognised under Commercial Arbitration Acts (CAAs) that govern domestic arbitration in Australian States and Territories. *See, e.g., Commercial Arbitration Act 2012* (WA), s. 27D [hereinafter, CAA 2012 (WA)].

107 *See* discussion in Section 5.2.3.2.5 *infra*.

108 Donahey, *supra* n. 8, at 77.

109 *Ibid*, at 74; Antaki, *supra* n. 1, at 113 (observing that while in China and other Asian countries arbitration and mediation are fully integrated, California and British Colombia adopted similar legislation allowing arbitrators to mediate disputes).

110 Kaufmann-Kohler, *supra* n. 12.

111 Donahey, *supra* n. 8, at 77. *British Columbia ICAA, supra* n. 103, s. 30(1) and Cal. Civ. Proc. Code Ann. §1297.301 (West 2013) are identical and provide as follows: it is not incompatible with an arbitration agreement for an arbitral tribunal to encourage settlement of the dispute and, with the agreement of the parties, the arbitral tribunal may use mediation, conciliation, or other procedures at any time during the arbitral proceedings to encourage settlement.

112 Kaufmann-Kohler & Kun, *supra* n. 70, at 492.

arbitrator's involvement in mediation.[113] Also, similarly to the Western institutions, such as ICC and the American Arbitration Association (AAA), BAC adopted a separate set of mediation rules.[114] Further to the BAC Mediation Rules, the mediation procedure is separated from the arbitration procedure, parties are allowed to choose a mediator who is not on the BAC's Panel of Mediators, and the majority of mediation fees are paid to the mediators directly to reduce the parties' costs.[115] By launching a separate set of mediation rules, the BAC intended to fulfil the parties' needs to resolve disputes through a multitude of ways.[116]

A study of the Asian Development Bank demonstrated that, with the expansion of Asian markets beyond national frontiers, the informal dispute settlement mechanisms that are used in East Asia are becoming less reliable and formal institutions and procedures with powers of decision and enforcement more important.[117]

4.4.3 Inter-influence of Anglo-American and Continental European legal traditions

Adaptations seem to be happening between the Anglo-American and Continental European legal systems. In Reiner's view, practitioners from the Anglo-American legal tradition may now be more prepared to accept mediation by the arbitrator, whereas those from the Continental European legal tradition may have become more aware of the risks that the combining of the roles of the arbitrator and mediator may pose.[118] Consequently, the latter might be more prepared to accept that in some cases mediation outside arbitration has some benefits.

For Newmark, however, there is a clear shift away from a traditional common-law approach towards a civil-law approach in facilitating settlement as part of arbitral proceedings.[119] Nottage's remarks are more cautious. He notes that while active facilitation of settlement by arbitrators in international arbitration mostly happens when arbitrators come from certain jurisdictions following the

113 China International Economic and Trade Arbitration Commission (CIETAC) Arbitration Rules, art. 47(8) (effective 1 Jan. 2015), available at <www.cietac.org/index.php?m=Page&a=index&id=106&l=en> (accessed 29 Mar. 2018); Beijing Arbitration Commission Arbitration Rules, art. 43 (effective 1 Apr. 2015), available at <www.bjac.org.cn/page/data_dl/bjac_guize_en.pdf> (accessed 29 Mar. 2018).

114 Kaufmann-Kohler & Kun, *supra* n. 70, at 492.

115 Kun, *supra* n. 44, at 240.

116 *Ibid* (referring to comments of Hongsong Wang, the former Secretary General of the BAC).

117 Böckstiegel, *supra* n. 89, at 300–301.

118 Andreas Reiner, *Bridges Between Mediation and Arbitration: The Mediator as Arbitrator?/ The Arbitrator as Mediator?* 31 (unpublished paper presented at Tenth Zagreb Arbitration Conference, 2002); *see also* First Summary Report of Mixed Mode Task Force, *supra* n. 40, at 16 (noting that even in the U.S. there is evidence that many neutrals have been given opportunities to use same neutral (arb)-med-arb and they often accept the challenge).

119 Newmark, *supra* n. 38, at 90.

Continental European tradition, particularly Switzerland, Germany, and Latin America, views have evolved in the common-law world that acknowledge that arbitrating is not fundamentally incompatible with mediating.[120]

The 2016 version of the UNCITRAL Notes on Organizing Arbitral Proceedings[121] might be a reflection of this kind of evolution, as it acknowledges that in 'appropriate circumstances, the arbitral tribunal may raise the possibility of a settlement between the parties'.[122] This contrasts with the 1996 version of the UNCITRAL Notes that merely observed that '[a]ttitudes differ as to whether it is appropriate for the arbitral tribunal to bring up the possibility of settlement'.[123] Berger and Jensen believe that despite the fact that the approach of the 2016 UNCITRAL Notes is still rather cautious, it reflects the general perception that the arbitrator's mandate is, in principle, compatible with becoming involved in parties' settlement efforts.[124]

Kaufmann-Kohler and Ehle identify a strong trend towards settlement and away from adjudication.[125] This seems to be a response to users' concerns that arbitration is becoming an increasingly inefficient and expensive process. More specifically, for Ehle, the trend clearly favours arbitrators as more actively involved settlement facilitators,[126] whereas for Kaufmann-Kohler the picture is 'more nuanced' as regards the involvement of arbitrators in settling their own cases.[127] Berger and Jensen side with Ehle, and they even very optimistically claim that settlement facilitation has already become a genuine part of the modern arbitrator's mandate, most practitioners have overcome the common law/civil law divide and facilitate settlement where necessary regardless of their cultural and legal background.[128]

120 Luke Nottage, *Arb-Med in Australia: The Time has Come*, Japanese Law and the Asia-Pacific ¶ 3 (31 Oct. 2007), available at <http://blogs.usyd.edu.au/japaneselaw/ArbMed.pdf> (accessed 29 Mar. 2018) (referring to the findings of Kaufmann-Kohler's empirical research); *see also* Kaufmann-Kohler, *supra* n. 12 (observing that current practice in the US shows that some judges get involved in settling their own cases and even do not hesitate to caucus with parties); *but see* Claude Thomson, *Med-Arb: A Fresh Look*, 1 (2006) (on file with the ICC Documentation & Research Centre) (stating that while the culture and tradition in many countries accepts the dual role of the neutral, the practice has not been widely adopted in North America).

121 The Notes describe matters relevant to the organisation of international arbitral proceedings and are intended to be used in a general and universal manner.

122 UNCITRAL, *UNCITRAL Notes on Organizing Arbitral Proceedings (2016)* 12 ¶ 72, available at <www.uncitral.org/pdf/english/texts/arbitration/arb-notes/arb-notes-2016-e.pdf> (accessed 29 Mar. 2018).

123 UNCITRAL, *UNCITRAL Notes on Organizing Arbitral Proceedings (1996)* 12 ¶ 47, available at <www.uncitral.org/pdf/english/texts/arbitration/arb-notes/arb-notes-e.pdf> (accessed 29 Mar. 2018).

124 Klaus Peter Berger & J. Ole Jensen, *The Arbitrator's Mandate to Facilitate Settlement*, 40 Fordham Int'l L.J. 887, 906 (Apr. 2017).

125 Kaufmann-Kohler, *supra* n. 12; Ehle, *supra* n. 1, at 88.

126 Ehle, *supra* n. 1, at 94.

127 Kaufmann-Kohler, *supra* n. 12.

128 Berger & Jensen, *supra* n. 124, at 916.

The above analysis indicates that dispute resolution practitioners in different parts of the world might be changing their views on the same neutral (arb)-med-arb due to the inter-influence of Western and East Asian cultures, on the one hand, and Anglo-American and Continental European legal traditions, on the other. Although there is variation in the literature as to what the emerging harmonisation trend is, most authors appear to agree that common-law practitioners are beginning to acknowledge that the roles of an arbitrator and a mediator are not fundamentally incompatible.

4.5 Conclusion

The divide in views of practitioners on whether the same neutral (arb)-med-arb is essentially a beneficial or flawed process can be partly explained by reference to practitioners' legal culture. This book has identified two key factors that appear to shape the practitioner's perception and use of the same neutral (arb)-med-arb. These are the practice of the judiciary and the way disputes are resolved in a particular jurisdiction.

Overall, while some civil-law systems have traditionally regarded promotion of settlement as the duty of judges and arbitrators, the common-law system has prohibited judges and arbitrators from being actively involved in settlement facilitation. In this context, one could contrast the inquisitorial legal traditions of Continental Europe with the adversarial approach of the Anglo-American legal system. Germany, Austria, and Switzerland stand out in Continental Europe as countries where judges and arbitrators systematically attempt to settle a dispute before them.

In some East Asian countries, where mediation is natural and closer to the mentality of its practitioners than litigation, the practice of arbitration resembles the German approach. The discussion of the East Asian approach to resolution of disputes is commonly held in the context of contrasting the Western world, which is often characterised as a litigious culture, with East Asian and Arab and Islamic societies, which are known for their emphasis on conciliation.

In Western countries, however, differences exist in the perception of the role of a judge. Anglo-American law countries have traditionally entrusted judges with adjudicating not settling disputes. In Continental Europe, Germany and countries following its tradition regard facilitation of settlement as a part of a judge's role, which is not the case for other Continental European countries. Nevertheless, it appears that, overall, Continental European countries have fewer objections to facilitation of settlement by judges than their Anglo-American counterparts.

In East Asia, arbitrators tend to play an active role in settling parties' dispute, due to a profound societal and philosophical preference for agreed solutions. China and Japan seem to be the foremost proponents of the practice of the combined role of an arbitrator and a mediator.

It appears, however, that differences between the Western and East Asian cultures, on the one hand, and between Continental European and

Anglo-American legal traditions, on the other hand, are diminishing. There is a shared view in the literature that common-law practitioners are beginning to recognise that the roles of an arbitrator and a mediator are not fundamentally incompatible. This might be an indication of an emerging harmonisation trend favouring the same neutral (arb)-med-arb.

This chapter together with the two other chapters of Part II (Chapters 2 and 3) constituted the theoretical foundation for the design of the empirical study conducted for the purposes of this book. Its results are presented and discussed in Part III (Chapter 5).

Part III

The empirical study

Part III comprises Chapter 5 that presents and discusses the key results of the two-phase empirical study carried out for the purposes of this book. The first phase employed a questionnaire to investigate the current use of combinations in international commercial dispute resolution and how combinations are perceived. Importantly, the study did not focus on the use and perception of the same neutral (arb)-med-arb, but it investigated the use and perception of all combinations. The second phase was undertaken through semi-structured interviews. It aimed to elicit views concerning the most significant questionnaire results.

5 Results of an empirical study of the use of mediation and arbitration in combination

5.1 Introduction

This chapter comprises two further sections. Section 5.2 is dedicated to the first phase of the empirical study. It begins by describing the methodology and the background of the questionnaire participants. Then it presents and discusses the key questionnaire results, after identifying several limitations. In particular, it examines the results related to the extent to which mediation is currently used in combination with arbitration at an international level, common triggers of the combined use of processes, the way in which the processes are combined most frequently, and the most common forms of recording the outcome of the combined use of mediation and arbitration. Section 5.2 concludes by summarising the questionnaire results significant for the second phase of the empirical study undertaken through semi-structured interviews.

Section 5.3, reports and discusses the interview results after describing the methodology and identifying the purpose of the interviews. In particular, it reports the results revealing perceptions as to barriers to the use of the same neutral (arb)-med-arb, the significance of the legal culture for the way combinations are conducted, the emergence of a harmonisation trend in the use of combinations, and the influence that the creation of an international enforcement mechanism for mediated settlement agreements might have on parties' willingness to use combinations. As specified in Section 5.3.2, the remaining part of the interview results is presented in Chapters 8 and 9.

5.2 Phase 1: The questionnaire[1]

5.2.1 Methodology

5.2.1.1 Process

The first phase of the study was conducted between February and June 2014. It involved the distribution of a questionnaire in paper and electronic form to a

1 The following published journal article contains aspects of this section: Dilyara Nigmatullina, *The Combined Use of Mediation and Arbitration in Commercial Dispute Resolution: Results from an International Study*, 33(1) J. Int. Arb. 37 (2016).

pool of participants as follows. Two hundred and eighty paper copies of the questionnaire were distributed at two international conferences: the 2014 ICC Mediation Week[2] and the APRAG 2014 Conference.[3] These conferences brought together international practitioners and legal academics from different legal cultures. The 2014 ICC Mediation Week assembled key experts in mediation and arbitration predominantly from Europe. The APRAG 2014 Conference mostly gathered international arbitration and mediation practitioners from the Asia Pacific region. A total of 33 responses were collected from both conferences, which represents a response rate of 12%. An invitation to complete the questionnaire online was published on LinkedIn[4] and circulated by the ICC and the Arbitration Institute of the Stockholm Chamber of Commerce (SCC).[5] Forty-eight online responses were received. The total number of completed questionnaires amounted to 81.[6]

5.2.1.2 *Purpose and design*

The overarching goal of the questionnaire was to gather data from international dispute resolution practitioners about the current use of mediation in combination with arbitration in international commercial dispute resolution.

The questionnaire contained 22 questions organised into three parts.[7] Questions 1–4 gathered background information about the participants. Questions 5–19 enquired into the participants' professional experience (if any) in the combined use of mediation and arbitration in international commercial dispute resolution over the previous five years. Through questions asked in this part, the study sought information on the following aspects of the combined use of processes:

- To what extent is a combination of mediation and arbitration used?
- Are there any regional variations in its use? Are there any variations in its use depending on the participants' legal background?
- Are many practitioners with experience in the combined use of mediation and arbitration qualified to practise as lawyers?

2 The 2014 International Chamber of Commerce (ICC) Mediation Week took place in Paris in Feb. 2014.

3 The 10th Anniversary Asia Pacific Regional Arbitration Group (APRAG) Conference took place in Melbourne in March 2014.

4 In particular, an invitation was posted in several interest groups, including International Arbitration, ADR Resources, and Latin American International Arbitration.

5 In particular, the ICC distributed the announcement and the link to the online questionnaire to its network, including through Facebook and Twitter pages. The SCC published the invitation to complete the questionnaire on its news webpage both in Russian and in English.

6 The background of the participants is described in Section 5.2.2 *infra*.

7 A copy of the questionnaire is provided in Appendix 2.

- How is the combined use of processes triggered? Are legislative provisions, where they are in place, relied upon? Do arbitration institutions become involved?
- What is the most popular way to combine mediation and arbitration? Are processes used in any particular sequence, or concurrently? Do neutrals have a single or dual role?
- Are caucuses used in the mediation stage of the combined use of processes?
- Is enforceability of the dispute resolution outcome a concern for parties? Do parties use the possibility of incorporating their settlement agreement into a consent award?

Questions 20–22 aimed at eliciting participants' views on the main benefits of the combined use of processes and the use of this dispute resolution approach in the future, irrespective of the participants' experience in this field.

5.2.1.3 Key terms

Given the fact that 'mediation' and 'the combined use of mediation and arbitration' might mean different things to different academics and practitioners[8] and to minimise the possibility of confusion, the questionnaire defined these terms and stated that

> 'Mediation' is used interchangeably with conciliation. Evaluative and facilitative styles of mediation are distinguished. A mediator adopting a facilitative style will not suggest specific options for settlement, express a view as to the merits of the dispute, or be directive on the outcome.
>
> 'The combined use of mediation and arbitration' refers to the actual use of the discrete processes of mediation and arbitration in combination. It includes any combination of processes in whatever order and whether conducted by the same or different neutrals.[9]

5.2.2 Participants

The pool of 81 participants comprised predominantly international commercial dispute resolution practitioners from 28 countries of the world.

8 David W. Plant, *The Arbitrator as Settlement Facilitator*, 17(1) J. Int'l. Arb. 143, 145 (Kluwer Law International 2000); Nancy M. Thevenin, *Caucusing and the Cross-Cultural Divide*, in *Contemporary Issues in International Arbitration and Mediation: The Fordham Papers 2012*, 367 (Arthur W. Rovine ed., Martinus Nijhoff 2013); *see* discussion regarding possible ways of combining mediation and arbitration, and various terms used to denote a combination of mediation and arbitration in Chapter 2 *supra*.

9 The same definition is used throughout this book, *see* Section 2.1 *supra*.

In segmenting the pool of the participants, their geographic distribution and legal background were taken into account. The latter factor is important because, as explained in Chapter 4, practitioners' perception of the same neutral (arb)-med-arb is often explained by reference to their legal culture. The participants were segmented into four main groups (see Figure 5.1). The largest two groups of the participants practised in Continental Europe (Continental Europe)[10] and in common-law countries in the Asia Pacific region (Common Law Asia Pacific).[11] Two other groups comprised participants practising in common-law and civil-law countries that did not fall into the largest two groups.[12]

The participants consisted almost entirely of lawyers (88.9%): three-quarters indicated that they were qualified to practise as a lawyer (75.3%); about 14% were qualified but not in practice at the time of the survey (13.6%). Only about 11% of the participants had never been qualified to practise as a lawyer (11.1%).

When asked about their most frequent professional role in international commercial dispute resolution over the previous five years (see Figure 5.2), most often the participants referred to the role of a counsel (38.3%), about 15%

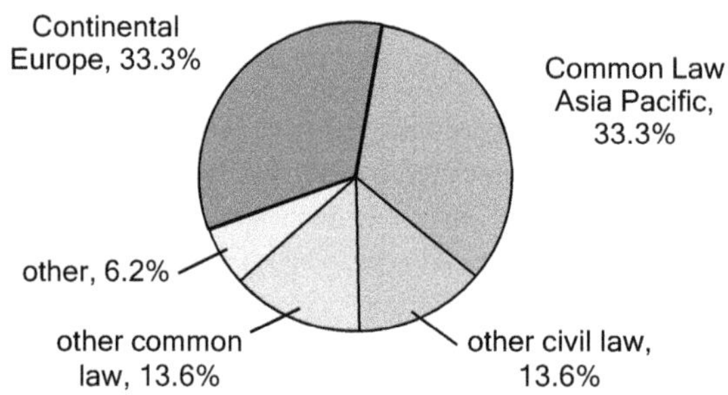

Figure 5.1 Legal system/region of practice

10 In particular, the participants practised in Austria (2.5%), Belgium (4.9%), Czech Republic (1.2%), France (3.7%), Germany (3.7%), Greece (2.5%), Italy (4.9%), the Netherlands (1.2%), Russia (3.7%), Spain (1.2%), Sweden (1.2%), Switzerland (1.2%), and Ukraine (1.2%).

11 In particular, the participants practised in Australia (14.8%), Hong Kong (9.9%), India (2.5%), New Zealand (1.2%), and Singapore (4.9%).

12 The 'other civil law' group included participants practising in Argentina (2.5%), Brazil (3.7%), China (1.2%), Ethiopia (1.2%), Mexico (1.2%), Taiwan (1.2%), and Turkey (2.5%). The 'other common law' group included participants from the United Kingdom (7.4%) and the United States (6.2%). The smallest group, 'other', included those who either indicated more than one primary country of practice (e.g., one participant referred to three countries: Switzerland, the United Kingdom, and the United States) (3.7%), or referred to a country with a hybrid legal system (Philippines) (1.2%), or indicated something other than a country (e.g., Global Litigation Counsel) (1.2%).

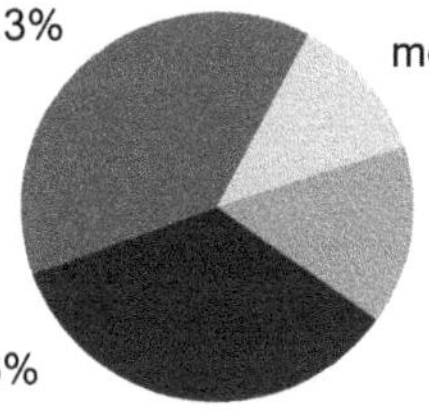

Figure 5.2 The most frequent professional role in international commercial dispute resolution over the last five years

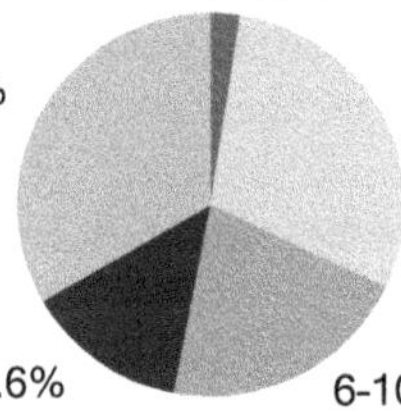

Figure 5.3 Approximate number of international commercial disputes over the last five years

of the participants chose the option of an arbitrator (14.8%), and about 12% of a mediator (12.3%).[13]

Almost all participants had been involved in international commercial disputes over the previous five years, though to varying degrees (see Figure 5.3). One-third of the participants had participated in more than 16 international commercial disputes (33.3%). Some participants in this group specified the approximate number of disputes they had been involved in over the previous five years as varying from about 20 to 800. About 30% of the participants were involved in one to five international commercial disputes in the five-year period (29.6%).

As explained in Section 5.2.3.1, the background of the questionnaire participants is an important factor to consider when interpreting the questionnaire results.

5.2.3 Limitations, results and discussion

This section presents the key questionnaire results and discusses them in the context of the literature, after identifying several limitations to the first phase of the empirical study.

13 The remaining participants (34.6%) included those who referred to a professional role other than as counsel, mediator, or arbitrator, e.g. an academic, expert witness, institutional case manager, arbitral tribunal secretary, or arbitrator's or mediator's assistant (23.5%); or referred to more than one most frequent professional role (9.9%); or indicated that they had not had any professional role in international commercial dispute resolution over the previous five years (1.2%).

5.2.3.1 Limitations

There are several limitations to the first phase of the empirical study. First, from a statistical point of view, the pool of 81 participants is a relatively small sample.[14] Second, the response rate to the questionnaire in paper form was relatively low, 12%. The response rate to the questionnaire in electronic form is impossible to calculate because of the way the electronic questionnaire data was collected.[15] Third, those who had some experience in the combined use of mediation and arbitration may have been more inclined to complete the questionnaire than those who did not have any experience in the combined use of processes. Fourth, the participants represented certain regions and legal cultures more than others. The majority of the participants reported practising either in Continental Europe or in Common Law Asia Pacific.[16] Also, the participants may have had a pre-existing interest in international commercial arbitration and mediation.[17] They may have been more supportive of their use, separately or in combination, than lawyers, in general, and in-house lawyers, in particular.[18] As a result, the questionnaire participants cannot be regarded as representative of dispute resolution practitioners worldwide.

Finally, although the questionnaire defined the term 'the combined use of mediation and arbitration', it did so broadly.[19] Consequently, in completing the questionnaire participants could have narrowed down the meaning of the term and used it to refer to a particular way of combining mediation and arbitration that they had experience of or were familiar with. Experiences of the participants varied. Some participants could have used the term as meaning a combination of mediation and arbitration involving only the same neutral or used only

14 However, researchers who conducted other empirical studies on international arbitration that involved even fewer participants regarded their sample size as appropriate. *See, e.g.*, Christian Bühring-Uhle et al., *Arbitration and Mediation in International Business*, 106 (2d ed., Kluwer Law International 2006) (stating that 53 respondents to a survey on international arbitration is not a small sample).

15 An invitation to complete the questionnaire online was published on LinkedIn and circulated by the ICC and SCC. It is not possible to identify the number of international dispute resolution practitioners and academics who saw the invitation to participate in the study and, consequently, it is impossible to calculate the response rate to the questionnaire in electronic form.

16 For example, practitioners from China and Japan, East Asian civil-law jurisdictions that are believed to be the foremost proponents of the practice of the same neutral arb-med-arb, participated in the study only minimally. Only one participant indicated China as a primary country of practice (1.2%); none of the participants indicated Japan as their primary country of practice.

17 This comment is particularly relevant to those attending the two international conferences where the questionnaire was distributed in paper form.

18 Although a choice of a dispute resolution mechanism is usually made by a party to the dispute in collaboration with in-house and external counsel, in-house counsel usually have the final say on this decision.

19 *See* the definition of the term in Section 5.2.1.3 *supra*.

sequentially. At the same time, other participants could have extended the meaning of the term to encompass, for example, the potential use of this dispute resolution approach,[20] whereas the questionnaire definition referred only to 'the actual use'. In view of all the above limitations, it is suggested that the questionnaire results cannot be generalised.

5.2.3.2 Participants' experience in the combined use of mediation and arbitration

The participants were asked about their experience as professionals in international commercial disputes involving the combined use of mediation and arbitration over the previous five years. Fifty-three participants stated that they had not had this kind of experience (65.4%), whereas 28 reported on their participation in disputes involving the combined use of processes (34.6%). Although about one-third of the participants of this study claimed experience in the combined use of processes, the particular way of combining mediation and arbitration that each of these participants referred to remained unclear. That uncertainty stemmed from the fact that the questionnaire provided a broad definition of 'the combined use of mediation and arbitration'.[21] Nevertheless, follow-up questions revealed the most common way of combining mediation and arbitration as experienced by the participants: the sequential use of processes with different neutrals in charge of the mediation and arbitration stages.[22]

All following questions in the second part of the questionnaire[23] were answered only by those participants who had experience in the combined use of processes. Some participants from this group chose not to answer certain questions.

5.2.3.2.1 PROFESSIONAL ROLE IN THE COMBINED USE OF MEDIATION AND ARBITRATION

The participants were asked to specify the professional roles they had in disputes involving the combined use of mediation and arbitration. In answering this question, they could select from four options. The answers to this question were not mutually exclusive. Most frequently the participants reported on their experience as counsel (see Table 5.1).

20 The potential combined use of mediation and arbitration can be illustrated by the following scenario. Parties incorporate into their contract a model multi-tiered clause of an arbitration institution. Once the dispute arises they resolve it in the mediation stage. The dispute never gets to the arbitration stage.

21 *See* the questionnaire definition of 'the combined use of mediation and arbitration' in Section 5.2.1.3 *supra* and discussion of its limitations in Section 5.2.3.1 *supra*.

22 *See* Sections 5.2.3.2.6 and 5.2.3.2.7 *infra*. Interestingly, this result contradicts views expressed in the literature. *See, e.g.*, Bobette Wolski, *Arb-Med-Arb (and MSAs): A Whole Which Is Less than, not Greater than, the Sum of Its Parts?* 6(2) Contemp. Asia Arb. J. 249, 260 (2013) (observing that med-arb (diff) does not seem to be used much).

23 These are the questions presented and discussed in Sections 5.2.3.2.1–5.2.3.2.8 *infra*. On parts of the questionnaire *see* Section 5.2.1.2 *supra*.

Table 5.1 Professional role in an international commercial dispute involving the combined use of mediation and arbitration

Answer options	*Response (%)*	*Response count*
As a counsel	57.1	16
As a mediator in a dispute involving arbitration with a different neutral	32.1	9
As an arbitrator in a dispute involving mediation with a different neutral	28.6	8
As a mediator and an arbitrator in the same dispute	17.9	5
Total		**28**

Note: although 28 participants answered this question, some of them selected more than one answer.

5.2.3.2.2 PROPORTION OF DISPUTES INVOLVING THE COMBINED USE OF PROCESSES OF THE OVERALL PRACTICE

The participants were asked to indicate the approximate proportion of disputes involving the combined use of mediation and arbitration of their overall international commercial dispute resolution practice over the previous five years (see Figure 5.4). In answering this question, the participants could select from six options. Twenty-seven participants answered this question. Almost half of them reported a minimal involvement of not more than 10% (48.1%) in the combined use of processes.

5.2.3.2.3 REGIONAL VARIATIONS IN THE COMBINED USE OF MEDIATION AND ARBITRATION

As reflected in Figure 5.1, overall the questionnaire participants evenly represented Common Law Asia Pacific and Continental Europe (33.3% each). However, a different picture emerged when the participants were asked about their experience with the combined use of mediation and arbitration. The questionnaire data revealed (see Figure 5.5) that the participants practising in Common Law Asia Pacific

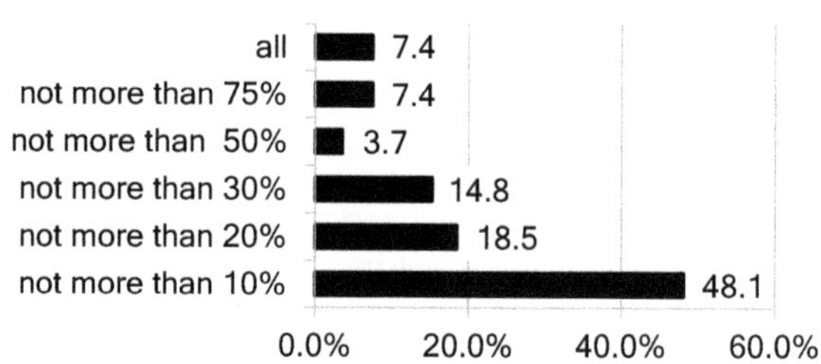

Figure 5.4 The approximate proportion of disputes involving the combined use of mediation and arbitration of the overall international commercial dispute resolution practice over the last five years

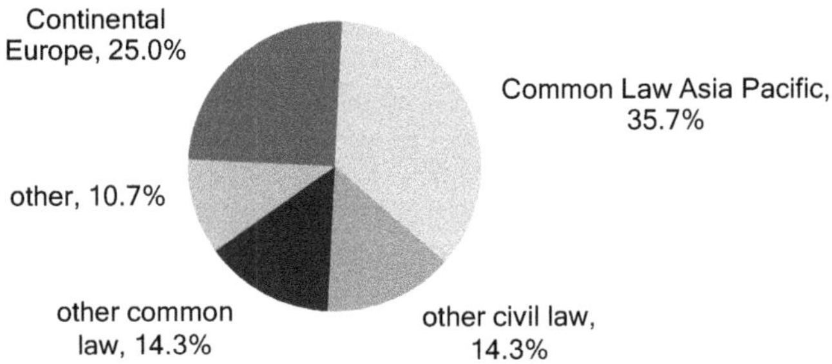

Figure 5.5 Legal system/region of practice (participants with experience in the combined use of mediation and arbitration)

experienced the combined use of mediation and arbitration more often (35.7%) than their colleagues from Continental Europe (25%).[24]

5.2.3.2.4 INTERRELATION BETWEEN PARTICIPANTS' QUALIFICATION TO PRACTISE AS A LAWYER AND THEIR EXPERIENCE IN THE COMBINED USE OF PROCESSES

The data shows that a large majority of practitioners with experience in the combined use of mediation and arbitration, regardless of the region of their practice, were qualified lawyers (85.7%), whereas about 14% of the participants did not hold a qualification to practise as a lawyer (14.3%). This result is comparable to the overall proportion of participants with and without legal qualifications: almost 90% of all participants indicated that they were qualified to practise as a lawyer (88.9%).

This result is no surprise in light of the professional background of the participants with experience in the combined use of mediation and arbitration (see Table 5.1). Most frequently these participants were involved in the combined use of processes as counsel (57.1%). More than one-quarter of the participants had been involved in the combined use of processes as arbitrators (28.6%), whereas about 18% had been involved as both mediators and arbitrators in the same dispute (17.9%). About 32% of the participants had acted as mediators in a combination of mediation and arbitration, where a different neutral was involved for the arbitration stage (32.1%).

While it is logical to expect that most professionals acting as counsel are qualified lawyers,[25] the necessity of this qualification for arbitrators is not self-evident.[26]

24 Compared to the overall proportion of the participants depending on their country of practice (*see* Figure 5.1), those who had experience with the combined use of mediation and arbitration constituted 37% of the overall number of Common Law Asia Pacific and 25.9% of Continental European participants.

25 Although arbitration laws and rules almost never require formal legal qualifications for counsel, in practice, parties would rarely instruct as counsel an individual who is not qualified.

26 Anyone can be appointed as an arbitrator. The choice of arbitrator usually depends on the subject-matter of the dispute. For example, it is not unusual for parties to choose an engineer for a building dispute.

However, commentators point out the desirability of appointing a lawyer as a neutral in international arbitrations.[27] Indeed, in general, an arbitrator should use the facts and the law to resolve the issues at stake.[28] While differences exist in the perception of the role of an arbitrator (whether it is confined to producing a binding award or whether it is to resolve a dispute, including by facilitating a settlement),[29] an arbitrator must be qualified to determine a dispute, if necessary. Similarly, neutrals having a dual role (acting as mediators and arbitrators in the same international commercial dispute) might be expected to be lawyers, because of the arbitration component of the combined use of processes.

A mediator's role differs significantly from that of an arbitrator. A mediator assists parties in settlement, which may involve narrowing the issues in dispute, helping parties understand each other, and revising a contract for the future.[30] Jones argues that non-lawyers (e.g., psychologists, business consultants, counsellors, and others) can make valuable contributions to mediation.[31] By embracing a wide range of professions, mediation can be informed by a number of perspectives. This will increase the number of available tools in the toolbox, which will enable mediation practitioners best help parties come to a settlement.[32]

In this study, only a minority of the participants with experience in the combined use of mediation and arbitration reported being non-lawyers (14.3%). This result can be explained by the fact that the participants' involvement solely as mediators in the combined use of processes was quite limited (32.1%). As mentioned above, many participants had experience acting as counsel, arbitrators, or

27 Alan Redfern et al., *Redfern and Hunter on International Arbitration* 259 (5th ed., Oxford University Press 2009) (observing that in international arbitrations before a sole arbitrator, it is usual to appoint a lawyer; where the arbitral tribunal consists of three arbitrators, at least one member should be a lawyer; a lawyer with suitable procedural and legal experience may better handle the frequently arising problems of procedure and of conflict of law rather than a person whose expertise lies in another area).

28 Julian D. M. Lew, *Multi-Institutional Conciliation and the Reconciliation of Different Legal Cultures*, in *New Horizons in International Commercial Arbitration and Beyond*, 12 ICCA Congress Series 421, 425 (Albert Jan van den Berg ed., Kluwer Law International 2005). As mentioned earlier, this is not the case if parties authorise the arbitrator to decide *ex aequo et bono*.

29 *See, e.g.*, Christopher Newmark, *Controlling Time and Costs in Arbitration*, in *Leading Arbitrators' Guide to International Arbitration* 81, 87–88 (Lawrence W. Newman & Richard D. Hill eds, 2d ed., Juris Publishing, Inc. 2008); Gabrielle Kaufmann-Kohler and Victor Bonnin, *Arbitrators as Conciliators: A Statistical Study of the Relation between an Arbitrator's Role and Legal Background*, ICCA 1, available at <www.arbitration-icca.org/media/0/12319144605970/00950003.pdf> (accessed 14 Jan. 2018); Fan Kun, *The Risks of Apparent Bias When an Arbitrator Acts as a Mediator: Remarks on Hong Kong Court's Decision in Gao Haiyan*, 13 Y.B. Private Int'l. L. 535, 536–537 (2011).

30 Lew, *supra* n. 28, at 425.

31 Doug Jones, *Various Non-binding (ADR) Processes*, in *New Horizons in International Commercial Arbitration and Beyond*, 12 ICCA Congress Series 367, 406 (Albert Jan van den Berg ed., Kluwer Law International 2005).

32 *Ibid.*

dual role neutrals in disputes involving the combined use of mediation and arbitration. The nature of these roles calls for, if not requires, a qualification to practise as a lawyer.

5.2.3.2.5 TRIGGERS FOR THE COMBINED USE OF MEDIATION AND ARBITRATION

The participants were asked to indicate what triggered[33] the combined use of processes in the dispute they were involved in (see Table 5.2). In answering this question, the participants could select from 11 options and specify any other trigger. The answers to this question were not mutually exclusive.

The participants identified **the suggestion of counsel** as the most frequent trigger for the use of a combination of mediation and arbitration (66.7%). When asked about countries of practice of those counsel, the participants referred to countries from all over the world.[34] However, the United States and the United Kingdom appeared to be the countries most frequently referred to,[35] which might reflect a traditional common-law trained approach,

Table 5.2 Triggers for the combined use of mediation and arbitration

Answer options	*Response (%)*	*Response count*
One or both parties' counsel suggestion	66.7	18
Specifically tailored contractual provision	51.9	14
Initiative of one or both parties	40.7	11
Model multi-tiered clause of an arbitration institute incorporated into parties' contract	25.9	7
Your suggestion	14.8	4
Arbitrator's suggestion	11.1	3
Provision in the applicable legislation	11.1	3
Provision in the rules of an arbitration institute	7.4	2
Mediator's suggestion	7.4	2
Combination of triggers	7.4	2
Suggestion of an arbitration institute	3.7	1
Other	11.1	3
Total		**27**

Note: although 27 participants answered this question, some of them selected more than one answer.

33 That is, what prompted the use of a combination of mediation and arbitration.

34 They specified, in particular, the following countries: Argentina, China, France, Germany, Hong Kong, India, Italy, Malaysia, Switzerland, the United Kingdom, and the United States.

35 The United States and the United Kingdom were mentioned by three participants each, France and Hong Kong by two, and the rest of the listed countries were referred to by one participant each.

where the initiative to settle is usually taken by counsel or parties themselves.[36]

Contrary to views expressed by some commentators that parties are reluctant to suggest using mediation because of the fear of appearing weak,[37] **parties** appeared to be relatively active in invoking the combined use of processes (40.7%).

A specifically tailored contractual provision requiring both the use of mediation and arbitration was the second most common trigger (51.9%). The result is not surprising, given the benefits that this kind of provision may offer. These include creating the possibility of settlement by bringing parties to the negotiating table and eliminating parties' fear to appear weak in suggesting mediation. However, not all commentators commend contractual commitments in advance to attempt mediation. For example, Jones observes that the disadvantage of a contractual commitment to mediation is that when a dispute arises, parties will generally know straight away whether there is any point in negotiating.[38] A better option could be to insert a general clause requiring that each party consider settling the dispute through mediation or to designate in the contract that a mediation clause applies only to certain disputes.[39]

Carter warns against leaving the drafting of clauses to parties because then parties 'rely on home-cooked individual recipes, which can be toxic'.[40] While arbitration clauses alone offer myriad examples of pathologies, the possibility of drafting chaos might be multiplied when several mechanisms are integrated. Arbitration institutions need to engage more actively in promulgation of multi-tiered dispute resolution clauses.[41]

The fact that only a limited number of arbitration institutes currently offer model multi-tiered clauses[42] may explain the questionnaire result that **a model multi-tiered clause** was relied upon to invoke the combined use of processes half as often as compared to a specifically tailored contractual provision (25.9%).

36 Jason Fry et al., *The Secretariat's Guide to ICC Arbitration* 264 (International Chamber of Commerce 2012).

37 *See, e.g.*, Bühring-Uhle et al., *supra* n. 14, at 262; Eric W. Fiechter, *Mediation – Timing Issues: When is the Right Time to Try Mediation: Before, During or After Arbitration or Court Proceedings?* 15 Croatian Arb. Y.B. 263, 271 (2008); Jacob Grierson & Annet van Hooft, *Arbitrating under the 2012 ICC Rules*, 57 (Kluwer Law International 2012).

38 Jones, *supra* n. 31, at 404–405.

39 *Ibid*, at 405.

40 James H. Carter, *Part I – Issues Arising from Integrated Dispute Resolution Clauses*, in *New Horizons in International Commercial Arbitration and Beyond*, 12 ICCA Congress Series 446, 447 (Albert Jan van den Berg ed., Kluwer Law International 2005).

41 *Ibid*, at 454.

42 *Ibid*, at 447 (adding that even if a model multi-tiered clause has been promulgated by an arbitration institute, it might not be free from ambiguity).

The combined use of processes rarely resulted from **a suggestion of an arbitrator** (11.1%) or **a mediator** (7.4%). Although Ehle calls for enhancing the arbitrator's mandate and transforming arbitrators into proactive settlement facilitators,[43] other commentators are more sceptical in this respect. For example, Greenwood considers that expectations that arbitrators would take a lead in suggesting the idea of a settlement are unrealistic.[44] Apart from requiring the making of certain assumptions about an arbitrator's role in the dispute resolution process,[45] these expectations place a heavy burden on the tribunal. More specifically, arbitrators might be facing competing issues: the need to issue a binding award, to observe due process and to maintain confidentiality.[46] They also need to be mindful of the time taken to reach a final award and the cost of reaching that award. Facilitation of settlement may not be a priority for the tribunal for more prosaic reasons, like lack of appropriate skills as a negotiator necessary to reach a settlement.[47] Naughton even doubts the wisdom of arbitrators who switch roles and recommends parties to refrain from granting arbitrators the power to do so, despite the difficulties of saying 'no' to a suggestion coming from their arbitrators.[48]

Few participants had experienced the combined use of mediation and arbitration pursuant to **a provision in the applicable legislation** (11.1%). Practitioners in jurisdictions with the legislation facilitating the combined use of processes by the same neutral for resolving international disputes, such as Singapore[49] and Hong Kong,[50] did not report any cases where this legislation applied in practice.[51] This result resonates with views of commentators who point out the paucity of the combined use of mediation and arbitration by the same neutral in Hong Kong and Singapore, despite its legislative

43 Bernd Ehle, *The Arbitrator as a Settlement Facilitator* in *Walking A Thin Line – What an Arbitrator Can Do, Must Do or Must Not Do, Recent Developments and Trends* 77, 94 (Bruylant 2010).

44 Lucy Greenwood, *A Window of Opportunity? Building a Short Period of Time into Arbitral Rules in order for Parties to Explore Settlement*, 27(2) Arb. Int'l. 199, 204–206 (2011).

45 *Ibid*, at 205–206 (observing that many international arbitrators still view their role as predominantly to render an enforceable arbitral award).

46 *Ibid*, at 204.

47 *Ibid*, at 204–205.

48 Philip Naughton, *The Role of Arbitrators and Arbitration Institutions in the Use of Alternatives for the Settlement of Disputes*, 73(1) Arb. 31, 37 (2007).

49 International Arbitration Act (Ch. 143A, 31 Dec. 2002), ss. 16–17 [hereinafter, Singapore IAA].

50 Arbitration Ordinance (Cap. 609, 1 Jun. 2011), L.N. 38 of 2011, ss. 32–33 [hereinafter, Hong Kong AO]. It appears that provisions encouraging arbitrators to act as mediators have been provided for in the Hong Kong AO since 1989. *See* Paul E. Mason, *The Arbitrator as Mediator, and Mediator as Arbitrator*, 28(6) J. Int'l. Arb. 541, 549 (2011).

51 Although, in Australia, the possibility for an arbitrator to act as a mediator is explicitly recognised by CAAs that govern domestic commercial arbitration in Australian States and Territories, *International Arbitration Act 1974* (Cth) governing international arbitration is silent in this respect.

recognition.[52] Notably, the legislative acts in both Singapore and Hong Kong expressly permit an arbitrator to act as a mediator (the same neutral arb-med-arb)[53] and a mediator to act as an arbitrator (the same neutral med-arb),[54] jointly referred to as the same neutral (arb)-med-arb.

The infrequent use of the same neutral (arb)-med-arb might be due to various factors. The legislative obligation of an arbitrator to disclose all confidential information from mediation that is material to arbitration to all parties in dispute seems to raise major concerns among academics and practitioners.[55] This obligation is regarded as the main stumbling block to hinder the use of the same neutral (arb)-med-arb because it prevents parties from being completely open in their discussions in mediation.[56] While a disclosure obligation may inhibit candid exchanges in mediation, it may be necessary to prevent offending Western notions of due process: the ultimate decision maker might have some material information of which one side is unaware and to which they have had no opportunity to respond.[57]

Additionally, one could attribute the infrequent use of the same neutral (arb)-med-arb in Hong Kong to the failure rate of mediation in the context of court proceedings where many parties apparently feel compelled to mediate pursuant to the Civil Justice Reforms.[58] The infrequent use might also be due to a relatively

52 *See, e.g.*, Fan Kun, *The New Arbitration Ordinance in Hong Kong*, 29(6) J. Int'l. Arb. 715, 720 (2012); Phillip Georgiou & Iain C. L. Seow, *Hong Kong Strengthens Position as Leading Jurisdiction for International Arbitration with Major Overhaul of Legislative Framework*, Lexology (22 Jul. 2011), available at <www.lexology.com/library/detail.aspx?g=24288c95-7f16-4ede-b7e7-41b1c8f8e1dc> (accessed 30 Mar. 2018); Claire Wilson, *The Arb-Med Hybrid in Hong Kong – Much Ado about Nothing?* Kluwer Mediation Blog (1 Feb. 2012), available at <http://kluwermediationblog.com/2012/02/01/the-arb-med-hybrid-in-hong-kong-much-ado-about-nothing/> (accessed 30 Mar. 2018); Luke Nottage, *In/formalisation and Glocalisation of International Commercial Arbitration and Investment Treaty Arbitration in Asia*, in *Formalisation and Flexibilisation in Dispute Resolution* 211, 227 (Joachim Zekoll, Moritz Bälz & Iwo Amelung eds, Brill 2014); Michael Hwang, *The Role of Arbitrators as Settlement Facilitators – Commentary*, in *New Horizons in International Commercial Arbitration and Beyond*, 12 ICCA Congress Series 571, 574–575 (Albert Jan van den Berg ed., Kluwer Law International 2005); Mason, *supra* n. 50, at 549; Kun, *supra* n. 29, at 541.

53 Singapore IAA, *supra* n. 49, s. 17; Hong Kong AO, *supra* n. 50, s. 33.

54 Singapore IAA, *supra* n. 49, s. 16; Hong Kong AO, *supra* n. 50, s. 32.

55 Justin D'Agostino, *Mediator-Arbitrators: The Perfect Match or No Love Lost? (A Valentine's Day Blog)*, Kluwer Arbitration Blog (15 Feb. 2011), available at <http://kluwerarbitrationblog.com/blog/2011/02/15/mediator-arbitrators-the-perfect-match-or-no-love-lost-a-valentines-day-blog/> (accessed 30 Mar. 2018); Georgiou & Seow, *supra* n. 52; Alexander Oddy et al., *Hong Kong Courts Consider the Mediation-Arbitration Procedure*, Lexology (8 Jun. 2011), available at <www.lexology.com/library/detail.aspx?g=dade4ce7-f513-411e-b9bf-57471a20133f> (accessed 30 Mar. 2018); Mason, *supra* n. 50, at 549–550.

56 Wilson, *supra* n. 52 (speaking about the situation in Hong Kong).

57 M. Scott Donahey, *Seeking Harmony: Is the Asian Concept of the Conciliator/Arbitrator Applicable in the West?* 50(2) Disp. Res. J. 74, 77 (Apr.–Jun. 1995).

58 D'Agostino, *supra* n. 55.

novel culture of mediation in this jurisdiction: arbitrators do not yet feel comfortable with mediating.[59] This attitude may change if more arbitrators and lawyers receive mediation training. In Singapore, practitioners might be cautious to actually implement the same neutral (arb)-med-arb, until individual dual role neutrals develop their own case law with some guidance from courts in a suitable test case.[60]

From a broader perspective, the scarce use of the legislative provisions might be due to the difficulty to 'move the mindset of lawyers trained in the common law tradition towards that of those from other legal traditions'.[61] It may not be a coincidence that legislation supporting the use of the same neutral (arb)-med-arb is adopted most often in common law jurisdictions where practitioners and the courts are 'culturally far less comfortable' with these processes than in civil law jurisdictions.[62] The provisions enacted in Hong Kong and Singapore will be discussed further on in Section 8.3.2.1.

The questionnaire results demonstrate that arbitration institutions play a very insignificant role in encouraging the combined use of mediation and arbitration. Only two participants of the study experienced a combination of mediation and arbitration pursuant to **a provision in the rules of an arbitration institution** (7.4%) and only one pursuant to **a suggestion of an arbitration institution** (3.7%).

The rare use of mediation and arbitration in combination pursuant to a suggestion of an arbitration institution, as reported by the study's participants, contrasts with the high demand for such initiatives, evidenced by empirical studies. For example, the 2013 International Mediation Institute (IMI) International Corporate Users ADR Survey found that arbitration providers are expected by about three-quarters of corporate users to be proactively encouraging parties to mediate their dispute.[63] In-house counsel, advocates, arbitrators, and mediators who participated in Bühring-Uhle's 2006 survey were of a similar opinion: three-quarters thought it was appropriate for an arbitration institution to explicitly suggest, at its own initiative, the use of mediation to the parties.[64]

59 Wilson, *supra* n. 52.
60 Hwang, *supra* n. 52, at 577.
61 Luke Nottage & Richard Garnett, *Top 20 Things to Change in or Around Australia's International Arbitration Act*, 6(1) Asian Int'l. Arb. J. 1, 36 (2010) (speaking about the situation in Singapore).
62 Campbell Bridge, *Med-Arb and Other Hybrid Processes – One Man's Meat Is Another Man's Poison*, 4 (unpublished paper presented at APRAG 2014, 10th Anniversary Conference, Australia 2014).
63 *IMI International Corporate Users ADR Survey (January-March 2013)*, International Mediation Institute (4 Apr. 2013), available at <www.fd.unl.pt/docentes_docs/ma/MFG_MA_23457.pdf> (accessed 30 Mar. 2018). The results are indicative, despite the non-scholarly nature of this survey.
64 Bühring-Uhle et al., *supra* n. 14, at 126.

While some commentators commend procedures that are already available in some arbitration institutions for offering possibilities to facilitate settlement,[65] others point out that arbitrators and arbitration institutions could be doing more to assist parties in settling disputes.[66]

Many dispute resolution institutions offer both arbitration and mediation services. However, few, if any, appear to make a continued effort to encourage parties to use mediation before or during arbitration proceedings administered by the institution.[67] The greater role that dispute resolution institutions need to play in promoting the use of mediation and arbitration in combination is explored in Section 9.4.

5.2.3.2.6 SINGLE OR DUAL ROLE OF A NEUTRAL IN THE COMBINED USE OF MEDIATION AND ARBITRATION

The participants were asked about the neutral who conducted mediation in the dispute involving the combined use of mediation and arbitration (see Figure 5.6). In answering this question, the participants could select from three options: the sole arbitrator, a member of the arbitral tribunal, or a neutral other than the sole arbitrator or a member of the arbitral tribunal. The

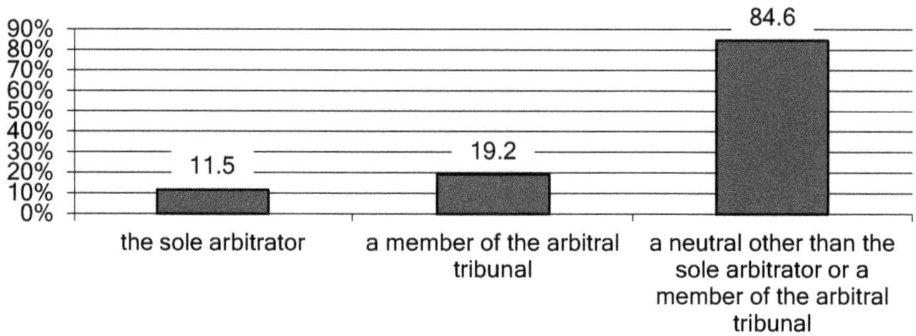

Figure 5.6 Who conducted mediation in a dispute involving the combined use of mediation and arbitration?

65 *See, e.g.*, Gerald Aksen, *Comments on Enforceability of Awards on the Role of Arbitrators as Settlement Facilitators*, in *New Horizons in International Commercial Arbitration and Beyond*, 12 ICCA Congress Series 565, 566 (Albert Jan van den Berg ed., Kluwer Law International 2005) (observing that the ICC Terms of Reference present a unique opportunity to facilitate settlement).

66 Newmark, *supra* n. 29, at 87.

67 *Ibid*, at 89; Jeremy Lack, *Appropriate Dispute Resolution (ADR): The Spectrum of Hybrid Techniques Available to the Parties*, in *ADR in Business: Practice and Issues across Countries and Cultures* vol. II 339, 379 (Arnold Ingen-Housz ed., Kluwer Law International 2011) (noting that ADR institutions should examine and create more links between the various processes they offer).

answers to this question were not mutually exclusive. Twenty-six participants answered this question.

The data shows that the involvement of different neutrals for the mediation and arbitration stages of the process is the most common way of using mediation and arbitration in combination (84.6%). Interestingly, all but one of the participants with a common-law background who responded to this question (12 out of 13) indicated their experience with this combination, whereas the participants with a civil-law background who responded to this question appeared to have experienced this combination less often (seven out of ten participants). The use of the sole arbitrator or a member of the arbitral tribunal as a mediator in the combined use of processes is limited (11.5% and 19.2%, respectively).[68]

The approach where different neutrals are in charge of the mediation and arbitration stages of the combined use of processes finds support among commentators. Fiechter observes that there is much to gain in keeping the functions of a mediator and arbitrator separate.[69] Similar views have been expressed by Masood,[70] Lang,[71] Costa Braga de Oliveira,[72] and Ross.[73] In fact, the involvement of different neutrals is one of the three ways to address concerns associated with the same neutral (arb)-med-arb discussed in Section 3.3, including the threat to the arbitrator's impartiality and the risk of a breach of due process. This and the other two ways, namely procedural modifications of the same neutral (arb)-med-arb and the implementation of safeguards for using the same neutral (arb)-med-arb, are explored further in Chapters 6, 7, and 8.

As discussed in Chapter 4, the practitioners' perception of the same neutral (arb)-med-arb is often explained by reference to the legal culture and, more specifically, the practice of the judiciary and the way that disputes are perceived and resolved in practitioners' home jurisdictions. While in common-law countries judges and arbitrators traditionally refrain from actively contributing to

68 The participants who experienced a sole arbitrator acting as a mediator practised in Belgium (3.85%), China (3.85%), and Hong Kong (3.85%). The participants who experienced a member of the arbitral tribunal acting as a mediator practised in China (3.85%), Hong Kong (3.85%), Italy (3.85%), and Mexico (3.85%). One participant in this group did not indicate primary country of practice (3.85%).

69 Eric W. Fiechter, *Mediation – Casting Issues: Can or Should the Same Person be Mediator, or Conciliator and Arbitrator?* 15 Croatian Arb. Y.B. 255, 261 (2008).

70 Ahmed Masood, *Settlement in International Arbitration: Comments on the CEDR Settlement Rules*, 76(2) Arb. 269, 276 (2010).

71 Jon Lang, *Med-Arb – An English Perspective*, 2(1) NYSBA New York Disp. Res. Law. 98, 102 (2009).

72 Pedro Alberto Costa Braga de Oliveira, *Designing Effective Med-Ard and Arb-Med Processes in Brazil*, 2(1) NYSBA New York Disp. Res. Law. 89, 89 (2009).

73 Donna Ross, *Med-Arb/Arb-Med: a More Efficient ADR Process or an Invitation to a Potential Ethical Disaster?* in *Contemporary Issues in International Arbitration and Mediation: The Fordham Papers 2012* 352, 358 (Arthur W. Rovine ed., Martinus Nijhoff 2013).

settlement, practices in civil-law countries vary. Nevertheless, Germany, Austria, Switzerland, Japan, and mainland China are often referred to as examples of civil-law countries where judges and arbitrators are eager to mediate cases that come before them.[74]

The questionnaire result showing that the most common way of using mediation and arbitration in combination is by involving different neutrals for the mediation and arbitration stages of the process (84.6%) may be explained by the legal background of the participants who reported experience with the combined use of mediation and arbitration.

The majority of these participants practised in Common Law Asia Pacific and in Continental Europe (see Figure 5.5). As discussed in Section 5.2.3.2.5, while legislative acts in Singapore and Hong Kong encourage arbitrators to act as mediators and mediators as arbitrators, these legislative provisions have rarely been used in practice. Dispute resolution practitioners trained in the common-law tradition still seem to be uncomfortable with these practices. Among the participants with a civil law background, very few reported practising in civil-law countries that are known for their favourable attitude to mediation by judges and arbitrators, namely Germany, Austria, Switzerland, Japan, and mainland China. More specifically, among participants with experience in the combined use of mediation and arbitration, only one practised in China and one in Switzerland. None practised in Germany, Austria, Switzerland, or Japan. The participant from Switzerland did not answer the question about the neutral who conducted mediation in the dispute involving the combined use of mediation and arbitration.

A preference for involving different neutrals for the mediation and arbitration stages of the combined use of processes demonstrated by the questionnaire participants contrasts with the results of another empirical study, the International Academy of Mediators and Straus Institute Survey on Mediator Practices and Perceptions (the IAM-Straus Institute survey).[75] One-hundred and thirty experienced mediators practising in different parts of the world, all fellows of the International Academy of Mediators, participated in this survey.[76] About 61% of the participants reported some experience in acting as both a mediator and an arbitrator in the same dispute (61.3%).[77] This result of the IAM-Straus Institute survey indicating a relatively frequent involvement of mediators as arbitrators in the same dispute is difficult to explain. Perhaps knowing the exact distribution of

74 *See* discussion in Sections 4.2 and 4.3 *supra*.

75 Thomas J. Stipanowich & Zachary P. Ulrich, *Commercial Arbitration and Settlement: Empirical Insights into the Roles Arbitrators Play*, 6 Y.B. On Arb. & Mediation 1, 27–28 (2014).

76 *Ibid*, at 27. The participants indicated that they 'regularly practised' in Africa; Asia, including the Middle East; Australia and New Zealand; Canada; Europe (both Western and Eastern, with a majority from the United Kingdom); Latin America; and the United States. About 90% (89.8%) of respondents indicated that they worked 'full time' at the time the survey was administered and devoted, on average, more than 70% of their work time to mediation practice.

77 *Ibid*, at 28.

participants by country could have provided a clue to this result. It would have been particularly interesting to know what proportion of the participants 'regularly practised' in China, Japan, Germany, Switzerland, and Austria. Nevertheless, the relatively frequent involvement of mediators as arbitrators in the same dispute may be attributed to the fact that mediators participating in that survey were asked to report on their overall experience rather than that over any particular period of time (e.g., over the last five years). The participants of the IAM-Straus Institute survey had, on average, over 18 years of mediation experience and had conducted, on average, about 1,500 mediations throughout their careers.[78] This extensive professional mediation experience of the IAM-Straus Institute survey's participants may provide an explanation for their more frequent (as compared to the participants of this study) involvement as mediators and arbitrators in the same dispute.

5.2.3.2.7 MEDIATION IN THE COMBINED USE OF PROCESSES: TIMING AND THE USE OF CAUCUSES[79]

Timing. The participants were asked to indicate when, in the combined use of processes, mediation had been used (see Table 5.3). In answering this

78 *Ibid*, at 27.

79 Apart from collecting data on these two aspects of mediation in combinations, the questionnaire investigated whether mediators are proactive rather than purely facilitative. Although many trainers still teach a purely facilitative model of mediation, Leathes highlights the need for mediators to learn how, when and whether to deploy evaluative and transformative techniques, depending on the circumstances. See Michael Leathes, *2020 Vision: Where in the World Will Mediation Be Within 10 Years?* International Mediation Institute (Nov. 2010), available at <www.imimediation.org/tools-and-resources/resources/reading-materials/> (accessed 30 Mar. 2018). Leathes' comments, however, refer to stand-alone mediation. When mediation is used as part of the same neutral (arb)-med-arb, commentators give different advice to mediators. They recommend mediators to refrain from being evaluative, not to opine on particular issues, to be careful not to express any definite opinion as to an appropriate outcome, and to avoid exerting any undue pressure. *See, e.g.*, Ross, *supra* n. 73, at 360; Richard P. Flake, *MED/ARB – A Viable ADR Vehicle? Nuances of Med/Arb—A Neutral's Perspective*, CEDIRES 7, available at <www.cedires.com/index_bestanden/FLAKE_http-www.cbylaw.com-filebin_files_flake_rpf-AAA_Med-Arb.pdf> (accessed 14 Jan. 2018); Alan L. Limbury, *Making Med-Arb Work*, 9(7) ADR Bulletin 1, 3 (2007); Andreas Reiner, *Bridges Between Mediation and Arbitration: The Mediator as Arbitrator?/The Arbitrator as Mediator?* 24 (unpublished paper presented at Tenth Zagreb Arbitration Conference, 2002). The questionnaire asked those who conducted mediation in a dispute involving the use of combinations to characterise their mediation style. Twenty-three participants answered this question. Surprisingly, 43.5% of these participants did not report any professional experience as mediators in international commercial disputes involving the combined use of processes when asked about it in one of the preceding questions. The majority of the remaining 56.5% participants with professional experience as mediators in combinations characterised their mediation style as facilitative (34.8%), while 8.7% said that their mediation style was evaluative; and 13% reported that their mediation style varied and could be facilitative, evaluative, or transformative. Most of those who characterised their mediation style as facilitative had acted as mediators in disputes that involved arbitration with a different neutral (21.7%). Due to the fact that 43.5% of

Table 5.3 Timing of mediation in the combined use of mediation and arbitration

Answer options	*Response (%)*	*Response count*
Before arbitration	74.1	20
After commencement of arbitration but before the hearing on the merits	70.4	19
After the hearing on the merits but before issuing the award	25.9	7
At the same time as arbitration	14.8	4
After issuing the award	11.1	3
Other	7.4	2
Total		27

Note: although 27 participants answered this question, some of them selected more than one answer.

question, the participants could select from five options and specify any other timing of mediation. The answers to this question were not mutually exclusive. About three-quarters of the participants had experienced mediation before arbitration (74.1%) and almost the same number reported the use of mediation after commencement of arbitration but before the hearing on the merits (70.4%). Those participants who selected more than one answer were asked to indicate the one that had applied most frequently. Nine participants answered this follow-up question and six of them referred to the use of mediation before arbitration.

The questionnaire results correspond to the views expressed by some commentators that the earlier mediation can be done, the better.[80] The process starting with mediation could potentially result in considerable savings of cost and time because only if all issues are not settled in mediation, do parties move to arbitration.[81] Hence, mediation conducted before arbitration may allow parties to avoid arbitration proceedings altogether.[82]

the participants who answered the question on the mediation style did not actually have any experience as mediators in combinations, the responses to this question are not discussed in this book any further.

80 Michael McIlwrath, *Anti-Arbitration: 10 Things To Do Before The Arbitration Gets Underway*, Kluwer Arbitration Blog (12 Nov. 2011), available at <http://kluwerarbitrationblog.com/blog/2011/11/12/anti-arbitration-10-things-to-do-before-the-arbitration-gets-underway/> (accessed 30 Mar. 2018); Stipanowich & Ulrich, *supra* n. 75, at 8 (noting that 'most business disputes are amenable to a negotiated resolution, and that there are multiple benefits associated with early, informal resolution of disputes'); *but see* Naughton, *supra* n. 48, at 31 (stating that the most difficult cases are often those referred to mediation before any proceedings have been commenced).

81 Ross, *supra* n. 73, at 363.

82 Bühring-Uhle et al., *supra* n. 14, at 251.

However, if parties have reached the stage of preparing for arbitration, the moment immediately before the initiation of arbitration may be inappropriate for mediation because then parties may focus more on how to win rather than how to reconcile their interests.[83] Also, parties' views on the case may be too one-sided, pre-arbitral mediation may be exploited for delay tactics, and parties may simply lack the necessary information on the merits of the dispute.[84] At that point, it may be preferable to formalise the dispute by initiating arbitration proceedings.[85]

After commencement of arbitration, mediation is thought to have more potential for success once parties have exchanged information at the preparatory phase of arbitration, which allows them to better estimate their respective strengths.[86] The chances of mediation being successful increase also because parties become aware of the costs and uncertainties of arbitration.[87] These arguments might explain the questionnaire result demonstrating frequent use of mediation after the commencement of arbitration but before the hearing on the merits.

The questionnaire data reveals that most frequently the combined use of mediation and arbitration involves the use of its mediation and arbitration components in sequence. The reference to mediation is usually made in the early stages of this dispute resolution approach: either before arbitration or after the commencement of arbitration but before the hearing on the merits. This result is understandable, as cost incentives exist for parties to resolve their dispute sooner rather than later.[88]

Use of caucuses. The participants were asked about the frequency of the use of caucuses in the mediation stage of the combined use of processes (see Figure 5.7). The data reveals that caucuses were used in mediation either in all (66.7%) or the majority of cases involving the combined use of processes (22.2%).

83 *Ibid*, at 264.

84 *Ibid*, at 252.

85 *Ibid*, at 264. Also, the initiation of arbitration is sometimes a deliberate settlement tactic, as it is supposed to create the necessary pressure on the other party to seriously negotiate. However, initiating arbitration may have an antagonising effect and change the frame for parties' interaction. *Ibid*, at 118.

86 *Ibid*, at 264–265; Michael E. Schneider, *Combining Arbitration with Conciliation*, in *International Dispute Resolution: Towards an International Arbitration Culture*, 8 ICCA Congress Series 57, 86 (Albert Jan van den Berg ed., Kluwer Law International 1998) (pointing out that while many views exist about the best moment for raising the idea of settlement discussions after the commencement of arbitration, normally parties should have been able to present the essence of their case).

87 Pierre Lalive, *The Role of Arbitrators as Settlement Facilitators – A Swiss View*, in *New Horizons in International Commercial Arbitration and Beyond*, 12 ICCA Congress Series 556, 563 (Albert Jan van den Berg ed., Kluwer Law International 2005); *but see* Arthur L. Marriott, *Arbitrators and Settlement*, in *New Horizons in International Commercial Arbitration and Beyond*, 12 ICCA Congress Series 533, 543 (Albert Jan van den Berg ed., Kluwer Law International 2005) (noting that, once fully involved in arbitration, parties may switch to a more adversarial mode and become less inclined to compromise).

88 Marriott, *supra* n. 87, at 542.

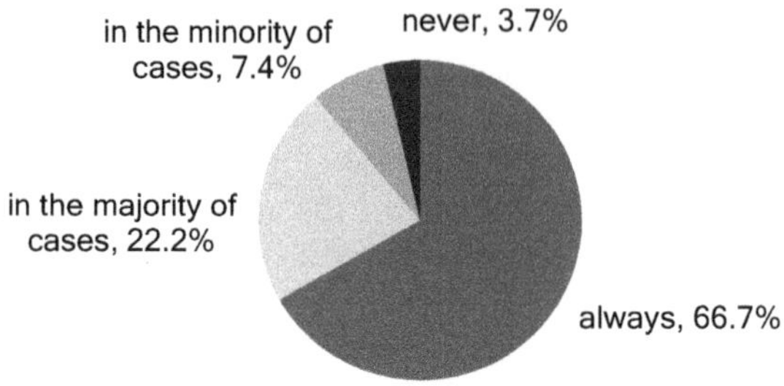

Figure 5.7 Use of caucuses in the mediation stage of the combined use of processes

These results are not surprising, given the fact that about 85% of the participants experienced the combined use of processes with different neutrals in charge of the mediation and arbitration stages (see Figure 5.6). Caucuses are problematic only in the context of the same neutral (arb)-med-arb. They raise no concerns if different neutrals conduct the mediation and arbitration stages, which is the case in this study. Consequently, there is nothing unusual in the result that caucuses were used in the mediation stage in all or the majority of cases.

The involvement of different neutrals is merely one of the three ways to address concerns associated with the same neutral (arb)-med-arb. These concerns may be addressed otherwise. For example, if parties want to keep the same neutrals for both roles, they may prohibit them from using caucuses altogether. Or, parties may allow caucusing but then require dual role neutrals either to disregard the disclosed facts or disclose them if mediation does not result in a settlement and parties have to move on to the arbitration stage. All options have their strengths and weaknesses and will be discussed in Chapters 6, 7, and 8.

5.2.3.2.8 RECORDING THE OUTCOME OF THE COMBINED USE OF MEDIATION AND ARBITRATION

The participants were asked to indicate how the outcome of the combined use of mediation and arbitration was recorded (see Figure 5.8). In answering this question, the participants could select from four options: in a mediated settlement agreement, in a consent arbitral award incorporating a mediated settlement agreement, in a regular arbitral award,[89] or in a court judgment. The participants could also specify any other form of recording the outcome. The answers to this question were not mutually exclusive. A mediated settlement agreement was used

89 That is, awards resulting from an arbitral tribunal's deliberations. In the context of the combined use of mediation and arbitration, usually an arbitrator will need to decide on a dispute and render an arbitral award if the parties do not settle in mediation.

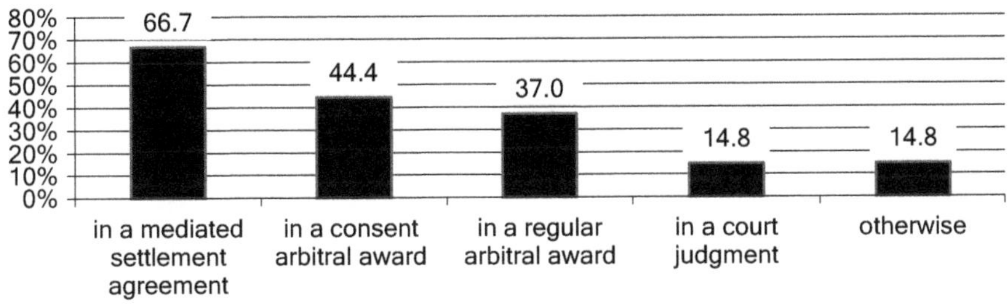

Figure 5.8 Recording the outcome of the combined use of mediation and arbitration

to record the outcome of the combined use of processes according to 18 of 27 participants who answered this question (66.7%). Those who selected more than one answer were asked to indicate the one that had been used most frequently. Eleven participants answered this follow-up question and seven of them selected recording the outcome of the combined use of processes in a mediated settlement agreement.

As discussed in Section 3.2.2, the current absence of a unified enforcement mechanism for international mediated settlement agreements is often seen as an obstacle to its greater use as a stand-alone method of international commercial dispute resolution. One of the frequently cited benefits of the combined use of mediation and arbitration is a possibility to convert a mediated settlement agreement into a consent award that is, arguably, enforceable all over the world pursuant to the New York Convention.

The questionnaire data, however, shows that the absence of a coherent enforcement mechanism for international mediated settlement agreements is not an obstacle to recording the outcome of the combined use of processes in this kind of agreement. On the contrary, two-thirds of the participants had experienced the combined use of mediation and arbitration resulting in a mediated settlement agreement (66.7%). Notwithstanding the existence of the established international enforcement mechanism for arbitral awards, neither consent nor regular arbitral awards had been used, according to the questionnaire participants, to a similar extent (44.4% and 37%, respectively). Moreover, the majority of those participants who had experienced various ways of recording the outcome of the combined use of processes referred to a mediated settlement agreement as the most frequently used option.

This suggests that the importance of establishing a unified enforcement mechanism for international mediated settlement agreements might be overstated: even in the absence of this mechanism in the majority of cases the outcome of the combined use of processes is recorded as a mediated settlement agreement. The possibility offered by the combined use of mediation and arbitration to incorporate a mediated settlement agreement into a consent arbitral award is used only to a limited extent.

One more issue related to the enforceability of the outcome of combinations needs to be explored here. The questionnaire data on the timing of mediation discussed in Section 5.2.3.2.7 revealed that in combinations, mediation is usually used either before arbitration or after the commencement of arbitration but before the hearing on the merits. If parties reach settlement in the mediation phase of a combination and want to incorporate it into a consent award, the timing of a mediated settlement agreement is important for the consent award's enforceability. This section turns now to examine this issue in more detail.

5.2.3.2.8.1 Timing of a mediated settlement agreement If a mediated settlement agreement terminates an arbitration process already in progress, it is generally recognised that the settlement agreements which are recorded in the consent award are enforceable under the New York Convention.[90] National laws and arbitral and mediation institutions authorise arbitrators to make an award in the form of the terms of settlement reached during arbitration.[91]

However, there is no clear and shared understanding in the literature of whether a mediator can be appointed as an arbitrator merely for the purposes of issuing a consent award. It is questionable whether a mediated settlement agreement will be enforced other than simply as a contract if the mediation part of the proceedings occurs apart from and before the arbitration part of the

90 Klaus Peter Berger, *International Economic Arbitration*, 582 (Kluwer Law and Taxation Publishers 1993) referred to in Carlos De Vera, *Arbitrating Harmony: 'Med-Arb' and the Confluence of Culture and Rule of Law in the Resolution of International Commercial Disputes in China*, 18 Colum. J. Asian L. 149, 161 n. 45 (2004); James T. Peter, *Med-Arb in International Arbitration*, 4 Revista de Arbitragem e Mediação 155, 158–159 n. 34 (2005); James T. Peter, *Note & Comment: Med-Arb in International Arbitration*, 8 Am. Rev. Int'l Arb. 83, 90 n. 34 (1997); Anthony Connerty, *ADR as a 'Filter' Mechanism: The Use of ADR in the Context of International Disputes*, 79(2) Arb. 120, 128 (2013); Ross, *supra* n. 73, at 362–363; Wolski, *supra* n. 22, at 261 n. 54 (noting, however, that this view is not universally accepted, with some authors noting that the proposition is 'untested').

91 *See, e.g.*, UK Arbitration Act 1996, c. 23, s. 51(2); Arbitration Law of the People's Republic of China, art. 51 (1994), Zhonghua Renmin Gongheguo Falu Huibian; UNCITRAL Arbitration Rules, art. 36.1 (effective 15 Aug. 2010), available at <www.uncitral.org/pdf/english/texts/arbitration/arb-rules-revised/arb-rules-revised-2010-e.pdf> (accessed 30 Mar. 2018); International Court of Arbitration of the International Chamber of Commerce (ICC) Rules of Arbitration, art. 33 (effective 1 Mar. 2017), available at <https://iccwbo.org/dispute-resolution-services/arbitration/rules-of-arbitration/> (accessed 30 Mar. 2018); London Court of International Arbitration (LCIA) Arbitration Rules, art. 26.9 (effective 1 Oct. 2014), available at <www.lcia.org/Dispute_Resolution_Services/lcia-arbitration-rules-2014.aspx> (accessed 30 Mar. 2018).

process, namely med-arb.[92] It appears important for the process to formally begin as arbitration, namely arb-med-arb.[93]

The major criticism related to med-arb is that, if mediation successfully resolves all differences, there is then no dispute capable of triggering a valid arbitration and, hence, generating an enforceable consent award.[94] As observed by Newmark and Hill, one cannot validly agree to appoint arbitrators where there is nothing for them to arbitrate.[95] Mustill and Boyd similarly note that it appears to be settled law that a procedure cannot be regarded as arbitration unless there is a formulated dispute in existence when the arbitrator is appointed.[96] Likewise, an agreement cannot be regarded as an arbitration agreement unless there is an existing dispute when the arbitrator is appointed.[97]

At the same time, similarly to other issues arising in the context of the combined use of mediation and arbitration, one's answer to the question of whether it is possible to enforce as a consent award a mediated settlement agreement concluded before the appointment of an arbitrator appears to be influenced by one's legal culture. When this possibility was discussed in the intergovernmental working group within the framework of preparation of the UNCITRAL ML on Conciliation, the opinions of the participants of that discussion differed. Some opined that it would be acceptable on the basis of experience in their countries, whereas others indicated that it would not work technically because to have arbitration one needs to have a dispute and there is none once a settlement has been reached.[98]

92 *See, e.g.*, Peter (1997), *supra* n. 90, at 90; De Vera, *supra* n. 90, at 161; Peter (2005), *supra* n. 90, at 158–159; Greenwood, *supra* n. 44, at 201–202; Brette L. Steele, *Enforcing International Commercial Mediation Agreements as Arbitral Awards under the New York Convention*, 54 UCLA L. Rev. 1385, 1401 (2007); José Maria Abascal Zamora, *Some Remarks on the UNCITRAL Model Law on International Commercial Conciliation*, in *New Horizons in International Commercial Arbitration and Beyond*, 12 ICCA Congress Series 415, 419–420 (Albert Jan van den Berg ed., Kluwer Law International 2005); Wolski, *supra* n. 22, at 262; Christopher Newmark & Richard Hill, *Can a Mediated Settlement Become an Enforceable Arbitration Award?* 16(1) Arb. Int'l. 81, 83–85 (2000); Yaraslau Kryvoi & Dmitry Davydenko, *Consent Awards in International Arbitration: From Settlement to Enforcement*, 40 Brook. J. Int'l L. 827, 864–865 (2014–2015).

93 *See, e.g.*, Alan L. Limbury, *Hybrid Dispute Resolution Processes – Getting the Best While Avoiding the Worst of Both Worlds?* in *CIArb's Mediation Compendium* 5 (A. Hudson-Tyreman et al. eds, London 2009); Nottage & Garnett, *supra* n. 61, at 35 n. 93; Newmark & Hill, *supra* n. 92, at 85.

94 *See, e.g.*, Zamora, *supra* n. 92, at 420; Wolski, *supra* n. 22, at 261.

95 Newmark & Hill, *supra* n. 92, at 83.

96 Michael J. Mustill & Stewart C. Boyd, *Commercial Arbitration*, 47 (2d ed., Butterworths 1989) quoted *ibid.*

97 *Ibid.*

98 Nadja Alexander, *International Comparative Mediation: Legal Perspectives (Global Trends in Dispute Resolution)*, 362 (Kluwer Law International 2009).

Practitioners' legal system emerged as a determinative factor in the approach taken to this question. Civil- and common-law legal systems appear to interpret differently the notion of a dispute as a condition precedent to arbitration, and the approach of the former is, arguably, broader.[99] As noted by the former Secretary of UNCITRAL, Jernej Sekolec, when debtors accept liability but claim that they do not have the money to pay, there is no dispute in common-law jurisdictions while there still may be one in civil-law countries.[100]

Nevertheless, a closer look at civil-law and common-law systems suggests that the approach is not consistent throughout either system.

5.2.3.2.8.2 Civil law jurisdictions Under Brazilian law, for example, parties cannot convert their mediated settlement agreement into a consent award if arbitration has not started before the parties' settlement is achieved, and any award recorded under such circumstances will be null and void.[101] However, settlement reached by the parties after the commencement of arbitration may be recorded as a consent award under the Brazilian Arbitration Act.[102] The same is possible in Mexico.[103]

Likewise, under Japanese law, if mediation takes place before arbitration and it leads to a settlement, a mediated settlement agreement is treated as no more than an agreement between the parties.[104] If, however, parties settle during arbitral proceedings, they may request the arbitral tribunal to make a ruling on agreed terms, which shall have the same effect as an arbitral award.[105]

Germany seems to have adopted the same approach. The conversion of a settlement agreement reached in mediation conducted prior to arbitration into an arbitral award on agreed terms further to the German Arbitration Act appears to be highly problematic because a dispute is a necessary precondition for arbitration.[106] Under the same conditions in France, on the contrary, a mediated settlement agreement can be converted into a consent award either by the mediator in the function of an

99 *Ibid*, at 363.

100 *Ibid.*

101 Costa Braga de Oliveira, *supra* n. 72, at 90.

102 Lei Ordinária 9.307, de 23.09.96 art. 28.

103 UNCITRAL, *Settlement of Commercial Disputes. Enforcement of Settlement Agreements Resulting from International Commercial Conciliation/Mediation. Compilation of Comments by Governments (A/CN.9/846/Add.3)*, 7 (4 Jun. 2015), available at <www.uncitral.org/uncitral/en/commission/working_groups/2Arbitration.html> (accessed 30 Mar. 2018).

104 UNCITRAL, *Settlement of Commercial Disputes. Enforcement of Settlement Agreements Resulting from International Commercial Conciliation/Mediation. Compilation of Comments by Governments (A/CN.9/846/Add.1)*, 6 (15 Apr. 2015), available at <www.uncitral.org/uncitral/en/commission/working_groups/2Arbitration.html> (accessed 30 Mar. 2018) [hereinafter, *Compilation of Comments Add.1*].

105 Chusai Ho [Arbitration Law] Law No. 138 of 2003 art. 38.

106 Art. 1053 Abs. 1 ZPO. *See also* Klaus Peter Berger, *Integration of Mediation Elements into Arbitration: 'Hybrid' Procedures and 'Intuitive' Mediation by International Arbitrators*, 19 (3) Arb. Int'l. 387, 389–390 & n. 16 (2003).

arbitrator or by a third party appointed for that purpose.[107] A similar possibility exists in Croatia[108] and Thailand.[109]

5.2.3.2.8.3 Common law jurisdictions In India, a mediated settlement agreement has the effect of a consent arbitral award even if arbitral proceedings have not commenced.[110] The same is possible even in the US. At least five US states – California, Texas, Ohio, North Carolina, and Oregon – expressly authorise in legislation the incorporation of a mediated settlement agreement concluded before commencement of arbitration into a consent award in international commercial disputes.[111] To benefit from the relevant provisions, a mediated settlement agreement must be in writing and signed by the parties (or their representatives) and the mediator.[112] In Bermuda, parties to an arbitration agreement may appoint a mediator, and any resulting settlement shall enjoy the status of a consent award and be enforced in an identical manner as a judgment to the same effect. Although the disputants must be parties to an arbitration agreement, it is not necessary for an arbitration procedure to commence before the appointment of a mediator.[113] Similar provisions can be found in the laws of Singapore[114] and Hong Kong.[115]

5.2.3.2.8.4 Institutional rules A number of institutional rules provide for the possibility of incorporating a mediated settlement agreement into an arbitral award even if mediation precedes arbitration.

Article 14 of the SCC Mediation Rules[116] states that

107 *Mediation: Principles and Regulation in Comparative Perspective*, 475–476 (Klaus J. Hopt & Felix Steffek eds, Oxford University Press 2012).

108 Conciliation Act (Official Gazette NN 18/11, 2011), art. 13(5) (allowing parties to formalise their mediated settlement agreement as a notarial deed, court settlement, or an arbitration award on agreed terms).

109 Although Thailand is a hybrid of many influences, it has a predominantly civil-law legal system. *Compilation of Comments Add.1, supra* n. 104, at 15–16 (noting that in Thailand parties may give the effect to the settlement agreement by agreeing to submit the dispute to an arbitral tribunal with a request to settle the dispute in accordance with the settlement agreement; the settlement agreement shall enjoy the same status and effect as a final award by an arbitral tribunal).

110 UNCITRAL, *Guide to Enactment and Use of the UNCITRAL Model Law on International Commercial Conciliation (2002)*, ¶ 91, available at <www.uncitral.org/uncitral/en/uncitral_texts/arbitration/2002Model_conciliation.html> (accessed 14 Jan. 2018) (citing ss. 73–74, Arbitration and Conciliation Act, Act No. 26 of 1996) [hereinafter, *Guide to ML on Conciliation*].

111 Cal. Civ. Proc. Code Ann. § 1297.401 (West 2013); Tex. Civ. Prac. & Rem. Code Ann. § 172.211 (West 2008); Ohio Rev. Code §2712.87 (2015); N.C. Gen. Stat. §1–567.84 (2013); Or. Rev. State. Ann. §36.546 (West 2015).

112 *Compilation of Comments Add.1, supra* n. 104, at 18.

113 Bermuda International Conciliation and Arbitration Act 1993, s. 20.

114 Singapore IAA, *supra* n. 49, ss. 16, 18.

115 Hong Kong AO, *supra* n. 50, ss. 32, 66(2).

116 Stockholm Chamber of Commerce (SCC) Mediation Rules (effective 1 Jan. 2014), available at <http://sccinstitute.com/dispute-resolution/rules/> (accessed 30 Mar. 2018).

> In case of settlement, the parties may, subject to the consent of the Mediator, agree to appoint the Mediator as an Arbitrator and request him/her to confirm the settlement agreement in an arbitral award.

Similar provisions are found in the Mediation Rules of the Court of Arbitration at the Polish Chamber of Commerce,[117] the International Commercial Mediation Rules of the Japan Commercial Arbitration Association (JCAA Mediation Rules),[118] the 2011 Domestic Arbitration Rules of the Korean Commercial Arbitration Board,[119] and elsewhere.[120]

The JCAA commented on the contradiction between the Japanese legislation treating a mediated settlement agreement reached before commencement of arbitration as merely an agreement, and Rule 11 of the JCAA Mediation Rules allowing parties under the same circumstances to appoint mediators as arbitrators and request them to make an arbitral award that incorporates the settlement agreement.[121] The JCAA explained that Rule 11 was introduced in view of the benefit of the final settlement of disputes for parties. To justify its approach, the JCAA referred to the view that even if parties have settled in mediation, the dispute may still exist between them in that, if parties request the arbitrator to make an arbitral award based on the agreed terms, the dispute has not been ultimately settled between parties and it will be finally settled when the arbitrator renders the arbitral award.[122] Although there have been no Japanese court decisions on this issue, in practice, same neutral med-arb can be found in a sufficient number of the domestic mediation cases, particularly at the dispute resolution centres operated by the local bar associations in Japan.[123]

117 Court of Arbitration at the Polish Chamber of Commerce (PCC) Mediation Rules (effective 1 Jan. 2015), § 8, available at <www.sakig.pl/en/arbitration/rules> (accessed 30 Mar. 2018).

118 Japan Commercial Arbitration Association (JCAA) International Commercial Mediation Rules (effective 1 Jan. 2009), rule 11, available at <www.jcaa.or.jp/e/mediation/docs/rules.pdf> (accessed 30 Mar. 2018).

119 Korean Commercial Arbitration Board (KCAB) Domestic Arbitration Rules (effective 1 Sep. 2011), arts. 18(2)-(3), available at <www.kcab.or.kr/jsp/kcab_eng/law/law_03_ex.jsp> (accessed 30 Mar. 2018). Interestingly, KCAB Domestic Arbitration Rules 2016 that superseded the Rules of 2011 do not contain any similar provision. Also, while the 2011 Rules used the term 'conciliation', the 2016 Rules speak about 'mediation'. Korean Commercial Arbitration Board (KCAB) Domestic Arbitration Rules (effective 30 Nov. 2016), available at <www.kcab.or.kr/jsp/kcab_eng/law/law_03_ex.jsp> (accessed 30 Mar. 2018).

120 *See, e.g.*, Society of Maritime Arbitrators (SMA) Conciliation Rules (effective 16 May 1988), art. 10(c), available at <www.smany.org/concilliation-rules.html> (accessed 30 Mar. 2018); Conciliation Centre at Croatian Chamber of Economy (CCCCE) Rules of Conciliation (effective 17 Jul. 2002), art. 6(2), available at <www.vsrh.hr/EasyWeb.asp?pcpid=286> (accessed 30 Mar. 2018)

121 *Compilation of Comments Add.1, supra* n. 104, at 6.

122 *Ibid.*

123 *Ibid.*

Despite the fact that the possibility of incorporating a mediated settlement agreement into an arbitral award exists in certain jurisdictions and under certain institutional rules even if the arbitrator is appointed after reaching the settlement, the enforceability of the resulting consent award is unclear and largely untested. For now, to ensure its enforceability, it is advisable that parties start the combined process with arbitration rather than mediation. While, as discussed in Chapter 3, the advantages and concerns associated with the same neutral med-arb and the same neutral arb-med-arb are generally the same, the enforceability of the outcome is the issue that makes the same neutral arb-med-arb preferable over the same neutral med-arb.

5.2.3.3 Main benefits and the future of the combined use of mediation and arbitration

All questionnaire participants were asked to share their views on the main benefits of the combined use of mediation and arbitration and the use of this dispute resolution approach in the future, regardless of their experience in this field. Although 77 and 79 participants answered these two questions, respectively, the particular way of combining mediation and arbitration that each of these participants referred to remained unclear. This was due to the fact that the questionnaire provided a broad definition of 'the combined use of mediation and arbitration'.[124]

5.2.3.3.1 MAIN BENEFITS OF THE COMBINED USE OF MEDIATION AND ARBITRATION

The participants were asked to identify the main benefits to parties of using a combination of mediation and arbitration (see Table 5.4). The participants could select from six options, including 'no benefits', and specify any other benefit. The answers to this question were not mutually exclusive.

The data shows that, overall, the participants had a positive attitude to the combined use of processes, with only 6.5% seeing no benefits to parties of using them. The benefits of the combined use of processes were attributed mostly to the mediation rather than to the arbitration component. The ability to preserve business relationships, faster resolution of the dispute, and its lower cost were rated as the top three benefits of the combined use of processes (72.7%, 67.5%, and 63.6%, respectively). About half of the participants perceived the high quality of the outcome[125] as a benefit of the combined use of processes (50.6%), whereas the possibility of obtaining an

124 *See* the questionnaire definition of 'the combined use of mediation and arbitration' in Section 5.2.1.3 *supra* and the discussion of its limitations in Section 5.2.3.1 *supra*.

125 As specified in the questionnaire, a high-quality outcome means that the outcome of a dispute resolution process is more in line with parties' needs (as compared to arbitration only).

Table 5.4 Main benefits to parties of using a combination of mediation and arbitration

Answer options	*Response (%)*	*Response count*
Ability to preserve business relationship	72.7	56
Faster resolution of their dispute (as compared to arbitration only)	67.5	52
Lower cost of resolution of their dispute (as compared to arbitration only)	63.6	49
High quality of the outcome, i.e., the outcome of a dispute resolution process is more in line with parties' needs (as compared to arbitration only)	50.6	39
Possibility of obtaining an enforceable arbitral award	31.2	24
Other	13	10
No benefits	6.5	5
Total		77

Note: although 77 participants answered this question, some of them selected more than one answer.

enforceable arbitral award was regarded as a benefit by about 31% of the participants (31.2%).

As discussed in Section 3.2.1, faster resolution of a dispute, its lower cost and the better quality of the outcome, as compared to arbitration only, are advantages often associated with the use of the same neutral (arb)-med-arb. In view of the broad questionnaire definition of 'the combined use of mediation and arbitration', the particular way of combining mediation and arbitration that each questionnaire participant referred to remained unclear.

Only about 31% of the participants perceived the possibility of obtaining an enforceable arbitral award as a benefit of the combined use of mediation and arbitration. On the one hand, this result is surprising because it contradicts the prevalent view among commentators that the possibility of incorporating a mediated settlement agreement into a consent arbitral award is a major advantage of using mediation and arbitration in combination.[126] This possibility is often seen as a remedy against, arguably, the key impediment to a more widespread use of mediation as a stand-alone method of international commercial dispute resolution: the absence of a coherent enforcement mechanism for international mediated settlement agreements.

On the other hand, this result is consistent with responses given to a question directed to the participants with experience in the combined use of mediation

126 *See* discussion in Section 3.2.2.2 *supra*.

and arbitration. These participants were asked about the way the outcome of the combined use of processes had been recorded. As discussed in Section 5.2.3.2.8, two-thirds of the participants had experienced the combined use of processes resulting in a mediated settlement agreement. Neither consent nor regular arbitral awards had been used, according to the participants, to a similar extent. Thereby, it appears that the possibility of incorporating a mediated settlement agreement into an arbitral award is neither perceived as a benefit of the combined use of processes nor availed of in practice.

It is notable that the questionnaire data revealed a contrast between the perception of combinations as beneficial processes and their infrequent use. A similar gap between the perception and use of combinations emerged from the Bühring-Uhle survey.[127] The author found that, despite a growing acceptance of explicit mediation elements in arbitration, these mediation elements are used less frequently than their general acceptance by practitioners might suggest.[128]

5.2.3.3.2 FUTURE OF THE COMBINED USE OF MEDIATION AND ARBITRATION

The participants were asked whether they wanted to see more use of a combination of mediation and arbitration for resolving international commercial disputes in the coming years. More than three-quarters of 79 participants answered 'yes' to this question (78.5%), whereas about 11% said 'no' (11.4%), and about 10% were not sure about their answer and selected the 'don't know' option (10.1%).[129] Although all participants were asked to comment on their answer, only 35 did so.

Most often the participants qualified the combined use of mediation and arbitration with reservations related to the conduct of both processes by the same neutral or the use of caucuses. These reservations were reiterated in the comments of those participants who were against or uncertain about the desirability of a wider use of this dispute resolution approach in the future.[130] The

127 Bühring-Uhle et al., *supra* n. 14, at 128.

128 *Ibid.*

129 The results of the GPC survey corroborate the desirability of more use of combinations. As noted in n. 23 of the Introduction chapter the GPC survey participants ranked combining adjudicative and non-adjudicative processes (e.g., arbitration/litigation with mediation/conciliation) and non-adjudicative dispute resolution methods (mediation or conciliation) second (45%) and third (43%) respectively in terms of processes that should be prioritised to improve the future of commercial dispute resolution. Pre-dispute or pre-escalation processes to prevent disputes were ranked as priority number one (51%). Greater emphasis on collaborative instead of adversarial processes was ranked first in response to the question about trends with the most significant influence on the future of commercial dispute resolution (57%). *Global Pound Conference Series 2016–17 Cumulated Data Results March 2016 – September 2017*, Global Pound, available at <http://globalpound.org/wp-content/uploads/2017/11/2017-09-18-Final-GPC-Series-Results-Cumulated-Votes-from-the-GPC-App-Mar.-2016-Sep.-2017.pdf> (accessed 14 Jan. 2018) [hereinafter, GPC Cumulated Data Results].

130 Concerns associated with the same neutral (arb)-med-arb are discussed in Section 3.3 *supra*.

participants frequently attributed both the benefits of the combined use of processes and its drawbacks to its mediation component.

5.2.4 Questionnaire results significant for the second phase of the empirical study

Section 5.2.3 presented and discussed the key questionnaire results. Four of them are significant for the second phase of the empirical study.

5.2.4.1 Result 1: Extent of use of combinations

All combinations are reported to be used to a relatively low extent in international commercial dispute resolution. Only about one-third of the questionnaire participants had had experience with them over the previous five years, almost half of whom reported that disputes involving combinations had constituted not more than 10% of their overall international commercial dispute resolution practice.

5.2.4.2 Result 2: Most common combination

The sequential use of processes with different neutrals in charge of the mediation and arbitration stages, namely diff neutral (arb)-med-arb, turned out to be the most common combination, whereas the use of the same neutral (arb)-med-arb appeared to be minimal only. This preference for diff neutral (arb)-med-arb can be explained by reference to the legal culture of the questionnaire participants with experience in combinations. The majority of these participants practised in Common Law Asia Pacific and Continental Europe. Among the participants with a civil-law background, very few reported practising in civil-law countries that are known for their favourable attitude to mediation by judges and arbitrators, namely Germany, Austria, Switzerland, Japan, and mainland China. The participants with a common-law background demonstrated a typical preference among common-law practitioners for using arbitration and mediation separately by involving different neutrals in each stage.

5.2.4.3 Result 3: Possibility of recording the outcome of combinations in a consent award

As noted in Sections 3.2.2 and 5.2.3.2.8, the possibility of converting a mediated settlement agreement into a consent arbitral award is one of the frequently cited benefits of combinations. The questionnaire participants, however, neither perceived this possibility as a benefit of combinations nor availed of it in practice.

5.2.4.4 *Result 4: Perception of combinations*

Almost all questionnaire participants recognised some benefits of combinations (93.5%). The ability to preserve business relationships, and faster and less expensive resolution of the dispute (as compared to arbitration only) were rated as the top three benefits. More than three-quarters of the participants supported the wider use of combinations in the coming years.

These four questionnaire results invited further enquiry that was undertaken through semi-structured interviews.

5.3 Phase 2: Interviews

5.3.1 Methodology

5.3.1.1 *Process*

The second phase of the study, semi-structured interviews, was conducted in March and April 2015. Thirteen professionals were invited to participate in a one-on-one interview, and six accepted the invitation. The interviewees were selected using purposive sampling. In particular, the selection was based on the interviewees' substantial professional experience in international commercial dispute resolution and highly probable professional experience with the combined use of mediation and arbitration, as evidenced by their publications and publicly available CVs. One interviewee was selected on the basis of the completed questionnaire that demonstrated experience with combinations and indicated willingness to participate in a follow-up interview. Considering the fact that practitioners' perception and, as demonstrated by the questionnaire data, use of the same neutral (arb)-med-arb can often be explained by reference to their legal culture, the study sought a balanced representation of both common-law and civil-law traditions among the interviewees. Of the six interviewees, three were from a civil-law jurisdiction, namely Belgium, Spain, and Switzerland. The remaining three originated from a common-law jurisdiction, namely Australia, Hong Kong, and the United States.

Five interviews were conducted in person and one by telephone. Each interview lasted 30–60 minutes. The interviewees were asked three introductory and six questions on the substance of the research.[131] All interviews were recorded using an audio digital recording device and transcribed into a Word document following the interviews. All interviewees have been given an opportunity to verify the accuracy of the data used in this book.

131 The interview schedule is provided in Appendix 3.

5.3.1.2 Purpose

The interview questions sought to elicit views concerning the most significant questionnaire results. Specifically, they covered the following matters:

- perceptions as to barriers to the use of the same neutral (arb)-med-arb;
- actual ways of overcoming barriers to the same neutral (arb)-med-arb (based on the participants' practice);
- perceptions as to the significance of a legal culture for the way the combined use of mediation and arbitration is conducted;
- perceptions as to the emergence of a harmonisation trend in the combined use of mediation and arbitration;
- perceptions as to the ways of enhancing the use of combinations;
- perceptions as to whether the introduction of an international enforcement mechanism for mediated settlement agreements might decrease parties' interest in the use of combinations.

5.3.1.3 Limitations

The interview results need to be interpreted with some caution. First, those interviewed were highly experienced international dispute resolution practitioners and were likely to have a pre-existing interest in international commercial arbitration and mediation. Hence, it is probable that the interviewees were more favourably disposed to the use of arbitration, mediation, and their combinations than dispute resolution practitioners in general. Second, the interviewees represented certain regions and legal cultures more than others. All three interviewees with the civil-law background were from Continental Europe. This happened because, despite the fact that an invitation to participate in an interview was sent to six potential interviewees originating from civil-law countries, including China and Japan, only those from Continental Europe accepted the invitation. As discussed in Section 4.3, while Germany, Austria, Switzerland, Japan, and China are frequently referred to as examples of civil-law countries where arbitrators are eager to mediate their own cases, differences exist between the German approach, on the one hand, and that of China and Japan, on the other hand. In particular, caucuses are uncommon for German judges and arbitrators, whereas they are widely used by their colleagues in China and Japan.

In view of these two limitations, the interview results cannot be extrapolated to all international dispute resolution practitioners.

5.3.2 Reporting

One part of the interview questions sought data on issues that have already been introduced in this and earlier chapters, whereas another part related to issues that are yet to be discussed in Chapters 8 and 9. Taking this point into account, the book will present and discuss in this chapter the results relevant to the issues that have already been introduced. The remaining results will be addressed in Chapters 8 and 9.

5.3.3 Results

5.3.3.1 Barriers to the use of the same neutral (arb)-med-arb

The questionnaire data revealed a rare use of combinations in general and a minimal use of the same neutral (arb)-med-arb in particular, with diff neutral (arb)-med-arb being the most common combination. The interviewees were asked to explain the rare use of the same neutral (arb)-med-arb. Most interviewees indicated that the extent of the use of this combination varied from country to country.

> Well, those empirical studies would not include China. Because the stats that I hear from say CIETAC ... is that there is a massive number of the arbitrations settled while mediation [is] in the process ... To leave China out of this debate [on the extent of the use of the same neutral (arb)-med-arb] is to ignore an elephant in the room.[132]
>
> I think you will be surprised that practice and the attitude is more spread than even I have thought ... I was surprised that it was not only the Chinese but also the Japanese, and Koreans and I think there was some other Asian group.[133]
>
> It's a cultural matter. In Switzerland and Germany there is a tradition to lead parties to a settlement. I would be very hesitant to do that in England.[134]

Some interviewees explained the rare use of the same neutral (arb)-med-arb by a particular mindset or a particular perception of the role of an arbitrator. For example:

> A lot of attorneys think in a compartmentalised way about the processes ... So often, if you are selected as a mediator, they want you to mediate. If you are selected as an arbitrator, they expect you to arbitrate. They don't choose you to be an all-purpose neutral ... There is just a mindset.[135]
>
> The big difference is the role model of the arbitrator. If the arbitrator considers himself as an impartial referee, he would not do this [act as a

132 Practitioner from Australia, Interview 2.
133 Practitioner from Switzerland, Interview 4.
134 Practitioner from Belgium, Interview 6.
135 Practitioner from the United States, Interview 5.

> mediator] ... whereas in these other jurisdictions, the arbitrator considers himself someone who has a dispute to solve and means, the way he resolves the dispute, do not matter.[136]

Two interviewees pointed out what they believed to be problematic issues in the use of the same neutral (arb)-med-arb.

> There are elements of arbitration which are potentially inconsistent with some of the techniques that make mediation very successful. And in particular the big issue for the combination of the processes is the caucus process.[137]

> There are problems with this process also. One of them is the arm-twisting, that the arbitrator or judge wants to avoid writing a judgment, and coerces parties.[138]

One interviewee considered that the rare use of the same neutral (arb)-med-arb stemmed from the reluctance to use mediation in general.

> In international arbitration, not talking about a concrete legal system ... there is no really great enthusiasm about formally conducting mediation, because ... formally instituting mediation will probably be not the last solution and at the end they [parties] might have to go to arbitration or litigation.[139]

5.3.3.2 Significance of the legal culture

All but one interviewee recognised the significant influence that the legal culture of counsel and neutral(s) has on the way a combination of mediation and arbitration is conducted. For example:

> I think US attorneys and ... to some extent US neutrals tend to be very doctrinaire about keeping mediation and arbitration separate ... there is a vast cultural difference say between a US situation or Germany and Switzerland or China where you have an experience with mixed roles. How it actually plays out is another thing ... So there is a spectrum of experience, it's affected by culture.[140]

> Probably the Chinese will be more open to it [the same neutral (arb)-med-arb] than, I would say, French. There is a tradition in Asian countries ... to settle rather than go to litigation or arbitration.[141]

136 Practitioner from Switzerland, Interview 4.
137 Practitioner from Australia, Interview 2.
138 Practitioner from Switzerland, Interview 4.
139 Practitioner from Spain, Interview 1.
140 Practitioner from the United States, Interview 5.
141 Practitioner from Belgium, Interview 6.

The interviewee who disagreed with the interviewees above, stated:

> I think the culture is not really an issue. I think the issue is the lawyers. If you are a law firm and this is your biggest client … you are going to convince your client that he should not settle.[142]

One interviewee emphasised the challenging task of an international arbitrator acting in a multicultural environment.

> Well, probably, the Chinese culture like other cultures, for instance, in Germany … they are very much in favour of mediating. Other cultures prefer not to mediate … International experienced arbitrators have to go through this clash of cultures and … be bold in trying to use one way or the other.[143]

Another interviewee pointed out the shortage of dispute resolution professionals who are open to new ideas and new ways of doing things.

> You're going to get both parties comfortable with the processes different from what they're used to … The baggage of legal culture is heavy. And there aren't a lot of lawyers who are interested in doing things differently.[144]

5.3.3.3 Harmonisation trend

Overall, interviewees appeared to be sceptical when asked whether they saw any harmonisation trend emerging in the combined use of mediation and arbitration, in general, and in relation to the same neutral (arb)-med-arb, in particular. The roots of their scepticism, however, varied.

The scepticism of one interviewee related to harmonisation efforts, in general.

> I don't believe in harmonisation … We have too many guidelines … too many harmonisation instruments. At the end we have to rely on the experience and capability of the arbitration tribunal and especially the chairman.[145]

Another interviewee pointed out the disparity in the practice of mediation around the world and the lack of international experience with it.

> To me it's too early to say that there is any harmonisation … There are lots of parts of the world … where there is a lot of [more] discussion of mediation … than there is any actual mediation of commercial cases …

142 Practitioner from Hong Kong, Interview 3.
143 Practitioner from Spain, Interview 1.
144 Practitioner from Australia, Interview 2.
145 Practitioner from Spain, Interview 1.

> That's not a basis for any kind of harmonisation. People don't even know what mediation is, if they have never mediated.[146]

Another interviewee criticised the focus of the ongoing debate on combinations.

> It's unfortunately been a debate that has not moved on in twenty years. Same arguments around at the conferences that I hear are being talked about. And there is not enough work being done to talk intelligently about it ... and to think more flexibly instead of debating it from the extremes of the spectrum.[147]

Yet another interviewee drew attention to differences in the underlying attitude to the use of mediation in arbitration in various countries and the limits to one's procedural flexibility.

> I would have thought that a German judge or arbitrator goes about it quite differently from a Chinese or Japanese ... But that is the underlying attitude ... Even depends on a dispute ... whether there is something that you can settle ... I think to some extent we are flexible but I have my own temperament, I have a certain way how I think things can be conducted most effectively.[148]

5.3.3.4 Enforceability of the outcome

Since at the time when interviews were conducted UNCITRAL had started considering the adoption of a convention on enforcement of settlement agreements resulting from international commercial mediation, one of the questions asked of the interviewees was whether they thought that combinations could become less attractive to parties if there were an international enforcement mechanism for mediated settlement agreements.

One interviewee disagreed that parties use a combination of mediation and arbitration to incorporate a mediated settlement agreement into an arbitral award.

> I don't think people arbitrate because they want to have an enforceable mediated outcome.[149]

Another interviewee expressed doubts that the adoption of the convention would make a difference.

146 Practitioner from the United States, Interview 5.
147 Practitioner from Australia, Interview 2.
148 Practitioner from Switzerland, Interview 4.
149 Practitioner from Australia, Interview 2.

> Probably the things might change because that's [the absence of an enforcement mechanism] one of the problems [with mediation]. But I mean, at the end to come to … settlement through mediation … you have to come to that and mediation does not always come to such a settlement of disputes.[150]

Many interviewees commented on whether an international enforcement mechanism for mediated settlement agreements was desirable in general. All, however, appeared to disapprove of the adoption of such a mechanism for various reasons. For example:

> I, however, disagree … that there should be a separate international regime for the enforcement of mediation outcomes … Trying to make it as if it's some sort of further enforceable obligation strikes at the heart of true consensus in the outcome of mediation.[151]

> I am troubled frankly by the fact that they are trying to create an international convention on mediation. All of this … regulatory superstructure being created for something that people have never experienced. I don't know how you can do that. I am somewhat cynical about it.[152]

> I am very sceptical about this convention … One of the biggest problems in the whole thing is … it is not practised domestically … In the US judges give some credence to settlement agreements in mediations in the US because they know the process … There is a problem if it comes from abroad … How can you then overcome this credibility gap simply by binding international convention?[153]

5.3.4 Discussion

5.3.4.1 Legal culture

Section 5.2.3.2.6 explained the questionnaire result that diff neutral (arb)-med-arb is used more frequently than the same neutral (arb)-med-arb by reference to the legal culture of practitioners with experience in combinations: practices in practitioners' home jurisdictions influence the way they perceive and use the same neutral (arb)-med-arb. The interview data supports this explanation. The interviewees observed that the extent of the use of the same neutral (arb)-med-arb varied from country to country. They referred to China, Japan, Korea, Germany,

150 Practitioner from Spain, Interview 1.
151 Practitioner from Australia, Interview 2.
152 Practitioner from the United States, Interview 5.
153 Practitioner from Switzerland, Interview 4.

and Switzerland as countries where arbitrators do not hesitate to act as mediators, while noting that this practice is uncommon for the United States and England. Given the fact that international dispute resolution involves neutrals and parties of different legal cultures, it appears desirable that more international dispute resolution practitioners become open to new ideas and ways of resolving disputes. International neutrals need to be capable and skilled to arrange a dispute resolution procedure in a way that accommodates parties from different legal cultures.[154]

5.3.4.2 Harmonisation trend

The interview data does not support a narrative in the literature addressed in Section 4.4 suggesting that there is an emerging harmonisation trend favouring the same neutral (arb)-med-arb: common-law practitioners are beginning to recognise that the roles of an arbitrator and a mediator are not fundamentally incompatible. The interview data revealed that it might be premature to talk about harmonisation. For harmonisation to occur it seems that many countries need to gain more experience with international commercial mediation. It appears that in some countries there is more discussion of mediation than its actual use in commercial cases. Rather than taking a rigid stance on whether the same neutral (arb)-med-arb is an appropriate process, it appears desirable that dispute resolution practitioners learn to look for opportunities that combinations offer and avail themselves only of those that are viable in light of the circumstances of each particular case.

154 An interesting issue pointed out by the interviewee from Hong Kong (cited in Section 5.3.3.2) is that lawyers rather than legal culture are an impediment to the wider use of mediation in combination with arbitration. Nottage notes in this respect that 'practices such as Arb-Med [same neutral arb-med-arb] come up against the "billable hours" model for funding legal practice – as well as defining career progression in large, increasingly multinational law firms'. *See* Nottage, *supra* n. 52, at 227. Similarly, Ali observes that financial pressures on lawyers prevent settlement: '[w]ith rates exceeding $650/hour, the potential financial impact of a quick settlement is … significant'. *See* Shahla F. Ali, *Barricades and Checkered Flags: An Empirical Examination of the Perceptions of Roadblocks and Facilitators of Settlement Among Arbitration Practitioners in East Asia and the West*, 19 Pac. Rim L. & Pol'y J. 243, 269 (2010). The results of a recent GPC survey echo the above opinions. Having identified that the future of commercial dispute resolution lies in the use of pre-escalation processes, combining adjudicative and non-adjudicative processes and non-adjudicative processes used on their own, the survey asked who was likely to be most resistant to change in commercial dispute resolution practice. All participants, including external lawyers themselves, overwhelmingly considered that the most resistant to change would be external lawyers (67%). *See* GPC Cumulated Data Results, *supra* n. 129. While the issue of lawyers opposing settlement is of growing concern, a further inquiry into this is beyond the scope of this book.

5.3.4.3 *Enforceability of the outcome*

The interview data further corroborates the questionnaire result that the possibility of incorporating a mediated settlement agreement into a consent award is not the reason why parties use a combination of mediation and arbitration. Also, in contrast to the strong narrative in the literature, which assumes there is a need for an international convention providing for enforceability of mediated settlement agreements, the interviewees questioned the necessity of such a convention and expressed various concerns related to this proposal. Their concerns include the lack of experience with mediation in some parts of the world, current absence of an enforcement mechanism for mediated settlement agreements on a domestic level, and the credibility gap should a party seek to enforce a mediated settlement agreement that originated from abroad.[155]

5.4 Conclusion

This chapter has presented and discussed the key results of the two-phase empirical study conducted for this research project. The first phase employed a questionnaire to investigate the current use of mediation in combination with arbitration in international commercial dispute resolution. The second phase, conducted through interviews, sought to elicit views of professionals concerning the most significant questionnaire results.

5.4.1 *Significant questionnaire results*

Section 5.2.4 identified four questionnaire results significant for the second phase of the empirical study. These are

155 Several jurisdictions voiced similar and other concerns when completing the UNCITRAL questionnaire on their legislation addressing enforcement of mediated settlement agreements. The UNCITRAL Secretariat circulated the questionnaire in 2014–2015 in view of considering the feasibility of a convention. *See, e.g.*, comments of the government of Austria in UNCITRAL, *Settlement of Commercial Disputes, Enforcement of Settlement Agreements Resulting from International Commercial Conciliation/Mediation. Compilation of Comments by Governments (A/CN.9/846)*, 5–6 (27 Mar. 2015), available at <www.uncitral.org/uncitral/en/commission/working_groups/2Arbitration.html> (accessed 6 Apr. 2018); comments of the government of Australia in UNCITRAL, *Settlement of Commercial Disputes. Enforcement of Settlement Agreements Resulting from International Commercial Conciliation/Mediation. Compilation of Comments by Governments (A/CN.9/846/Add.2)*, 4 (22 Apr. 2015), available at <www.uncitral.org/uncitral/en/commission/working_groups/2Arbitration.html> (accessed 30 Mar. 2018); comments of the Government of Russia in UNCITRAL, *Settlement of Commercial Disputes. Enforcement of Settlement Agreements Resulting from International Commercial Conciliation/Mediation. Compilation of Comments by Governments (A/CN.9/846/Add.4)*, 4 (12 Jun. 2015), available at <www.uncitral.org/uncitral/en/commission/working_groups/2Arbitration.html> (accessed 6 Apr. 2018). While the need for a convention providing for enforceability of mediated settlement agreements is a fascinating issue to consider in the current international commercial dispute resolution environment, a further inquiry into this is beyond the scope of this book.

1 All combinations are used to a relatively low extent in international commercial dispute resolution.
2 Diff neutral (arb)-med-arb is the most common combination. The use of the same neutral (arb)-med-arb is minimal only.
3 The ability to convert a mediated settlement agreement into a consent award is neither perceived as a benefit of combinations nor availed of in practice.
4 All combinations are widely perceived as beneficial processes. The ability to preserve business relationships, and faster and less expensive resolution of the dispute (as compared to arbitration only) emerged as their top three benefits.

5.4.2 *Interview results*

The interview results presented in this chapter relate to two of the four significant questionnaire results (Results 2 and 3). The interview results concerning the remaining two significant questionnaire results (Results 1 and 4) will be presented and discussed in Chapter 9. Chapter 8 will present and discuss more interview results concerning questionnaire Result 2. There is a reason why the interview results concerning questionnaire Result 2 are presented in two different chapters. While the interview results presented in this chapter seek to explain the minimal use of the same neutral (arb)-med-arb, those presented in Chapter 8 explore ways to increase the use of this combination by addressing concerns associated with it. The interview results concerning questionnaire Results 2 and 3 presented in this chapter are as follows:

1 When asked to explain the minimal use of the same neutral (arb)-med-arb, the interviewees observed that the extent of the use of this combination varied from country to country. In this way, the interviewees further supported the earlier explanation of this questionnaire result by reference to the practitioners' legal culture: practitioners' perception and use of the same neutral (arb)-med-arb largely depends on practices in their home country. Contrary to the narrative in the literature, assuming that there is an emerging harmonisation trend favouring the same neutral (arb)-med-arb, the interview data reveals that it might be premature to talk about harmonisation.
2 The interview data further corroborates the questionnaire result that the ability to convert a mediated settlement agreement into a consent arbitral award is not the reason why parties use combinations.

Diff neutral (arb)-med-arb (the most common combination according to the questionnaire participants) has been praised for avoiding concerns associated with the same neutral (arb)-med-arb[156] analysed in Section 3.3. At the same time, the

156 Wolski, *supra* n. 22, at 259.

same neutral (arb)-med-arb has been discussed in the literature as the process with the most potential for the increased time and cost efficiency of dipute resolution, along with other advantages, as compared to any other combination. The book turns now to examining in Part IV ways to address concerns associated with the same neutral (arb)-med-arb.

Part IV

Solutions

Section 3.3 identified two principal groups of concerns associated with the same neutral (arb)-med-arb: behavioural concerns that surface in the mediation stage and procedural concerns that arise in the arbitration stage. The key behavioural concerns are parties' reluctance to be open in their discussions with mediators, the inhibited conduct of mediators, parties' use of mediation as a tactical tool, and the abuse of power by mediators resulting in the coercion of parties into a settlement. The procedural concerns include the danger that arbitrators will appear or actually be biased and the risk that the process may offend the principles of due process.

Part IV consists of three chapters and investigates ways to address behavioural and procedural concerns associated with the same neutral (arb)-med-arb. It identifies and evaluates three major ways the concerns can be addressed. First, through the involvement of different neutrals in each, mediation and arbitration, phase of a combined process. Second, by modifying the same neutral (arb)-med-arb procedure. Third, by implementing relevant safeguards for using the same neutral (arb)-med-arb. These three ways are discussed in Chapters 6, 7, and 8, respectively.

Most of the combinations examined in Chapters 6 and 7 were introduced and defined in Chapter 2. Chapters 6 and 7 explore these processes further, identifying their strengths and weaknesses and giving specific examples of their use. The use of combinations is illustrated mostly through cases anecdotally reported by dispute resolution practitioners.[1] Chapter 8 identifies and examines two key safeguards for using the same neutral (arb)-med-arb – party voluntary and informed consent to the process – and two main safeguard options for reducing concerns related to the use of caucuses.

1 It should be acknowledged that these cases are impossible to verify and their reporting may be tainted by the practitioner's subjective interpretation of the circumstances of the case.

6 Involvement of different neutrals in combinations as a way to address concerns associated with the same neutral (arb)-med-arb

6.1 Introduction

This chapter evaluates the involvement of different neutrals as a way to address concerns associated with the same neutral (arb)-med-arb. Section 6.2 examines diff neutral (arb)-med-arb, the most common combination, according to the questionnaire participants. Section 6.3 analyses combinations involving different neutrals as mediators and arbitrators other than diff neutral (arb)-med-arb. These are shadow mediation, co-med-arb, and four other combinations suggested by dispute resolution institutions. Section 6.4 examines (arb)-med-arb opt-out – a combination that allows any party independently to call for a different neutral to act as the arbitrator after completion of the mediation phase of the process.

6.2 Diff neutral (arb)-med-arb

Bühring-Uhle et al. consider that the only solution to overcome the confusion of roles and the resulting interference between mediation and arbitration when both processes are conducted by the same neutral, is to conduct mediation and arbitration as two distinct processes.[2] A clear separation can be achieved through having different persons perform the two tasks.[3]

Diff neutral (arb)-med-arb or the involvement of different neutrals in a sequential use of mediation and arbitration is widely supported in the literature on combinations.[4] Fiechter emphasises that it is for good reasons that

2 Christian Bühring-Uhle et al., *Arbitration and Mediation in International Business* 249 (2d ed., Kluwer Law International 2006).

3 *Ibid.*

4 *See, e.g.*, Ahmed Masood, *Settlement in International Arbitration: Comments on the CEDR Settlement Rules*, 76(2) Arb. 269, 276 (2010); Bobette Wolski, *Arb-Med-Arb (and MSAs): A Whole Which Is Less than, not Greater than, the Sum of Its Parts?* 6(2) Contemp. Asia Arb. J. 249, 260 (2013); Su Yin Anand, *The Risks of Arbitration-Mediation: Hong Kong Courts Decline to Enforce PRC Arbitral Award*, 16(2) Arb. News (Newsletter of the International Bar Association Legal Practice Division) 40, 42 (2011); Harold I. Abramson, *Protocols for International*

most mediation rules set the principle that mediators may not act as arbitrators, unless all participating parties ask a mediator to arbitrate the dispute.[5] In most cases, the parties will feel more comfortable if the mediator hands over the arbitration proceedings to a different neutral. The CEDR Commission on Settlement in International Arbitration (CEDR Commission) prefers diff neutral arb-med-arb over the same neutral arb-med-arb that involves the use of caucuses in the mediation stage.[6] Diff neutral (arb)-med-arb turned out to be the most common combination, according to the questionnaire participants.

6.2.1 Advantages and disadvantages of diff neutral (arb)-med-arb

There are at least three advantages of diff neutral (arb)-med-arb. The first obvious advantage of this process is that it eliminates the risk of compromising the procedural integrity of arbitration and undermining the efficacy of mediation,[7] i.e. procedural and behavioural concerns associated with the use of the same neutral (arb)-med-arb. Second, the involvement of two different neutrals might improve the quality of both processes if a process expert is chosen as a mediator and a legal or technical specialist as an arbitrator.[8] Third, arbitrators' power to confirm the agreement as an award is subject to their consent.[9] This 'health check' of the settlement by someone other than the mediator might be particularly valuable where mediators do not have a legal qualification.

Arbitrators Who Dare to Settle Cases, 10 Am. Rev. Int'l Arb. 1, 3 (1999); Jeremy Lack, *Appropriate Dispute Resolution (ADR): The Spectrum of Hybrid Techniques Available to the Parties*, in *ADR in Business: Practice and Issues across Countries and Cultures* vol. II 339, 373 (Arnold Ingen-Housz ed., Kluwer Law International 2011); J. Martin H. Hunter cited in Christian Bühring-Uhle, *Arbitration and Mediation in International Business: Designing Procedures for Effective Conflict Management* 209 (Kluwer Law International 1996); Richard Hill, *MED-ARB: New Coke or Swatch?* 13(1) Arb. Int'l. 105, 107 (1997); Brian A. Pappas, *Med-Arb and the Legalisation of Alternative Dispute Resolution*, 20 Harv. Negot. L. Rev. 157, 160 & 201–202 (Spring 2015).

5 Eric W. Fiechter, *Mediation – Casting Issues: Can or Should the Same Person be Mediator, or Conciliator and Arbitrator?* 15 Croatian Arb. Y.B. 255, 260 (2008).

6 Safeguards for Arbitrators Who Use Private Meetings with Each Party as a Means of Facilitating Settlement (Final Report of the CEDR Commission on Settlement in International Arbitration, Appendix 2), ¶ 6, available at <www.cedr.com/about_us/arbitration_commission/> (accessed 14 Jan. 2018). The starting preference of the CEDR Commission is the same neutral arb-med-arb that does not involve the use of caucuses.

7 Bühring-Uhle et al., *supra* n. 2, at 249; Srikant Deekshitha & Arka Saha, *Amalgamating the Conciliatory and the Adjudicative: Hybrid Processes and Asian Arbitral Institutions*, III(1) Indian J. Arb. L. 76, 79 (Jodhpur 2014); Christopher Newmark & Richard Hill, *Can a Mediated Settlement Become an Enforceable Arbitration Award?* 16(1) Arb. Int'l. 81, 86 (2000).

8 Bühring-Uhle et al., *supra* n. 2, at 249; Deekshitha & Saha, *supra* n. 7, at 79.

9 Newmark & Hill, *supra* n. 7, at 86.

The obvious disadvantages of using two individuals are additional costs and time, as compared to the same neutral (arb)-med-arb.[10] Unless a dispute is settled in the mediation phase, there is little saving in time and cost in diff neutral (arb)-med-arb.[11] If the dispute proceeds or goes back to the arbitration stage, however, additional expenses may be reduced by authorising mediators to provide arbitrators with an agreed list of issues that are and are not in dispute.[12]

A field experiment conducted at the Dispute Settlement Center in New York revealed other disadvantages of diff neutral med-arb as compared to the same neutral med-arb.[13] In the former, mediators appeared to be less involved in the case, and disputants were not as motivated to reach agreement as in the latter.[14]

6.2.2 Diff neutral (arb)-med-arb and legal culture

In Section 5.2.3.2.6, the book explained the questionnaire result that the most common combination is diff neutral (arb)-med-arb by referring to the legal culture of the participants with experience in combinations. Most of these participants practised in Common Law Asia Pacific and Continental Europe, with very few originating from countries known for their favourable attitude to mediation by arbitrators, such as Germany, Austria, Switzerland, Japan, and mainland China.

This questionnaire result combined with the reviewed literature indicates that practitioners who come from countries that disapprove of the same neutral acting as a mediator and arbitrator, in particular, view diff neutral (arb)-med-arb as a solution to concerns associated with the same neutral (arb)-med-arb. Many of these practitioners would have been those trained in the common-law system that has traditionally demonstrated a preference for the separate use of mediation and arbitration by involving different neutrals as mediators and arbitrators.[15]

10 *Ibid; see also* Bernd Ehle, *The Arbitrator as a Settlement Facilitator* in *Walking A Thin Line – What an Arbitrator Can Do, Must Do or Must Not Do, Recent Developments and Trends* 77, 85 (Bruylant 2010); Wolski, *supra* n. 4, at 258–259; Claire Wilson, *The Arb-Med Hybrid in Hong Kong – Much Ado about Nothing?* Kluwer Mediation Blog (1 Feb. 2012), available at <http://kluwermediationblog.com/2012/02/01/the-arb-med-hybrid-in-hong-kong-much-ado-about-nothing/> (accessed 31 Mar. 2018).

11 Wolski, *supra* n. 4, at 258–259.

12 *Ibid*, at 259.

13 Dean G. Pruitt, *Process and Outcome in Community Mediation*, 11(4) Negotiation J. 365 (Oct. 1995).

14 *Ibid*, at 368.

15 Some empirical data from the US provides evidence of this preference for separating adjudicative and non-adjudicative functions. *See*, Roselle L. Wissler, *Court-Connected Settlement Procedures: Mediation and Judicial Settlement Conferences*, 26 Ohio St. J. on Disp. Resol. 271, 297–298 (2011) (reporting results of the 2008 survey where Ohio lawyers ranked the five settlement procedures in order of overall preference, from most to least preferred, as follows: mediation with staff mediators, settlement conferences with judges not assigned to the case, mediation with private mediators, settlement conferences with judges assigned to the case, and mediation with volunteer mediators).

While Singapore is one of the few common-law jurisdictions that have adopted legislation facilitating the use of the same neutral (arb)-med-arb, its main mediation and arbitration centres, the SIMC and the SIAC, jointly promote a combined process that involves different neutrals in the mediation and arbitration stages.

The two centres offer their combined services through an arb-med-arb clause[16] that entails the application of the SIAC-SIMC Arb-Med-Arb Protocol.[17] In accordance with this protocol, a party may start arbitration, proceed to mediation after appointment of the tribunal, and revert to the tribunal to incorporate a settlement agreement into a consent award. Unless parties agree otherwise, the arbitrators and the mediators are different persons.[18] They are separately and independently appointed by the SIAC and the SIMC, respectively, under the applicable arbitration and mediation rules of each centre. It appears that, since its introduction in November 2014 and as of November 2017, the SIAC-SIMC Arb-Med-Arb Protocol has been used in nine cases.[19] It is known that in at least three of these cases parties managed to settle in mediation.[20]

In Hong Kong, there is a similar disparity between the legislation facilitating the use of the same neutral (arb)-med-arb and the rules of Hong Kong's main international arbitration institution, which discourage the use of this process. The Mediation Rules of the Hong Kong International Arbitration Centre (HKIAC) differ from the provisions of the Arbitration Ordinance. Article 14 of the Mediation Rules prohibits the parties from appointing the mediator as adjudicator, arbitrator or representative, counsel or expert witness of any party in any subsequent adjudication, arbitration or judicial proceedings whether arising out of the mediation or any other dispute in connection with the same contract.[21] Unlike the approach taken by the SIAC-SIMC that establishes the involvement of different neutrals as a default rule, Article 14 is not a default provision. Consequently, parties cannot change it. HKIAC's

16 Singapore International Mediation Centre, *The Singapore Arb-Med-Arb Clause*, available at <http://simc.com.sg/the-singapore-arb-med-arb-clause/> (accessed 14 Jan. 2018).

17 Singapore International Mediation Centre, *SIAC-SIMC Arb-Med-Arb Protocol*, available at <http://simc.com.sg/siac-simc-arb-med-arb-protocol/> (accessed 14 Jan. 2018).

18 Singapore International Mediation Centre, *What is Arb-Med-Arb?* available at <http://simc.com.sg/arb-med-arb/> (accessed 14 Jan. 2018).

19 Markus Altenkirch & Anindya Basarkod, *Arb-Med-Arb: What is it and how can it help the parties to solve their disputes efficiently?* Global Arbitration News (20 Nov. 2017), available at <https://globalarbitrationnews.com/arb-med-arb-what-is-it-and-how-can-it-help-the-parties-to-solve-their-disputes-efficiently/> (accessed 31 Mar. 2018).

20 *Press Release: Singapore International Mediation Centre (SIMC) Announces Case Numbers for 2014/2015*, Singapore International Mediation Centre (16 Mar. 2016), available at <http://simc.com.sg/press-release-singapore-international-mediation-centre-simc-announces-case-numbers-for-20142015/> (accessed 31 Mar. 2018).

21 Hong Kong International Arbitration Centre (HKIAC) Mediation Rules (effective 1 Aug. 1999), available at <www.hkiac.org/mediation/rules/hkiac-mediation-rules> (accessed 31 Mar. 2018).

Arbitration Rules do not appear to provide for any mixing of mediation and arbitration either.

This disparity in both Singapore and Hong Kong between the legislation and the rules of the jurisdictions' main dispute resolution centres can be explained by the conflicting influences of the Chinese tradition and Western standards. As observed in Section 4.4, Kaufmann-Kohler has no doubt that the provisions on the same neutral (arb)-med-arb were included in the Hong Kong and Singapore arbitration statutes because of the influence of the Chinese tradition.[22] While China is commonly regarded as a foremost proponent of the practice of using the same neutral as a mediator and an arbitrator, this practice seems to be disfavoured in the West. SIAC-SIMC and HKIAC appear to integrate the rules of Western institutional arbitration regimes into their own rules to standardise their mediation and arbitration procedures for Western parties resolving their disputes in Hong Kong and Singapore.[23]

6.2.3 Anecdotally reported cases

6.2.3.1 Resolution of a dispute in the mediation stage of diff neutral arb-med-arb

In the following three cases, parties who intended to use diff neutral arb-med-arb succeeded in resolving their dispute in the mediation stage. They did not need to go back to arbitration, which allowed them to make substantial savings of time and money. These cases illustrate the best-case scenario for diff neutral arb-med-arb in terms of time and cost efficiency.

6.2.3.1.1 INTERNATIONAL METALS CASE

In a case involving international metals arbitration in London, the parties agreed to attempt mediation with a leading London mediator.[24] The sole arbitrator was requested to stay the arbitration proceedings, which were being conducted under the rules of a London commodities association. The mediation was successful and the parties signed an agreement embodying the terms of settlement.

22 Gabrielle Kaufmann-Kohler, *When Arbitrators Facilitate Settlement: Towards a Transnational Standard*, Clayton Utz, available at <www.claytonutz.com/ialecture/2007/transcript_2007.html> (accessed 14 Jan. 2018).

23 Carlos De Vera, *Arbitrating Harmony: 'Med-Arb' and the Confluence of Culture and Rule of Law in the Resolution of International Commercial Disputes in China*, 18 Colum. J. Asian L. 149, 192 (2004) (speaking about the HKIAC Rules).

24 Anthony Connerty, *ADR as a 'Filter' Mechanism: The Use of ADR in the Context of International Disputes*, 79(2) Arb. 120, 130 (2013) (reporting a case from his own professional experience where he acted as co-counsel together with in-house corporate counsel in that case).

6.2.3.1.2 MISSING CONTRACTUAL BASE CASE

In this case, the parties agreed to try mediation in Bern after exchanging the first submissions in arbitration proceedings in Zurich.[25] It became clear during mediation that a situation had arisen which had not been contemplated in the initial contract, yet the contract had not been adjusted. The contract turned out to be totally inappropriate to deal with the situation. In one single mediation session, the parties imagined a fair contract for the future and then applied the solution retroactively.

Commenting on this case, Fiechter argues that the arbitrator could never have acted as the mediator because to succeed, the parties were to explore scenarios that could have been detrimental to their positions as expressed in arbitration.[26] It would have been unthinkable for them to admit before the arbitrator that the contract on the basis of which they had based their respective positions was simply not an adequate basis for their relationship. In this case, Fiechter's point may be true due to the particular circumstances of the case, which Fiechter only partially discloses; however, it would be a far stretch to say that arbitrators should never act as mediators in similar situations. Whether to do it or not will depend on numerous factors, including the legal background of the participants of a dispute resolution process. For instance, as noted in Section 4.3, the same neutral arb-med-arb is common practice for Chinese practitioners.

6.2.3.1.3 BRAZILIAN SHAREHOLDERS CASE

In this case, the involvement of a professional mediator led to a settlement of one of the biggest shareholders' disputes in Brazil's corporate history: Casino's (France) acquisition of Pao de Açucar – a leading supermarket chain in Brazil.[27] After more than two years of a ruthless shareholding dispute for the control of the Brazilian supermarket chain, William Ury was appointed as a mediator to help parties settle their dispute. With William Ury's involvement, the parties reached a simple two-page agreement. This contained only seven points and specified the parties' agreement to settle all disputes, complaints, or claims related to their partnership in Brazil, and bring to an end all arbitration cases brought by them throughout the dispute.

6.2.3.2 Resolution of a dispute in the arbitration stage of diff neutral arb-med-arb

In the following two cases, parties did not settle in the mediation stage of diff neutral arb-med-arb and had to return to arbitration. Despite this, in the first

25 Fiechter, *supra* n. 5, at 259.

26 *Ibid.*

27 Andrea Maia, *Solving Complex Problems – Thinking out of the Box*, Kluwer Mediation Blog (25 Oct. 2013), available at <http://kluwermediationblog.com/2013/10/25/solving-complex-problems-thinking-out-of-the-box/> (accessed 31 Mar. 2018).

case, the parties still benefitted from the mediation stage by using it to agree on the relevant facts, which substantially reduced the number of issues left for the subsequent arbitration. This differed from what happened in the second case, where parties failed to reach any kind of agreement in the mediation stage of diff neutral arb-med-arb.

6.2.3.2.1 COMMODITY DELIVERY CASE

The dispute involved several deliveries of a commodity, the price of which had fluctuated considerably and the quality of which was challenged.[28] The contract was cancelled and damages resulted from the impossibility of selling the commodity on similar terms at the time when the buyer notified the seller about the cancellation. The parties appointed an arbitrator but agreed to try mediation first. Although the dispute could not be resolved in mediation, mediation enabled the parties to sort out numerous issues and to agree on the facts that were relevant. The arbitrator's task therefore became limited to establishing the few decisive disputed facts before rendering his award. This case demonstrates how the mediation stage of diff neutral arb-med-arb, even if it does not create conditions for resolving the dispute entirely, can be used to streamline arbitration, saving the parties time and money.

6.2.3.2.2 NORTH SEA OIL-DRILLING CASE

This case illustrates an expensive and time-consuming scenario for diff neutral arb-med-arb. In this case, the parties returned to arbitration after the mediation stage had resulted in no agreement at all. The parties were in a dispute concerning sub-sea oil-drilling structures for use in the North Sea.[29] The claimant commenced arbitral proceedings. Part way through arbitration, the parties decided to try mediation and appointed a separate mediator. Numerous joint and private sessions took place throughout the two days allocated for mediation. The sessions involved the parties' representatives, including lawyers, the commercial director of one party, and the sub-contract manager of the other; and expert witnesses. By the end of the second day the parties agreed to adjourn the mediation so that discussions could continue. Further discussions took place but no agreement was reached. The arbitration resumed.

6.3 Involvement of different neutrals in combinations other than diff neutral (arb)-med-arb

Although diff neutral (arb)-med-arb eliminates most of the procedural and behavioural concerns associated with the same neutral (arb)-med-arb, it is not

28 Fiechter, *supra* n. 5, at 257–258.

29 Connerty, *supra* n. 24, at 132–134 (reporting a case from his own professional experience where he was appointed as the sole mediator).

always a cost- and time-efficient combination. Parties may benefit from using processes like shadow mediation and co-med-arb because apart from eliminating many concerns associated with the same neutral (arb)-med-arb, these processes appear to be more time efficient than diff neutral (arb)-med-arb.[30] This section explores shadow mediation, co-med-arb, and four other combinations suggested by dispute resolution institutions.

6.3.1 Shadow mediation

In shadow mediation, mediators attend arbitration hearings and at promising moments during the proceedings, such as at the beginning or end of each hearing day, conduct mediation. By attending arbitration hearings, mediators educate themselves about the facts of the case, which reduces the time that will need to be spent on mediation. This aspect of shadow mediation makes this process more time efficient than diff neutral (arb)-med-arb. However, similarly to diff neutral (arb)-med-arb, shadow mediation is not a cost-efficient process due to the involvement of two neutrals.

According to Hunter, a process resembling shadow mediation is frequently employed in practice. In particular, Hunter observes that there are numerous documented examples of mediators being appointed by the parties to work independently of, and in parallel with, arbitral tribunals: the mediator receives all the materials received by the tribunal and reviews these materials with the parties to evaluate the strengths and weaknesses of their positions.[31] The following case illustrates the potential of shadow mediation to achieve financial savings.

6.3.1.1 Multi-party construction dispute

In a complex multi-party construction dispute with eight parties and claims and counterclaims totalling close to USD 9 million, three arbitrators were appointed and up to 50 hearing days were anticipated.[32] A retired judge was appointed as a mediator to 'shadow' the arbitration proceedings as an initially passive observer, being informed about the case and ready to step in as soon as the parties thought mediation attempts might make sense. The mediator tried to mediate twice: first,

30 Donna Ross, *Med-Arb/Arb-Med: A More Efficient ADR Process or an Invitation to a Potential Ethical Disaster?* in *Contemporary Issues in International Arbitration and Mediation: The Fordham Papers 2012* 352, 358 (Arthur W. Rovine ed., Martinus Nijhoff 2013); *see also* Bühring-Uhle et al., *supra* n. 2, at 261 (referring to shadow mediation as an example of cooperation between two neutrals that may increase the efficiency of the combined use of mediation and arbitration by different neutrals).

31 J. Martin Hunter, *Commentary on Integrated Dispute Resolution Clauses*, in *New Horizons in International Commercial Arbitration and Beyond*, 12 ICCA Congress Series 470, 472 (Albert Jan van den Berg ed., Kluwer Law International 2005).

32 This case was administered by the American Arbitration Association. Reported in Bühring-Uhle et al., *supra* n. 2, at 261–262.

after a pre-hearing conference, which did not result in a settlement; and second, on the day of the main hearing, where a breakthrough occurred in mediation. Once each side had given a summary presentation of its case, the mediator met with all parties and engaged in intensive negotiations and shuttle diplomacy. After one and a half days, he was able to broker an agreement not only between the two main parties in dispute but also among the various subcontractors. The compensation for the mediator, who had spent a total of four days observing the arbitration and conducting the mediation and who charged the same per diem fee as the arbitrators, could easily be covered by the deposit the parties had made to cover the costs of the arbitration. Although the estimated costs of arbitration are not known, the savings achieved through the mediated settlement were around USD 500,000–750,000.[33]

6.3.2 Co-med-arb

In co-med-arb, the arbitrator attends the joint mediation sessions but does not participate in caucusing. If no settlement is reached in mediation, the arbitrator renders an award with or without additional hearings and documents, depending on the particular circumstances of the case. The key feature of co-med-arb is that mediation is divided into an open and a confidential phase.[34]

The most commonly given advantage of co-med-arb is that it reduces concerns associated with the same neutral (arb)-med-arb.[35] In particular, parties may be interested in using co-med-arb because it seems to eliminate concerns of partiality, coercion, and withholding of information by parties,[36] while protecting the confidentiality and purpose of caucuses.[37] In addition, the fact that the joint session serves to instruct both the mediator and the arbitrator, makes co-med-arb streamlined.[38] If the dispute is not settled in mediation, no time is lost because the arbitrator is already aware of the facts of the case. In summary, co-med-arb seeks to preserve the efficiency gains of a mediation process with the impartiality of an arbitration process.[39]

33 *Ibid*, at 262.

34 David C. Elliott, *Med/Arb: Fraught with Danger or Ripe with Opportunity*, 34 Alta. L. Rev. 163, 178 (1995–1996); James T. Peter, *Note & Comment: Med-Arb in International Arbitration*, 8 Am. Rev. Int'l Arb. 83, 102 (1997).

35 *See, e.g.*, Alan L. Limbury, *Hybrid Dispute Resolution Processes – Getting the Best While Avoiding the Worst of Both Worlds?* in *CIArb's Mediation Compendium* 9 (A. Hudson-Tyreman et al. eds, London 2009); Elliott, *supra* n. 34, at 178.

36 Peter, *supra* n. 34, at 102; *see also* Steven Friel, *Arbitration in Context (Chapter 3)*, in *Arbitration in England, with Chapters on Scotland and Ireland* 31, 42 (Julian D. M. Lew, Harris Bor, et al. eds, Kluwer Law International 2013) (regarding co-med-arb as a solution to the potentially 'chilling' effect of the same neutral med-arb).

37 Wolski, *supra* n. 4, at 269.

38 Peter, *supra* n. 34, at 102.

39 Elliott, *supra* n. 34, at 178.

Similarly to diff neutral (arb)-med-arb and shadow mediation, the disadvantage is that the involvement of an extra neutral makes co-med-arb cost-intensive.[40] Even if parties manage to settle in mediation and no arbitration award is needed, the arbitrator has to be paid anyway.[41]

6.3.3 Other combinations suggested by dispute resolution institutions

A number of dispute resolution institutions offer parties the use of model multi-tiered clauses that are generally similar to one another. They often prescribe that parties mediate as the first step, then, if required, arbitrate as the second step (that is, diff neutral med-arb). For example, one of the ICC model clauses provides:

> In the event of any dispute arising out of or in connection with the present contract, the parties shall first refer the dispute to proceedings under the ICC Mediation Rules. If the dispute has not been settled pursuant to the said Rules within [45] days following the filing of a Request for Mediation or within such other period as the parties may agree in writing, such dispute shall thereafter be finally settled under the Rules of Arbitration of the International Chamber of Commerce by one or more arbitrators appointed in accordance with the said Rules of Arbitration.[42]

The London Court of International Arbitration and the SCC have similar provisions.[43] However, several dispute resolution institutions around the world suggest different combinations summarised below.

6.3.3.1 Centre de Médiation et d'Arbitrage de Paris: simultaneous and independent mediation and arbitration

In France, the Centre de Médiation et d'Arbitrage de Paris (CMAP) provides for simultaneous, parallel, and independent mediation and arbitration proceedings in

40 Wolski, *supra* n. 4, at 269; Limbury, *supra* n. 35, at 9.

41 Peter, *supra* n. 34, at 103.

42 International Court of Arbitration of the International Chamber of Commerce, *Suggested Clauses for ICC Mediation: Clause D: Obligation to Refer Dispute to the ICC Mediation Rules, Followed by Arbitration if Required*, available at <https://iccwbo.org/publication/suggested-icc-mediation-clause-english-version/> (accessed 14 Jan. 2018).

43 London Court of International Arbitration, *Recommended Clauses: Mediation and Arbitration*, available at <www.lcia.org/Dispute_Resolution_Services/LCIA_Mediation_Clauses.aspx> (accessed 14 Jan. 2018); Arbitration Institute of the Stockholm Chamber of Commerce, *Model Mediation Clause – Combined Clause*, available at <www.sccinstitute.com/dispute-resolution/model-clauses/english/> (accessed 14 Jan. 2018).

a case, using different individuals as mediators and arbitrators.[44] This option mitigates concerns related to caucuses in the context of the same neutral (arb)-med-arb.[45]

The CMAP approach has found some supporters. For example, Santos and de la Garcia recommend, among others, a dispute settlement clause providing for conciliation proceedings immediately after the arbitration proceedings have commenced, and without suspending or interrupting said proceedings.[46]

6.3.3.2 International Centre for Dispute Resolution: concurrent arbitration-mediation

In the United States, the International Centre for Dispute Resolution (ICDR) has developed a model 'concurrent arbitration-mediation' clause (concurrent clause) that obligates parties to mediate at some point after the initiation of arbitration. This clause is as follows:

> Any controversy or claim arising out of or related to this contract, or a breach thereof, shall be resolved by arbitration administered by the International Centre for Dispute Resolution in accordance with its International Arbitration Rules. Once the demand for arbitration is initiated, the parties agree to attempt to settle any controversy or claim arising out of or relating to this contract or a breach thereof by mediation administered by the International Centre for Dispute Resolution under its International Mediation Rules. Mediation will proceed concurrently with arbitration and shall not be a condition precedent to any stage of the arbitration process.[47]

As noted by Andersen, the ICDR vice president, the ICDR presumes that arbitrators will not be mediators and that mediators will not be arbitrators in the same case, unless parties expressly agree otherwise after full disclosure of the risks involved.[48] Parties can remove any doubts about this by expressly specifying: 'Absent agreement of the parties, no mediator appointed pursuant to this

44 Centre de Médiation et d'Arbitrage, *Autres modes alternatifs de règlement des conflits*, available at <www.cmap.fr/notre-offre/les-autres-modes-alternatifs-de-resolution-des-conflits/> (accessed 14 Jan. 2018).

45 Renzo Maria Morresi, *The Use of Med-Arb-Like Mechanisms in Italy and Other European Countries*, 2(1) NYSBA New York Disp. Res. Law. 106, 108 (2009).

46 Santos and de la Garcia quoted in Michael E. Schneider, *Combining Arbitration with Conciliation*, in *International Dispute Resolution: Towards an International Arbitration Culture*, 8 ICCA Congress Series 57, 74 (Albert Jan van den Berg ed., Kluwer Law International 1998).

47 International Centre for Dispute Resolution, *Guide to Drafting International Dispute Resolution Clauses*, 5, available at <www.icdr.org/sites/default/files/document_repository/ICDR_Guide_Drafting_Clauses.pdf> (accessed 14 Jan. 2018).

48 Steven K. Andersen, *ICDR Offers Concurrent Mediation/Arbitration Clause*, 63 Disp. Res. J. 15, 16 (Nov. 2008–Jan. 2009).

agreement shall serve as an arbitrator and no arbitrator shall serve as a mediator'.[49]

Parties may decide to mediate whenever they believe it would be most productive, as long as it is prior to the issuance of the award. Mediation proceeds on a parallel track with arbitration, which alleviates concerns that a party can use mediation as a tactic to delay arbitration. If parties settle during the concurrent mediation, the concurrent clause allows the arbitral tribunal to incorporate the parties' settlement in an award pursuant to the ICDR International Arbitration Rules.[50] Interestingly, the ICDR Guide to Drafting International Dispute Resolution Clauses does not justify the use of mediation after commencement of arbitration, for reasons related to concerns about the subsequent enforceability of the outcome.[51] It takes into account parties' concerns that early mediation will not allow them sufficient time to understand the case, making negotiations more perilous.[52]

6.3.3.3 Judicial Arbitration and Mediation Services, Inc.: mediator-in-reserve

Judicial Arbitration and Mediation Services, Inc. (JAMS), another dispute resolution centre in the United States, has developed a mediator-in-reserve policy for international arbitrations that it administers.[53] This policy provides that within one week of the commencement of an international arbitration, a list of suggested mediators is sent to the parties. The parties are encouraged to select a mediator from the list, who is placed in reserve during arbitration. This mediator-in-reserve is available to the parties to assist in settlement if, at any time in arbitration, all parties agree to use the mediator's assistance. Parties are not charged for the appointment of the mediator-in-reserve, and they do not incur any fees unless and until they choose to use the mediator's services. The mediator-in-reserve is not informed of the parties' selection until and unless the parties decide to request the mediator's services. The parties are not bound to use the mediator-in-reserve and may, at any time, mutually select another mediator to assist in their settlement. The arbitrator(s) have no knowledge of the identity of the mediators-in-reserve or whether the parties may have engaged their services at any point in arbitration.

It is not a coincidence that the three above examples promoting the use of combinations involving different neutrals as mediators and arbitrators are offered by the US and French arbitration institutions. The ICDR concurrent arbitration-mediation and JAMS Mediator-in-Reserve are processes that accord and align

49 *Ibid.*

50 *Ibid.*

51 *See* discussion in Section 5.2.3.2.8 *infra*.

52 *Guide to Drafting International Dispute Resolution Clauses, supra* n. 47, at 5.

53 JAMS, *JAMS Mediator-in-Reserve Policy for International Arbitrations*, available at <www.jamsinternational.com/mediator-in-reserve-policy-international-arbitration> (accessed 14 Jan. 2018).

with the traditional approach of the common-law system that does not allow judges and arbitrators to be actively involved in facilitation of settlement, as explained in Section 4.2. As for the combination available at the CMAP, again it reflects the practice of French judges and arbitrators who, as observed in Section 4.2, appear to be reluctant to become involved in the settlement of their own cases, despite the fact that the French CCP expressly regards conciliation as one of their functions.

It is difficult to say which of the three processes (ICDR concurrent arbitration-mediation, CMAP simultaneous and independent mediation and arbitration, or JAMS mediator-in-reserve) has more potential of saving costs as compared to the others. In all three cases, even if parties settle in mediation, they can do so only after the commencement of arbitration. This means that in all three cases parties would have already incurred costs related to arbitration. If parties do not settle in mediation, in all three cases arbitration will run its full course.

6.3.3.4 Baltic and International Maritime Council: combination

A final example of a combination involving different neutrals as a mediator and an arbitrator is a dispute resolution provision available at the Baltic and International Maritime Council (BIMCO).[54] This provision allows a party, once arbitration has commenced, at any time, to refer the dispute or part thereof to mediation by serving on the other party a written mediation notice.

If the other party agrees to mediate, the parties need to agree on a mediator within 14 calendar days, failing which, on the application of either party, a mediator will be appointed by the Arbitration Tribunal or such person as the Tribunal may designate for that purpose. The mediation is to be conducted in accordance with parties' agreement or, in the event of disagreement, as may be set by the mediator.

If the other party does not agree to mediate, that fact may be brought to the attention of the Tribunal and may be taken into account by the Tribunal when allocating the costs of the arbitration between the parties.

If parties agree to mediate, the arbitration procedure continues during mediation but the Tribunal may take the mediation timetable into account when setting the timetable for arbitration. The mediation process is without prejudice and confidential, and no information or documents disclosed during it can be revealed to the Tribunal, except to the extent that they are disclosable under the law and procedure governing the arbitration.

Although this BIMCO provision does not oblige parties to mediate after commencement of arbitration, the fact that an award of costs can be made

54 BIMCO, *BIMCO Standard Dispute Resolution Clause 2016*, available at <www.bimco.org/contracts-and-clauses/bimco-clauses/dispute_resolution_clauses> (accessed 14 Jan. 2018).

against a party who refuses to mediate creates a strong incentive for a party receiving a suggestion to mediate to accept it.[55]

The four combinations presented in this section provide alternatives to diff neutral (arb)-med-arb. All four combinations involve different neutrals acting as a mediator and an arbitrator. This, similarly to the situation with diff neutral (arb)-med-arb, eliminates behavioural and procedural concerns associated with the same neutral (arb)-med-arb, and makes the dispute resolution process more expensive than the same neutral (arb)-med-arb. The four combinations, however, may be more time-efficient than diff neutral (arb)-med-arb, because in all four cases mediation proceeds on a parallel track with arbitration. In diff neutral (arb)-med-arb, arbitration and mediation are used in sequence.

6.4 (Arb)-med-arb opt-out: potential involvement of different neutrals in (arb)-med-arb

Behavioural and procedural concerns associated with the same neutral (arb)-med-arb may be allayed to a certain extent by (arb)-med-arb opt-out – a process that allows each party independently to call for a different person to act as the arbitrator after completion of the mediation stage of the process.[56]

Panchu even argues that it is neither just nor effective to bind parties at the commencement of arbitration or mediation to enter into the second process on the failure of the first.[57] To ensure party autonomy and choice, Panchu considers it important that the parties exercise their choice whether to engage in the same neutral (arb)-med-arb as close as possible to when the second process can commence.[58] If mediation is attempted and has not succeeded, then the mediator becomes an arbitrator only if both parties are willing at that stage. Similarly, in the case of arb-med-arb, each party must be willing to mediate after arbitration hearings; however, as pointed out in Section 3.1, concerns arise when arbitration follows mediation and the former mediator acts as an arbitrator. No concerns are raised when the arbitrator takes on the role of a mediator. Taking this into account, it appears that obtaining parties' consent to the former mediator becoming the arbitrator is much more important in terms of alleviating concerns associated with the same neutral (arb)-med-arb than the former arbitrator becoming the mediator.

55 Hunter, *supra* n. 31, at 474.

56 Bühring-Uhle et al., *supra* n. 2, at 253; James T. Peter, *Med-Arb in International Arbitration*, 4 Revista de Arbitragem e Mediação 155, 164 (2005); Peter, *supra* n. 34, at 99; John T. Blankenship, *Developing Your ADR Attitude: Med-Arb, a Template for Adaptive ADR*, 42 (11) Tennessee Bar J. 28, 37 (2006); Edna Sussman, *Developing an Effective Med-Arb/ Arb-Med Process*, 2(1) NYSBA New York Disp. Res. Law. 71, 71 (2009); Klaus Peter Berger, *Integration of Mediation Elements into Arbitration: 'Hybrid' Procedures and 'Intuitive' Mediation by International Arbitrators*, 19(3) Arb. Int'l. 387, 394 (2003); Limbury, *supra* n. 35, at 9.

57 Sriram Panchu, *Arb-Med and Med-Arb Are Well-Suited to Meeting India's ADR Needs*, 2(1) NYSBA New York Disp. Res. Law. 103, 104–105 (2009).

58 *Ibid*, at 104.

(Arb)-med-arb opt-out allows parties to avoid being submitted to a binding decision by the former mediator. Parties may choose to do so if, based on the conduct in mediation, they doubt the mediator's impartiality, or if they have disclosed highly sensitive information that might influence the decision.[59]

6.4.1 Advantages and disadvantages of (arb)-med-arb opt-out

(Arb)-med-arb opt-out may appeal to parties for at least three reasons.[60] First, it allows parties to express reservations as to the neutral's impartiality and ability to decide on the dispute. If parties consider that the neutral can no longer act impartially, they can appoint a new arbitrator to render the award. This upholds the integrity of the process and the award. Second, (arb)-med-arb opt-out increases the likelihood that parties will be candid in mediation. This is because parties know that if they do not reach a settlement in mediation, they can appoint another neutral as the arbitrator. Third, (arb)-med-arb opt-out might eliminate the issue of coercion. As discussed in Section 3.3.1.4, vesting the authority to decide on the dispute in the same person who mediates, creates enormous power in a dual role neutral in the same neutral (arb)-med-arb. The dual role neutral may use the threat of an award to coerce parties into settlement in the mediation stage. Mediators in (arb)-med-arb opt-out do not have this kind of power, because mediators cannot be sure that they will act as arbitrators, as parties still need to decide on this issue. Concerns related to the same neutral acting as a mediator and an arbitrator may even prove unfounded once parties are engaged in the process.[61] Or, the mere existence of a right to veto the process could create an atmosphere which eliminates the need to actually do so.[62]

Parties may refrain from using (arb)-med-arb opt-out for at least three reasons. First, parties may lose the incentive to settle created by the neutral's authority to decide. As discussed in Section 3.2.5, this incentive is one of the six advantages attributed to the same neutral (arb)-med-arb. Second, if parties proceed with the new arbitrator, the process transforms into mediation followed by arbitration conducted by two different neutrals. This leads to higher costs and lengthier proceedings, as compared to the same neutral (arb)-med-arb.[63] However, unlike where the parties simply agree to mediate and then (if mediation does not result in a settlement) to arbitrate their dispute by a different neutral, in (arb)-med-arb opt-out the chance that the parties will keep the same neutral for both stages seems to be higher.[64] Finally, if the parties choose to continue with the same

59 Bühring-Uhle et al., *supra* n. 2, at 253–254.

60 *Ibid*, at 254; Peter, *supra* n. 34, at 99–100; Blankenship, *supra* n. 56, at 37.

61 Blankenship, *supra* n. 56, at 37.

62 *Ibid*.

63 Peter, *supra* n. 34, at 100; Ross, *supra* n. 30, at 365; Limbury, *supra* n. 35, at 9.

64 Peter, *supra* n. 34, at 100 n. 76.

neutral, the risk of a breach of due process, a major procedural concern associated with the same neutral (arb)-med-arb discussed in Section 3.3.2.2, remains.[65]

Similarly to other combinations, (arb)-med-arb opt-out is a valuable dispute resolution option that parties may find useful, depending on the particular circumstances of their case. Before agreeing to use (arb)-med-arb opt-out, it is essential that parties inform themselves about the advantages and disadvantages associated with this combination. Their decision to use (arb)-med-arb opt-out must be an informed decision. The same requirement applies to the use of other combinations.

6.4.1.1 Case requiring enforcement in China

The following case illustrates the best-case scenario for (arb)-med-arb opt-out, namely when the parties manage to settle in the mediation stage and the terms of their settlement are incorporated into a consent award. In a dispute between a Canadian and a US party, which involved manufacturing activities in China and required enforcement in China, the dispute resolution process started as mediation.[66] Considering the need for enforcement in China, the mediator recommended that parties use med-arb so that, if they reach a resolution, it could be incorporated into a consent award and thus be enforceable. As the recommendation to use med-arb came from the mediator, she considered it necessary for the parties' informed consent to the process to provide that either party could elect to have someone other than the mediator serve as the arbitrator if the matter did not settle. So, in fact, the parties agreed to use med-arb opt-out. However, the matter did settle and the terms of the parties' agreement were incorporated into a consent award. Apparently, all participants of the process, including the mediator were comfortable with the fact that the mediator was appointed as the arbitrator merely for the purposes of issuing a consent award.[67]

6.4.2 Med-arb opt-out and the potential to reach an agreement in mediation

Med-arb opt-out (more so than arb-med-arb opt-out) might be the combination that creates the best conditions for parties to reach an agreement in mediation.[68]

65 Limbury, *supra* n. 35, at 9.

66 This case is reported by Edna Sussman who acted as a dual role neutral in it. *Summary Report of the First Meeting in September 23–24, 2016 of the International Task Force on Mixed Mode Dispute Resolution: Inaugural Summit at Pepperdine University, Malibu, CA, USA*, International Mediation Institute 20–21 (2017), available at <www.imimediation.org/about-imi/who-are-imi/mixed-mode-task-force/> (accessed 31 Mar. 2018).

67 As observed in Section 5.2.3.2.8, the enforceability of this kind of consent award is unclear and largely untested. To ensure enforceability, it is advisable that parties start the combined process with arbitration.

68 Peter, *supra* n. 34, at 117.

The analysis of the following four different consequences that can result from the mediation phase of all combinations leads to this conclusion.

First, the mediation phase may lead to an agreement that resolves all issues in dispute. This is obviously the preferred outcome and the main goal of mediation.[69] However, it appears that most of the discussion of mediation focuses exclusively on this possibility. The possibility of reaching a partial agreement is not considered sufficiently.

Second, the mediation phase may end with an agreement on a cooperative concept to resolve the dispute. This is an agreement that transforms the dispute from a rights-based arbitration focused on the past, into an interest-based arbitration focused on the determination of a new contract. In this way, legal issues are diminished and business interests are emphasised. This result can be illustrated by a situation where parties, instead of quarrelling over the damages, agree to an imposed licence for which the fee has yet to be determined.[70]

Third, the mediation phase may result in an agreement on a streamlined procedure or a consensus on factual and legal issues.[71] If parties do not manage to reach any of the two previously mentioned types of agreements, they can still agree on other matters that may assist them with settling their dispute. For example, parties may agree on how to proceed to settle their dispute, negotiate to eliminate certain disputed issues, or elaborate procedural rules (such as 'last offer arbitration') and rules concerning the process style. If the applicable law is in question, parties could agree on a particular law to apply to the entire dispute or to a certain part thereof.[72]

Fourth, the mediation phase may result in no agreement at all.[73] Peter laments that this outcome is too often perceived as the only alternative to an agreement that disposes entirely of the dispute (option one). Parties may benefit more from mediation used either as a stand-alone mechanism or as part of a combination if more neutrals conducting mediation work towards achieving a partial agreement (options two and three).[74] Considering that efficiency is one of the important benefits that combinations can contribute to international arbitration,

69 *Ibid*, at 115–116.

70 *Ibid*, at 116 (another example would be the Washington Agreement in the IBM-Fujitsu case discussed in Section 9.5.3 *infra*).

71 *Ibid.*

72 *Ibid.*

73 *Ibid.*

74 *Ibid; see also* Thomas J. Stipanowich & Zachary P. Ulrich, *Commercial Arbitration and Settlement: Empirical Insights into the Roles Arbitrators Play*, 6 Y.B. On Arb. & Mediation 1, 9 (2014) (pointing out that over the years, there have been efforts to 'think outside the box' of the linear framework of stepped dispute resolution by exploiting its potentialities in different ways; for example, even where substantive issues cannot be resolved in mediation, mediators may focus on facilitating agreements regarding dispute resolution process elements and helping parties to set the stage for arbitration proceedings with features that are effectively tailored to the issues in hand).

combinations that encourage or at least allow termination of the mediation phase by a partial agreement might be more favourable than others.

The chance that the mediation phase will end with a partial agreement as per options two and three above appears to be higher if the mediation phase takes place prior to the arbitration phase. Beginning with arbitration may make parties focus from the very beginning on the arbitration process, which determines (psychologically and technically) to a large extent how the dispute's settlement is approached.[75] The focus on the arbitration process may diminish the possibility that parties will change the track they are already on, and agree to a partial settlement, as described in options two and three above.[76] This lessens the attractiveness of combinations starting with arbitration, such as co-med-arb or arb-med-arb.[77]

Combinations that begin with mediation, like the same neutral med-arb and med-arb opt-out become more appealing because they appear to create good conditions for parties to reach an agreement in mediation. What may make med-arb opt-out preferable over the same neutral med-arb is that it reduces many concerns associated with the use of the same neutral med-arb. It has, however, its own disadvantages, as compared to the same neutral (arb)-med-arb, as discussed in Section 6.4.1.

6.4.3 Med-arb opt-out and CIArb's hybrid process

In 2008, the Australian branch of the Chartered Institute of Arbitrators (CIArb) prepared what it regarded as draft hybrid dispute resolution rules.[78] These provided for a process that resembles med-arb opt-out. Although these rules have never come into force, the approach taken by the drafters is interesting to consider because it is another example of how mediation and arbitration can be used in combination.

The process in the draft rules differs from med-arb opt-out in at least two respects. First, it calls for the appointment of two neutrals at the commencement of proceedings, with one neutral staying in reserve and stepping in only if the first neutral resigns. Second, the first neutral mediates the dispute after being appointed as the arbitrator. The default provisions of the rules authorise the first neutral to caucus with the parties but forbid expressing any opinion as to the likely outcome of the dispute if it were to go to arbitration. If mediation results in a settlement, the first neutral, upon request by the parties, produces a consent award. If mediation does not result in a settlement, the first neutral proceeds as an arbitrator. Before the first neutral does so, the parties must provide a written

75 Peter, *supra* n. 34, at 117.

76 *Ibid.*

77 *Ibid.*

78 All materials related to the CIArb draft hybrid dispute resolution rules were provided by Albert Monichino in an email of 31 Mar. 2014.

authority acknowledging that they agree to the first neutral continuing to act as an arbitrator, that they have had an opportunity to obtain legal advice before agreeing to such continuation, and that they have no objection to the first neutral conducting the arbitration.

A first neutral who proceeds as an arbitrator must disregard any information from caucuses and is prohibited from disclosing it. A first neutral who is unable to continue impartially as an arbitrator after mediation must resign. In that case, the second neutral will act as an arbitrator. Similarly, the first neutral will resign if any party objects to the first neutral continuing to act as an arbitrator. The first and the second neutrals are not allowed to discuss with each other anything said or done in the mediation phase of the process.

While it is not clear why the rules did not come into force, it is likely that, even if put into effect, the rules would not have gained popularity due to being cumbersome and limiting parties' autonomy to design their own process.

6.5 Conclusion

The involvement of different neutrals in combinations is the first of three ways to address concerns associated with the same neutral (arb)-med-arb. The main advantage of combinations involving different neutrals as mediators and arbitrators is that they eliminate concerns associated with the same neutral (arb)-med-arb. Their main disadvantage, as compared to the same neutral (arb)-med-arb, is additional costs and time, due to the involvement of different neutrals. The questionnaire findings combined with the literature review indicate that diff neutral (arb)-med-arb is viewed as a solution to concerns associated with the same neutral (arb)-med-arb mostly by common-law practitioners. This is due to the traditional common-law preference for the separate use of mediation and arbitration by involving different neutrals as mediators and arbitrators.

Anecdotally reported cases on the use of diff neutral arb-med-arb demonstrate that despite the involvement of different neutrals, this combination can still save the parties time and money. Even if the parties do not manage to resolve their dispute in the mediation stage, they can use mediation to agree on matters that may assist them in the following arbitration stage. For example, they may agree on disputed or undisputed facts. Using the mediation stage of diff neutral arb-med-arb in this way can increase the time and cost efficiency of the process.

Combinations such as shadow mediation and co-med-arb appear to be more time-efficient than diff neutral (arb)-med-arb. In shadow mediation, mediators attend arbitration hearings and do not need any time to educate themselves about the facts of the case at the commencement of mediation. In co-med-arb, arbitrators become aware of the facts of the case by attending joint mediation sessions, which saves time if arbitration is needed.

Some dispute resolution institutions administer other combinations involving different neutrals: JAMS mediator-in-reserve, BIMCO combination, ICDR concurrent arbitration-mediation, and CMAP simultaneous and independent mediation and arbitration. Similarly to diff neutral (arb)-med-arb, the involvement of different neutrals in these four processes eliminates concerns associated with the same neutral (arb)-med-arb, but increases costs of dispute resolution, as compared to the same neutral (arb)-med-arb; however, these processes may be more time-efficient than diff neutral (arb)-med-arb because in all four cases mediation proceeds on a parallel track with arbitration. In diff neutral (arb)-med-arb, mediation and arbitration are used in sequence.

(Arb)-med-arb opt-out allows each party independently to call for a different person to act as the arbitrator after completion of the mediation stage. This alleviates behavioural concerns associated with the same neutral (arb)-med-arb, particularly, parties' reluctance to be open in mediation and the abuse of power by a mediator resulting in the coercion of parties into a settlement. If parties decide to proceed with a different person as the arbitrator, the process transforms into diff neutral (arb)-med-arb. Med-arb opt-out (more so than arb-med-arb opt-out) appears to create the best conditions for parties to reach an agreement in mediation, as compared to other combinations.

7 Procedural modifications of the same neutral (arb)-med-arb as a way to address concerns associated with this process

7.1 Introduction

This short chapter considers the second way to address concerns associated with the same neutral (arb)-med-arb. This is by modifying the same neutral (arb)-med-arb procedure. The effect of these procedural modifications on concerns associated with the same neutral (arb)-med-arb, however, is different from that of combinations involving different neutrals discussed in Chapter 6. While the latter effectively eliminate these concerns, the former mostly reduce them.

This is because the procedural modifications still involve the use of the same neutral as a mediator and arbitrator. What changes is the arbitration part of the process (MEDALOA), or the sequence in which mediation and arbitration are used (arb-med), or who among a three-member tribunal conducts mediation (mediation by only some members of a three-member arbitration tribunal). These three procedural modifications of the same neutral (arb)-med-arb are explored in Sections 7.2, 7.3, and 7.4, respectively.

7.2 MEDALOA

Some of the behavioural and procedural concerns raised by the same neutral (arb)-med-arb may be eased by modifying the arbitration part of the process and incorporating last offer arbitration into it.[1]

As defined in Section 2.3.6, MEDALOA (mediation and last offer arbitration) means a process that starts with mediation and, if parties do not settle in the mediation stage, each party submits a 'last offer' to dual role neutrals who choose between them. While MEDALOA is commonly discussed as a modification of the same neutral med-arb, it is equally relevant to the same neutral arb-med-arb; if

1 Richard P. Flake, *MED/ARB – A Viable ADR Vehicle? Nuances of Med/Arb—A Neutral's Perspective*, CEDIRES 8–9, available at <www.cedires.com/index_bestanden/FLAKE_http-www.cbylaw.com-filebin_files_flake_rpf-AAA_Med-Arb.pdf> (accessed 14 Jan. 2018); Royden Hindle, *Mixing it up: Medarb Re-visited*, ¶ 40[g] (unpublished paper prepared for the AMINZ Seminar 'Current issues in Arbitration', Mar. 2014).

mediation does not result in a settlement and dual role neutrals resume as arbitrators, parties may authorise them to choose between the parties' last offers.

While not a complete cure for concerns associated with the same neutral (arb)-med-arb, this change gives parties an opportunity to resolve the case in the mediation phase, and also has the virtue of 'limiting' the award that can be issued by neutrals if the process goes to the arbitration phase. Two high-profile US cases illustrate the use of MEDALOA.

In the first case, Conoco Inc. and Browning Ferris Industries became involved in an environmental clean-up dispute over responsibility for paying to clean up a holding pond in which hazardous chemicals had been dumped.[2] After three years of fruitless litigation and increasing cost and complexity, the parties agreed to MEDALOA. Nine months of mediation settled most issues and narrowed the difference between the parties over liability. The mediator became the arbitrator and chose one of the last offers made by each party.

The second case, Federal Deposit Insurance Corporation and Chery, Bekart and Holland, involved a claim that auditors had misrepresented the status of a bank which had defaulted.[3] After spending $2 million in fees and costs without getting to trial, the parties agreed to mediation and, ultimately, to last offer arbitration to settle the remaining issues.

Thomas Stipanowich recalls a MEDALOA case from his own practice.[4] The case related to insurance coverage associated with a mining disaster and was stuck in federal court for a decade. In mediation, parties managed to make progress on some issues while still reaching no agreement on others. When the mediator raised with each party the possibility of using a last offer arbitration to resolve the matter, both parties expressed interest in the idea. The parties then discussed the idea with each other, after which they requested the mediator to act as the arbitrator. Once the mediator and the parties discussed the practical and legal concerns, the parties conferred and, thereafter, confirmed their intent to have the mediator arbitrate. The mediator agreed and helped them organise a process. Within two weeks the matter was finally resolved.

A review of the literature shows that MEDALOA is a combination well known in the United States. Last offer or 'baseball' arbitration (one of the two key components of MEDALOA) was conceived in the United States and was originally used to resolve salary disputes in Major League Baseball.[5]

2 Reported in David C. Elliott, *Med/Arb: Fraught with Danger or Ripe with Opportunity*, 34 Alta. L. Rev. 163, 165 (1995–1996).

3 *Ibid.*

4 In this case, Stipanowich first became involved as a mediator. The case is reported in *Summary Report of the First Meeting in September 23–24, 2016 of the International Task Force on Mixed Mode Dispute Resolution: Inaugural Summit at Pepperdine University, Malibu, CA, USA*, International Mediation Institute 13 (2017), available at <www.imimediation.org/about-imi/who-are-imi/mixed-mode-task-force/> (accessed 31 Mar. 2018) [hereinafter, First Summary Report of Mixed Mode Task Force].

5 Christian Borris, *Final Offer Arbitration from a Civil Law Perspective*, 24(3) J. Int'l. Arb. 307, 307 (2007).

Continental European and East Asian practitioners do not appear to be familiar with the concept of MEDALOA. Only one reference to a variation of MEDALOA has been found in the literature outside the context of the United States. Moti Mironi, an Israeli practitioner trained in the US, reports a commercial dispute between an Israeli and Austrian company, in which the same neutral played three different roles – mediator, conciliator, and arbitrator.[6] The court referred the dispute to the mediator. The mediation was to be conducted over two days. On the second day, the mediator became a conciliator, which allowed him to be evaluative and make proposals. When parties appeared to be at an impasse, the neutral suggested that they consider last offer arbitration to resolve the issues that were still open. The parties agreed and submitted their last offers. The neutral then explained the advantages of open last offer arbitration – a process in which the parties see each other's last offers and have an opportunity to negotiate a settlement – which the parties agreed to try. After about half an hour of negotiation, the parties asked the neutral (now as arbitrator) to render a decision, which he did. While the parties appeared to be very satisfied with the flexibility, effectiveness, and finality of the process, the neutral felt frustrated because it was clear to him that what had been decided in arbitration was not the best solution for both parties.

7.2.1 Advantages and disadvantages of MEDALOA

The incorporation of last offer arbitration is likely to result in the parties putting their best settlement foot forward in the mediation phase of the proceeding,[7] being reasonable[8] and less prone to inflate their offer lest it not be chosen.[9] Moreover, MEDALOA may reduce the risk of bias, since the arbitrator does not decide on a dispute but chooses between last offers proposed by the parties.[10] The neutral may even continue mediation after the last offers are submitted to see whether a compromise could be reached.[11] As a variation of MEDALOA, parties may agree that any of them may opt out of the process after exchanging last offers but before presenting them to the neutral for consideration.[12] Both

6 Mironi acted as a neutral in this case. The case is reported in First Summary Report of Mixed Mode Task Force, *supra* n. 4, at 19–20.

7 Flake, *supra* n. 1, at 9; *see also* Borris, *supra* n. 5, at 311 (noting that by including last offer arbitration, the parties are given an additional incentive to continue mediation in good faith—more so than in the case of med-arb).

8 Claude Thomson, *Med-Arb: A Fresh Look*, 5 (2006) (on file with the ICC Documentation & Research Centre).

9 Donna Ross, *Med-Arb/Arb-Med: a More Efficient ADR Process or an Invitation to a Potential Ethical Disaster?* in *Contemporary Issues in International Arbitration and Mediation: The Fordham Papers 2012* 352, 362 (Arthur W. Rovine ed., Martinus Nijhoff 2013).

10 *Ibid.*

11 Flake, *supra* n. 1, at 9.

12 Thomson, *supra* n. 8, at 7.

parties are then in a position to decide whether an award against them will be within a range that they can accept.

One of MEDALOA's limitations appears to be its relative inability to solve the dispute on something other than strictly monetary terms.[13] Also, dual role neutrals are not allowed to settle the dispute in the way they consider appropriate, even if neither party submits a last offer which seems reasonable to them, which may occur, for example, in cases of multi-issue disputes.[14] Arbitrators, however, may manage this situation by asking parties to submit more than one last offer.

7.2.2 Use of MEDALOA in the domestic v. international context

Interestingly, the drivers behind the use of MEDALOA in the domestic context might not exist in the international setting.[15] It appears that in the United States, an important rationale behind the use of MEDALOA in the domestic context is that US arbitrators tend to compromise and 'split the baby'. Assuming arbitrators will 'split the baby', parties may hesitate to compromise in the mediation phase of the same neutral (arb)-med-arb to gain more when the arbitrator eventually comes to the stage of making a decision. MEDALOA, however, seems to compel parties to make reasonable concessions because arbitrators are more likely to choose the last offer they decide is more balanced. The process appears to drive parties towards a compromised settlement, which may enhance the success of the mediation phase of the process. Also, it seems the process becomes even more attractive, the more the issue lacks well-defined rights for decision-making purposes.

In international arbitration, however, it appears to be less common for arbitrators to 'split the baby'. Consequently, in the United States, parties may be less hesitant to seek a compromise in the mediation phase of the same neutral (arb)-med-arb in an international context rather than in the domestic context. Although this might eliminate the main incentive to agreeing to MEDALOA in international arbitration, MEDALOA may still be suitable for certain disputes. It is better to leave the decision whether to use it until the dispute has actually emerged.

As noted above, it appears that for now MEDALOA has gained ground in US practice only. Given the advantages that MEDALOA offers, it seems reasonable to suggest that more efforts need to be made to increase the awareness of Continental European and East Asian practitioners of the existence of this combination.

13 *Ibid*; Flake, *supra* n. 1, at 9.

14 James T. Peter, *Note & Comment: Med-Arb in International Arbitration*, 8 Am. Rev. Int'l Arb. 83, 102 (1997).

15 *Ibid*, at 101–102.

7.3 Arb-med

As defined in Section 2.3.6, arb-med is a process beginning with arbitration resulting in an award that is placed in a sealed envelope and kept confidential. Then the former arbitrator becomes a mediator. If parties do not settle in mediation, the award is revealed and becomes binding. Otherwise, the neutral never discloses the award.

Oghigian recalls his experience as a dual role neutral in arb-med in three cases,[16] each involving one Japanese and one American party.[17] In all three cases, Oghigian prepared a formal arbitral award after the arbitration hearing, met with parties, and placed an envelope with the signed and sealed arbitral award on the table. After informing parties that he was fully discharged of his duties as an arbitrator, he suggested that if parties agreed in writing, he could attempt to mediate. All participants (including the neutral) could at any time terminate the process. In all three cases, parties eagerly accepted the suggestion and the matter was successfully mediated and settled.

Oghigian refers to arb-med as the most effective way to disarm a possible challenge to a dual role neutral's ability to maintain impartiality in both roles in the same neutral (arb)-med-arb.[18] More pragmatic commentators suggest that when compared to the same neutral (arb)-med-arb, arb-med could be considered the lesser of the alleged evils, as it raises fewer ethical concerns.[19]

7.3.1 Advantages of arb-med

In arb-med, mediation occurs after a decision has been reached on the merits of the case. This eliminates a concern associated with the same neutral (arb)-med-arb that in rendering their decision arbitrators may be partial, further to parties' disclosures during mediation.[20]

Arb-med also prevents parties from using mediation strategically,[21] which is another concern commonly associated with the use of the same neutral (arb)-med-arb.[22] In the same neutral (arb)-med-arb, there is a fear that parties may use

16 Haig Oghigian, *Perspectives from Japan: A New Concept in Dispute Resolution – the Mediation – Arbitration Hybrid*, 2(1) NYSBA New York Disp. Res. Law. 110, 111 (2009).

17 *Ibid* (observing that he draws no particular inference from the origin of the parties but states it as a common feature for the record).

18 *Ibid.*

19 Ross, *supra* n. 9, at 359; James T. Peter, *Med-Arb in International Arbitration*, 4 Revista de Arbitragem e Mediação 155, 164–168 (2005); Edna Sussman, *Developing an Effective Med-Arb/ Arb-Med Process*, 2(1) NYSBA New York Disp. Res. Law. 71, 71 (2009); Edna Sussman, *Combinations and Permutations of Arbitration and Mediation: Issues and Solutions*, in *ADR in Business: Practice and Issues across Countries and Cultures* vol II 381, 384–385 (Arnold Ingen-Housz ed., Kluwer Law International 2011).

20 *See* discussion of this concern in Section 3.3.2.1 *supra*.

21 Oghigian, *supra* n. 16, at 112.

22 *See* discussion in Section 3.3.1.3 *supra*.

mediation to present their position, not with a genuine view to achieving a settlement but, tactically, to lay the groundwork for the subsequent arbitration phase of the process. Since mediation in arb-med occurs after arbitration resulting in an award, parties cannot use mediation tactically to influence the arbitrators' decision.

Another advantage of arb-med is that parties seem to demonstrate less grandstanding and belligerence in post-arbitral mediation because they may feel that they have been given the opportunity to put their best case in the adversarial setting. Also, by the time of mediation, each side has a fair idea of its strengths and weaknesses, which may make them receptive to exploring settlement avenues with someone who knows the file very well.[23]

Parties' motivation to achieve settlement in the mediation part of arb-med has been confirmed empirically in a 2002 study by Conlon, Moon, and Ng. They conducted a field experiment in which they examined the impact of the same neutral med-arb and arb-med on various dispute outcomes.[24] These researchers found that disputants in arb-med settled in the mediation phase of their procedure more frequently than did disputants in the same neutral med-arb.[25]

The following case involving the use of a variation of arb-med illustrates how the process prompts parties to be reasonable and conciliatory in post-arbitral mediation. In that case, the parties agreed to engage in arbitration hearings, after which the arbitrator was to place the arbitration award in a sealed envelope.[26] The parties, too, were to submit last offers in sealed envelopes, after which they were to engage in mediation with the arbitrator as mediator. If mediation failed to produce an agreement, the parties were to open the envelopes and whichever party had the number closest to the arbitration award was to prevail. One of the parties (that previously expressed great confidence in its case) came up with more flexible offers, which led to a resolution. Hirsh, who reported this case, concludes that the process succeeded in putting pressure on parties to be reasonable in bargaining.[27]

Arb-med appears to reduce one more concern commonly associated with the same neutral (arb)-med-arb and discussed in Section 3.3.1.2 – the inhibited conduct of a mediator. Oghigian recalls his feelings as a mediator in the mediation part of arb-med: he felt both liberated and empowered.[28] He felt liberated because he could be assertive and somewhat opinionated, without risking that someone could claim bias. The arbitral award was already on the table and at any

23 Sriram Panchu, *Arb-Med and Med-Arb Are Well-Suited to Meeting India's ADR Needs*, 2(1) NYSBA New York Disp. Res. Law. 103, 104 (2009).

24 Donald E. Conlon et al., *Putting the Cart Before the Horse: The Benefits of Arbitrating Before Mediating*, 87(5) J. App. Psychol. 978 (2002).

25 *Ibid*, at 982.

26 This case was reported by Merril Hirsh in First Summary Report of Mixed Mode Task Force, *supra* n. 4, at 19.

27 *Ibid*.

28 Oghigian, *supra* n. 16, at 112.

point either party could end mediation. He felt empowered because having acted as an arbitrator he knew the weak points of each party's case and could move them towards a possible compromise solution with a free hand and foreknowledge. In Oghigian's view, arb-med allowed him to play a much more effective role as a mediator.[29] While this can definitely be the case, the mediation style adopted by Oghigian could make parties feel as though they are being coerced into accepting his solution. To avoid this risk, arbitrators-turned-mediators could consider adopting a facilitative, interests-based approach because the purpose of arb-med is to allow parties to forge their own settlement, rather than accept the decision of the arbitrator.[30]

Arb-med seems to be particularly useful when parties have an ongoing relationship and when they want some degree of control and finality.[31] Oghigian reports that in all three above-mentioned arb-med cases where he acted as a dual role neutral, parties although in a significant commercial dispute, expressly stated their intent to continue their business relationship.[32] The real driver in the use of arb-med may have been the ultimate wish of the parties to continue their commercial relationships.[33] Arb-med may be a preferred option in countries where the enforceability of a mediated settlement agreement reached before commencement of arbitration as a consent award might be an issue.[34] Anecdotal evidence suggests that the process can be of help in business negotiations, not just in dispute resolution.[35]

7.3.2 Disadvantages of arb-med

Arb-med does not save time and costs.[36] Regardless of whether parties manage to settle their case in the mediation phase, the arbitration process will run its full course. Thus, there appears to be no incentive to eliminate a time-consuming and

29 *Ibid.*
30 Ross, *supra* n. 9, at 359.
31 *Ibid.*
32 Oghigian, *supra* n. 16, at 111.
33 Andrew Burr, *Med-Arb: A Viable Hybrid Solution?* 8 Les Arbitres Internationaux 57, 72 (2005) (commenting on Oghigian's experience).
34 *Ibid.*
35 Jeremy Lack, *Appropriate Dispute Resolution (ADR): The Spectrum of Hybrid Techniques Available to the Parties*, in *ADR in Business: Practice and Issues across Countries and Cultures* vol. II 339, at 358 n. 19 (Arnold Ingen-Housz ed., Kluwer Law International 2011) referring to Michael Leathes et al., *Einstein's Lessons in Mediation*, Managing Intellectual Property 23 (Jul./Aug. 2006) (presenting a case study describing how arb-med was used in business negotiations when the parties disagreed on an issue of price).
36 Peter, *supra* n. 14, at 100; Srikant Deekshitha & Arka Saha, *Amalgamating the Conciliatory and the Adjudicative: Hybrid Processes and Asian Arbitral Institutions*, III(1) Indian J. Arb. L. 76, 81 & 93 (Jodhpur 2014); Claire Wilson, *The Arb-Med Hybrid in Hong Kong – Much Ado about Nothing?* Kluwer Mediation Blog (1 Feb. 2012), available at <http://kluwermediationblog.com/2012/02/01/the-arb-med-hybrid-in-hong-kong-much-ado-about-nothing/> (accessed 31 Mar. 2018).

cost-intensive arbitration for parties in reaching a settlement.[37] While going through an entire arbitration process requires substantial money and time, engaging in mediation after arbitration will involve even more time and money.[38]

Also, having gone through the highly adversarial arbitration process, parties may have psychological difficulties working through the issues together. They might be reluctant to make the effort to engage in mediation after trying to convince arbitrators to decide in their favour.[39] Instead of focusing on reaching a settlement in mediation, each party might attempt to figure out what neutrals decided in the sealed arbitral award. This makes it difficult for neutrals to test the BATNA and to avoid signalling their views.[40] If one party thinks that neutrals' behaviour indicates that they have issued an award in its favour, this party may be less willing to engage in mediation and negotiate with another party.[41] Nevertheless, as noted in Section 7.3.1, the available empirical data demonstrates that parties settle more frequently in the mediation phase of arb-med than in the same neutral med-arb.[42]

Analysing the results of their field experiment, Conlon, Moon, and Ng identify three environments in which the same neutral med-arb might still be preferable to arb-med: when there is significant time pressure, when the financial costs of paying for a third party need to be minimized, and when there is considerable hostility between disputants.[43] In the last situation, beginning with the more adversarial arbitration phase might be unwise because it may further heighten animosity between the parties, making it unlikely that mediation will be successful.

7.3.3 Arb-med and a hybrid hearing in Queensland

In 2012, the Queensland Civil and Administrative Tribunal introduced a process called a 'hybrid hearing',[44] which resembles to a large extent arb-med. In a hybrid hearing, parties attend a hearing first, and then attend a mediation after the hearing. Both the hearing and the mediation take place on

37 Peter, *supra* n. 14, at 100–101.
38 *Ibid*, at 100.
39 *Ibid.*
40 Brian A. Pappas, *Med-Arb and the Legalisation of Alternative Dispute Resolution*, 20 Harv. Negot. L. Rev. 157, 186 (Spring 2015).
41 Peter, *supra* n. 14, at 101; Roman Rewald & Kimberly Jachimek Weil, *Expanding ADR in Poland: Mediation and Arbitration Together*, Lexology 3, available at <http://documents.lexology.com/63de58ab-0582-410b-97aa-1c6f490e7f67.pdf> (accessed 14 Jan. 2018); *but see* Deekshitha & Saha, *supra* n. 36, at 80 (noting that the fact that neither party can be certain that the award is in their favour encourages cooperation in the mediation stage).
42 Conlon et al., *supra* n. 24, at 983.
43 *Ibid.*
44 Queensland Civil and Administrative Tribunal, *Hybrid Hearings* (effective 3 Sep. 2012), available at <www.qcat.qld.gov.au/using-qcat/practice-directions#2012> (accessed 31 Mar. 2018).

the same day. The award is sealed in an envelope following the hearing. If parties are unable to reach agreement on all issues in mediation, the envelope is opened and the decision becomes binding. Both the adjudicative and mediatory functions are performed by the same neutral. However, the neutral is not allowed to meet with any of the parties in a private session in mediation. A hybrid hearing might be useful when the issues in dispute are simple, the amount involved is not large, and the hearing can be expedited and simplified.[45] It is, however, unlikely to be suitable for the majority of international commercial disputes due to their complexity and high amounts at stake.

7.4 Modifications relevant to a three-member tribunal

In arb-med-arb, an arbitral tribunal consisting of three arbitrators offers significant flexibility in configuring a pathway towards helping parties settle a case. Involvement in mediation of only some members of the tribunal is a way to reduce concerns associated with the same neutral (arb)-med-arb. At least four configurations of a panel have been identified.[46]

First, mediation may be conducted by the two co-arbitrators, while reserving the chair for the arbitration hearing.[47] This would ensure that the chair is not privy to and, consequently, not influenced by confidential information. If settlement efforts are unsuccessful, the chair could serve as a sole arbitrator. Alternatively, all three arbitrators could hear the case.

Second, the chair could serve as the mediator, preserving the relative impartiality of the co-arbitrators.[48] If the case does not settle, the three-person panel would hear the case but it may be agreed that only the two co-arbitrators would issue an award. A tie between the two co-arbitrators could be broken by the chair.

Third, when three arbitrators are selected, one co-arbitrator could serve as a mediator while the chair and another co-arbitrator function only as arbitrators. This arrangement would preserve the impartiality of two arbitrators.[49] If the case does not settle, the remaining two arbitrators would issue the award. If the two arbitrators reach an impasse, then the third arbitrator-turned-mediator would be available to break the tie.

45 Bobette Wolski, *Arb-Med-Arb (and MSAs): A Whole Which Is Less than, not Greater than, the Sum of Its Parts?* 6(2) Contemp. Asia Arb. J. 249, 264 (2013).

46 Harold I. Abramson, *Protocols for International Arbitrators Who Dare to Settle Cases*, 10 Am. Rev. Int'l Arb. 1, 13–15 (protocol 8) (1999).

47 *Ibid*, at 13–14; *see also* Su Yin Anand, *The Risks of Arbitration-Mediation: Hong Kong Courts Decline to Enforce PRC Arbitral Award*, 16(2) Arb. News (Newsletter of the International Bar Association Legal Practice Division) 40, 42 (2011); Sussman (2009), *supra* n. 19, at 71; Sussman (2011), *supra* n. 19, at 385.

48 Abramson, *supra* n. 46, at 14.

49 *Ibid*, at 14–15.

Fourth, three arbitrators could serve as a mediation team, although this poses a significant risk of arbitrators' impartiality being compromised.[50]

Abramson gives recommendations on the type of activity arbitrators can engage in each of the four configurations. For example, in the first configuration, Abramson suggests that if parties authorise two co-arbitrators to caucus, they should be allowed to do so only as a team – each co-arbitrator should avoid any ex parte contact with the appointing party.[51] In the last configuration, Abramson recommends that the arbitrators consider limiting themselves in mediation to employing the least intrusive techniques. These include encouraging the participants to try settling the case on their own, requesting parties with settlement authority to be present, helping participants define legal and factual issues in dispute, or suggesting at an appropriate moment that the parties 'split the difference'. However, it appears that the decision in respect of the kind of mediation techniques that arbitrators should use in each of the four configurations should be left until the moment the arbitral tribunal is constituted. The kind of techniques to use will depend on the particular circumstances of a case, including the legal culture of the participants of a dispute resolution process.

7.4.1 Anecdotally reported cases

Five anecdotally reported cases illustrate how various configurations of a three-member tribunal play out in international arbitration cases.

7.4.1.1 Mediation by a party-appointed arbitrator

7.4.1.1.1 GENERAL ELECTRIC COMPANY (GEC) CASE

In this case, parties settled in mediation by a party-appointed arbitrator during arbitral proceedings.[52] There had been a series of commercial disputes between the same parties under different contracts. These had resulted in two ad hoc arbitrations and a court proceeding in a southern European country. Claims and counterclaims amounted to a small amount less than USD 1 million.

The chairman of the joint tribunal constituted for both arbitrations observed that the costs of arbitration seemed to be disproportionate to any amounts that could be recovered. He asked if parties wanted to discuss the possibility of

50 *Ibid*, at 15.

51 *Ibid*, at 13–14.

52 Michael McIlwrath, *Anti-Arbitration: It's Not Hard to Mediate During Arbitral Proceedings*, Kluwer Arbitration Blog (13 Sep. 2011), available at <http://kluwerarbitrationblog.com/2011/09/13/anti-arbitration-its-not-hard-to-mediate-during-arbitral-proceedings/> (accessed 31 Mar. 2018) (sharing his own experience as an in-house counsel at General Electric Company); also reported in Paul E. Mason, *The Arbitrator as Mediator, and Mediator as Arbitrator*, 28(6) J. Int'l. Arb. 541, 546 (2011).

subjecting all three pending disputes to mediation before one of the co-arbitrators, noting her qualifications in the field.

Both sides expressed interest. The co-arbitrator indicated she would accept the appointment by the parties if they would allow her to resign as arbitrator if a settlement was not reached or if she or either of the parties felt that her impartiality as arbitrator had been compromised by information she had received. If she resigned, the party that had nominated her (the respondent in this case) would be permitted to appoint a new co-arbitrator to replace her, without prejudice to its position or any delay in the arbitration. It was important to safeguard the appointing party's right to designate an arbitrator of choice should the mediation fail and there might exist any doubts about confidential information that had been shared.

The parties agreed to mediation under these conditions, and the hearing was adjourned. The parties reconvened the following week with the co-arbitrator acting as a mediator. All three disputes were rapidly settled. As noted by a participant of the process, the parties used the positive feelings about the settlement to re-establish relationships that had been severed.[53]

7.4.1.2 Mediation by the chairman of a tribunal

In the following two cases the chairman of a tribunal acted as a mediator.

7.4.1.2.1 COMECON CASE

In a dispute between a Western private company and a state trading organization (STO) of a country from what was then the Council for Mutual Economic Assistance (COMECON), the parties met with the arbitral tribunal to prepare the terms of reference and organise the procedure.[54] At a certain point, it became apparent that the parties were interested in settling. The chairman of the tribunal offered assistance but pointed out that, should the settlement attempt fail, he and his colleagues would have to decide the outcome of the dispute. The parties agreed to a mediation attempt by the chairman. In mediation, parties reached agreement on the essential elements of a settlement. The STO representatives found the settlement acceptable but requested to arrange it as a settlement proposal from the chairman of the tribunal. The chairman prepared the proposal, emphasising that it was made on the basis of his current understanding of the case and, had the case proceeded to the arbitration, different conclusions could have been reached. The proposal was delivered to the parties. Once the parties

53 McIlwrath, *supra* n. 52.

54 Michael E. Schneider, *Combining Arbitration with Conciliation,* in *International Dispute Resolution: Towards an International Arbitration Culture*, 8 ICCA Congress Series 57, 82 (Albert Jan van den Berg ed., Kluwer Law International 1998) (reporting a case from his personal experience).

returned to their respective headquarters, they notified the chairman that they had accepted the proposal and requested the tribunal to issue an award by consent.

7.4.1.2.2 HONG KONG CASE

In a Hong Kong arbitration, an overseas party claimed damages from a Chinese party for a delay in completing a building project.[55] The claimed amount approached USD 1 million and there were counterclaims. At the hearing, both parties asked the chair of the tribunal to mediate. Before proceeding with mediation, the participants discussed the procedure. The minutes of the agreed outcome of discussions provided for a 'standstill' in the arbitration for two months pending the chair's efforts to mediate, that the chair could contact or meet with the parties separately or together (and without lawyers) at his choice, that everything said or done for the purpose of mediation could not be referred to at the arbitration, and that the mediator should continue to act as the third arbitrator if mediation failed. The mediator caucused with the parties and then met them at a joint session before sending them off to discuss the matter between themselves. After some hours a settlement was concluded.

The parties settled at the figure which beforehand the mediator had privately indicated to the paying party as his best guess of the lowest figure that the other party would be likely to accept in settlement. As a result, the parties saved some HKD 1.5 million of estimated tribunal costs for a hearing scheduled to last three weeks. In the view of the mediator, nothing said or seen during his discussions with the parties would have inhibited him in the least from continuing with arbitration if it had gone ahead.[56]

7.4.1.3 Mediation by all three members of a tribunal

7.4.1.3.1 ICC CASE

In an ICC case relating to a dispute between a Chinese and a German party, a tribunal comprised an American chairman and Chinese and German co-arbitrators.[57] The parties agreed that, a day before the hearing, the tribunal would conduct mediation and, if no settlement was reached, the tribunal would

55 Michael Thomas, *Mediation at Work in Hong Kong*, 58(1) Arb. 29 (1992) (reporting his own recollections of a Hong Kong case where he was appointed as the chair and then as the mediator); also reported in Michael Hwang, *The Role of Arbitrators as Settlement Facilitators – Commentary,* in *New Horizons in International Commercial Arbitration and Beyond*, 12 ICCA Congress Series 571, 579–580 (Albert Jan van den Berg ed., Kluwer Law International 2005); Burr, *supra* n. 33, at 72–73.

56 Thomas, *supra* n. 55, at 29; Hwang, *supra* n. 55, at 580.

57 This case was personally observed by Fan Kun. Fan Kun, *Arbitration in China: A Legal and Cultural Analysis* 242 (Hart Publishing 2013).

proceed with the arbitration hearing. During mediation, the tribunal explained the procedure, reconfirmed the parties' consent, and verified the authority of the mediation participants to settle. In caucuses, the tribunal tried to make each party aware of the strengths and weaknesses of its case. Although the parties did not reach settlement in mediation, the differences between them were substantially narrowed. The next day, the members of the tribunal commenced the arbitration hearing, reminded the parties that they were acting now as arbitrators and that nothing said or heard during mediation could be used in arbitration. The hearing lasted the whole day, after which the parties were invited to exchange further submissions. At the dinner after the hearing, the parties chose to sit at the same table, and some negotiation could have taken place then. In a couple of months, the parties reached a settlement and the arbitration claims were withdrawn.

7.4.1.3.2 JAPAN COMMERCIAL ARBITRATOR ASSOCIATION (JCAA) CASE

In a JCAA case, two of three arbitrators were trained in the common-law tradition, though both had vast experience in Japan.[58] On the suggestion of one party, the entire arbitral tribunal acted as mediators, which resulted in a settlement.[59] To deal with some traditional common-law concerns, a mediation agreement was arranged providing for some safeguards and matters of procedure. In reporting this case, Goodrich does not specify what safeguards and matters of procedure the mediation agreement provided for. He notes, however, that they were of a kind described in the final section of his article. That section indicates that parties should record in their mediation agreement, among other things, their consent to the same neutral arb-med-arb, the time for mediation to occur, and whether the dual role neutral is allowed to caucus with the parties.[60] In Goodrich's view, a key reason for the success of the process was the participants' acceptance of the legitimacy of the process.

7.4.1.4 Commentary

It is not clear from the available information what mediation techniques dual role neutrals used in the GEC and COMECON cases. The available information reveals divergent expectations of dual role neutrals in these two cases as to their role in subsequent arbitration if mediation did not result in a settlement. In the GEC case, the dual role neutral indicated that she would resign if she or either of the parties felt that her impartiality had been compromised by information she

58 Mark Goodrich, *Arb-med: Ideal Solution or Dangerous Heresy?* 15(1) Int'l Arb. L. Rev. 12, 15 (2012) (reporting a case from his own professional experience).

59 The fact that in this and previous case all three members of the tribunal acted as mediators transforms this process to the same neutral (arb)-med-arb. The safeguards for using the same neutral (arb)-med-arb are discussed in Chapter 8 *infra*.

60 Goodrich, *supra* n. 58, at 18.

had received in mediation. The dual role neutral in the COMECON case left parties no choice, by stating that if mediation did not lead to a settlement, he and his colleagues would have to decide the outcome of the dispute.[61]

The position taken by the dual role neutral in the GEC case is preferable. It finds support in soft-law instruments, such as the CEDR Rules for the Facilitation of Settlement in International Arbitration (CEDR Rules)[62] and the IBA Guidelines on Conflicts of Interest in International Arbitration (IBA Guidelines on CIIA),[63] and is advocated by Kaufmann-Kohler.[64] There is, however, one difference between the position of the latter three and the former. Contrary to the dual role neutral in the GEC case, the CEDR Rules, IBA Guidelines on CIIA, and Kaufmann-Kohler suggest that the decision on resignation should be left to the discretion of a dual role neutral only.

In the ICC case, the three-member tribunal made sure that the parties consenting to give mediation a try understood what the mediation procedure entailed, when the mediation phase was over, and how they needed to treat during arbitration the information revealed in the mediation phase.

In the Hong Kong and JCAA cases, mediating arbitrators addressed concerns associated with their dual roles by discussing and arranging mediation agreements with the parties. These specified matters of procedure and provided for safeguards. The safeguards addressed issues such as parties' consent to the process, caucusing, and the use of information from mediation in subsequent arbitration. These will be explored in Chapter 8.

It is not clear from the available information whether the reason for the conduct of mediation by one member of the tribunal (in three of the five presented cases) was to reduce concerns associated with the involvement of the entire tribunal as mediators. However, all five cases demonstrate that mediation by some or all members of a three-member tribunal may create conditions for parties to settle, which saves them time and money.

7.5 Conclusion

Procedural modifications of the same neutral (arb)-med-arb are the second of three ways to address concerns associated with this process. Procedural

61 A similar position was taken by the arbitrator-mediator in the Hong Kong case.

62 CEDR Rules for the Facilitation of Settlement in International Arbitration (Nov. 2009), art. 7, available at <www.cedr.com/about_us/arbitration_commission/Rules.pdf> (accessed 31 Mar. 2018).

63 International Bar Association (IBA) Guidelines on Conflicts of Interest in International Arbitration (2014), general standard 4(d), available at <www.ibanet.org/Publications/publications_IBA_guides_and_free_materials.aspx> (accessed 14 Jan. 2018).

64 Gabrielle Kaufmann-Kohler, *When Arbitrators Facilitate Settlement: Towards a Transnational Standard*, Clayton Utz, available at <www.claytonutz.com/ialecture/2007/transcript_2007.html> (accessed 14 Jan. 2018).

modifications discussed in this chapter are MEDALOA, arb-med, and modifications relevant to a three-member tribunal.

MEDALOA appears to ease some of the behavioural and procedural concerns raised by the same neutral (arb)-med-arb. In particular, the incorporation of last offer arbitration is likely to reduce the risk of a dual role neutral's bias because the arbitrator does not decide on a dispute but chooses between the last offers proposed by parties.

In arb-med, the risk of arbitrator bias further to confidential disclosures in mediation is excluded because mediation occurs after an arbitral award has been issued. The same factor prevents parties from using mediation tactically to influence the arbitrator's decision. Empirical research shows that parties settle more frequently in the mediation phase of arb-med than in the mediation phase of the same neutral med-arb. The disadvantage of starting with arbitration is that arb-med saves little time and few costs.

Arbitral tribunals consisting of three arbitrators offer significant flexibility for configuration in the mediation phase. This assists in reducing concerns associated with the same neutral (arb)-med-arb, particularly those related to the risk of arbitrator bias. For example, two co-arbitrators may conduct mediation, while reserving the chair of the tribunal for the arbitration hearing. This would ensure that the chair is not privy to any confidential information. If mediation does not result in a settlement, the chair could serve as a sole arbitrator.

If, given the particular circumstances of a case, parties consider that they can benefit from using the same neutral (arb)-med-arb, they need to consider the third way to address concerns associated with the same neutral (arb)-med-arb. This is through the implementation of safeguards for using this process. These safeguards are explored in the next chapter.

8 Safeguards for using the same neutral (arb)-med-arb as a way to address concerns associated with this process

8.1 Introduction

This chapter explores the third way to address concerns associated with the same neutral (arb)-med-arb, the implementation of safeguards for using this process. As discussed in Section 3.3, the same neutral (arb)-med-arb risks undermining the efficacy of mediation (behavioural concerns) and jeopardising the integrity of arbitration (procedural concerns). The arbitrator's prior involvement in mediation, particularly in caucuses, may deprive parties of their right to an impartial tribunal and due process. As a result, the arbitrator and the award resulting from the same neutral (arb)-med-arb may be challenged.

To protect the arbitrator and the award from a challenge, many authors propose safeguards for using the same neutral (arb)-med-arb.[1] Some authors

1 *See, e.g.*, Gabrielle Kaufmann-Kohler, *When Arbitrators Facilitate Settlement: Towards a Transnational Standard*, Clayton Utz, available at <www.claytonutz.com/ialecture/2007/transcript_2007.html> (accessed 14 Jan. 2018); John T. Blankenship, *Developing Your ADR Attitude: Med-Arb, a Template for Adaptive ADR*, 42(11) Tennessee Bar J. 28, 36 (2006); Andrew Burr, *Med-Arb: A Viable Hybrid Solution?* 8 Les Arbitres Internationaux 57, 64–66 (2005); David W. Plant, *The Arbitrator as Settlement Facilitator*, 17(1) J. Int'l. Arb. 143, 145–146 (Kluwer Law International 2000); David W. Plant, *We Must Talk Because We Can: Mediating International Intellectual Property Disputes* (International Chamber of Commerce 2008) discussed in Jeremy Lack, *Appropriate Dispute Resolution (ADR): The Spectrum of Hybrid Techniques Available to the Parties*, in *ADR in Business: Practice and Issues across Countries and Cultures* vol. II 339, 375–376 (Arnold Ingen-Housz ed., Kluwer Law International 2011); Jacob Rosoff, *Hybrid Efficiency in Arbitration: Waiving Potential Conflicts for Dual Role Arbitrators in Med-Arb and Arb-Med Proceedings*, 26(1) J. Int'l. Arb. 89, 93–94 (2009); Andreas Reiner, *Bridges Between Mediation and Arbitration: The Mediator as Arbitrator?/The Arbitrator as Mediator?* 27–28 (unpublished paper presented at Tenth Zagreb Arbitration Conference, 2002); Bernd Ehle, *The Arbitrator as a Settlement Facilitator* in *Walking A Thin Line – What an Arbitrator Can Do, Must Do or Must Not Do, Recent Developments and Trends* 77, 87–94 (Bruylant 2010); Justin D'Agostino, *Mediator-Arbitrators: The Perfect Match or No Love Lost? (A Valentine's Day Blog)*, Kluwer Arbitration Blog (15 Feb. 2011), available at <http://kluwerarbitrationblog.com/blog/2011/02/15/mediator-arbitrators-the-perfect-match-or-no-love-lost-a-valentines-day-blog/> (accessed 3 Apr. 2018);

focus on a limited number of key issues, whereas others address almost every aspect of the process. This chapter synthesises the suggestions of various authors and the empirical data collected for this book to identify two key safeguards for using the same neutral (arb)-med-arb: (1) party voluntary and informed consent; and (2) two safeguard options for reducing concerns related to the use of caucuses.

The majority of commentators suggest safeguards for situations when arbitrators act as mediators.[2] Others address the opposite situation, when mediators act as arbitrators[3] or refer to both options simultaneously.[4] As noted in Section 3.1, concerns arise whenever arbitration follows mediation and the same neutral

Michael E. Schneider, *Combining Arbitration with Conciliation,* in *International Dispute Resolution: Towards an International Arbitration Culture*, 8 ICCA Congress Series 57, 85–96 (Albert Jan van den Berg ed., Kluwer Law International 1998); Michael Hwang, *The Role of Arbitrators as Settlement Facilitators – Commentary,* in *New Horizons in International Commercial Arbitration and Beyond*, 12 ICCA Congress Series 571, 578 (Albert Jan van den Berg ed., Kluwer Law International 2005); Royden Hindle, *Mixing it up: Medarb Re-visited,* ¶ 40 (unpublished paper prepared for the AMINZ Seminar 'Current issues in Arbitration', Mar. 2014); Mark Goodrich, *Arb-Med: Ideal Solution or Dangerous Heresy?* 8, White & Case (30 Mar. 2012), available at <www.whitecase.com/publications/article/arb-med-ideal-solution-or-dangerous-heresy> (accessed 3 Apr. 2018); Peter Talbot, *Should an Arbitrator or Adjudicator Act as a Mediator in the Same Dispute?* 67(3) Arb. 221, 229 (Aug. 2001); Alan L. Limbury, *Making Med-Arb Work*, 9(7) ADR Bulletin 1, 3–4 (2007); Thomas J. Brewer & Lawrence R. Mills, *Combining Mediation & Arbitration*, 54(4) Disp. Res. J. 32, 36–38 (1999); Su Yin Anand, *The Risks of Arbitration-Mediation: Hong Kong Courts Decline to Enforce PRC Arbitral Award*, 16(2) Arb. News (Newsletter of the International Bar Association Legal Practice Division) 40, 41–42 (2011); Harold I. Abramson, *Protocols for International Arbitrators Who Dare to Settle Cases*, 10 Am. Rev. Int'l Arb. 1, 8–16 (1999).

2 Ehle, *supra* n. 1, at 87; Burr, *supra* n. 1, at 64; Plant (2000), *supra* n. 1, at 145–146; Kaufmann-Kohler, *supra* n. 1; Schneider, *supra* n. 1, at 85–86; Goodrich, *supra* n. 1, at 8; Anand, *supra* n. 1, at 41–42.

3 Julian D. M. Lew, *Multi-Institutional Conciliation and the Reconciliation of Different Legal Cultures,* in *New Horizons in International Commercial Arbitration and Beyond*, 12 ICCA Congress Series 421, 426–427 (Albert Jan van den Berg ed., Kluwer Law International 2005); Claude Thomson, *Med-Arb: A Fresh Look,* 5 (2006) (on file with the ICC Documentation & Research Centre).

4 Hindle, *supra* n. 1, at ¶¶ 8, 40 (discussing safeguards for the use of what she calls 'med-arb', which means the same neutral (arb)-med-arb); Brewer & Mills, *supra* n. 1, at 34–37 (although Mills and Brewer define med-arb broadly, as any ADR procedure combining mediation and arbitration in sequence (either by the same or different neutrals and starting either with mediation or arbitration), when they describe advantages and disadvantages of med-arb and its safeguards, they seem to narrow the meaning down to the same neutral (arb)-med-arb); J. Brian Casey, *Arbitration Law of Canada: Practice and Procedure,* 16–17 (JurisNet 2005) (addressing situations when the arbitrator acts as a mediator during the arbitral process or where a person mediates and then, if there is no settlement, sits as an arbitrator); Donna Ross, *Med-Arb/Arb-Med: A More Efficient ADR Process or an Invitation to a Potential Ethical Disaster?* in *Contemporary Issues in International Arbitration and Mediation: The Fordham Papers 2012* 352, 358, 363–366 (Arthur W. Rovine ed., Martinus Nijhoff 2013) (speaking about the same neutral (arb)-med-arb and referring to the same neutral arb-med-arb as a form derivative from the same neutral med-arb).

performs the functions of a mediator and an arbitrator. Thus, unless otherwise specified, all safeguards discussed here are in relation to both the same neutral med-arb and the same neutral arb-med-arb, referred to jointly as the same neutral (arb)-med-arb.

This chapter comprises two sections. Section 8.2 analyses the fundamental safeguard for using the same neutral (arb)-med-arb: party voluntary and informed consent to the process. It explores whether consent incorporates the waiver of the right to challenge the arbitrator and the award on the ground of the arbitrator's participation in mediation. Section 8.3 examines two main safeguard options for reducing concerns related to the use of caucuses and assesses their strengths and weaknesses.

8.2 Consent and waiver

8.2.1 Consent

8.2.1.1 The importance of consent

When the same neutral acts as a mediator and arbitrator, party consent is a critical safeguard[5] that must be observed to protect the arbitrator and the award from a challenge on the ground of the arbitrator's participation in mediation. The requirement for consent is in accordance with the consensual nature of arbitration and mediation as well as the parties' procedural autonomy.

The vast majority of legislative acts and institutional arbitration and mediation rules all over the world allow arbitrators to act as mediators and mediators to act as arbitrators if parties expressly agree upon that.[6] The legislation and rules, however, differ in their starting preference. For example, the starting preference of both the UNCITRAL ML on Conciliation and UNCITRAL Conciliation Rules is that a conciliator should not take the role of an arbitrator.[7] Article 12 of the ML on Conciliation provides:

5 *See, e.g.*, Goodrich, *supra* n. 1, at 8; Barry C. Bartel, *Med-Arb as a Distinct Method of Dispute Resolution: History, Analysis, and Potential*, 27 Willamette L. Rev. 661, 689–691 (1991); Hwang, *supra* n. 1, at 578; Ariel Ye, *Commentary on Integrated Dispute Resolution Systems in the PRC*, in *New Horizons in International Commercial Arbitration and Beyond*, 12 ICCA Congress Series 478, 482 (Albert Jan van den Berg ed., Kluwer Law International 2005) (citing Professor Kaplan who endorses the combination of mediation and arbitration subject to the agreement of the parties and two other conditions so as to ensure justice); Abramson, *supra* n. 1, at 16 (protocol 12); Burr, *supra* n. 1, at 64; Jesus Almoguera, *Arbitration and Mediation Combined. The Independence and Impartiality of Arbitrators*, in *Liber Amicorum Bernardo Cremades* 101, 130 (M. A. Fernandez-Ballesteros & David Arias eds., La Ley 2010).

6 *See, e.g.*, Appendix 4 to the CEDR Final Report, which contains a table of existing legislative provisions from around the world on this issue.

7 UNCITRAL Model Law on International Commercial Conciliation (effective 24 Jun. 2002), art. 12, available at <www.uncitral.org/pdf/english/texts/arbitration/ml-conc/03-90953_Ebook.pdf> (accessed 3 Apr. 2018); UNCITRAL Conciliation Rules (effective 23 Jul. 1980), arts. 19, 1(2), available at <www.uncitral.org/pdf/english/texts/arbitration/conc-rules/conc-rules-e.pdf> (accessed 3 Apr. 2018).

> Unless otherwise agreed by the parties, the conciliator shall not act as an arbitrator in respect of a dispute that was or is the subject of the conciliation proceedings or in respect of another dispute that has arisen from the same contract or legal relationship or any related contract or legal relationship.

The ICC Mediation Rules take the same view.[8] Likewise, Section 80(a) of the Indian Arbitration and Conciliation Act 1996 prohibits a conciliator from transforming to an arbitrator, unless parties agree otherwise.[9] However, a different approach is taken by the same Indian Act towards the reverse transformation of an arbitrator to a conciliator. Section 30(1) of the Act states:

> It is not incompatible with an arbitration agreement for an arbitral tribunal to encourage settlement of the dispute and, with the agreement of the parties; the arbitral tribunal may use mediation, conciliation or other procedures at any time during the arbitral proceedings to encourage settlement.[10]

The Bangladesh Arbitration Act and the International Commercial Arbitration Acts (ICAAs) of Canadian common law provinces, except for Northwest Territories and Nunavut, likewise, allow arbitral tribunals to encourage settlement and, if parties agree, to use mediation, conciliation or other procedures.[11] The position taken by the Canadian ICAAs contrasts with that of the Ontario Arbitration Act (OAA) governing domestic arbitration in that province. Rather than expressing its starting preference, the OAA prohibits arbitrators from acting as mediators. Section 35 of the OAA states:

> The members of an arbitral tribunal shall not conduct any part of the arbitration as a mediation or conciliation process or other similar process that might compromise or appear to compromise the arbitral tribunal's ability to decide the dispute impartially.[12]

As discussed in Section 6.2.2, in Hong Kong, Article 14 of the HKIAC Mediation Rules prohibits the reverse transformation of the mediator to an adjudicator

8 International Court of Arbitration of the International Chamber of Commerce (ICC) Mediation Rules (effective 1 Jan. 2014), art. 10(3), available at <www.iccwbo.org/products-and-services/arbitration-and-adr/mediation/rules/> (accessed 3 Apr. 2018) [hereinafter, ICC Mediation Rules].

9 Arbitration and Conciliation Act, Act No. 26 of 1996.

10 *Ibid.*

11 Arbitration Act, Act No. I of 2001, s. 22(1). In Canada *see, e.g., British Columbia International Commercial Arbitration Act*, R.S.B.C. 1996, c. 233, s. 30(1); *Alberta International Commercial Arbitration Act*, R.S.A. 2000, c. I-5, s. 5.

12 *Ontario Arbitration Act*, S.O. 1991, c. 17, s. 35.

or an arbitrator.[13] This contrasts with the provisions of the Hong Kong Arbitration Ordinance that allow arbitrators to act as mediators and mediators to act as arbitrators, provided parties consent to this in writing.[14]

The starting preferences, arguably, reflect the general position taken by a particular jurisdiction, organisation, or institution on whether the same neutral can act as a mediator and an arbitrator. The above examples from India, Canada, and Hong Kong demonstrate that these jurisdictions are not yet completely settled on whether the same neutral can serve as both a mediator and an arbitrator.

Before embarking on the same neutral (arb)-med-arb, neutrals need to ensure that they have the clear authority of both parties or clear statutory authority, to serve as both a mediator and an arbitrator.[15] Absent clear authority, the dual role neutral, the process, and the result may become susceptible to allegations of unfairness, whereas if parties know what to expect from the process and accept it voluntarily, they may be less likely to undermine the result, even if they are not completely satisfied with it.[16]

8.2.1.2 Form of consent

According to Berger, parties' implied agreement to the same neutral (arb)-med-arb should be sufficient if there is a shared intention and neither party is coerced into the process.[17] The following examples from case law, however, show the necessity of parties' express consent to the process.

8.2.1.2.1 *GASKIN V. GASKIN*

In the US case *Gaskin v. Gaskin*,[18] the court noted that mediation encourages candid disclosure, including disclosure of confidential information to a mediator. This creates the potential for a problem if the mediator, over the objection of one of the parties, becomes the arbitrator of the same or a related dispute.[19] The

13 Hong Kong International Arbitration Centre (HKIAC) Mediation Rules (effective 1 Aug. 1999), available at <www.hkiac.org/mediation/rules/hkiac-mediation-rules> (accessed 3 Apr. 2018).

14 Arbitration Ordinance (Cap. 609, 1 Jun. 2011), L.N. 38 of 2011, ss. 32, 33 [hereinafter, Hong Kong AO].

15 Bartel, *supra* n. 5, at 691.

16 *Ibid; but see* Geoff Lawday, *Hybrid Dispute Resolution Processes* 4 (unpublished paper presented at 'Mediation in a Global Village – Cross-cultural and International Aspects of Mediation and Negotiation', Germany 2009) (noting that parties' consent does not eliminate concerns associated with the same neutral (arb)-med-arb and practical and legal weaknesses remain when the process moves from one stage to the other).

17 Klaus Peter Berger, *Integration of Mediation Elements into Arbitration: 'Hybrid' Procedures and 'Intuitive' Mediation by International Arbitrators*, 19(3) Arb. Int'l. 387, 393 (2003).

18 *Gaskin v. Gaskin*, No. 2-06-039-CV, 2006 WL 2507319 (Tex. App. Fort Worth, 21 Sep. 2006).

19 Edna Sussman, *Developing an Effective Med-Arb/ Arb-Med Process*, 2(1) NYSBA New York Disp. Res. Law. 71, 72 (2009); Edna Sussman, *Combinations and Permutations of Arbitration and Mediation: Issues and Solutions*, in *ADR in Business: Practice and Issues across Countries and Cultures* vol II 381, 388 (Arnold Ingen-Housz ed., Kluwer Law International 2011).

court concluded that it would be improper for the mediator to act as the arbitrator in the same or related dispute 'without the express consent of the parties'.

8.2.1.2.2 *MARCHESE V. MARCHESE*

Following the court decision in *Marchese v. Marchese*,[20] contracting parties in Ontario can expressly opt for the same neutral arb-med-arb. In that case, the Court of Appeal for Ontario held that an agreement between parties to submit to the same neutral arb-med-arb was enforceable despite a provision in the province's domestic arbitration statute that prohibits arbitrators from conducting any part of arbitration as mediation.[21] The court stated that if the prohibition applied to the same neutral arb-med-arb (a point that the court held it did not need to decide), the prohibition could be waived by the parties' mutual decision to engage in the same neutral arb-med-arb.

It is a common view in the literature that parties' consent must be recorded in writing.[22] The legislation in Hong Kong and Singapore, and the ICC Mediation Rules require parties' written consent for an arbitrator to act as a mediator and a mediator to act as an arbitrator.[23] Considering the seriousness of concerns associated with the same neutral (arb)-med-arb in some jurisdictions, this book suggests that, unless the form of consent is regulated in the applicable legislation or rules, it is good practice to record parties' consent to the process in writing.

8.2.1.3 Timing of consent

In the same neutral arb-med-arb, it may be impractical to authorise an arbitrator to serve as a mediator in advance,[24] although this apparently

20 *Marchese v. Marchese* (2007), 219 O.A.C. 257 (C.A.), MacPherson, Sharpe and Juriansz, JJ.A.

21 Barry Leon & Alexandra Peterson, *Med-Arb in Ontario: Enforceability of Med-Arb Agreement Confirmed by Court of Appeal*, 2(1) NYSBA New York Disp. Res. Law. 92, 92 (2009).

22 *See, e.g.*, Ehle, *supra* n. 1, at 88; Hwang, *supra* n. 1, at 578; Goodrich, *supra* n. 1, at 8; Hindle, *supra* n. 1, at ¶ 40[a]; Lew, *supra* n. 3, at 428; Toshio Sawada, *Hybrid Arb-Med: Will West and East Never Meet?* 14(2) ICC Int'l Ct. Arb. Bull. 29, 36 (Fall 2003); Reiner, *supra* n. 1, at 27; Schneider, *supra* n. 1, at 87; Ross, *supra* n. 4, at 363; Plant (2000), *supra* n. 1, at 146 (pointing out that the arbitrator may agree to participate in settlement discussion only with the express written agreement of all parties and their counsel and only in accordance with the terms and conditions of the parties' express agreement). *See also* Safeguards for Arbitrators Who Use Private Meetings with Each Party as a Means of Facilitating Settlement (Final Report of the CEDR Commission on Settlement in International Arbitration, Appendix 2), ¶ 7.2, available at <www.cedr.com/about_us/arbitration_commission/> (accessed 14 Jan. 2018) [hereinafter, CEDR Appendix 2].

23 Hong Kong AO, *supra* n. 14, s. 33(1); International Arbitration Act (Ch. 143A, 31 Dec. 2002), s. 17(1) [hereinafter, Singapore IAA]; ICC Mediation Rules, *supra* n. 8, art. 10(3).

24 Plant (2000), *supra* n. 1, at 146 n. 2.

happens in some jurisdictions.[25] Parties are better off permitting arbitral proceedings to unfold to the extent sufficient to build trust between them and the arbitrator as a potential mediator. If parties want their arbitrator to mediate, at the moment when the arbitrator commences mediation at the latest, parties should confirm their consent to the process and clarify all points that may give rise to difficulties, which should be recorded in writing.[26] One of the points that parties need to specify is the actions to be taken in respect of arbitration if mediation terminates without success.[27] In particular, to ensure that the neutral in mediation avoids conduct that could later taint arbitration, it is highly recommended that parties specify up front whether the mediator will later become the arbitrator. This recommendation is relevant to both the same neutral arb-med-arb and the same neutral med-arb.[28]

At the same time, written consent of parties before the mediation phase of the same neutral (arb)-med-arb may be insufficient to protect the arbitrator or the award from a challenge. A safer approach might be to obtain renewed consent from parties every time the process shifts from mediation to arbitration and vice versa and, particularly, after termination of mediation and before commencement of the arbitration phase, as parties may change their position.[29] It is in the interest of neutrals to verify that they have the parties' written consent before changing hats.

The CEDR Commission recommends that parties insert a requirement of the second consent to be given upon termination of mediation, and before the mediator resumes as an arbitrator.[30] It should be noted that this CEDR Commission's recommendation relates to situations when parties authorise an

25 Edna Sussman reports seeing some contracts, mostly coming from California, that specifically provide for the same neutral arb-med-arb. In accordance with these contracts, only the neutral can withdraw if not comfortable proceeding to arbitration, while parties must accept the same neutral as the mediator and the arbitrator. *Summary Report of the First Meeting in September 23–24, 2016 of the International Task Force on Mixed Mode Dispute Resolution: Inaugural Summit at Pepperdine University, Malibu, CA, USA*, International Mediation Institute 21 (2017), available at <www.imimediation.org/about-imi/who-are-imi/mixed-mode-task-force/> (accessed 3 Apr. 2018) [hereinafter, First Summary Report of Mixed Mode Task Force].

26 Schneider, *supra* n. 1, at 87; Goodrich, *supra* n. 1, at 8.

27 Goodrich, *supra* n. 1, at 8; Bernardo M. Cremades, *Overcoming the Clash of Legal Cultures: The Role of Interactive Arbitration,* 14(2) Arb. Int'l. 156, 164 (1998) (calling for setting the terms under which arbitration shall continue if mediation between parties does not prove possible, establishing these conditions in the clearest possible fashion to prevent challenge of the arbitrator or the award).

28 Schneider, *supra* n. 1, at 87 (speaking about the same neutral arb-med-arb); Richard P. Flake, *MED/ARB – A Viable ADR Vehicle? Nuances of Med/Arb—A Neutral's Perspective*, CEDIRES 8, available at <www.cedires.com/index_bestanden/FLAKE_http-www.cbylaw.com-filebin_files_flake_rpf-AAA_Med-Arb.pdf> (accessed 14 Jan. 2018) (addressing the same neutral med-arb).

29 Ross, *supra* n. 4, at 364.

30 CEDR Appendix 2, *supra* n. 22, at ¶ 7.3.

arbitrator to caucus during mediation.[31] According to the CEDR Commission, the second consent is more effective than the one at an earlier stage because parties give it in the knowledge of developments during mediation. Australian Commercial Arbitration Acts (CAAs) even require parties' second consent on or after the termination of the mediation proceedings to enable the former mediator to resume arbitration.[32] What the CEDR Commission and CAAs propose is (arb)-med-arb opt-out. As discussed in Section 6.4, (arb)-med-arb opt-out is a process with advantages and disadvantages that parties may find useful, depending on the particular circumstances of the case. The English case of *Glencot* illustrates the consequences of the parties' disagreement as to whether the same person should go back to the role of an adjudicator after unsuccessful mediation.

8.2.1.3.1 GLENCOT

In the *Glencot* case,[33] the parties to a construction dispute met with the adjudicator for an adjudication hearing at a hotel. Before the adjudication hearing the parties negotiated and seemed to reach substantial agreement on a figure. They informed the adjudicator about their agreement. They then discovered that they had not agreed whether a discount should be applied to the figure. They both asked the adjudicator to mediate between them. He agreed, adding that if negotiations failed he would resume his role as adjudicator. He then presided over six hours of talks, which failed to bring an agreed resolution of the dispute. The defendant asked the adjudicator to withdraw. The claimant wanted the adjudicator to continue and he did so, ultimately giving a decision in the claimant's favour. The claimant sought to enforce the award by way of summary judgment, but the application was successfully resisted on grounds of partiality on the part of the adjudicator.

In the High Court proceedings, Judge Humphrey Lloyd QC applied the apparent bias test. This test essentially asks whether the relevant circumstances would lead a fair-minded and informed observer to conclude that there was a real possibility or a real danger that the tribunal was biased. On the facts of the case, Judge Lloyd found that caucuses in mediation could have conveyed information

31 As will be explained in Section 8.3.1 *infra*, the starting point of the CEDR Commission is that arbitrators who facilitate settlement may not caucus with the parties. *See* CEDR Rules for the Facilitation of Settlement in International Arbitration (Nov. 2009), art. 5(2), available at <www.cedr.com/about_us/arbitration_commission/Rules.pdf> (accessed 3 Apr. 2018).

32 *See, e.g., Commercial Arbitration Act 2012* (WA), ss. 27D(1), 27D(4).

33 *Glencot Development & Design Ltd v. Ben Barrett & Son (Contractors) Ltd* (2001) EWHC Technology 15 (13 Feb. 2001). *See* discussion of this case in Jon Lang, *Med-Arb – An English Perspective*, 2(1) NYSBA New York Disp. Res. Law. 98, 98–101 (2009); Rosoff, *supra* n. 1, at 90–91; Herbert Smith Freehills, *UK: Can Adjudicators Get Involved?* Mondaq (12 Nov. 2001), available at <www.mondaq.com/x/14136/Property+Litigation/Can+Adjudicators+Get+Involved> (accessed 3 Apr. 2018); Hwang, *supra* n. 1, at 573–574; Lucy Greenwood, *A Window of Opportunity? Building a Short Period of Time into Arbitral Rules in order for Parties to Explore Settlement*, 27(2) Arb. Int'l. 199, 208 (2011).

or impressions which subsequently influenced the adjudicator's decision. Judge Lloyd also noted that as the discussions during the mediation were heated, it would have been understandable if the adjudicator-mediator had formed some view about one or both of the parties. Further, the adjudicator-mediator was also asked to form a view about the credibility of the applicant's case without any documentary evidence or basis. In view of these facts, the judge decided that the adjudicator's conduct was such that there was a danger of apparent bias.

8.2.1.4 Consent as a result of parties' voluntary choice

It is essential that the same neutral (arb)-med-arb is voluntarily chosen by parties.[34] Parties should not be coerced into the process. This may occur, for example, if one party suggests to the other in the presence of arbitrators that arbitrators should attempt to mediate the dispute. While the other party may have no wish to mediate, it may feel coerced into the process for fear that refusing to do so may give arbitrators the impression of weakness of its position or reluctance to cooperate. Alternatively, arbitrators might suggest that they act as mediators. In this case, both parties may feel coerced into the process because of the fear of causing some negative reaction from arbitrators if they refuse their suggestion. In either case, Bartel believes that all concerns associated with the same neutral arb-med-arb will surface due to the fact that the process has not been voluntarily chosen by the parties.[35]

Nevertheless, consent is more likely to be uncoerced if a suggestion to mediate comes from a party rather than arbitrators.[36] The arbitrators' suggestion may be interpreted as an order that, if not followed, will alienate arbitrators from a party who refuses their suggestion. If arbitrators raise the idea of assisting parties in their settlement attempts, they must exercise caution.[37] Parties should have no doubt that arbitrators are willing to decide a dispute and all the issues that the parties fail to settle. If arbitrators are prepared to assist parties in their settlement attempt at a later stage in the proceedings, parties should be made aware of this from the start, so that they can express any reservations.

Comments of the US practitioner interviewed for this study echoed the concern about coercing parties into the process. He noted,

> I have been involved in cases where arbitrators said: let me mediate this case. And my client . . . was feeling tremendous pressure because he did not want to offend the arbitrator . . . I think that's absolutely terrible for an arbitrator to say: let me mediate this and putting pressure on the parties.[38]

34 Bartel, *supra* n. 5, at 689–691; Almoguera, *supra* n. 5, at 130.
35 Bartel, *supra* n. 5, at 689.
36 Abramson, *supra* n. 1, at 9.
37 Burr, *supra* n. 1, at 64.
38 Practitioner from the United States, Interview 5.

The following case vividly illustrates the expressed concern. In a very large and complex case in Texas, the multi-party contract included an arbitration clause providing for the appointment of the arbitrator by a court if the parties could not agree.[39] When a dispute arose, it became necessary to apply to a judge to appoint the arbitrator. Apparently, the appointee had never arbitrated but was a highly successful mediator. From the very beginning of the arbitration proceedings, the arbitrator urged the parties to allow him to switch to the role of mediator. It is known that at least one of the parties was very reluctant to allow the arbitrator to mediate but was afraid that, if it did not agree to let him do so, it would offend him and diminish its chances for a favourable result in arbitration. This party eventually agreed to mediate. It is, however, highly questionable whether the arbitrator's actions were ethically proper and respected party autonomy.

The US practitioner interviewed for this study shared his approach as neutral to ensuring that parties choose the same neutral (arb)-med-arb voluntarily:

> I was always very careful about saying: it's not my expectation that I would play multiple roles. It was only when they [parties] raised the issue about whether I could play the role, we would talk about the problems with that. Then they would have to go … and confirm between themselves and then come back jointly and report. And I did not want a situation where one party would say: oh we want you; and the other party would say: no, we don't. I don't want to put any pressure on people.[40]

The same practitioner succinctly summarised how he deals with concerns related to the same neutral (arb)-med-arb:

> To me it's a combination of proper education, surfacing the concerns, but then giving people the space to make their own decision away from the arbitrator or the mediator.[41]

This points to another essential element of a solution to concerns associated with the same neutral (arb)-med-arb, which the practitioner refers to here as 'proper education', i.e., the need to inform parties of the behavioural and procedural concerns associated with the process.

39 This case is reported by Thomas Stipanowich who was called in privately to advise one of the parties. First Summary Report of Mixed Mode Task Force, *supra* n. 25, at 18–19.

40 Practitioner from the United States, Interview 5.

41 *Ibid.* These comments addressed questionnaire Result 2 (minimal use of the same neutral (arb)-med-arb). *See* a summary of the significant questionnaire results in Section 5.4 *supra*.

8.2.1.5 Informed consent

Parties must not only choose the process voluntarily, they should also be able to make an informed decision.[42] Unless parties understand what the process involves and voluntarily choose it, agreeing to the same neutral arb-med-arb may do more harm than good in the long run.[43] The question is how to ensure that parties' consent is informed.

The literature gives different answers to this question. Most authors limit themselves to general recommendations. For example, Flake considers it essential for parties to agree on methodology and record their agreement prior to the commencement of the same neutral med-arb.[44] Talbot suggests that, when shifting from one process to another in arb-med-arb, parties must be made fully aware of the implications. They should enter a written agreement identifying the ground rules, and the neutral must ensure clarity as to the direction of the process.[45] Goodrich advises against arbitrators engaging in mediation unless all parties are legally represented and have the opportunity to receive legal advice on the implications.[46] He further notes that, before any mediation occurs, the parties and the dual role neutral should draw up a written document that records the parties' consent and contains other key aspects of the procedure.[47]

Mills and Brewer regard active client counselling, by both counsel and the neutral, combined with written agreements by parties as the best way to secure genuine informed consent of the parties to the same neutral (arb)-med-arb.[48]

42 *See, e.g.*, Ehle, *supra* n. 1, at 89; Kaufmann-Kohler, *supra* n. 1; Bartel, *supra* n. 5, at 691; Brewer & Mills, *supra* n. 1, at 36; Fan Kun, *The Risks of Apparent Bias When an Arbitrator Acts as a Mediator: Remarks on Hong Kong Court's Decision in Gao Haiyan*, 13 Y.B. Private Int'l. L. 535, 551 (2011); Abramson, *supra* n. 1, at 9; *but see* Brian A. Pappas, *Med-Arb and the Legalisation of Alternative Dispute Resolution*, 20 Harv. Negot. L. Rev. 157, 190–200 (Spring 2015) (noting that even when the same neutral (arb-med-arb) is selected through a process of informed consent, it does not provide for party self-determination for five main reasons: lawyers and the increased legalisation of mediation curtail party self-determination; increasing the legality of mediation by making the mediator also the arbitrator further curtails party self-determination; informed consent to formal processes is not the same as informed consent to informal processes; barriers to educating clients and their advocates about the dangers of the process make achieving truly informed consent difficult; and, even assuming self-determination to use the process, issues with educated party choice exist beyond the initial agreement).

43 Bartel, *supra* n. 5, at 691.

44 Flake, *supra* n. 28, at 4.

45 Talbot, *supra* n. 1, at 229; *see also* Burr, *supra* n. 1, at 64 (suggesting that when the arbitrator commences mediation, all parties should be made aware that they are entering a new stage of the proceedings and all points giving rise to the conflict and differences must be clarified).

46 Goodrich, *supra* n. 1, at 8; *see also* Abramson, *supra* n. 1, at 16 (observing in protocol 12 that to increase the likelihood of parties making an informed decision, they should be given a disclosure statement on the advantages and risks of the neutral performing two roles).

47 Goodrich, *supra* n. 1, at 8.

48 Brewer & Mills, *supra* n. 1, at 36.

Contrary to the general recommendations of the above authors, Mills and Brewer recommend six specific steps:[49]

1 Counsel for parties interested in the same neutral (arb)-med-arb should inform their clients about advantages and disadvantages of the process.[50]
2 Parties who wish to employ the same neutral (arb)-med-arb following such counselling should enter into a written pre-dispute agreement providing for possible use of the same neutral (arb)-med-arb before any disputes have arisen.[51]
3 The pre-dispute agreement should provide that the same neutral (arb)-med-arb cannot be required unless both parties still agree to use it after the dispute has arisen.[52]
4 After the dispute has arisen, and if the parties still agree that the same neutral (arb)-med-arb is their preferred process, they should execute a detailed written protocol specifying how the process is to be conducted.[53]
5 When invited to serve as a dual role neutral, the neutral should take reasonable steps to ascertain that parties understand possible advantages and disadvantages of the process.[54] For example, the neutral may require parties to execute a retention agreement that summarises the possible disadvantages of the same neutral (arb)-med-arb, which, once arranged, should leave little doubt of parties' informed consent to employ the same neutral (arb)-med-arb process. Thus, if parties have followed other recommendations to ensure informed consent to the same neutral (arb)-med-arb before execution of such a retention agreement, it would be the third time parties would have agreed in writing to employ the procedure before it began: once in the pre-dispute agreement, then in the written protocol to submit a particular dispute to the same neutral (arb)-med-arb, and, finally, in executing the neutral's retention agreement. Parties who are this clear about the procedure they wish to employ to resolve their dispute should be free to commit to the same neutral (arb)-med-arb process.
6 Finally, once the process begins, the neutral must strictly adhere to the written protocol negotiated and agreed to by the parties.[55]

These six steps can serve as a roadmap to ensuring that parties' consent to the same neutral (arb)-med-arb is informed. This should prevent challenges to an

49 *Ibid*, at 36–37.
50 *Ibid*, at 36.
51 *Ibid*, at 36–37 (suggesting a draft of a pre-dispute ADR clause).
52 *Ibid*, at 36 (observing that this should enhance the likelihood that the procedure is employed only in cases where the parties clearly understand and agree that the procedure is appropriate for the particular dispute at issue).
53 *Ibid*, at 36–38 (suggesting a draft of a protocol).
54 *Ibid*, at 37.
55 *Ibid*.

arbitrator and an award on the grounds of the arbitrator's participation in mediation. It may be unnecessary to implement all of them. What can be useful for parties intending to use the same neutral (arb)-med-arb is to consider these steps and select those that suit their particular circumstances.

Although there is a variation in the level of prescription in the literature as to how to ensure that parties' consent is informed, two steps appear to be essential. First, a dual role neutral needs to verify that parties have received legal advice on the implications of the process. Second, parties and a dual role neutral need to arrange a written document that records parties' consent to the process and specifies other key aspects of the procedure. Both steps need to occur before a dual role neutral embarks on the mediation stage of the same neutral (arb)-med-arb.

Parties need to clearly understand nuances, imperfections, and ethical issues associated with the process because not every case is appropriate for the same neutral (arb)-med-arb.[56] Many parties will not wish to accept the imperfections inherent therein. However, parties need to be allowed to knowingly and voluntarily consent to having the same neutral mediate and arbitrate if they believe that the benefits outweigh the risks.[57] Thereby, it appears that the strongest argument for acceptance of the same neutral (arb)-med-arb originates with parties – parties' interests overrule ethical principles.[58]

Given the implications of the same neutral (arb)-med-arb, the process appears to be better adapted to sophisticated parties.[59] These are parties who have a good understanding of the process, its risks, and its possible shortcomings. In the commercial context, parties tend to be sophisticated and can be fully informed of any ethical problems and decide to waive objections they may have to the process.[60] This, according to Phillips, makes parties' informed consent to same neutral (arb)-med-arb critical.[61] Nevertheless, even where such consent is given, it may be argued that consent is not given on a fully informed basis if the parties are not aware of all the matters that have been discussed in caucuses.[62] As

56 Flake, *supra* n. 28, at 4.

57 Ross, *supra* n. 4, at 366; Arthur L. Marriott, *Arbitrators and Settlement*, in *New Horizons in International Commercial Arbitration and Beyond*, 12 ICCA Congress Series 533, 541 (Albert Jan van den Berg ed., Kluwer Law International 2005) (observing that the risks are understood by the parties who consent to the combination of roles, expressing a clear wish to settle the case, and suggesting practitioners should pay the parties the compliment of recognising that they understand what they are doing).

58 Richard Fullerton, *The Ethics of Mediation-Arbitration*, 38(5) Colorado Law. 31, 37 (2009); Gerald F. Phillips, *Same-Neutral Med-Arb: What Does the Future Hold?* 2(1) NYSBA New York Disp. Res. Law. 75, 75–76 (2009); Thomson, *supra* n. 3, at 5; Bartel, *supra* n. 5, at 691–692; Lack, *supra* n. 1, at 378.

59 Ross, *supra* n. 4, at 363; Julie Brienza, *ADR Doing Two Things at Once Can Be Problematic*, 34 Trial 19 (1998) cited in Thomson, *supra* n. 3, at 8.

60 Phillips, *supra* n. 58, at 75–76; Brewer & Mills, *supra* n. 1, at 36.

61 Phillips, *supra* n. 58, at 76.

62 CEDR Appendix 2, *supra* n. 22, at ¶ 5 (adding that whether the parties' consent is effective may also vary under different laws).

discussed in Section 8.2.2.3, questions arise regarding whether and, if so, to what extent parties can waive their rights to an impartial tribunal and due process.

A question that emerges from the review of the literature is whether, by giving their informed consent to the same neutral (arb)-med-arb, parties automatically waive the right to challenge the arbitrator and the award on the ground of the arbitrator's participation in mediation. In short, does parties' informed consent to the process imply waiver? This is the question that this chapter turns now to examine.

8.2.2 *Waiver*

8.2.2.1 *Does parties' informed consent to the process imply waiver?*

Before addressing this question, it is necessary to clarify what rights in particular a waiver is meant to waive. To do this, the book proposes to look back at Section 3.3.2 that discussed two procedural concerns associated with the same neutral (arb)-med-arb. The first is the danger of the arbitrators appearing or actually becoming biased because of the information received in mediation. The inability of parties to hear and respond to the issues raised by each of them in caucuses with mediators, who later becomes arbitrators, gives rise to the second procedural concern, a failure to adhere to the rules of due process. In the context of the same neutral (arb)-med-arb, a waiver means that parties are presumed to waive their right to challenge arbitrators and the award on two specific grounds: first, partiality of arbitrators due to their participation in mediation; and, second, failure to adhere to the rules of due process due to the arbitrators' participation in caucuses. The effect of parties' waiver of the right to challenge arbitrators and the award on these two grounds will be discussed in Section 8.2.2.3.

For now, let us return to the posed question: does parties' informed consent to the process imply waiver? A review of the literature shows that commentators are not yet settled on this question. Three main views have been identified. According to the first view, parties' informed consent implies a waiver of the right to challenge the arbitrator and the award, if mediation does not lead to settlement.[63] The reasoning behind this view is that the parties are not obliged to have the same person act as a mediator and an arbitrator.[64] Their deliberate choice of the process must constitute an implied waiver to challenge the dual role neutral for complying with their agreement.[65]

63 *See, e.g.*, Kaufmann-Kohler, *supra* n. 1; Lew, *supra* n. 3, at 428 (noting that written consent of all parties to the mediator acting as arbitrator should, on its own, prevent mediation from giving reason to challenge the arbitrator on the grounds of lack of impartiality); Ross, *supra* n. 4, at 363 (warning parties that, if they provide informed written consent, they must be aware that they may be waiving their right to due process).

64 Rosoff, *supra* n. 1, at 94.

65 *Ibid.*

According to the second view, informed consent and waiver are alternative options. For example, Blankenship refers to parties' informed consent and/or knowing waiver as one of the safeguards for using the same neutral (arb)-med-arb.[66] This means that parties can either give their informed consent or knowing waiver. Both, in Blankenship's understanding, have the same effect.

Third, some consider that apart from expressly consenting in writing to the arbitrator acting as a settlement facilitator, parties need to expressly waive any right to challenge the arbitrator or the award on the ground of the arbitrator's participation in mediation.[67]

Support for the first view has been found in some soft-law instruments and case law.

For example, the IBA Guidelines on CIIA that are widely consulted when arbitrators evaluate whether they need to make disclosures to the parties about potential conflicts before accepting appointments specify:

> An arbitrator may assist the parties in reaching a settlement of the dispute, through conciliation, mediation or otherwise, at any stage of the proceedings. However, before doing so, the arbitrator should receive an express agreement by the parties that acting in such a manner shall not disqualify the arbitrator from continuing to serve as arbitrator. *Such express agreement shall be considered to be an effective waiver of any potential conflict of interest* that may arise from the arbitrator's participation in such a process, or from information that the arbitrator may learn in the process. If the assistance by the arbitrator does not lead to the final settlement of the case, the parties remain bound by their waiver.[68]

The DIS Rules demonstrate a similar approach to the issue of waiver.[69] However, even in those cases where the DIS Rules do not apply but the seat of arbitration is Germany, a waiver may be dispensable.[70] Thus, German courts have repeatedly

66 Blankenship, *supra* n. 1, at 36.

67 *See, e.g.,* Plant (2000), *supra* n. 1, at 146; Ehle, *supra* n. 1, at 93; Schneider, *supra* n. 1, at 87; Goodrich, *supra* n. 1, at 8; Anand, *supra* n. 1, at 42; Burr, *supra* n. 1, at 64; Abramson, *supra* n. 1, at 6 (protocols 10 and 12); Klaus Peter Berger & J. Ole Jensen, *The Arbitrator's Mandate to Facilitate Settlement*, 40 Fordham Int'l L.J. 887, 913 (Apr. 2017).

68 International Bar Association (IBA) Guidelines on Conflicts of Interest in International Arbitration (2014), general standard 4(d) (emphasis added), available at <www.ibanet.org/Publications/publications_IBA_guides_and_free_materials.aspx> (accessed 14 Jan. 2018) [hereinafter, IBA Guidelines on CIIA].

69 This is because Section 32 of the DIS Rules authorising the tribunal to facilitate settlement at any stage is considered to already protect arbitrators against any challenges. Berger & Jensen, *supra* n. 67, at 912, referring to Siegfried H. Elsing, *Germany as a Place for International and Domestic Arbitrations – General Overview, in Arbitration in Germany: The Model Law in Practice* 3 (Karl-Heinz Böckstiegel et al. eds., 2d ed., Kluwer Law International 2015) and Daniele Favalli & Max K. Hasenclever, *The Role of Arbitrators in Settlement Proceedings*, 23 Mealey's Int'l Arb. Rep. 1, 3–4 (Jul. 2008).

70 Berger & Jensen, *supra* n. 67, at 912.

denied challenges on the ground of an arbitrator's involvement in settlement discussions to which the parties consented, even in the absence of an express waiver of the right to challenge an arbitrator.[71]

In *Duncan & Davis Nurseries New Plymouth Ltd. v. Honnor Block Ltd.*,[72] the High Court of New Zealand appeared to also side with commentators holding the first view. In that case, the parties to the dispute agreed to mediation and appointed the mediator, Ms Dean, QC. In their settlement agreement, parties included a clause 23 providing that if 'there is any dispute as to the terms of, or implementation of, this agreement the parties will appoint the mediator [Ms Dean] to determine any such dispute'.[73] Subsequently, the respondent contacted the mediator, asking her to arbitrate two disputes between the parties. The applicant requested Ms Dean to withdraw as arbitrator, which Ms Dean disregarded and proceeded to arbitrate the dispute. The applicant then filed an application with the High Court of New Zealand to remove Ms Dean as arbitrator. The court dismissed that application.

The court found that the applicant was aware of the grounds for challenging the arbitrator when it signed the settlement agreement containing clause 23. Therefore, the applicant was aware of situations that would give rise to justifiable doubts as to the arbitrator's impartiality when the appointment was made and, because of that, could not sustain a challenge to the arbitrator. The result was that the applicant had waived the right to challenge Ms Dean on the basis of her involvement as a mediator when the applicant signed the settlement agreement.[74] It should be noted that the High Court differentiated the situation of the same neutral med-arb from the situation in this case, where parties had already concluded mediation before they agreed that the mediator would become the arbitrator.[75] Nevertheless, the reasoning in this decision suggests that, if parties agree to the same neutral (arb)-med-arb, then they have implicitly waived their right to challenge the arbitrator or the award on the ground of arbitrator's participation as a mediator.[76]

The CEDR Commission appears to support both the first and third views. This is because the CEDR Commission distinguishes the situation when the same neutral arb-med-arb does not involve the use of caucuses from the situation when it does, and provides a different set of rules for each situation. The CEDR Rules apply to the former, whereas Appendix 2 to the Final Report of the CEDR Commission (CEDR Appendix 2) applies to the latter. Article 3(3) of the CEDR Rules specifies that by agreeing to apply the CEDR Rules

71 *Ibid* (referring to Oberlandesgericht [OLG] [Highest Regional Court] 3 Jan. 2008, Zeitschrift Schiedsverfahren [Schiedsvz]102, 104 (2008) (Ger.)).

72 *Duncan & Davis Nurseries New Plymouth Ltd. v. Honnor Block Ltd.*, 14 Jun. 2005, High Court of New Zealand, ¶ 6. HC Auckland, CIV 2005-404-2513 (2005) [hereinafter, *Duncan & Davis*] discussed in Rosoff, *supra* n. 1, at 95; Hindle, *supra* n. 1, at ¶12.

73 *Duncan & Davis, supra* n. 72, at ¶ 2.

74 Rosoff, *supra* n. 1, at 95.

75 Hindle, *supra* n. 1, at ¶12.

76 Rosoff, *supra* n. 1, at 95.

> The Parties agree that the Arbitral Tribunal's facilitation of settlement in accordance with these Rules will not be asserted by any Party as grounds for disqualifying the Arbitral Tribunal (or any member of it) or for challenging any award rendered by the Arbitral Tribunal.

In other words, parties' consent to the same neutral arb-med-arb that does not involve the use of caucuses, implies a waiver of the right to challenge the arbitrator and the award, if mediation does not lead to settlement, which corresponds to the first view.

The third view is supported by the CEDR Appendix 2, which provides safeguards for using the same neutral arb-med-arb that involves the use of caucuses. Paragraph 5 of the CEDR Appendix 2 states:

> If the parties have not consented to the mediator/conciliator resuming as arbitrator, and have not waived any right to object arising out of his role as mediator/conciliator, the arbitrator and/or his award may therefore be subject to challenge.

The use of the conjunction 'and' means that both consent and waiver are required to protect the arbitrator and the award from challenge.

In addition, paragraph 7.5 of the CEDR Appendix 2 specifies that

> The consent should include a statement that the parties will not at any later time use the fact that the arbitrator has acted as a mediator/conciliator as a basis for challenging the arbitrator or any award which the arbitrator may make (either alone or as part of a tribunal).

By indicating the need for both written consent and waiver, the CEDR Appendix 2 sides with commentators holding the third view.

This dual approach taken by the CEDR is not surprising. As discussed in Section 8.3.1, where no caucuses are held, the problem of due process does not arise and the issue of arbitrators' partiality becomes less problematic. This is the most probable reason for the CEDR not to require an express waiver for the same neutral arb-med-arb that does not involve the use of caucuses. The same neutral arb-med-arb that involves the use of caucuses, on the contrary, raises very serious concerns due to the danger that arbitrators may lose their impartiality and due to the risk of failure to adhere to the rules of due process. These serious concerns appear to be the reason why the CEDR requires a separate waiver for the situation of the same neutral arb-med-arb that involves the use of caucuses.

8.2.2.2 Should parties arrange for consent and waiver?

It is likely that parties' informed consent implies a waiver of their right to challenge the arbitrator and the award on the ground of the arbitrator's participation in mediation. It might, however, be impractical and could potentially jeopardise the entire arbitration if parties do not sign an express waiver.[77] In view of this, it is suggested that, unless the issue of waiver is regulated in the applicable legislation or rules, parties should specifically arrange an express written waiver of their right to challenge the arbitrator and the award on the ground of the arbitrator's participation in mediation.

It was argued in Section 8.2.1.3 that parties' consent to the same neutral (arb)-med-arb should be reiterated every time the process shifts from mediation to arbitration and vice versa. Likewise, it would be wise to sign written waivers between stages within the process, accepting that the neutral may continue to act on a different basis at each stage of the process.[78] This should also ensure that parties are able to differentiate between different roles that the same person takes at different times.

8.2.2.3 The effect of waiver

As noted in Section 8.2.2.1, parties' informed consent to the process and waiver are presumed to mean that parties waive their right to challenge arbitrators and the award on two specific grounds: first, partiality of arbitrators due to their participation in mediation; second, failure to adhere to the rules of due process due to the arbitrators' participation in caucuses. The first ground can be invoked in both situations – the same neutral (arb)-med-arb involving the use of caucuses or not – although in the former, the risk that arbitrators may become biased is undoubtedly higher. The second ground can be invoked only if the same neutral (arb)-med-arb involves the use of caucuses. This section will first investigate the effect of parties' waiver of the right to challenge arbitrators and the award on the first ground. Then it will explore the effect of parties' waiver of the right to challenge arbitrators and the award on the second ground.

8.2.2.3.1 WAIVER OF THE RIGHT TO AN IMPARTIAL TRIBUNAL

In international arbitration, arbitrators are expected to be independent and impartial.[79] At the same time, the preponderance of opinion favours the view that parties can waive the impartiality requirement to a large extent.[80] This view

77 *Ibid.*

78 Lack, *supra* n. 1, at 378.

79 James T. Peter, *Med-Arb in International Arbitration*, 4 Revista de Arbitragem e Mediação 155, 161 & 158 n. 28 (2005). Interestingly, in a three-member tribunal the 'American rule' is that party-appointed arbitrators are not subject to the impartiality requirement. *Finkelstein v. Smith*, 326 So 2d 39, 40 (Fla. App. 1976) ('Arbitrators appointed by disputants to a tripartite panel are expected by the disputants and should be understood by the courts to act as partisans – only one step removed from the controversy').

80 Almoguera, *supra* n. 5, at 121.

is supported by UNCITRAL ML on Arbitration,[81] the IBA Guidelines on CIIA,[82] and some court decisions.[83]

For example, Kaufmann-Kohler refers to a decision of the European Court of Human Rights on fair trial under Article 6 of the European Convention on Human Rights, which might be enlightening by analogy.[84] In that case, an arbitrator disclosed a conflict of interest, but parties consented to him acting as arbitrator anyway. One party later challenged the award alleging the arbitrator's bias as a result of his conflict of interest. The award was upheld by the national courts and the European court refused to set aside that decision. It held that the party had unequivocally consented to waive the requirement of impartiality. The unequivocal waiver given by a party who was represented by counsel and fully informed had to be enforced. It might be assumed from this case that arbitrators can act as mediators and their challenge or the challenge of the award is unlikely to be sustained, provided parties waive the requirement of impartiality.

Another example is the *Duncan* case, discussed in Section 8.2.2.1, where the High Court of New Zealand dismissed the application to remove the arbitrator who previously acted as the mediator. In this case the applicant was aware of a situation that could give rise to justifiable doubts as to the arbitrator's impartiality when the appointment was made and, thereby, could not sustain a viable challenge to the arbitrator.[85]

8.2.2.3.1.1 The effect of waiver of the right to an impartial tribunal depending on the point in time when it is given Pitkowitz and Richter suggest that two situations be distinguished, depending on the point in time when parties consent to the same neutral med-arb.[86] These authors hold the view that parties' informed consent implies a waiver of the right to challenge the arbitrator and the award on the ground of the arbitrator's participation in mediation.

The first situation is when parties agree at the outset, before using the same neutral med-arb, that, if mediation fails, they will proceed to

81 UNCITRAL Model Law on International Commercial Arbitration art 12(2) (effective 7 Jul. 2006), available at <www.uncitral.org/pdf/english/texts/arbitration/ml-arb/07-86998_Ebook.pdf> (accessed 3 Apr. 2018).

82 IBA Guidelines on CIIA, *supra* n. 68, ¶ 2.1.2 at 20. A prior involvement in the dispute by the arbitrator, including as mediator, constitutes a waivable conflict of interest under the IBA red list.

83 Rosoff, *supra* n. 1, at 93 (pointing out that parties successfully waive their right to challenge arbitrators for their conduct as mediators in many same neutral (arb)-med-arb proceedings in the United States).

84 Kaufmann-Kohler, *supra* n. 1.

85 *Duncan & Davis, supra* n. 72.

86 Matthias M. Pitkowitz & Marie-Therese Richter, *May a Neutral Third Person Serve as Arbitrator and Mediator in the Same Dispute?* 4 Schieds VZ 225, 228–229 (2009).

arbitration and former mediators will act as arbitrators.[87] It might be assumed that such agreements have to be binding on parties, who should not be allowed to object to the appointment of former mediators as arbitrators before and if the dispute proceeds to the arbitration stage.[88] This is the position taken by the IBA Guidelines on CIIA.[89] Allowing parties to object would be equivalent to the unilateral revocation of one's consent. This would make an agreement concerning the neutral impracticable in business life because no one could reasonably rely on it. Nevertheless, parties still preserve their right to challenge arbitrators during the proceedings if they consider that arbitrators demonstrate partiality. They can also challenge the award if it reveals arbitrators' bias.

The second situation is when parties initially decide only to mediate their dispute and, once the mediation efforts fail, they choose to proceed with arbitration. It is then that the parties appoint former mediators as arbitrators. Future arbitrators, however, have to disclose all circumstances that might raise reasonable doubts about their impartiality and independence. If, despite the disclosure, parties appoint former mediators as their arbitrators, they might be presumed to have waived their right to challenge arbitrators for reasons connected with their service as mediators. An argument against this view would be that any waiver will only apply to the parties if consent is given on a fully informed basis.[90] If something emerges during the course of arbitration that raises fresh doubts as to the arbitrators' impartiality, the earlier consent might become ineffective.[91] An illustration of such a situation might be that one party may know something about the mediation stage of the process and share this information subsequently with the other party, which makes them both wonder about the impartiality of a mediator-turned-arbitrator.

Hence, it appears that in both discussed situations, parties' waiver of the right to challenge arbitrators or the award is not absolute. If arbitrators manifest bias during or after arbitration, parties may still challenge them as arbitrators and the award. This view finds support in the literature.[92]

87 *Ibid,* at 229.

88 *Ibid.*

89 IBA Guidelines on CIIA, *supra* n. 68, general standard 4(d) (addressing the situation of the same neutral arb-med-arb).

90 Lang, *supra* n. 33, at 101.

91 *Ibid.*

92 *See, e.g.,* Casey, *supra* n. 4, at 17; Plant (2008), *supra* n. 1 discussed in Lack, *supra* n. 1, at 376; Rosoff, *supra* n. 1, at 98.

8.2.2.3.1.2 Importance of a timely challenge on the ground of partiality A party's challenge of the arbitrator and the award stands little chance of success if parties have given informed consent to the process and expressly waived the impartiality requirement. Nevertheless, as observed in Section 8.2.2.3.1.1, parties' waiver of the right to challenge the arbitrator and the award is not absolute. A party may still challenge the arbitrator and the award if the arbitrator manifests bias during or after arbitration. If a party believes that it has reasons to challenge the arbitrator or the award, it should do it promptly. This is because otherwise a party will waive its right to challenge the award on that basis at a later stage.[93] Section 73(1) of the English Arbitration Act, for example, provides that a party loses the right to object to any irregularity affecting the tribunal or the proceedings if it continues to take part in the arbitral proceedings without making any objection, either forthwith or within the allowed time. The IBA Guidelines on CIIA allow a party 30 days to raise an objection, failing which the party will be deemed to have waived the right to object.[94]

Two cases illustrate the importance of a timely challenge. The first case, *ASM Shipping Ltd of India v. TTMI Ltd of England*,[95] shows that a party is not permitted to hedge, to hang on to a possible challenge on grounds of bias pending the award and to complain only if they lose. In that case Morison J. said:

> In my judgment, by taking up the award, at the very least, the owners had lost any right they may have had to object to X QC's continued involvement in that part of the arbitral process. It is unacceptable to write making further objections after the hearing was concluded. X QC had made his decision not to recuse himself, rightly or wrongly, at the beginning of the third day. Owners were faced with a straight choice: come to the court and complain and seek his removal as a decision maker or let the matter drop. They could not get themselves into a position whereby if the award was in their favour they would drop their objection but make it in the event that the award went against them. A 'heads we win and tails you lose' position is not permissible in law as section 73 makes clear. The threat of objection cannot be held over the head of the tribunal until they make their decision and could be seen as an attempt to put unfair and undue pressure upon them.[96]

One of the two main issues that emerged in the second *Gao Haiyan* case[97] was whether the failure of a party to raise the issue of bias in arbitration resulted in a

93 Ross, *supra* n. 4, at 364; Lang, *supra* n. 33, at 100–101.

94 IBA Guidelines on CIIA, *supra* n. 68, general standard 4(a).

95 *ASM Shipping Ltd of India v. TTMI Ltd of England* (2006), EWCA Civ 1341 (16 Oct. 2006) [hereinafter, *ASM Shipping*].

96 Cited in Lang, *supra* n. 33, at 101.

97 *Gao Haiyan v. Keeneye Holdings Ltd* [2012] 1 HKRLD 627 (CA); *Gao Haiyan v. Keeneye Holdings Ltd* [2011] 3 HKC 157.

waiver of a right to do so at the stage of enforcement.[98] It appears to be one of the first cases in which the enforcement of an award arising from the same neutral arb-med-arb was considered.[99] The case is also interesting because it traces the positions of the parties step by step following the same neutral arb-med-arb proceedings up to the enforcement stage. As noted in the Introduction chapter, some commentators attribute to *Gao Haiyan* the recent emergence of the same neutral arb-med-arb as a 'hot topic' among practitioners.[100]

The dispute arose out of a share transfer agreement and a supplementary share transfer agreement (Agreements) signed in 2008 between Gao Haiyan and her husband (the Applicants) and Keeneye Holdings Limited and New Purple Golden Resources Development Limited (the Respondents). The Applicants disputed the validity of the Agreements. The Respondents commenced arbitration before the Xi'an Arbitration Commission of China (XAC). The XAC Rules permit parties to agree to mediate during arbitration, and the arbitrators to act as the mediators. At the end of the first hearing in December 2009, the arbitral tribunal (the Tribunal) suggested that the parties mediate, to which the parties agreed. The Tribunal decided to propose that the parties settle the case with the Respondents paying RMB 250 million to the Applicants and authorised the Secretary General of XAC (Pan) and one member of the Tribunal (Zhou) to contact the parties with the proposal. On 27 March 2010 over dinner in a hotel in Xi'an, Pan and Zhou informed 'a person related to' the Respondents (Zeng) that the Tribunal was going to find that the Agreements were valid but the Respondents had to pay RMB 250 million as compensation. Zeng was asked to 'work on' the Respondents. Both the Respondents and the Applicants rejected the settlement and arbitration resumed.[101] No complaint was brought about the conduct of Pan and Zhou. In June 2010, the Tribunal rendered an award that differed from the suggestion voiced over dinner. The Tribunal declared the

98 The second issue was whether the way the mediation had been conducted created apparent bias sufficient to refuse the enforcement of the award for being contrary to public policy. This issue is discussed in Section 9.5.2.

99 Kun, *supra* n. 42, at 538.

100 Justin D'Agostino, *Arb-Med Procedures and Enforcement in Hong Kong: The Crest of the Waiver?* Kluwer Arbitration Blog (16 Jan. 2012), available at <http://kluwerarbitrationblog.com/2012/01/16/arb-med-procedures-and-enforcement-in-hong-kong-the-crest-of-the-waiver/> (accessed 3 Apr. 2018); Matthew Townsend & James Rogers, *Arbitral Procedure and Med-Arb from English and Chinese Eyes*, 7(1) Global Arb. Rev. (2011); Michael Davison & Timothy Hill, *Med-Arb under Scrutiny*, 6(3) Global Arb. Rev. (2011); *Arbitration Update for the New Year 2012* (event by HK45 Arbitration Group, Hong Kong 12 Jan. 2012); *International Arbitration: The View from England and China* (event by the General Council of the Bar of England & Wales and the China Britain Law Institute, Beijing 22 Nov. 2011); *Hot Topics in International Arbitration 2011* (event by SJ Berwin, London 19 Sep. 2011) referred to in Zhuang-Hui Wu, *Enforcement of an Award Rendered Following Arb-Med Proceedings*, 27(1) Mealey's Int'l Arb. Report 1, 8 n. 120 (2012).

101 *Gao Haiyan v. Keeneye Holdings Ltd* [2011] 3 HKC 157 at ¶ 22 (setting out in more detail the circumstances in which the mediation was conducted).

Agreements invalid and recommended that the Respondents pay the Applicants RMB 50 million as compensation.

The Respondents challenged the award at the Xi'an Intermediate People's Court of Shaanxi (XIPCS) contending that the difference in the outcome was due to Pan's manipulation and the Tribunal's 'favouritism and malpractice'. The application was dismissed.

The Applicants then sought to enforce the award in Hong Kong. While the first ex parte application was granted, the Respondents appealed the order granting enforcement. They relied on Article 40E(3) of the Arbitration Ordinance (Cap 391) then in force, whereby the enforcement of an award may be refused if enforcement would be against public policy.

The Hong Kong High Court found that the meeting over a private dinner created apparent bias and refused to enforce the award for being contrary to public policy.[102] The court also found that the Respondents had not waived their right to raise bias by not complaining about the events of 27 March 2010 in the resumed arbitration.[103] Had the Respondents complained about bias, they would have risked antagonising the Tribunal and turning the Tribunal against them.[104]

About eight months later, the Hong Kong Court of Appeal reversed the High Court's judgment on appeal of the Applicants and held that the Applicants could enforce the award.[105] The Court of Appeal found that by failing to raise their objections in a timely fashion during arbitration, the Respondents had waived their right to do so at the stage of enforcement.[106]

Although the court determined that a clear case of waiver had been established, it proceeded in any case to consider whether the events of 27 March 2010 caused concerns of bias sufficient to give rise to the issue of public policy. The court was not satisfied that a case of apparent bias had been established, certainly not such that would lead the court to refuse the enforcement of the award.[107] Thus, the Court of Appeal upheld the award.

One of the important implications of the Court of Appeal ruling is that parties need to raise their objections to any procedural defects, including arbitrator's bias, in the course of the arbitral proceedings.[108] Otherwise, parties will be held to have waived their right to object.[109]

102 *Ibid* (the reasoning of the Court is discussed in Section 9.5.2 *infra*).

103 *Ibid,* at ¶¶ 84–85.

104 *Ibid,* at ¶ 87.

105 *Gao Haiyan v. Keeneye Holdings Ltd* [2012] 1 HKRLD 627 (CA).

106 *Ibid,* at ¶ 69.

107 *Ibid,* at ¶¶ 103–104, 106 (the reasoning of the court is discussed in Section 9.5.2 *infra*).

108 Friven Yeoh & Desmond Ang, *Reflections on Gao Haiyan – Of 'Arb-Med', 'Waivers', Cultural Contextualisation of Public Policy Arguments,* 29(3) J. Int'l. Arb. 285, 297 (2012); Wu, *supra* n. 100, at 9.

109 Wu, *supra* n. 100, at 9.

8.2.2.3.2 WAIVER OF THE RIGHT TO DUE PROCESS

It was noted in Section 3.3.2 that the same neutral (arb)-med-arb may offend the principles of due process because parties have no possibility to hear and respond to the issues raised by each of them in caucuses with the mediator who later becomes an arbitrator. The question is whether parties can waive their due process rights.

There is no clear and shared view in the literature on this issue. Commentators express contrasting views in this respect. Some raise serious doubts that parties can waive their due process rights.[110] For example, Pryles examines the UNCITRAL ML on Arbitration and notes that while parties enjoy very broad freedom in selecting the procedure to be followed, some ML provisions are mandatory and cannot, therefore, be excluded or modified by the parties.[111] While the ML does not expressly say so, Pryles considers it almost certain that a court would construe Article 18 as mandatory. Article 18 provides that '[t]he parties shall be treated with equality and each party shall be given a full opportunity of presenting his case'. Pryles concludes that if parties agreed that only the claimant would be heard in arbitration, this agreement would be struck down as invalid on account of Article 18 of the ML.[112] Section 33(1)(a) of the Arbitration Act 1996 (UK) resembles Article 18 of the ML. It provides that the tribunal 'shall act fairly and impartially as between the parties, giving each party a reasonable opportunity of putting his case and dealing with that of his opponent'. This section is mandatory because it is listed in Schedule 1 of the Act.

Pryles' view is supported by Holtzmann and Neuhaus, who observed:

> The freedom of the parties [under the Model Law] is subject only to the provisions of the Model Law, that is, to its mandatory provisions. The most fundamental of such provisions, from which the parties may not derogate, is the one contained in paragraph (3) [Art. 18 in the final text].[113]

110 *See, e.g.*, Leon & Peterson, *supra* n. 21, at 93 (noting that it remains an open question whether procedural fairness requirements tie the hands of the dual role neutral in the mediation phase and impede the use of caucuses); Christian Bühring-Uhle et al., *Arbitration and Mediation in International Business*, 264 (2d ed., Kluwer Law International 2006) (referring to an argument that the principles of natural justice cannot be set aside by parties' agreement, and, consequently, the validity of the award cannot be assured by means of a written consent to the dual role of the neutral); Michael Pryles, *Limits to Party Autonomy in Arbitral Procedure*, ICCA 3, available at <www.arbitration-icca.org/articles.html?author=Michael_Pryles&sort=author> (accessed 14 Jan. 2018) (arguing that parties cannot opt out of the rules of natural justice).

111 Pryles, *supra* n. 110, at 3.

112 *Ibid.*

113 Cited *ibid.*

A similar view was taken by the New Zealand Hamilton High Court in *Acorn Farms Ltd v. Schnuriger*.[114] The court considered it clear that it was beyond the power of parties to contract out of the fundamental requirements of due process. Consequently, it would be legally impossible to commit parties by contract to the same neutral (arb)-med-arb process in which the parties agreed that no breach of due process by the mediation phase of the same neutral (arb)-med-arb would be a ground for challenging an award that might result if completion of a formal arbitration proved necessary.

Some commentators disagree with this view and argue that waiving due process rights is not as outrageous as it may sound[115] and parties can do so provided they have considered the implications of this choice in the light of a particular dispute.[116] One supporter of this view, Elliott, speaks about the tension between the competing concepts of due process, which does not favour mixing mediation and arbitration processes and party autonomy that allows parties to resolve their dispute by whatever means, including by involving a dual role neutral.[117] According to Elliott, increasingly, although not universally, the party autonomy view seems to be winning the battle. Some case law provides support to this view. For example, the South Australian *Duke Group* case demonstrates that the Australian courts might allow caucuses with a judge or arbitrator where the parties consent beforehand.[118] The judge in that case referred to the following principles:

> It would be inconsistent with basic notions of fairness that a judge should take into account, or even receive, secret or private representations on behalf of a party or from a stranger with reference to a case which he has to decide.[119]

114 *Acorn Farms Ltd v. Schnuriger* [2003] 3 NZLR 121, at 2 ¶ 26 [hereinafter, *Acorn Farms*].

115 Sawada, *supra* n. 22, at 30 (concluding this after analysing the meaning of natural justice and its role as a mostly supplementary source for filling the gaps of the positive law); *see also* Blankenship, *supra* n. 1, at 36 (noting that the denial of due process is a criticism that can be overstated); Schneider, *supra* n. 1, at 94 (observing that the due process problem is much less serious than descriptions often suggest).

116 Talbot, *supra* n. 1, at 228; *see also* Alan L. Limbury, *Hybrid Dispute Resolution Processes – Getting the Best While Avoiding the Worst of Both Worlds?* in *CIArb's Mediation Compendium* 9 (A. Hudson-Tyreman et al. eds, London 2009) (noting that, to avoid difficulties with the same neutral med-arb while retaining caucuses in the mediation phase, parties may agree, either at the outset or before each stage, that the arbitrator does not need to observe the rules of procedural fairness when mediating, thus enabling caucuses); Lack, *supra* n. 1, at 374 (observing that a party may waive its due process rights if it is aware of the risk, trusts the neutral to act fairly and impartially and wants the mediator to act as arbitrator even after caucusing); Berger & Jensen, *supra* n. 67, at 914–915 (differentiating between a situation before a dispute has arisen and when arbitration is underway and suggesting that, while parties cannot waive their due process rights in the former, it is perfectly possible to do so in the latter).

117 David C. Elliott, *Med/Arb: Fraught with Danger or Ripe with Opportunity*, 34 Alta. L. Rev. 163, 169 (1995–1996).

118 *The Duke Group Ltd (in liq) v. Alamain Investments Ltd* [2003] SASC 272 [hereinafter, *Duke Group*] discussed in Limbury, *supra* n. 116, at 11–12; Limbury, *supra* n. 1, at 3.

119 *Re JRL; Ex parte CJL* (1986) 161 CLR 342 at 350 per Mason J cited in Limbury, *supra* n. 116, at 12 n. 26; Limbury, *supra* n. 1, at 3 n. 11.

> ... save in the most exceptional cases, there should be no communication or association between a judge and one of the parties (or the legal advisers or witnesses of such a party) otherwise than in the presence of or with the previous knowledge *or consent* of the other party.[120]

The words 'or consent' clearly indicate that caucuses with a judge or arbitrator are permissible where the parties consent beforehand, which accords with the principle of party autonomy.[121]

However, the debate on ability to waive due process rights does not seem to be over, except in those few jurisdictions that have addressed the issue directly. For example, in Australia, section 27 of the former Commercial Arbitration Acts (governing domestic arbitration) expressly permitted waiver of the right to due process.[122] The ability of parties to waive their due process rights in Australia was supported by the *Duke Group* case. This, however, is not possible for parties in New Zealand, as demonstrated by the *Acorn Farms* case. Some UK cases have suggested that the Human Rights Act 1998, which implemented the European Convention on Human Rights, may preclude waiver of the right to due process guaranteed by Article 6 of the Convention.[123] However, this may apply only to court proceedings, because other cases have held that parties to arbitration waive their Article 6 rights in the interests of privacy and finality.[124] In any event, some degree of legal risk to the award remains, since this point is not settled in many jurisdictions.[125]

The absence of a definite answer to the question of whether parties can waive their due process rights has prompted law and rule makers and commentators to come up with various solutions to minimise the risk of breach of due process and arbitrators' bias arising from the arbitrators' participation in caucuses. These will be discussed in the next section.

120 Per McInerney J in *R v. Magistrates' Court at Lilydale; Ex parte Ciccone* [1973] VR 122 at 127 (emphasis added), cited with approval by Gibbs CJ and Mason J in *Re JRL; Ex parte CJL* (1986) 161 CLR 342 at 346, 350 cited in Limbury, *supra* n. 116, at 12 n. 27.

121 Limbury, *supra* n. 116, at 12.

122 *See, e.g., Commercial Arbitration Act 1984* (NSW), s. 27(3) discussed in Alan L. Limbury, *Making Med-Arb Work in Australia*, 2(1) NYSBA New York Disp. Res. Law. 84, 85 (2009). Current CAAs address concerns related to the breach of due process differently. This will be discussed in Section 8.3.2.1 *infra*.

123 Limbury, *supra* n. 116, at 13 n. 29 (referring to *Halsey v. Milton Keynes General NHS Trust* (2004) EWCA Civ 576 (11 May 2004) and *Glencot Development & Design Ltd v. Ben Barrett & Son (Contractors) Ltd* (2001) EWHC Technology 15 (13 Feb. 2001)).

124 *Ibid,* at 13 n. 30 (referring to *Nordström-Janzon v. Netherlands* (ECHR 28101/95, 27 Nov. 1996); *North Range Shipping Ltd v. Seatrans Shipping Corp.* (2002) EWCA Civ 405 (14 Mar. 2002), cited with approval in *ASM Shipping, supra* n. 95).

125 Bühring-Uhle et al., *supra* n. 110, at 264 (concluding that, in the large majority of cases, full-intensity mediation in the shadow of arbitration will only be advisable if it is conducted by someone other than the arbitrator).

8.3 Safeguards related to caucuses

Although caucuses are widely regarded as invaluable in mediation,[126] their use becomes a fundamental concern in the context of the same neutral (arb)-med-arb[127] due to the risk of breach of due process and arbitrator's bias. Virtually all commentators proposing safeguards for using the same neutral (arb)-med-arb address the issue of caucuses. It is recommended that parties using the same neutral (arb)-med-arb at least specify whether caucuses are allowed.[128] Some commentators suggest a range of options, and, depending on the circumstance of each particular case, parties may choose the one that suits them the best.[129] Having analysed options suggested by different commentators that often overlap, this book has identified two main options:[130]

1 to exclude caucusing and conduct mediation in joint sessions only;
2 to caucus and, if parties do not settle in mediation and the dispute proceeds to arbitration, authorise the neutral
   (a) to disclose the information from caucuses to the other party before starting/resuming arbitration; or
   (b) to disregard the information from caucuses.

126 Bobette Wolski, *Arb-Med-Arb (and MSAs): A Whole Which Is Less than, not Greater than, the Sum of Its Parts?* 6(2) Contemp. Asia Arb. J. 249, 265 (2013); Brette L. Steele, *Enforcing International Commercial Mediation Agreements as Arbitral Awards under the New York Convention*, 54 UCLA L. Rev. 1385, 1403–1404 (2007); *but see* Nancy M. Thevenin, *Caucusing and the Cross-Cultural Divide*, in *Contemporary Issues in International Arbitration and Mediation: The Fordham Papers 2012*, 368–369 (Arthur W. Rovine ed., Martinus Nijhoff 2013) (observing that the role of caucuses in mediation has been the subject of debate in recent years and some authors propose that mediation should be conducted in joint sessions only).

127 Leon & Peterson, *supra* n. 21, at 93; Burr, *supra* n. 1, at 65; Bühring-Uhle et al., *supra* n. 110, at 263.

128 *See, e.g.*, Hindle, *supra* n. 1, at ¶ 40[c]; Burr, *supra* n. 1, at 64; Goodrich, *supra* n. 1, at 8; Ross, *supra* n. 4, at 364; Reiner, *supra* n. 1, at 28; Schneider, *supra* n. 1, at 87; Hwang, *supra* n. 1, at 578.

129 Each commentator suggests two or three options. *See, e.g.*, Sriram Panchu, *Arb-Med and Med-Arb Are Well-Suited to Meeting India's ADR Needs*, 2(1) NYSBA New York Disp. Res. Law. 103, 104 (2009); Hindle, *supra* n. 1, at ¶ 21; Kaufmann-Kohler, *supra* n. 1; Bartel, *supra* n. 5, at 686–688; Emilia Onyema, *The Use of Med-Arb in International Commercial Dispute Resolution*, 12 Am. Rev. Int'l Arb. 411, 417–418 (2001); Thomson, *supra* n. 3, at 3, 6–7; Ross, *supra* n. 4, at 364; Schneider, *supra* n. 1, at 94–96; M. Scott Donahey, *Seeking Harmony: Is the Asian Concept of the Conciliator/Arbitrator Applicable in the West?* 50(2) Disp. Res. J. 74, 77 (Apr.–Jun. 1995); M. Scott Donahey, *The Asian Concept of Conciliator/Arbitrator: Is It Translatable to the Western World?* 9–10 (on file with the ICC Documentation & Research Centre); Elliott, *supra* n. 117, at 175–176. Although the starting point of the CEDR Rules is 'no caucusing', the CEDR Commission offers safeguards to minimise risks involved in the approach that uses caucuses. CEDR Appendix 2, *supra* n. 22, at ¶ 7.1.

130 The list does not include options that have already been discussed in Chapters 6 and 7.

Both options are either promoted by legislation/rules or effectively practised in different countries of the world. Each option will be explored now in more detail.

8.3.1 The 'no caucusing' approach

The exclusion of caucuses from the mediation phase of the same neutral (arb)-med-arb should eliminate most of the behavioural and procedural concerns associated with this process discussed in Section 3.3.[131] Where no caucuses are held, the problem of due process does not arise and the issue of arbitrator's bias becomes less problematic.[132] Disallowing dual role neutrals from caucusing in the mediation stage also avoids committing in advance to additional clauses that attempt to minimise due process concerns related to that practice, such as those prohibiting the use of confidential information or requiring its disclosure.[133] The benefits of these clauses and concerns expressed in their respect are addressed in Section 8.3.2.

The 'no caucusing' approach is practised in parts of Continental Europe, particularly in Germany and countries following its tradition.[134] As noted in

131 *See, e.g.*, Ehle, *supra* n. 1, at 86, 92–93; Kaufmann-Kohler, *supra* n. 1; Onyema, *supra* n. 129, at 420; Sussman (2009), *supra* n. 19, at 71; Luke Nottage, *Arb-Med and New International Commercial Mediation Rules in Japan*, Japanese Law and the Asia-Pacific (21 Jul. 2009), available at <http://blogs.usyd.edu.au/japaneselaw/2009/07/arbmed_and_new_international_c_1.html> (accessed 3 Apr. 2018); Luke Nottage, *International Commercial Arbitration Developments in Model Law Jurisdictions: Japan Seen from Australia,* 29 JCAA Newsletter 3, 5–6 (Dec. 2012); Luke Nottage, *Drafting Arbitration Clauses to Minimise Costs and Delays in International Commercial Arbitration: An Asia-Pacific Perspective*, Japanese Law and the Asia-Pacific (16 May 2011), available at <http://blogs.usyd.edu.au/japaneselaw/2011/05/> (accessed 3 Apr. 2018); Ross, *supra* n. 4, at 363; Abramson, *supra* n. 1, at 12–13 (protocol 7); Hindle, *supra* n. 1, at ¶ 21[a]; Srikant Deekshitha & Arka Saha, *Amalgamating the Conciliatory and the Adjudicative: Hybrid Processes and Asian Arbitral Institutions*, III(1) Indian J. Arb. L. 76, 95 (Jodhpur 2014).

132 Peter, *supra* n. 79, at 174–175; James T. Peter, *Note & Comment: Med-Arb in International Arbitration*, 8 Am. Rev. Int'l Arb. 83, 114 (1997); *see also* Berger & Jensen, *supra* n. 67, at 915 (recommending to avoid caucuses because of the risk of the arbitrator's bias and expressing fewer concerns about the risk of breach of due process considering that, after commencement of arbitration, parties can waive their due process rights).

133 Luke Nottage, *Arb-Med in Australia: The Time has Come*, Japanese Law and the Asia-Pacific ¶ 6 (31 Oct. 2007), available at <http://blogs.usyd.edu.au/japaneselaw/ArbMed.pdf> (accessed 3 Apr. 2018).

134 Peter, *supra* n. 132, at 111; Christian Bühring-Uhle, *Arbitration and Mediation in International Business: Designing Procedures for Effective Conflict Management* 191, 195 (Kluwer Law International 1996); Christopher Newmark, *Controlling Time and Costs in Arbitration,* in *Leading Arbitrators' Guide to International Arbitration* 81, 88 (Lawrence W. Newman & Richard D. Hill eds., 2d ed., Juris Publishing, Inc. 2008); Peter, *supra* n. 79, at 174; Arthur Marriott, *Litigate, Arbitrate, Mediate – Frustrate? Breaking the Dispute Deadlock,* Clayton Utz, available at <www.claytonutz.com/ialecture/2005/transcript_2005.html> (accessed 14 Jan. 2018); Luke Nottage, *International Commercial Arbitration in Australia: What's New and What's Next?* 30(5) J. Int'l. Arb. 465, 490 (2013) (observing that the 'no caucusing' approach is common for international arbitrations involving arbitrators from Switzerland and some other European countries); Lack, *supra* n. 1, at 374 (noting that

Section 4.2, in facilitating settlement, German judges and arbitrators usually do not try to depart from the level of the legal issues to reveal the underlying interests of parties. This makes the issue of bias of even less concern in Germany.[135] The possible bias of an arbitrator due to a prejudgment of the case does not seem to be considered a serious problem in German proceedings.[136]

The Rules of some arbitration institutions and ADR providers promote the 'no caucusing' approach. For example, Article 5(2) of the CEDR Rules prohibits arbitral tribunals from meeting with any party separately or obtaining information from any party that is not shared with other parties.[137] Or, Section 8 of the IBA's Rules of Ethics for International Arbitrators explicitly discourages separate meetings where the arbitrator discusses settlement terms with only one of the parties at a time, because normally this would disqualify an arbitrator from any future participation in arbitration.[138] The CIArb International Practice Guideline 7 and COMA Med-Arbitration Rules demonstrate a similar approach.[139]

Another example is contained in the ICC Rules of Arbitration.[140] Article 24(1) of these Rules requires the arbitral tribunal to convene a case management conference to consult the parties on appropriate procedural measures to be adopted, including the techniques described in Appendix IV entitled 'Case Management Techniques'. Paragraph (h)(ii) of Appendix IV suggests, in particular, that, where agreed between the parties and the arbitral tribunal, the arbitral tribunal may take steps to facilitate settlement of the dispute, provided that every effort is made to ensure that any subsequent award is enforceable at law. The Secretariat's Guide to ICC Arbitration expands on this issue and recommends the

mediation in joint sessions only is quite common for Austria, Germany, and the Netherlands; the approach, however, is not widely used in Anglo-Saxon mediations); *but see* Richard Hill, *MED-ARB: New Coke or Swatch?* 13(1) Arb. Int'l. 105, 106 (1997) (observing that some Swiss arbitrators even go so far as to have ex parte communications (with the agreement of both parties) in order to seek a negotiated settlement).

135 Peter, *supra* n. 79, at 174–175; Peter, *supra* n. 132, at 113–114.

136 Peter, *supra* n. 79, at 175; Peter, *supra* n. 132, at 114.

137 This is a starting point. The Commission, however, offers safeguards that may minimise the risks involved in the approach that involves caucusing with parties. CEDR Appendix 2, *supra* n. 22, at ¶ 2.5.

138 International Bar Association (IBA) Rules of Ethics for International Arbitrators (1987), s. 8, available at <www.ibanet.org/Document/Default.aspx?DocumentUid=B21F3C32-190E-4FB0-9750-5459AE4E8498> (accessed 14 Jan. 2018).

139 Chartered Institute of Arbitrators (CIArb), *Practice Guideline 7: Guidelines for Arbitrators on the Use of ADR Procedures*, art 5, available at <www.ciarb.org/docs/default-source/practice-guidelines-protocols-and-rules/international-arbitration-guidelines-2011/2011adrprocedures.pdf?sfvrsn=10> (accessed 14 Jan. 2018); Colorado Mediators & Arbitrators Med-Arbitration Rules of Procedure, Rule MA-9(1) (effective 1 Nov. 2013), available at <http://coma.com/rules/med-arbitration#Rule%20MA-1.%20Purpose%20of%20Med-Arbitration%20Proceedings> (accessed 3 Apr. 2018).

140 International Court of Arbitration of the International Chamber of Commerce (ICC) Rules of Arbitration (effective 1 Mar. 2017), available at <https://iccwbo.org/dispute-resolution-services/arbitration/rules-of-arbitration/> (accessed 3 Apr. 2018).

arbitral tribunal to verify whether the chosen approach may give rise to concerns either at the place of arbitration or at likely places of enforcement, before adopting a settlement procedure that requires its participation.[141] The Guide specifies that any form of separate party caucusing is likely to give rise to such concerns.

The 'no caucusing' approach has also found support in case law. For example, in a New Zealand case, *Acorn Farms,* the Hamilton High Court held that the dual role neutral may not receive information without the knowledge of both parties, which rules out the possibility of caucusing at any stage of the process. The High Court considered it clear that it was beyond the power of parties to contract out of the fundamental requirements of due process.[142] The exclusion of caucuses was one of the five suggested precautions if arbitration is to be combined with mediation in New Zealand.[143]

Four of six practitioners interviewed for this study reported[144] that they refrain from caucusing with parties in the context of the same neutral (arb)-med-arb.[145] Two of them considered that their approach was conditioned by their legal and cultural background. In particular, the practitioner from Spain noted,

> I think there are different methods depending on, let's say, the legal culture in different countries. In my personal activity ... I prefer, if I try to mediate, I have to do that in the presence of everybody and with total transparency.[146]

The Australian practitioner, who does not caucus, pointed out China as a country where caucusing is a common practice. He observed,

> I am not comfortable with caucusing as an arbitrator. It's my cultural background. I know in China it's done all the time and it seems to work. But I don't myself feel sufficiently comfortable to do it.[147]

The Swiss practitioner admitted that although he had not done much caucusing himself, he did not see caucusing as very problematic.

141 Jason Fry et al., *The Secretariat's Guide to ICC Arbitration* 264–265 (International Chamber of Commerce 2012).

142 *Acorn Farms, supra* n. 114, at 2 ¶ 26.

143 *Ibid*, at ¶ 27. *See also* David A R Willams and Amokura Kawharu, *Arbitration and Dispute Resolution*, 2012 N.Z. L. Rev. 487, 490–491 (2012) (referring to this case to emphasise that arbitrators should only meet with parties in joint sessions).

144 All interviewed practitioners were asked how they deal with concerns related to the same neutral (arb)-med-arb (in particular, those related to the use of caucuses) in their practice. This question addressed questionnaire Result 2. *See* a summary of the significant questionnaire results in Section 5.4 *supra*.

145 The remaining two interviewees reported that they caucus with the parties in the mediation stage of the same neutral (arb)-med-arb. Their responses are reported in Section 8.3.2 *infra*.

146 Practitioner from Spain, Interview 1.

147 Practitioner from Australia, Interview 2.

> No. I have not done this [caucusing when acting as a mediator and an arbitrator in the same case]. But in one case – yes, I did some ... I would think the concern about caucusing is overdone and exaggerated. I think the concern with caucusing is more what the arbitrator acting as mediator would say himself about the prospective of the party with whom he is discussing ... especially if it is unilateral and used to coerce the party into a settlement.[148]

The Belgian practitioner, similarly to the above three, reported that he did not use caucuses in the mediation stage of the same neutral (arb)-med-arb.

> I have not done it because it is very dangerous to caucus ...[149]

However, contrary to the above three, this practitioner observed that he was against the use of the same neutral (arb)-med-arb, in principle. He said:

> I would never accept to be a conciliator; nobody would do that in Continental Europe. The only country that I know where they do that is in China.[150]

A theme that emerges from the above responses is that despite the fact that the four practitioners do not use caucuses themselves, at least half of them recognise that the same neutral (arb)-med-arb involving the use of caucuses is a common practice in some countries due to the legal culture.

Indeed, the attitude to the use of caucuses in the context of the same neutral (arb)-med-arb, similarly to the question of whether it is appropriate for the same neutral to act as a mediator and arbitrator, appears to be closely linked to the legal culture of a practitioner.[151] As observed in Section 4.3, the literature and some empirical evidence suggest that caucuses are widely used in the same neutral (arb)-med-arb in China and Japan, whereas they are uncommon for German judges and arbitrators. For the Chinese, caucusing is, arguably, not a serious problem because they seem to believe that the parties would not reveal to the mediator during the mediation phase any facts that the neutral could not have found out from the record.[152] Chinese arbitrators

148 Practitioner from Switzerland, Interview 4.

149 Practitioner from Belgium, Interview 6.

150 *Ibid.*

151 Kaufmann-Kohler, *supra* n. 1; CEDR Appendix 2, *supra* n. 22, at ¶ 8 (recognising that concerns about caucuses may not arise where the arbitration takes place in jurisdictions where the courts consider caucuses to be a common and accepted practice).

152 Gabrielle Kaufmann-Kohler & Fan Kun, *Integrating Mediation into Arbitration: Why It Works in China*, 25(4) J. Int'l. Arb. 479, 491 (2008); Fan Kun, *Arbitration in China: A Legal and Cultural Analysis* 168 (Hart Publishing 2013) (contrasting the Western world with the Oriental world); *see also* Donahey (ICC), *supra* n. 129, at 10 (observing that it is unclear whether parties actually convey any confidential information to the neutral during the mediation phase, and, if so, how it is dealt with.

seem to perceive caucusing as the best way to clarify the positions and to facilitate a negotiated settlement.[153] De Vera suggests that because of the dominance of cultural expectations over law in China, the restoration of harmony is the primary goal of a dispute resolution process regardless of the way this is achieved.[154] While not a matter of concern in China and Japan, in the Western world caucuses are regarded as one of the major dangers of the same neutral (arb)-med-arb because they may compromise the impartiality of an arbitrator and parties' due process rights[155] and raise other concerns discussed in Section 3.3. That is why the 'no caucusing' approach appears to be widely supported by Western practitioners and academics.

8.3.2 The caucusing approach: the use of information disclosed in caucuses in subsequent arbitration

Although caucuses are not necessarily an indispensable part of mediation,[156] their elimination may do more harm than good.[157] Barring caucuses might prevent the use of a process stage that many mediators consider vital for settlement efforts to be successful.[158] This will affect the efficiency of the mediation phase of the process.[159] Although not every mediation requires caucuses, the ability to caucus to explore parties' position and interests in confidence is regarded as an important part of the mediation process.[160]

Two of six interviewed practitioners said that they use caucuses in the mediation phase of the same neutral (arb)-med-arb. The Hong Kong practitioner who

153 Kaufmann-Kohler & Kun, *supra* n. 152, at 488.

154 Carlos De Vera, *Arbitrating Harmony: 'Med-Arb' and the Confluence of Culture and Rule of Law in the Resolution of International Commercial Disputes in China*, 18 Colum. J. Asian L. 149, 184 (2004).

155 *Ibid*; Nottage (2009), *supra* n. 131 (noting that European civil-law jurisdictions and the Anglo-Australian variant of the common-law tradition appear to remain sceptical about caucuses due to concerns about natural justice and bias tainting arbitrators).

156 Reiner, *supra* n. 1, at 24 (referring to his own experience of many mediations in the course of arbitration that were successful without caucuses).

157 Bartel, *supra* n. 5, at 687; Abramson, *supra* n. 1, at 12–13 (recommending in protocol 7 that the dual role neutral should refrain from caucusing, while observing, at the same time, that many settlers believe that caucuses create a unique opportunity for neutrals to help parties vent anger, clarify positions, and assess the acceptability of alternative settlement options).

158 Abramson, *supra* n. 1, at 12; Thomson, *supra* n. 3, at 3.

159 Deekshitha & Saha, *supra* n. 131, at 95–96 (observing that elimination of caucuses will inevitably decrease the efficiency of the mediation phase of the process); Nottage, *supra* n. 133, at ¶ 6 (noting that mediation in joint sessions only may have some chilling effect on parties' willingness to express views aimed at achieving settlement); Rosoff, *supra* n. 1, at 92 (observing that it should be entirely possible, although perhaps not as effective, for a dual role neutral to conduct mediation in joint sessions only).

160 Hindle, *supra* n. 1, at ¶ 20; Abramson, *supra* n. 1, at 12–13; Leon & Peterson, *supra* n. 21, at 93; Thomson, *supra* n. 3, at 7; Bartel, *supra* n. 5, at 687.

reported using caucuses in the mediation phase of the same neutral (arb)-med-arb at all times[161] emphasised the benefits of doing so. He noted,

> Actually it [caucusing] helps ... once you start to talk to your clients in the private sessions ... they start thinking: I have to spend more money, more time and everything is basically unpredictable and maybe I will have to go to appeal. May be if I settle within a reasonable area, I will get something done.[162]

It appears that one of the purposes of caucuses for this practitioner is to make sure that parties are aware about costs and delays that the arbitration process will involve. This approach may create a healthy pressure on parties to settle. It may also make parties feel coerced into settlement. These two options were discussed in Sections 3.2.5 and 3.3.1.4, respectively. A competent and experienced neutral would usually know how to achieve the first and avoid the second.

The US practitioner reported that in his experience caucuses were either used or not depending on whether the process started with mediation or arbitration. He said,

> Where I had been mediating ... yes, I had been caucusing. So, at this point when they [parties] say: we would like you now to arbitrate, we will have to talk about the fact that I have already caucused ... Where I had been appointed as an arbitrator and then put on the hat of the mediator, as far as I recall ... the entire mediation took place with everyone in a single room, in joint sessions.[163]

In short, this practitioner used caucuses in the mediation stage of the same neutral med-arb but did not in the mediation stage of the same neutral arb-med-arb. A possible explanation for this approach is that in the former case the practitioner was not aware that he would be asked to arbitrate until the completion of the mediation process. Consequently, the use of caucuses in mediation did not raise the concerns that are typically raised in the context of the same neutral (arb)-med-arb. This differed from the situation in the latter case, where the practitioner acted as a mediator after being appointed as an arbitrator. This should have brought concerns associated with the use of caucuses in the

161 This practitioner was selected to participate in an interview on the basis of the completed questionnaire (first phase of the empirical study) that demonstrated experience with combinations. This practitioner answered ‘always’ to the questionnaire question whether caucuses were used in mediation (the mediation stage of combinations). This practitioner reported experience as a dual role neutral, as a mediator in a dispute that involved arbitration with a different neutral, and as an arbitrator in a dispute that involved mediation with a different neutral.

162 Practitioner from Hong Kong, Interview 3.

163 Practitioner from the United States, Interview 5.

mediation stage of the same neutral (arb)-med-arb to the surface. It is likely that the practitioner refrained from using caucuses in this situation as a precaution.

As noted in Section 8.3.1, the CEDR is a proponent of the 'no caucusing' approach. At the same time, it says nothing against caucusing if this approach is acceptable to the courts of all jurisdictions which might have reason to evaluate the validity of the tribunal's award or if the parties explicitly consent to this approach and its consequences.[164] The latter point finds support in case law and the literature.

The South Australian *Duke Group* case discussed in Section 8.2.2.3.2 demonstrates that the Australian courts are likely to allow caucuses with a judge or arbitrator where the parties consent beforehand.[165] Similarly, in the literature, despite the scepticism surrounding the use of caucuses, commentators suggest that caucuses are permissible, provided parties consent to their use on a fully informed basis and put necessary safeguards in place.[166] Lack argues that the use of caucuses in the mediation phase of the same neutral (arb)-med-arb clearly calls for involvement of separate neutrals. He considers, however, that, provided special measures are implemented, the dual role neutrals can still engage in caucuses.[167] In Lack's view this is primarily a matter that should be left to the parties to decide.

Abramson suggests that caucuses are less risky if mediation is focused on solely forward-looking solutions, such as a continuing business relationship, instead of on backward-looking issues that typically arise in arbitration.[168] If mediation can be separated in time or subject matter from the issues in arbitration, a dual role neutral is much less likely to be affected by off-the-record information disclosed during mediation in the subsequent arbitration stage.

Overall, rules, case law, literature, and interview data support the use of caucuses in the mediation stage of the same neutral (arb)-med-arb, provided parties explicitly consent to it and the necessary safeguards are in place. The book turns now to examine two main safeguards for using caucuses in the same neutral (arb)-med-arb. To do so, the book draws on experiences of jurisdictions where the use of caucuses in the context of the same neutral (arb)-med-arb is permitted by law or is an accepted practice.

164 Final Report of the CEDR Commission on Settlement in International Arbitration (Nov. 2009), ¶ 2.4.3, available at <www.cedr.com/about_us/arbitration_commission/> (accessed 3 Apr. 2018). The CEDR recommends that the arbitrators explain to the parties the risks associated with caucuses and take necessary steps to minimise the risks, especially with respect to confidential information obtained in caucuses.

165 *Duke Group, supra* n. 118.

166 *See, e.g.,* Elliott, *supra* n. 117, at 167; Schneider, *supra* n. 1, at 95; Abramson, *supra* n. 1, at 13.

167 Lack, *supra* n. 1, at 373.

168 Abramson, *supra* n. 1, at 13.

8.3.2.1 A 'disclosure' rule

To protect an arbitrator against claims for bias and to meet due process requirements, the legislators in Singapore,[169] Hong Kong,[170] and Australia[171] require dual role neutrals, before resuming arbitral proceedings, to disclose to all parties as much of the confidential information obtained via prior caucuses as they consider material to the arbitral proceedings.

Although the disclosure may inhibit candid exchanges in mediation, it appears to be necessary not to offend the principles of due process, particularly as understood in the Anglo-American legal system,[172] because a decision maker might possess material information of which one side is unaware and to which it has had no opportunity to respond.[173] If due process requirements are met, the award should be safe against attack on this ground in the courts of the country where it is made and in any country of enforcement..[174]

Apart from minimising concerns relating to the breach of due process, the approach in Singapore, Hong Kong, and Australia is commended for leaving it up to arbitrators to decide what information they will rely on in making their decisions.[175] Only the information relied on must be disclosed to all parties. Arbitrators may equally decide that they will not rely on any information revealed in caucuses in making their decision. If either party wishes, it may submit evidence presented to the dual role neutral in mediation in arbitration once it resumes.[176]

Article 24(3) of the UNCITRAL ML on Arbitration also imposes a disclosure requirement on dual role neutrals by stating:

> All statements, documents, or other information supplied to the arbitral tribunal by one party shall be communicated to the other party.

Contrary to the approach taken by the legislators in Singapore, Hong Kong, and Australia, the requirement of disclosure under the UNCITRAL ML is not limited to the information that is material to the arbitral proceedings, but covers 'all statements, documents, or other information' supplied to arbitrators. Commentators on the UNCITRAL ML emphasise the mandatory nature

169 Singapore IAA, *supra* n. 23, s. 17 (3).

170 Hong Kong AO, *supra* n. 14, s. 33(4).

171 In Australia, the 'disclosure' rule is provided under the legislation governing domestic, but not international, arbitration. *See, e.g., Commercial Arbitration Act 2010* (NSW) s. 27D(7) [hereinafter, CAA 2010 (NSW)]; *Commercial Arbitration Act 2013* (Qld) s. 27D(7).

172 Lawday, *supra* n. 16, at 8; *see also* Donahey (ICC), *supra* n. 129, at 9–10 (referring to a threat posed by caucuses to the Western notions of due process).

173 Donahey (1995) *supra* n. 129, at 77; Donahey (ICC), *supra* n. 129, at 9–10; Schneider, *supra* n. 1, at 96.

174 Marriott, *supra* n. 57, at 545; Schneider, *supra* n. 1, at 96.

175 Marriott, *supra* n. 57, at 545.

176 *Ibid.*

of Article 24(3)[177] and note that its violation will most likely lead to the annulment of the award or the refusal of the award's enforcement.[178]

The UNCITRAL ML disclosure requirement applies in countries that base their legislation on the UNCITRAL ML and have adopted its Article 24(3) without amendment. For example, that is the case for New Zealand, where Article 24(3) of the First Schedule to the Arbitration Act 1996 repeats word for word the disclosure requirement contained in Article 24(3) of the UNCITRAL ML.

The New Zealand Court of Appeal endorsed the view that rather than being a default provision, Article 24(3) encapsulates an inalienable procedural right. The Court of Appeal observed that although the parties in arbitration have significant autonomy in setting up the arbitral process, it is not open to them to exclude Article 24(3).[179]

This research did not find any cases from other countries where courts would comment on the nature of Article 24(3) of the UNCITRAL ML adopted without amendment into countries' national legislation. However, taking into account the view of commentators on the UNCITRAL ML and the position of the New Zealand Court of Appeal, one might expect that courts in other countries will be inclined to regard Article 24(3) as a mandatory rather than a default provision. Thereby, if jurisdictions adopting the UNCITRAL ML intend to allow caucuses, it might be worth considering adding a specific legislative provision that would limit the requirement of disclosure to the confidential information obtained via prior caucuses that arbitrators consider material to the arbitral proceedings.

Even if it is not required under the applicable legislation, a number of commentators insist on the disclosure of all material information from mediation as a measure to manage concerns related to impartiality and due process.[180] Some

177 *See, e.g.*, Howard M. Holtzmann et al., *A Guide to the 2006 Amendments to the UNCITRAL Model Law on International Commercial Arbitration: Legislative History and Commentary*, 674 (Kluwer Law International 2015); Stavros L. Brekoulakis et al., *UNCITRAL Model Law, Chapter V, Article 24 [Hearings and written proceedings]*, in *Concise International Arbitration* 885–886 (Loukas A. Mistelis ed., 2d ed., Kluwer Law International 2015).

178 Brekoulakis et al., *supra* n. 177, at 885.

179 Hindle, *supra* n. 1, at ¶¶ 16–17 referring to *Methanex Motunui v. Spellman* [2004] 3 NZLR 454. Hindle observes that in view of this decision, in New Zealand, it might be necessary for neutrals to keep an accurate record of any and all information that is given to them in caucuses in case it needs to be disclosed later. *Ibid*, at ¶ 40[e]. Keeping an accurate record can turn into a very time-consuming task.

180 *See, e.g.*, Thomson, *supra* n. 3, at 5; Anand, *supra* n. 1, at 42; Houzhi Tang, *Combination of Arbitration with Conciliation – Arb-Med*, in *New Horizons in International Commercial Arbitration and Beyond*, 12 ICCA Congress Series 547, 554 (Albert Jan van den Berg ed., Kluwer Law International 2005) (adding that dual role neutrals should warn parties in the course of caucusing against giving any substantive information which they do not want the neutral to disclose to the other party); Ye, *supra* n. 5, at 482 (citing Professor Kaplan who endorses the combined use of mediation and arbitration by the same neutral under three conditions, including the disclosure of all material facts discovered in mediation if mediation efforts do not bring a settlement).

even suggest sample clauses. For example, Thomson, a Canadian practitioner, proposes the following clause:[181]

> If caucusing (meetings separately with each party) is used during the mediation process, any statements in caucusing which might influence the decision of the Mediator/Arbitrator will be revealed to the other side prior to the decision of the Mediator/Arbitrator (this will not apply if the parties reach an agreement).

8.3.2.1.1 CONCERNS RELATED TO THE 'DISCLOSURE' RULE

The Hong Kong, Singaporean, and Australian provisions raise three main concerns for some practitioners and academics.

8.3.2.1.1.1 Concern № 1: disclosure requirement The major concern relates to the obligation of a dual role neutral to disclose to all parties to arbitration, information that the neutral considers material to the arbitral proceedings.[182]

First, it puts the dual role neutral in a difficult position by requiring the neutral to take a view about what information is 'material' and how exactly to disclose it.[183] Furthermore, mediations usually take place in an informal fashion with few notes taken, which makes it difficult for the neutral to record everything accurately. It might happen that one party will object to the disclosure made by the neutral as not reflecting an accurate summary of what was said. Also, it would seem to open up the neutral to subsequent challenges as to what should have been disclosed.[184] In response to this criticism, the Hong Kong Law Revision Commission has suggested that, if the dual role neutral sends each party a list of the issues disclosed in confidence by that party that the dual role neutral regards as 'material' prior to any disclosure of that information, thereby allowing the party to comment to the dual role neutral prior to such disclosure, the chances of error in the process will be quite small.[185] In any case, no disclosure requirement will eliminate the possibility that one

181 Thomson, *supra* n. 3, at 7.

182 Goodrich, *supra* n. 1, at 6–7; Claire Wilson, *The Arb-Med Hybrid in Hong Kong – Much Ado about Nothing?* Kluwer Mediation Blog (1 Feb. 2012), available at <http://kluwermediationblog.com/2012/02/01/the-arb-med-hybrid-in-hong-kong-much-ado-about-nothing/> (accessed 3 Apr. 2018).

183 Goodrich, *supra* n. 1, at 7; Wolski, *supra* n. 126, at 263; Ross, *supra* n. 4, at 361 (observing that instead of determining what information is material, it might be more convenient for the neutral to simply disclose everything); Thomson, *supra* n. 3, at 7; Deekshitha & Saha, *supra* n. 131, at 92.

184 Goodrich, *supra* n. 1, at 7 (noting that one might say that, because the matters were confidential, the other party would find it difficult to mount a challenge; however, if the obligation to disclose is not enforceable, Goodrich wonders why give the neutral this difficult responsibility).

185 Donahey (1995), *supra* n. 129, at 77 n. 31; Donahey (ICC), *supra* n. 129, at 11 n. 31.

party will believe that the dual role neutral has been told a lie by the other party in caucuses but has chosen not to reveal it or withdraw.[186]

Second, parties' knowledge about possible disclosure may impede the success of mediation.[187] The parties are unlikely to be candid and forthcoming in caucuses if they know that information might be passed onto the other party.[188]

8.3.2.1.1.2 Concern № 2: ability to withdraw consent The legislative rules in Hong Kong and Singapore are also criticised for allowing a party to first agree that the arbitrator can mediate and later to withdraw its consent.[189] For example, Section 33(1) of the Hong Kong Arbitration Ordinance provides:

> If all parties consent in writing, and for so long as no party withdraws the party's consent in writing, an arbitrator may act as a mediator after the arbitral proceedings have commenced.

The Australian legislation governing domestic arbitration even prohibits dual role neutrals from conducting subsequent arbitration proceedings unless parties re-authorise them in writing to do so after mediation that did not result in settlement. For example, Section 27D(4) of the New South Wales' Commercial Arbitration Act 2010 (NSW) states:

> An arbitrator who has acted as mediator in mediation proceedings that are terminated may not conduct subsequent arbitration proceedings in relation to the dispute without the written consent of all the parties to the arbitration given on or after the termination of the mediation proceedings.

In both cases (Hong Kong and Singapore, on the one hand, and Australia, on the other) the legislation gives each party a veto over whether the dual role neutral can continue. There is a fear that parties may use this veto tactically to remove an arbitrator who is seen as unfavourable or simply to delay proceedings.[190]

186 Bartel, *supra* n. 5, at 687.
187 Goodrich, *supra* n. 1, at 7; Kaufmann-Kohler, *supra* n. 1; Wolski, *supra* n. 126, at 263; Deekshitha & Saha, *supra* n. 131, at 92; Wilson, *supra* n. 182; Schneider, *supra* n. 1, at 96.
188 Wolski, *supra* n. 126, at 263.
189 Goodrich, *supra* n. 1, at 7.
190 *Ibid; but see* Deekshitha & Saha, *supra* n. 131, at 96–97 (commending the requirement of the second consent in CAA 2010 (NSW), *supra* n. 171, s. 27D for mitigating the risk of bias and violation of principles of natural justice to a large extent and advocating for incorporation of a second consent requirement into the existing framework of the Hong Kong and Singaporean law because this will allow parties, after disclosure of the material information, to check for the danger of bias and act accordingly to protect their interests).

8.3.2.1.1.3 Concern № 3: limitation of party autonomy Finally, these provisions may infringe the autonomy of the parties in determining how they can regulate their (arb)-med-arb process.[191] It appears that attempts to encourage the practice of the same neutral (arb)-med-arb through the legislation in Hong Kong and Singapore have had the opposite effect,[192] which is supported by the empirical data collected for this book. As discussed in Section 5.2.3.2.5, none of the questionnaire participants practising in Singapore and Hong Kong reported any cases where this legislation applied in practice. Goodrich argues that countries which have traditionally embraced same neutral (arb)-med-arb seem to have managed perfectly well without any mandatory laws.[193] It is, therefore, desirable that any legislative regulation of the same neutral (arb)-med-arb be more circumscribed and that it respect more fully party autonomy. It could include a caveat that parties should receive adequate legal advice on the concerns raised by the process before entering into it.[194]

8.3.2.2 A 'disregard' rule

An alternative approach to dealing with information from caucuses to minimise bias and due process concerns is a so-called 'disregard' rule. In accordance with this rule, the dual role neutral when acting as an arbitrator is to take no account of material information obtained in caucusing and base the award only on evidence presented in arbitration. The 'disregard' rule has many supporters.[195] For some commentators, this rule is a better approach, as compared to the 'disclosure' rule,[196] if it is felt necessary to regulate the way of dealing with information from mediation rather than leave this question to parties and their legal advisers.[197]

The disregard rule is sometimes referred to as the Chinese solution/approach.[198] The Chinese appear to have no problem with disregarding information from caucuses.[199] They believe that if judges and jurors are trusted to be capable of

191 Goodrich, *supra* n. 1, at 6.

192 *Ibid,* at 8.

193 *Ibid,* at 6.

194 *Ibid,* at 8.

195 *See, e.g.,* Plant (2000), *supra* n. 1, at 146; Reiner, *supra* n. 1, at 27; Burr, *supra* n. 1, at 68; Leon & Peterson, *supra* n. 21, at 93; Bühring-Uhle et al., *supra* n. 110, at 249; Michael E. Schneider, *Combining Arbitration with Conciliation*, 1 Transnat'l Disp. Mgmt 9, 27–28 (2004); Marriott, *supra* n. 57, at 545; Limbury, *supra* n. 1, at 3; Abramson, *supra* n. 1, at 15 (Protocol 9).

196 Goodrich, *supra* n. 1, at 7; Deekshitha & Saha, *supra* n. 131, at 96.

197 Goodrich, *supra* n. 1, at 7.

198 Kaufmann-Kohler, *supra* n. 1; Wolski, *supra* n. 126, at 262; *but see* Donahey (ICC), *supra* n. 129, at 10 (observing that in Chinese practice once the mediator determines that efforts at mediation have failed, it is uncertain how the evidence that the mediator has received in confidence is treated and whether it influences any award that may be issued).

199 Wolski, *supra* n. 126, at 263.

disregarding inadmissible evidence, one should not doubt the ability of well-trained arbitrators to remain impartial despite the information obtained in mediation.[200] The 2015 CIETAC Arbitration Rules[201] contain a provision that prohibits the use of any information from mediation in the subsequent arbitration. Article 47(9) of the 2015 CIETAC Arbitration Rules provides:

> Where conciliation is not successful, neither party may invoke any opinion, view or statement, and any proposal or proposition expressing acceptance or opposition by either party or by the arbitral tribunal in the process of conciliation as grounds for any claim, defense or counterclaim in the subsequent arbitral proceedings, judicial proceedings, or any other proceedings.

The Chinese Arbitration Law does not have any similar provision. The disregard rule appears to be practised in the United States due to the statutory protection of mediation confidentiality.

8.3.2.2.1 US COURTS APPLYING THE 'DISREGARD' RULE

Indeed, in the US, general mediation confidentiality statutes, court rules, and other laws provide for the confidentiality of mediation communications without exception for the same neutral (arb)-med-arb.[202] This means that communications made in both private and joint mediation sessions cannot be used in the subsequent arbitration stage.[203] Case law, discussed below, demonstrates that courts examine not only whether parties consented to the same neutral (arb)-med-arb but also whether they agreed to the use of mediation communications in subsequent arbitration.

The Ohio Court of Appeals in *Bowden v. Weickert*[204] dealt with an arbitrator who attempted to mediate the dispute. Upon failure of the mediation process,

200 *Ibid*; Kaufmann-Kohler & Kun, *supra* n. 152, at 491; Kun, *supra* n. 152, at 168.

201 China International Economic and Trade Arbitration Commission (CIETAC) Arbitration Rules (effective 1 Jan. 2015), available at <www.cietac.org/index.php?m=Page&a=index&id=106&l=en> (accessed 3 Apr. 2018).

202 Kristen M. Blankley, *Keeping a Secret from Yourself? Confidentiality When the Same Neutral Serves Both as Mediator and as Arbitrator in the Same Case*, 63 Baylor L. Rev. 317, 338–339 (Spring 2011). Unif. Mediation Act ss. 4, 5, 7A U.L.A. 117 (Supp. 2010) [hereinafter, UMA]. Even those US states that have not adopted the UMA may also provide for the confidentiality of mediation communications, which should be checked by the same neutral (arb)-med-arb's participants before engaging in the process. *Ibid*, at 342 & n. 100.

203 Similar prohibitions against the admission of mediation communications in arbitration can be found in the legislation of other countries. *See, e.g.,* Bermuda International Conciliation and Arbitration Act s. 10 (1993); Indian Arbitration and Conciliation Act, Act No. 26 of 1996, s. 81; Uganda Arbitration and Conciliation Act s. 66 (2000). For more examples, *see* Ellen E. Deason, *Combinations of Mediation and Arbitration with the Same Neutral: A Framework for Judicial Review*, 5 Y.B. On Arb. & Mediation 219, 227 n. 47 (2013).

204 *Bowden v. Weickert*, No. S-02-017, 2003 WL 21419175 (Ohio App. 6 Dist. 20 Jun. 2003) discussed in Sussman (2009), *supra* n. 19, at 72; Sussman (2011), *supra* n. 19, at 387–388; Blankley, *supra* n. 202, at 346–351.

the dual role neutral returned to his role as arbitrator and rendered the award. The court reviewed the same neutral arb-med-arb and delineated the nature of the agreement necessary for this kind of process:

> At a minimum, the record must include clear evidence that the parties have agreed to engage in a med-arb process [same neutral arb-med-arb], by allowing a court-appointed arbitrator to function as the mediator of their dispute. The record must also contain: (1) evidence that the parties are aware that the mediator will function as an arbitrator if the mediation attempt fails; (2) a written stipulation as to the agreed method of submitting their disputed factual issues to an arbitrator if the mediation fails; and (3) evidence of whether the parties agree to waive the confidentiality requirements imposed on the mediation process ... in the event that their disputes are later arbitrated.

Finding that the arbitrator had relied on information obtained in his role as mediator in violation of statutory protections of mediation confidentiality and that there had been no explicit agreement by the parties regarding the use of confidential information, the court held that the use of the same neutral as arbitrator and mediator rendered the arbitrator's decision 'arbitrary and capricious' on its face. The award was set aside.[205]

In *Town of Clinton v. Geological Services Corp*,[206] a Massachusetts superior court reiterated the reasoning of Bowden and further stated that waiver of mediation privilege must be explicitly made and that consenting to the same neutral arb-med-arb procedure would not automatically and implicitly result in a waiver of mediation confidentiality.

California's Second District Court of Appeals held in *John Eisendrath v. Superior Court*[207] that there can be no implied waiver of mediation privilege. Mediation communications could only be disclosed with the express consent of all participants (as distinguished from parties), including the disputants, other non-parties in attendance, and the mediator.

At the same time, as demonstrated by the next case, the court will not necessarily vacate the award even in the absence of an express consent on the use of confidential information in limited circumstances.

205 *See also Township of Aberdeen v. Patrolmen's Benevolent Association*, Local 163, 669 A.2d 291, 294 (N.J. Super. Ct. App. Div. 17 Jan. 1996) (where the Superior Court of New Jersey vacated the award on the ground that the arbitrator improperly relied upon information he learned during the mediation process but that was not presented at the arbitration hearing when rendering the arbitration decision) discussed in Blankley, *supra* n. 202, at 356–358.

206 *Town of Clinton v. Geological Servs. Corp.*, No. 04-0462A, 2006 WL 3246464, at §1 (Mass. Super. 8 Nov. 2006) (Unreported Memo) discussed in Deekshitha & Saha, *supra* n. 131, at 90; Blankley, *supra* n. 202, at 351–354.

207 *John Eisendrath v. Superior Court* (2003 DJDAR 5849) discussed in Andrew Tuch, *Dispute Resolution Update*, 6(9) ADR Bulletin 184, 186–187 (2004).

In *Logan v. Logan*,[208] the losing party sought to set aside the award on the grounds that the dual role neutral referred to confidential information from mediation in his arbitration award. The court noted that:

> If there was an improper reference to the mediation in the arbitration proceedings, this would constitute grounds for vacating or modifying the arbitration order and subsequent judgment, if the reference materially affected appellants' substantial rights.

However, on the facts before it, the court refused to set aside the award, stating that it was not convinced that the reference in the arbitration order to matters that occurred in mediation 'materially affected substantial rights'.

As shown in the next case, where parties have consented, the use of confidential information by the arbitrator in the award will not provide a basis for vacating the award.

In *U.S. Steel Mining Company v. Wilson Downhole Services*,[209] the parties had agreed to have the mediator serve as the arbitrator if mediation failed to lead to a resolution and empowered the mediator, now arbitrator, to select between the parties competing proposals in baseball arbitration. The parties expressly authorised the dual role neutral to rely on confidential mediation disclosures in reaching his decision. The parties' agreement provided:

> The Parties anticipate that ex parte communications with the Arbitrator will occur during the course of the mediation. The Parties agree that the Arbitrator, in evaluating each Party's best and final offer, may rely on information he deems relevant, whether obtained in an ex parte communication or otherwise, in making the final Award.

In attacking the award, the challenging party claimed fraud in the presentation of information in the mediation. The court held that such evidence of fraud had to be clear and convincing and no such finding could be made on the facts presented in the face of the consent given.

Although none of the US courts in the abovementioned cases specifically endorsed the same neutral (arb)-med-arb, courts appeared to support parties' choice of using this process under certain conditions. First and foremost, parties need to express in writing their intent to engage in the same neutral (arb)-med-arb. Second, parties are to specify whether they waive the confidentiality of mediation communications if the neutral becomes the arbitrator and proceeds

208 *Logan v. Logan*, No. F051606, 2007 WL 2994640 (Cal. App. 5 Dist. 16 Oct. 2007) discussed in Sussman (2009), *supra* n. 19, at 72–73; Sussman (2011), *supra* n. 19, at 389.

209 *U.S. Steel Mining Company v. Wilson Downhole Services*, No 02:00CV1758, 2006 WL 2869535 (W.D. Pa. 5 Oct. 2006) discussed in Sussman (2009), *supra* n. 19, at 72; Sussman (2011), *supra* n. 19, at 388.

to render an arbitration award. Interestingly, Blankley recommends that parties record their choice in writing, regardless of whether they agree to waive or maintain the confidentiality of mediation communications.[210] Parties who choose the latter option must be aware that subsequent arbitration would require a full presentation in front of the arbitrator, even if that presentation is substantially duplicative of information discussed at mediation.[211] This might deprive parties of one of the benefits of the same neutral (arb)-med-arb – the ability to have a truncated arbitration hearing because neutrals familiarised themselves with the case during the mediation stage.[212]

8.3.2.2.2 CRITIQUE OF THE 'DISREGARD' RULE

The ability of any neutral to disregard information disclosed in caucuses is the subject of discussion in the literature.[213] Some commentators contend that arbitrators should have no problem with following a disregard rule, whereas others argue that this is unachievable in practice. This difference in views, similarly to the difference in views on whether it is appropriate to use caucuses in the same neutral (arb)-med-arb, can be explained by reference to the practitioners' legal culture.[214] Lew observes that, while in China awards tend to be based solely on what is heard in arbitration, not in mediation,[215] for Western minds it seems impossible that arbitrators can mentally disregard everything heard in the mediation phase.[216] Even if arbitrators believe in their capacity to do so, parties are unlikely to accept this, particularly when a decision is made against them.[217] This might well be the case. The available case law from the United States presented in Section 8.3.2.2.1, however, demonstrates that parties may succeed in vacating an arbitral award rendered by arbitrators who previously acted as mediators only if there is a reference to confidential information from mediation in the arbitral award without parties' explicit agreement to it. In *Logan v. Logan*, the court even stated that for an award to be vacated, the reference to confidential information (to which parties did not explicitly agree) needs to materially affect party's substantial rights. It appears that in the absence of a reference to confidential information from mediation in an arbitral award (to which parties did not explicitly agree), a party's challenge of the award in the United States stands little chance of success.

210 Blankley, *supra* n. 202, at 366. Her own choice, however, is for parties to waive confidentiality of mediation communications, at least, with respect to anything said in joint sessions. *Ibid.*
211 Blankley, *supra* n. 202, at 366.
212 *Ibid*, at 342.
213 *See, e.g.*, Lew, *supra* n. 3, at 426.
214 *Ibid.*
215 *Ibid* (quoting Tang Houzhi).
216 *Ibid.*
217 *Ibid.*

8.3.2.2.2.1 Reasons why arbitrators may have no problem with following the 'disregard' rule Some commentators are convinced that arbitrators should have little difficulty in following the disregard rule[218] and state that concerns about possible contamination of neutrals by receiving information in caucuses are overstated.[219] After all, all decision makers are taught to decide only on the basis of properly admitted applicable evidence.[220] These commentators draw parallels between judges and arbitrators and suggest that if one presumes that judges are able to render decisions based only upon admissible evidence and that they are capable of blocking out extraneous, yet potentially prejudicial, matters, there is no reason why dual role neutrals cannot be afforded the same presumption.[221]

Also, the requirement to disregard information from caucuses appears to be little different in principle from other occasions in which arbitrators are aware of certain matters but are required to disregard them in reaching their decision. For example, arbitrators may have to consider and rule on the admissibility of certain evidence, and, if they hold that it is inadmissible, they need to disregard it.[222] Apart from inadmissible evidence, arbitrators may be required to disregard information that is not presented in arbitration, such as public documents or information in the media.[223] Arbitrators, generally, often receive documents and information of which they take note and to which the other party replies only months later in the responding statement.[224] Arbitrators read the initial material with a critical mind, expecting that the other side will respond to most of what is said in these statements, and it is unlikely that dual role neutrals will react differently to information revealed in caucuses where their critical sense is likely to be sharpened.[225]

Any concerns about possible contamination of arbitrators by receiving information in caucuses can be reduced by requiring dual role neutrals upon conclusion of mediation to inform parties whether they feel able to conduct arbitration impartially.[226] In particular, dual role neutrals need to report whether, in

218 *See, e.g.*, Mark Goodrich, *Arb-med: Ideal Solution or Dangerous Heresy?* 15(1) Int'l Arb. L. Rev. 12, 17 (2012); Goodrich, *supra* n. 1, at 7; Marriott, *supra* n. 57, at 544.

219 Marriott, *supra* n. 57, at 544; Thomson, *supra* n. 3, at 8; Schneider, *supra* n. 1, at 94 (noting that arbitrators generally are not quite as gullible as critics of caucusing seem to presume).

220 Marriott, *supra* n. 57, at 544.

221 *Ibid*; Peter, *supra* n. 79, at 160; Thomson, *supra* n. 3, at 8.

222 Goodrich, *supra* n. 1, at 7; *see also* Schneider, *supra* n. 1, at 94 (observing that sometimes improperly submitted arguments are rejected after the arbitrators have become aware of them); Marriott, *supra* n. 57, at 544 (noting that arbitrators often get documents or hear testimony that is irrelevant but may be prejudicial to one side, which they must and do disregard in reaching their decisions).

223 Rosoff, *supra* n. 1, at 97.

224 Schneider, *supra* n. 1, at 94.

225 *Ibid.*

226 Limbury, *supra* n. 1, at 3; Limbury, *supra* n. 122, at 85.

formulating the award, they feel able to disregard confidential information from mediation. If dual role neutrals feel that they are unable to ignore confidential information, these neutrals should resign.[227] The IBA Guidelines on CIIA and CEDR Appendix 2 contain the same recommendation.[228] Alternatively, parties may expressly permit dual role neutrals to continue as arbitrators and to use confidential information in arbitration.[229]

Considering that courts may vacate awards or disqualify arbitrators if they manifest partiality in the arbitration proceedings or in the award, arbitrators need to ensure that they do not rely in arbitration on anything learned in mediation.[230] To achieve this, dual role neutrals may provide at the outset of the arbitration phase a written statement of what they apprehend to be the issues to be determined and the facts as then understood, and invite parties to comment on it, including to object to the admissibility of any of the facts. Admitted facts would provide a starting point for the arbitration phase.[231]

8.3.2.2.2.2 Reasons why arbitrators may find it difficult to follow the 'disregard' rule Some authors argue that the idea of erasing things from one's mind is an artificial one and unrealistic in practice: '[u]nlike a computer keyboard, one could not simply press a "delete" key or "empty trash can"'.[232] The requirement to disregard does not avoid the risk that arbitrators may be influenced by what they have heard in caucuses.[233] This is because 'bias is such an insidious thing that, even though a person may in good faith believe that he was acting impartially, his mind may unconsciously be affected by bias'.[234]

The argument that an arbitrator should be able to block out information as a judge does when applying the rules of evidence appears to be insufficient to

227 Limbury, *supra* n. 1, at 3; Limbury, *supra* n. 122, at 85; Rosoff, *supra* n. 1, at 97 (observing that it may only be in extreme circumstances where a dual role neutral may feel compelled to resign or refuse appointment because of a bias created in mediation; for that to happen the confidential information from mediation would have to create a bias that the dual role neutral could not ignore).

228 IBA Guidelines on CIIA, *supra* n. 68, general standard 4(d); CEDR Appendix 2, *supra* n. 22, at ¶ 7.6.

229 Limbury, *supra* n. 1, at 3.

230 *Ibid*; Limbury, *supra* n. 122, at 86.

231 Limbury, *supra* n. 116, at 10.

232 Lawrence G. S. Boo, *Commentary on Issues Involving Confidentiality,* in *New Horizons in International Commercial Arbitration and Beyond*, 12 ICCA Congress Series 523, 528 (Albert Jan van den Berg ed., Kluwer Law International 2005); *see also* Nottage, *supra* n. 133, at ¶ 6 (noting that the requirement to disregard 'is probably unrealistic in practice').

233 Kaufmann-Kohler, *supra* n. 1; Lang, *supra* n. 33, at 100 (observing that it is arrogant to suggest that there is no chance for a neutral to become influenced in rendering an award by what has been said by the parties in private during the mediation stage); Deekshitha & Saha, *supra* n. 131, at 96 (noting that the disregard rule does not resolve the issue of residual inherent bias, which owing to its psychological and subconscious nature is not something a procedural rule can eliminate).

234 Lang, *supra* n. 33, at 100 (quoting Lord Goff from *R v. Gough* [1993] UKHL 1 (20 May 1993)).

overcome the problem of apprehended bias.[235] The rules of evidence relate to legally relevant facts which can be consciously blocked out for decision purposes, that is, the particular facts and their impact on the decision can be rationally determined. And even then, the available empirical data demonstrates that judges do not disregard inadmissible information when making substantive decisions in civil and criminal cases because, arguably, they simply cannot ignore it much of the time.[236] The empirical data further shows that judges are less able to ignore inadmissible evidence when making factual determinations that they consider less amenable to judicial review.[237] Pappas concludes that arbitrators facing little risk of review are probably even less able not to consider mediation communications during the arbitration phase.[238]

Additionally, arbitrators may have difficulty with consciously blocking out information conveyed during mediation because of its legal irrelevance: unlike under the rules of evidence, such legally irrelevant information should not have an impact on the outcome of the case in the first place.[239] As no rational connection exists between such legally irrelevant information and the outcome of the decision, it is not possible to rationally isolate the information which should be blocked out.[240] The dual role neutral may subconsciously and for whatever reason become more understanding and supportive of a particular party's position after becoming aware of certain facts. This kind of information is hard to consciously block out.[241]

At the same time, impartiality, being understood as a complete lack of opinion, is psychologically impossible.[242] Even if arbitrators or mediators start as impartial, they will at a certain point become biased, even if unconsciously so.[243] Also, impartiality could never be understood in an absolute way, which would exclude preconceptions, because neutrals who have lived in the world 'will invariably come to a case with perspectives and beliefs and preconceptions that bear the stamp of their past experiences'.[244]

235 Peter, *supra* n. 132, at 93–94.

236 Andrew J. Wistrich et al., *Can Judges Ignore Inadmissible Information? The Difficulty of Deliberately Disregarding*, 153 U.Pa.L.Rev. 1251, 1323 (Mar. 2005) (reporting the results of experiments designed to test the ability of trial judges to disregard inadmissible information).

237 *Ibid*, at 1324.

238 Brian A. Pappas, *Med-Arb: The Best of Both Worlds May Be Too Good to Be True: A Response to Weisman*, 19 Disp. Resol. Mag. 42, 42 (2013).

239 *Ibid*; Limbury, *supra* n. 122, at 85 (making an interesting observation: while in court proceedings or arbitration all parties are aware of the evidence that has been ruled inadmissible, in the same neutral (arb)-med-arb only one party knows what confidential information it has confided to the neutral).

240 Peter, *supra* n. 132, at 94.

241 *Ibid.*

242 Almoguera, *supra* n. 5, at 128; Peter, *supra* n. 79, at 158 n. 28.

243 Almoguera, *supra* n. 5, at 128 (quoting Jeremy Lack).

244 Peter, *supra* n. 79, at 158 n. 28 citing Alan Scott Rau, *Integrity in Private Judging*, 38 S. Tex. L. Rev. 485, 488 (1997).

Moreover, according to some commentators, it is not only unrealistic to expect mediators-turned-arbitrators, when making an arbitration award, to put aside their awareness of underlying interests that surfaced in mediation, but it may well lessen the quality of the decision and affect the efficiency of the process, even if it is theoretically and practically possible to do so.[245] A dual role neutral cannot and should not be expected to merely block out information gleaned from mediation because this is the reason why parties have chosen the same neutral (arb)-med-arb instead of opting for diff neutral (arb)-med-arb.[246]

Nevertheless, in view of all the discussed concerns raised about both the disclosure and disregard rule, some commentators remain pessimistic about the ability to overcome them and advocate either the elimination of caucuses altogether or the use of the alternative approaches examined in Chapters 6 and 7.[247]

One of the major concerns associated with the use of caucuses in the same neutral (arb)-med-arb is the risk of breach of due process due to the arbitrator's participation in caucuses. It was noted in Section 8.2.2.3.2 that for the moment there is no definite answer to the question of whether parties can waive their due process rights. Both the disclosure and disregard rule minimise but do not eliminate the risk of breach of due process. To remedy this situation, the book suggests that jurisdictions permitting the same neutral (arb)-med-arb involving the use of caucuses should specify that parties using this process waive their due process rights on the ground of arbitrator's participation in caucuses.

8.4 Conclusion

This chapter has investigated the third way to address behavioural and procedural concerns associated with the same neutral (arb)-med-arb, the implementation of safeguards for using the same neutral (arb)-med-arb. It has identified two key safeguards that parties need to consider and should implement if they choose the same neutral (arb)-med-arb as their dispute resolution mechanism: party consent and one of the two safeguard options for reducing concerns related to the use of caucuses.

8.4.1 Safeguard 1: party consent

Party written consent is the first and critical safeguard for using the same neutral (arb)-med-arb that must be observed to protect the arbitrator and the award

245 Elliott, *supra* n. 117, at 167; Peter, *supra* n. 132, at 94 (adding that it is not even possible to exclude all information in general gained during mediation from being considered in arbitration; this would render the efficiency argument obsolete).

246 De Vera, *supra* n. 154, at 186.

247 Nottage, *supra* n. 133, at ¶6 (criticising both the disregard rule for being 'unrealistic in practice' and the disclosure rule for going 'too far' and advocating a 'no caucusing' approach); Kun, *supra* n. 42, at 554 (observing that neither approach appears to be capable of totally eliminating the risks of potential contamination of neutrals when they are exposed to information in caucuses, and suggesting the consideration of alternative approaches).

from a challenge on the ground of the arbitrator's participation in mediation. Party consent is required in accordance with the consensual nature of arbitration and mediation and parties' procedural autonomy. To be valid, party consent needs to satisfy two essential criteria. First, consent must be a result of parties' voluntary choice, which means that parties cannot be coerced into the process. One of the ways to ensure that parties choose the same neutral (arb)-med-arb voluntarily is through allowing them to discuss separately and between themselves (outside the neutral's presence) any process design option. Second, consent must be informed, which means that parties must be fully aware of the risks and concerns associated with the same neutral (arb)-med-arb.

Apart from giving their informed and voluntary consent, and unless the issue of waiver is regulated in the applicable legislation or rules, it is advisable that parties arrange an express written waiver of their right to challenge the arbitrator and the award on the ground of the arbitrator's participation in mediation. In the absence of such an express written waiver, it is arguable that parties' written consent to the process will imply the said waiver.

Although it is widely recognised that parties can waive the impartiality requirement, the waiver is not absolute. If arbitrators manifest bias during or after arbitration, parties may still challenge them or the award. It is unclear whether parties can waive their due process rights. While some commentators believe that this is entirely possible, provided parties have considered implications of this choice in light of a particular dispute, others disagree or at least question this possibility. The few jurisdictions that addressed this issue directly reached contrasting conclusions in its respect. The ability of parties to waive their due process rights in Australia was supported by the *Duke Group* case. This, however, might not be possible for parties in countries that base their legislation on the UNCITRAL ML and have adopted its Article 24(3) without amendment, for example New Zealand, which was demonstrated by the *Acorn Farms* case. The debate is ongoing, and some risk to the award remains because this issue is not settled in many jurisdictions. The absence of a definite answer to the question of whether parties can waive their due process rights has prompted law and rule makers and commentators to come up with various solutions to minimise the risk of breach of due process and arbitrators' partiality due to their participation in caucuses.

8.4.2 Safeguard 2: safeguards related to caucuses

The book has identified two main safeguard options for reducing concerns related to the use of caucuses, both having their strengths and weaknesses. The first option is to exclude caucuses altogether and to conduct mediation in joint sessions only. Where no caucuses are held, the problem of due process does not arise, and the issue of arbitrators' bias due to their participation in mediation becomes less problematic. This approach is practised in European countries following the Germanic tradition and is recommended by the CEDR, CIArb, COMA, and the ICC. However, this 'no caucusing' approach is criticised for eliminating a mediation process stage that may be vital for settlement efforts to be successful.

The second option is to allow caucuses and to specify what dual role neutrals are to do with the information from caucuses if mediation efforts do not result in a settlement and dual role neutrals need to resume as arbitrators.

One way is to require dual role neutrals, before resuming as arbitrators, to disclose to all parties as much of the confidential information from caucuses as they consider material to the arbitral proceedings (the 'disclosure' rule). This is the approach taken by the legislators in Singapore, Hong Kong, and Australia. In jurisdictions that base their legislation on the UNCITRAL ML and have adopted its Article 24(3) without amendment, for example, New Zealand, the requirement of disclosure is not limited to information that is material but extends to all information provided to dual role neutrals in caucuses.

Alternatively, dual role neutrals may be required when acting as arbitrators to disregard any information obtained in caucuses and to base their award only on evidence properly presented in arbitration (the 'disregard' rule). This approach is practised in China and the United States.

Both the disclosure and disregard rule have flaws. The former may, for example, deter parties from being open in caucuses and thereby inhibit the entire mediation process. The latter is often criticised for not avoiding the risk that arbitrators may become influenced by what they have heard. Both the disclosure and disregard rule minimise but do not eliminate the risk of breach of due process. To remedy this situation, the book suggests that jurisdictions permitting the same neutral (arb)-med-arb involving the use of caucuses should specify that parties using this process waive their due process rights on the ground of the arbitrators' participation in caucuses.

This book does not advocate for any of the presented safeguard options for reducing concerns related to the use of caucuses in particular. Neither does it advocate for any of three ways to address concerns associated with the same neutral (arb)-med-arb discussed in Part IV (Chapters 6, 7, and 8). Which safeguard or way is appropriate to use will depend on the particular circumstances of the case, including the jurisdictions that are the place of arbitration and the award's enforcement and the legal culture of the participants of the dispute resolution process.

Part V

The way forward

The questionnaire data presented and discussed in Chapter 5 reveals a contrast between the infrequent use of combinations in international commercial dispute resolution and the overwhelmingly positive perception of their potential benefits.[1] Only about one-third of the participants reported experience with combinations (34.6%) whereas 93.5% acknowledged that the use of combinations was beneficial to parties. Faster resolution of a dispute and its lower cost (as compared to arbitration only) were among the top three benefits, as rated by the questionnaire participants. Considering the current discontent of users with costs and delays in arbitration proceedings, the questionnaire participants appeared to regard combinations as a remedy against these limitations of arbitration. This shows that there is scope for a more widespread use of combinations.

Part V explores initiatives, including those suggested in the interviews conducted for this study, that could enhance the use of the same neutral (arb)-med-arb and other combinations in international commercial dispute resolution. So far, the discussion of combinations has revolved around one combination, the same neutral (arb)-med-arb. Other combinations examined in Chapters 6 and 7 have been largely overlooked and addressed mostly in the context of ways to address concerns associated with the same neutral (arb)-med-arb. This needs to change. Combinations other than the same neutral (arb)-med-arb should be considered as valuable dispute resolution options as well.

1 *See* questionnaire Results 1 and 4 in Section 5.4 *supra*.

9 Initiatives to enhance the use of the same neutral (arb)-med-arb and other combinations in international commercial dispute resolution

9.1 Introduction

This final chapter proposes four initiatives to enhance the use of combinations in international commercial dispute resolution. Sections 9.2 and 9.3 examine how the use of combinations can be supported through the adoption of legislation and development of international guidelines. Section 9.4 analyses how dispute resolution institutions can contribute to enhancing the use of combinations. Section 9.5 emphasises the importance of consistent efforts to build the capacity of dispute resolution practitioners. It argues that in the international commercial dispute resolution environment of today more practitioners need to be trained in both mediation and arbitration. It calls for dispute resolution practitioners to learn and enhance their knowledge on how to overcome cultural differences and adopt a flexible approach to process design.

9.2 Adopt legislation supporting the use of combinations

The first initiative to enhance the use of combinations in international commercial dispute resolution is to adopt legislation promoting their use.[2] The author advocates for incorporating a succinct provision that recognises the possibility of using combinations, rather than specifies the details of the process.

As observed in Section 5.2.3.2.5, legislation supporting the use of the same neutral (arb)-med-arb has been adopted more often in common-law jurisdictions where practitioners are not comfortable with the process. Although legislation in

2 This initiative is in line with the results of the GPC survey where in response to two questions – (1) Who has the potential to be most influential in bringing about change in commercial dispute resolution practice? and (2) Who has the greatest responsibility for taking action to promote better access to justice? – the first ranked answer was governments/ministries of justice. *Global Pound Conference Series 2016–17 Cumulated Data Results March 2016 – September 2017*, Global Pound, available at <http://globalpound.org/wp-content/uploads/2017/11/2017-09-18-Final-GPC-Series-Results-Cumulated-Votes-from-the-GPC-App-Mar.-2016-Sep.-2017.pdf> (accessed 14 Jan. 2018) [hereinafter, GPC Cumulated Data Results].

Hong Kong and Singapore expressly recognises the same neutral (arb)-med-arb and regulates its use in detail, commentators point out the paucity of its use, which is confirmed by the empirical data collected for this book.[3]

The research shows that in China and Japan, arbitrators actively assist parties in settling their disputes due to the deeply rooted tradition of conflict avoidance.[4] The legal basis for facilitation of settlement is established in the countries' respective arbitration laws. It appears, however, that arbitrators in both countries attempted to mediate their cases even before enactment of these laws.

Contrary to the detailed legislative provisions in Hong Kong and Singapore, relevant provisions in China and Japan merely acknowledge the possibility of facilitation of settlement, provided parties consent to that. In China, Article 51 of the Arbitration Law provides:

> The arbitration tribunal may carry out conciliation prior to giving an award. The arbitration tribunal shall conduct conciliation if both parties voluntarily seek conciliation. If conciliation is unsuccessful, an arbitration award shall be made promptly.[5]

Article 38(4) of the Japanese Arbitration Law authorises an arbitral tribunal or one or more arbitrators designated by it to attempt to settle a civil dispute subject to the arbitral proceedings, if consented to by the parties.[6]

In Australia, the ability of an arbitrator to act as a mediator is recognised under Commercial Arbitration Acts (CAA) that govern domestic arbitration in Australian States and Territories.[7] The CAAs' provisions regulating the use of the same neutral (arb)-med-arb are as detailed as the corresponding provisions in Hong Kong and Singapore, although different in some respects.[8] Similarly to the provisions in Hong Kong and Singapore, the relevant provisions of the Australian CAAs seem to have been applied in practice rarely.[9]

3 *See* discussion in Section 5.2.3.2.5 *supra*.

4 *See* discussion in Section 4.3 *supra*.

5 Arbitration Law of the People's Republic of China (1994), Zhonghua Renmin Gongheguo Falu Huibian.

6 Chusai Ho [Arbitration Law] Law No. 138 of 2003.

7 *See, e.g., Commercial Arbitration Act 2012* (WA), s. 27D.

8 The relevant provisions of the Australian CAAs differ from those contained in the laws of Hong Kong and Singapore in that they require parties' written consent twice: first, for arbitrators to act as mediators (s. 27D(1)) and, second, to continue as arbitrators if mediation does not result in a settlement (s. 27D(4)).

9 Richard Garnett & Luke Nottage, *The 2010 Amendments to the International Arbitration Act: A New Dawn for Australia?* 7(1) Asian Int'l. Arb. J. 29, 43 (2011). The predecessor of s. 27D, s. 27 of the Uniform Commercial Arbitration Acts had little impact and was not used much. *See* Luke Nottage & Richard Garnett, *Top 20 Things to Change in or Around Australia's International Arbitration Act*, 6(1) Asian Int'l. Arb. J. 1, 36 (2010); Arthur Marriott, *Litigate, Arbitrate, Mediate – Frustrate? Breaking the Dispute Deadlock*, Clayton Utz, available at <www.claytonutz.com/ialecture/2005/transcript_2005.html> (accessed 14 Jan. 2018).

The express recognition of the same neutral (arb)-med-arb in the Australian legislation regulating domestic arbitration contrasts with the gap in the legislation regulating international arbitration – the International Arbitration Act 1974 (IAA). In 2010, following a near two-year review process, the amended IAA came into force. Although public submissions made during the IAA review process raised the issue of the same neutral (arb)-med-arb and suggested this process be recognised expressly, the revised IAA remained silent in this respect. Analysing the impact of the new IAA regime, Nottage observes that little has changed in positioning Australia as a plausible arbitral venue in the Asia-Pacific region and advocates for a new round of IAA amendments.[10] Nottage recommends that one of the amendments should address the same neutral arb-med-arb. He suggests that instead of incorporating provisions allowing caucusing and requiring disclosure as in the legislation of Hong Kong and Singapore, the IAA should clarify that the same neutral arb-med-arb is permissible if it does not involve caucusing.[11]

The legislative recognition of only one particular variation of the same neutral (arb)-med-arb, however, might be unhelpful, be it the same neutral arb-med-arb with no caucuses or the combination promoted by the legislators in Hong Kong and Singapore. This type of recognition will inevitably limit parties' choice and prevent them from considering other combination possibilities and exercising their autonomy when selecting the most suitable process for their specific dispute.

What appears to be important is to make parties aware and remind them that they have a choice of dispute resolution options and empower them to select the process that best suits their needs. This can be achieved by incorporating a general legislative provision stating that if parties agree, the arbitral tribunal, its member, or a different neutral may, among others, act as a mediator and assist parties in reaching settlement. The author argues that the provision should be worded affirmatively to signal to parties that their choice of a dispute resolution process will be supported. The provision could provide as follows:

> With the written agreement of the parties, the arbitral tribunal, its member, or a different neutral may use mediation or other processes at any time during the arbitral proceedings to facilitate settlement.

The author suggests that no further procedural details should be specified, as this will inevitably restrict parties' choice. The decision on procedural details should be left to the participants of each particular case. Before taking the decision,

10 Luke Nottage, *International Commercial Arbitration in Australia: What's New and What's Next?* 30(5) J. Int'l. Arb. 465, 465 (2013).

11 *Ibid,* at 489. He remains, however, quite sceptical as to the prospect of even this kind of amendment, observing that 'it will be difficult to achieve'. Luke Nottage, *In/formalisation and Glocalisation of International Commercial Arbitration and Investment Treaty Arbitration in Asia*, in *Formalisation and Flexibilisation in Dispute Resolution* 211, 227 (Joachim Zekoll, Moritz Bälz & Iwo Amelung eds, Brill 2014).

parties should be encouraged to seek legal advice on the available combinations, advantages, and concerns associated with them. A sentence could be added to the above provision:

> The arbitral tribunal may encourage parties to seek legal advice on processes that may assist with settlement, and the benefits and risks associated with these processes.

In this context, it could be useful to have a dispute resolution adviser to assist parties in selecting the most suitable and efficient dispute resolution process for their dispute.[12] Empirical data, however, suggests that assisting parties in understanding their dispute resolution options so that they can make an informed decision on which one to use is the task of external lawyers and in-house counsel, rather than a special dispute resolution adviser.[13] The same empirical data also shows that currently the needs of the parties in terms of the information about available dispute resolution options are not satisfied and there is much scope for improvement in this respect.[14] In any case, it will help if parties can be directed to a set of guidelines addressing various combinations and safeguards for their use. Developing guidelines is the second of the suggested initiatives.

9.3 Develop international guidelines for using combinations

For Goodrich, developing guidelines internationally is a better approach in dealing with a gulf in views between practitioners of different legal cultures on the same neutral (arb)-med-arb than passing legislation in countries where the process is rarely used.[15] However, the author argues that passing legislation and developing international guidelines are complementary initiatives.

There is a common call in the literature to elaborate a set of guidelines addressing acceptable same neutral (arb)-med-arb procedures.[16] This should

12 This was an idea suggested in one of the interviews conducted by Shahla Ali for her PhD project. *See* Shahla Ali, *International Arbitration and Mediation in East Asia: Examining the Role of Domestic Legal Culture and Globalization on Shaping East Asian Arbitration* 218 (PhD thesis, University of California, 2007).

13 The GPC survey participants regarded external lawyers (59%) and in-house lawyers (55%) as primarily responsible for ensuring that parties understand their dispute resolution process options and the possible consequences of each process before deciding which one to use. GPC Cumulated Data Results, *supra* n. 2.

14 The GPC survey participants referred to the insufficient knowledge of options available to resolve disputes as the second main obstacle parties face when seeking to resolve commercial disputes (52%), with the first main obstacle being financial or time constraints (59%). *Ibid.*

15 Mark Goodrich, *Arb-Med: Ideal Solution or Dangerous Heresy?* 8, White & Case (30 Mar. 2012), available at <www.whitecase.com/publications/article/arb-med-ideal-solution-or-dangerous-heresy> (accessed 4 Apr. 2018).

16 *See, e.g., ibid*; Justin D'Agostino, *Mediator-Arbitrators: The Perfect Match or No Love Lost? (A Valentine's Day Blog),* Kluwer Arbitration Blog (15 Feb. 2011), available at

be of assistance, particularly where the practice of the same neutral (arb)-med-arb is not accepted at present.[17] A set of guidelines could also lay the groundwork for a broader appreciation of the opportunities that exist for resolving arbitrated cases through settlement.[18] Actually, the basis for the proposed set of guidelines already exists. These are the CEDR Rules elaborated by the CEDR Commission.

9.3.1 The CEDR Rules

The CEDR Rules are the first major international effort to focus specifically on settlement during arbitration.[19] These rules have been commended for recognising the differences between civil- and common-law tradition and providing a menu appropriate for different tribunals and different nationalities of parties.[20] Ehle regards them as a step towards establishing a transnational standard for encouraging settlement of disputes[21] and transforming arbitrators into proactive settlement facilitators, while establishing safeguards.[22]

At the same time, the CEDR Rules have drawn criticism. In particular, roles envisioned for arbitrators in facilitation of settlement have been criticised for falling short of a consensus model and being somewhat controversial.[23] Particularly US arbitrators may feel uncomfortable in taking the steps listed in Article 5 of the CEDR Rules in settling the parties' dispute.[24] Steps such as presenting preliminary views or offering suggested settlement terms risk projecting 'arbitration tribunals into a much more forthright role as settlement facilitators' as compared to other initiatives such as the ICC Techniques.[25]

<http://kluwerarbitrationblog.com/blog/2011/02/15/mediator-arbitrators-the-perfect-match-or-no-love-lost-a-valentines-day-blog/> (accessed 4 Apr. 2018); Thomas J. Stipanowich & Zachary P. Ulrich, *Commercial Arbitration and Settlement: Empirical Insights into the Roles Arbitrators Play*, 6 Y.B. On Arb. Mediation 1, 29–31 (2014) (proposing to elaborate guidelines for US practitioners that reflect current US practice but that take note of developing international norms).

17 D'Agostino, *supra* n. 16.

18 Stipanowich & Ulrich, *supra* n. 16, at 29.

19 *Ibid*, at 14.

20 Stephen Bond (quote from Conference 26/11/09), available at <www.cedr.com/about_us/arbitration_commission/arbcomsampledirections.php> (accessed 14 Jan. 2018); *but see* Klaus Peter Berger & J. Ole Jensen, *The Arbitrator's Mandate to Facilitate Settlement*, 40 Fordham Int'l L.J. 887, 911 (Apr. 2017) (observing that 'despite their common-law origin, the CEDR Rules adopt . . . 'Germanic' approach . . .').

21 Bernd Ehle, *The Arbitrator as a Settlement Facilitator* in *Walking A Thin Line – What an Arbitrator Can Do, Must Do or Must Not Do, Recent Developments and Trends* 77, 86–87 (Bruylant 2010).

22 *Ibid*, at 94.

23 Stipanowich & Ulrich, *supra* n. 16, at 14.

24 *Ibid*.

25 *Ibid*, at 15.

The CEDR Rules have also been criticised for failing to address significant areas of settlement facilitation process.[26] In particular, although engaging in facilitation of settlement is still a controversial practice for many international arbitrators, the CEDR Rules seem to take for granted that arbitrators will not hesitate to do it. In the case of three-member tribunals, as compared to sole arbitrators, issues are exacerbated because the Rules appear to assume that a tribunal of three arbitrators would act with one mind, and provide no assistance to help arbitrators overcome cultural, conceptual, and technical differences of approach between themselves.[27]

Apart from failing to address the consensus-building exercise carried out by the tribunal about the decision to facilitate settlement, the Rules appear to be silent on the timing and trigger of the settlement facilitation process and the possibility of a shift in the perception of the tribunal's authority, both by the parties and within the tribunal, as a consequence of the tribunal's facilitation of settlement.[28] Any future guidelines should be elaborated taking into account and responding to these criticisms of the CEDR Rules.

It is important to note that, as mentioned in Section 8.2.2.1, the CEDR Commission provides rules and safeguards for two variations of the same neutral arb-med-arb. While the CEDR Rules apply to the same neutral arb-med-arb that does not involve the use of caucuses, the CEDR Appendix 2 establishes safeguards for using the same neutral arb-med-arb that involves the use of caucuses. In this way, the CEDR Commission provides parties with guidance on two variations of the same neutral arb-med-arb (with and without caucuses).

9.3.2 Proposed Guidelines on Combinations

The author advocates for the guidelines to encompass combinations other than the same neutral (arb)-med-arb, including those involving different neutrals and procedural modifications of the same neutral (arb)-med-arb. The CEDR Rules, CEDR Appendix 2, and this book can be of help when elaborating this kind of guidelines. The guidelines need to define various combinations, specify the benefits and risks associated with them, and provide safeguards for their use. They should emphasise the importance of ensuring that a combination that parties intend to use does not offend legislative provisions at the place of arbitration and the place of the award's enforcement. Where possible, combinations addressed in the guidelines could be accompanied by a brief overview of positions taken by different jurisdictions to them. In fact, elaboration of this kind of guidelines is one of the goals of the International Task Force on Mixed Mode

26 Sophie Nappert & Dieter Flader, *A Psychological Perspective on the Facilitation of Settlement in International Arbitration — Examining the CEDR Rules*, 2(2) J. Int'l Disp. Settlement 459, 462 (2011).

27 *Ibid*, at 465.

28 *Ibid*, at 466–470.

Dispute Resolution (Task Force) established in 2016 by the College of Commercial Arbitrators, the International Mediation Institute, and the Straus Institute for Dispute Resolution, Pepperdine School of Law.[29]

9.3.3 Mixed Mode Task Force

The Task Force aims to examine and seek to develop criteria for ways of combining different dispute resolution processes that may involve the interplay between public or private adjudicative systems (e.g., litigation, arbitration, or adjudication) with non-adjudicative methods that involve the use of a neutral (e.g., conciliation or mediation), whether in parallel, sequentially, or as integrated processes, which the Task Force has called 'Mixed Mode Scenarios'.[30]

The Task Force comprises international experts in arbitration, adjudication, conciliation, litigation, and mediation and is divided into six Working Groups focusing, respectively, on the following subjects:[31]

1 mediators using non-binding evaluations and making settlement proposals;
2 mediators setting the stage for adjudicative processes and other dispute resolution options (e.g., guided choice processes);
3 neutrals 'changing hats' (e.g., med-arb, arb-med, or arb-med-arb);
4 arbitrators setting the stage for settlement;
5 consent awards and the enforceability of mediated settlement agreements;
6 possible interactions between adjudicative and non-adjudicative neutrals.

The Task Force's final work product is expected to be an online collection of resources (and possibly a book) that will include sections on the subjects covered by each of the Working Groups.[32] Among other issues, the online collection is to contain best practices or guidelines aimed at practitioners, dispute resolution professionals, business users, and others.[33]

9.4 A greater role for dispute resolution institutions

As observed in Section 5.2.3.2.5, the questionnaire result showing that combinations are rarely used, pursuant to a suggestion of an arbitration institution, contrasts with the high demands for such initiatives. Dispute resolution

29 CCA/IMI/ Straus Institute International Task Force on Mixed Mode Dispute Resolution, *Memo on the Task Force and Project*, International Mediation Institute 1 (5 Apr. 2016), available at <www.imimediation.org/about-imi/who-are-imi/mixed-mode-task-force/#about> (accessed 4 Apr. 2018).

30 International Mediation Institute, *Mixed Mode Task Force: About*, available at <www.imimediation.org/about-imi/who-are-imi/mixed-mode-task-force/#about> (accessed 14 Jan. 2018).

31 *Ibid.*

32 Letter to Working Group 2 Task Force Member (28 Aug. 2017) (on file with author).

33 *Memo on the Task Force and Project, supra* n. 29, at 3.

institutions are urged to examine and create more links between different processes they offer.[34] By doing so, they can provide parties with greater choice and create opportunities for less expensive, faster, and better outcomes (as compared to arbitration only), minimising the risk of the process itself becoming part of the problem.[35]

More specifically, arbitration institutions could consider implementing a rule that, as a matter of routine, would oblige the arbitration institution or the arbitrator at a certain point to suggest that parties consider using mediation.[36] An example of this kind of rule is contained in Article 21.3 of the 2016 ACICA Arbitration Rules, although it does not refer specifically to mediation:

> The Arbitral Tribunal shall raise for discussion with the parties the possibility of using other techniques to facilitate settlement of the dispute.[37]

To remove the burden of suggesting mediation from arbitrators, rules of arbitration institutions could provide for a standard, obligatory, short (two-week) settlement window in the arbitral procedure.[38] Ideally, this hypothetical window should open after establishing the tribunal, once parties have seen the initial pleadings, but before the cost-intensive phase of arbitration.[39] Within this window of time, parties could consider using alternative means to resolve their dispute. Rather than requiring parties to mediate or negotiate, rules could give parties the possibility of doing so. The tribunal would not even need to know whether settlement had been explored by the parties.

Arbitration institutions may introduce the idea of a mediation window through another standard procedure. Following the designated stage, the institution could send a letter to the parties saying,

> at this stage, as a matter of routine, we ask whether the parties would be interested in having a mediator appointed who is not the arbitrator and has

34 Jeremy Lack, *Appropriate Dispute Resolution (ADR): The Spectrum of Hybrid Techniques Available to the Parties,* in *ADR in Business: Practice and Issues across Countries and Cultures* vol. II 339, 379 (Arnold Ingen-Housz ed., Kluwer Law International 2011).

35 *Ibid.*

36 James T. Peter, *Note & Comment: Med-Arb in International Arbitration*, 8 Am. Rev. Int'l Arb. 83, 103 (1997); James T. Peter, *Med-Arb in International Arbitration*, 4 Revista de Arbitragem e Mediação 155, 167–168 (2005) (observing that the rule could help parties make the first move in respect of mediation after commencement of arbitration, as they might be afraid to appear weak).

37 Australian Centre for International Commercial Arbitration (ACICA) Arbitration Rules (effective 1 Jan. 2016), available at <http://acica.org.au/acica-services/acica-rules-2016> (accessed 4 Apr. 2018).

38 Lucy Greenwood, *A Window of Opportunity? Building a Short Period of Time into Arbitral Rules in order for Parties to Explore Settlement*, 27(2) Arb. Int'l. 199, 208–209 (2011).

39 *Ibid*, at 209.

nothing else to do with the case and will have nothing to do with it if the mediation fails.[40]

Marriott even suggests that we should learn from the experience of court-attached mediation schemes and make mediation mandatory, authorising the arbitrator to direct parties to mediate either with the arbitrator or a different person.[41] According to Marriott, in England, where such schemes are voluntary, the take-up rate is 5% or less, while statistical evidence from various jurisdictions shows a similarly high rate of success, regardless of whether the case is referred voluntarily or by compulsion.[42] Marriott, however, does not indicate the sources of the statistical evidence he is referring to. In fact, mandatory court-related mediation is still a controversial subject.[43] The author argues against mandatory mediation in the context of arbitration. To use mediation or not should be left to parties to decide, in accordance with the consensual nature of mediation. Instead of obliging parties to use mediation, arbitration rules should merely nudge parties into considering the use of mediation in arbitration.

Rules could encourage not only arb-med-arb, but also the reverse process, med-arb. The Mediation Rules of the World Intellectual Property Organization (WIPO) illustrate this.[44] Article 14(b) of the Rules provides that where the mediator believes that any issues in dispute between the parties are not susceptible to resolution through mediation, the mediator may propose, for the consideration of the parties, procedures that may lead to the most time and cost-efficient settlement of those issues. In particular, the mediator may propose:

1 an expert determination of one or more particular issues;
2 arbitration;
3 the submission of last offers of settlement by each party and arbitration conducted on the basis of those last offers pursuant to an arbitral procedure in which the mission of the arbitral tribunal is confined to determining which of the last offers shall prevail.

40 Bond quoted in Christian Bühring-Uhle et al., *Arbitration and Mediation in International Business*, 262–263 (2d ed., Kluwer Law International 2006).

41 Arthur L. Marriott, *Arbitrators and Settlement*, in *New Horizons in International Commercial Arbitration and Beyond*, 12 ICCA Congress Series 533, 546 (Albert Jan van den Berg ed., Kluwer Law International 2005).

42 *Ibid.*

43 *See, e.g.*, Nadja Alexander, *Global Trends in Mediation: Riding the Third Wave*, in *Global Trends in Mediation* 1, 25 (Nadja Alexander ed., 2d ed., Kluwer Law International 2006) (referring to legal debates over mandatory court-related mediation due to the classical definition of mediation as a voluntary process and observing that voluntary court-related mediation may be a much more powerful tool than mandatory mediation for changing disputing cultures and reducing abuse of the mediation process).

44 World Intellectual Property Organization (WIPO) Mediation Rules (effective 1 Jan. 2016), available at <www.wipo.int/amc/en/mediation/rules/newrules.html#7a> (accessed 4 Apr. 2018).

This WIPO rule, initiatives such as the implementation of an arbitration rule that, as a matter of routine, opens a settlement window for parties to mediate (if they want) or obliges an arbitrator to suggest that parties consider using mediation, and procedures from the CMAP, ICDR, JAMS, and BIMCO discussed in Section 6.3.3, illustrate how bridges can be built between mediation and arbitration. Even separate organisations can cooperate to provide parties with more dispute resolution options. The SIAC-SIMC Arb-Med-Arb Protocol discussed in Section 6.2.2 is an example of this kind of cooperation, which hopefully will inspire dispute resolution centres in other countries to revise and enhance the dispute resolution services that they currently offer.

The importance of having arbitration rules that encourage the use of mediation was emphasised by two practitioners interviewed for this study when they were asked what needed to be done to enhance the use of combinations in international commercial dispute resolution.[45] The Hong Kong practitioner noted,

> If you have a formal set of rules, for example ICC Rules ... when you are arranging the Terms of Reference, you can ask then: are you keen on doing mediation? ... If you actually have the empowerment from the rules that allow you to do this, the chances are that you can achieve more.[46]

Similar thoughts were expressed by the Australian practitioner, who observed,

> I am a great believer in innovation, but I have so many arbitrations where my co-arbitrators run a mile from my suggestion that we should do something to encourage settlement ... if I had a rules system which said we should think about it I could get them to think about it, I could open their minds to the possibility.[47]

Clearly there is scope for dispute resolution institutions to enhance the use of combinations by creating links between mediation and arbitration services and expanding parties' choice of dispute resolution solutions.

9.5 Build capacity of dispute resolution practitioners

Section 3.4 addressed the challenging task for dual role neutrals in the same neutral (arb)-med-arb. They must be skilled and experienced in both mediation and arbitration and capable of effectively switching from one to another. The author argues that, to be truly effective in promoting the use of combinations in international commercial dispute resolution, the first three initiatives proposed

45 This interview question related to questionnaire Result 1. *See* a summary of the significant questionnaire results in Section 5.4 *supra*.

46 Practitioner from Hong Kong, Interview 3.

47 Practitioner from Australia, Interview 2.

above need to be accompanied by considerable efforts to build the capacity of dispute resolution practitioners. The crucial role that adequate training of dispute resolution practitioners has in boosting the use of combinations was highlighted by a practitioner from Spain. In response to a question on how the use of combinations could be enhanced, he proposed,

> To rely on very experienced arbitrators ... I think a lot has been done and it's much more a question of ... training of the young people more than elaborating documents and guidelines and something like that.[48]

9.5.1 Training in both mediation and arbitration

The use of combinations will not increase unless there is a concerted effort to train more dispute resolution practitioners in both mediation and arbitration so they can gain experience in both. This suggestion is particularly relevant to the same neutral (arb)-med-arb due to the high demands of a dual role. However, knowledge and experience in both mediation and arbitration can pave the way for wider use of combinations in general. This is because, while parties rely on lawyers' guidance regarding what dispute resolution mechanisms to use,[49] lawyers recommend mechanisms that they are familiar with.[50]

Commonly cited expressions that 'the process is only as good as the neutral'[51] and 'arbitration is as good as arbitrators'[52] are equally applicable to the same neutral (arb)-med-arb: by and large, the process is as good as the dual role neutral facilitating it. Therefore, it is essential to ensure that dual role neutrals are skilled professionals who have the trust of all parties, are experienced in both mediation and arbitration, and are capable of handling the challenges presented by the special nature of the same neutral (arb)-med-arb.[53] The complex task of

48 Practitioner from Spain, Interview 1.

49 *See* discussion in Brian A. Pappas, *Med-Arb and the Legalisation of Alternative Dispute Resolution*, 20 Harv. Negot. L. Rev. 157, 192–193 & nn. 190–195 (Spring 2015).

50 The GPC survey participants regarded familiarity with a particular type of dispute resolution process as the most influential factor when in-house counsel or external lawyers recommend parties procedural options for resolving a commercial dispute (59%). GPC Cumulated Data Results, *supra* n. 2.

51 Donna Ross, *Med-Arb/Arb-Med: A More Efficient ADR Process or an Invitation to a Potential Ethical Disaster?* in *Contemporary Issues in International Arbitration and Mediation: The Fordham Papers 2012* 352, 366 (Arthur W. Rovine ed., Martinus Nijhoff 2013).

52 Fan Kun, *The Risks of Apparent Bias When an Arbitrator Acts as a Mediator: Remarks on Hong Kong Court's Decision in Gao Haiyan*, 13 Y.B. Private Int'l. L. 535, 550 (2011).

53 Ross, *supra* n. 51, at 366; Peter Talbot, *Should an Arbitrator or Adjudicator Act as a Mediator in the Same Dispute?* 67(3) Arb. 221, 229 (Aug. 2001); Royden Hindle, *Mixing it up: Medarb Re-visited*, ¶ 40[f] (unpublished paper prepared for the AMINZ Seminar 'Current issues in Arbitration', Mar. 2014); Su Yin Anand, *The Risks of Arbitration-Mediation: Hong Kong Courts Decline to Enforce PRC Arbitral Award*, 16(2) Arb. News (Newsletter of the International Bar Association Legal Practice Division) 40, 42 (2011); Julian D. M. Lew,

dual role neutrals may well be a reason why many neutrals are reluctant to offer the same neutral (arb)-med-arb services.[54] In this context, capacity building comes to the fore.

It is time to make greater efforts to familiarize arbitrators with the practice of mediating[55] and the particularities of proceedings which incorporate elements of mediation.[56] This can be done through more training of arbitrators in mediation practice.[57] For mediators, it would be useful to receive training in arbitration. Dispute resolution practitioners, in general, could engage more actively in learning about mediation, arbitration, and the ways in which these processes can be combined. The increased awareness of dispute resolution practitioners about various combinations will contribute to expanding the toolkit of available dispute resolution solutions.

The current challenge of finding professionals capable of effectively handling both roles[58] can be addressed by initiatives such as Arbitrator Intelligence

Multi-Institutional Conciliation and the Reconciliation of Different Legal Cultures, in *New Horizons in International Commercial Arbitration and Beyond*, 12 ICCA Congress Series 421, 428 (Albert Jan van den Berg ed., Kluwer Law International 2005); Geoff Lawday, *Hybrid Dispute Resolution Processes* 8 (unpublished paper presented at 'Mediation in a Global Village – Cross-cultural and International Aspects of Mediation and Negotiation', Germany 2009); Claude Thomson, *Med-Arb: A Fresh Look,* 5 (2006) (on file with the ICC Documentation & Research Centre); Andreas Reiner, *Bridges Between Mediation and Arbitration: The Mediator as Arbitrator?/The Arbitrator as Mediator?* 28 (unpublished paper presented at Tenth Zagreb Arbitration Conference, 2002); Michael F. Hoellering, *Comments on the Growing Inter-Action of Arbitration and Mediation*, in *International Dispute Resolution: Towards an International Arbitration Culture*, 8 ICCA Congress Series 121, 123 (Albert Jan van den Berg ed., Kluwer Law International 1998); John T. Blankenship, *Developing Your ADR Attitude: Med-Arb, a Template for Adaptive ADR*, 42(11) Tennessee Bar J. 28, 36 (2006); Harold I. Abramson, *Protocols for International Arbitrators Who Dare to Settle Cases*, 10 Am. Rev. Int'l Arb. 1, 9 (protocol 1) (1999).

54 Richard Fullerton, *The Ethics of Mediation-Arbitration*, 38(5) Colorado Law. 31, 38 (2009); Christian Bühring-Uhle, *Arbitration and Mediation in International Business: Designing Procedures for Effective Conflict Management* 249 (Kluwer Law International 1996).

55 Gabrielle Kaufmann-Kohler & Fan Kun, *Integrating Mediation into Arbitration: Why It Works in China*, 25(4) J. Int'l. Arb. 479, 492 (2008).

56 Michael E. Schneider, *Combining Arbitration with Conciliation,* in *International Dispute Resolution: Towards an International Arbitration Culture*, 8 ICCA Congress Series 57, 97 (Albert Jan van den Berg ed., Kluwer Law International 1998); *see also* Claire Wilson, *The Arb-Med Hybrid in Hong Kong – Much Ado about Nothing?* Kluwer Mediation Blog (1 Feb. 2012), available at <http://kluwermediationblog.com/2012/02/01/the-arb-med-hybrid-in-hong-kong-much-ado-about-nothing/> (accessed 4 Apr. 2018) (suggesting enhancing the awareness of the same neutral arb-med-arb's advantages in Hong Kong).

57 Wilson, *supra* n. 56.

58 Carlos De Vera, *Arbitrating Harmony: 'Med-Arb' and the Confluence of Culture and Rule of Law in the Resolution of International Commercial Disputes in China*, 18 Colum. J. Asian L. 149, 159 (2004); Lawday, *supra* n. 53, at 7; Barry Leon & Alexandra Peterson, *Med-Arb in Ontario: Enforceability of Med-Arb Agreement Confirmed by Court of Appeal*, 2(1) NYSBA New York Disp. Res. Law. 92, 92 (2009); Peter (2005), *supra* n. 36, at 163; Peter (1997), *supra* n. 36, at 98.

(formerly known as the International Arbitrator Information Project). This is a non-profit, interactive informational network that aims to promote transparency, fairness, and accountability in the selection of international arbitrators by increasing and equalising access to critical information about arbitrators and their decision making.[59] In this online resource, each arbitrator is expected to have a webpage that would include standard biographic information, links to publicly available awards associated with the arbitrator, academic and professional publications, and, more importantly, information about case-management skills, predilections, and demeanour as an adjudicator.[60] Currently, the information about an arbitrator's case-management skills is usually collected through ad hoc, piecemeal, and individualised inquiries. This information may lack objectivity. The online resource aspires to provide a more cost-effective, systematic, and accessible source for this critical information, by collecting reliable quantitative feedback from users and counsel about the key features of arbitrator decision making. Information is expected to be collected through the Arbitrator Intelligence Questionnaire that allows users to provide feedback on specific topics such as case management, document disclosure, and award rendering.[61] By promoting transparency and making information about arbitrators more readily available to anyone interested, Arbitrator Intelligence aims to increase arbitrator accountability, to make the selection process more fair and predictable, and to create better opportunities for new and diverse arbitrators.[62] Although this resource is focused on arbitrators, it could also include information on dual role neutrals, which would facilitate the finding of skilled and experienced professionals capable of acting as mediators and arbitrators. This could remove one of the obstacles to a wider acceptance of the same neutral (arb)-med-arb as a viable dispute resolution mechanism.

It is not only dispute resolution practitioners that need to be trained in both mediation and arbitration, but students as well.[63] The latter can be educated about the possibilities of combining mediation and arbitration through moot court competitions similar to the annual Willem C. Vis International Commercial Arbitration Moot Competition. The International ADR Mooting Competition (ADR Moot) already provides students with an opportunity to act as both a

59 Arbitrator Intelligence, *About*, available at <www.arbitratorintelligence.org/about/> (accessed 26 Jan. 2018).

60 Catherine A. Rogers, *The International Arbitrator Information Project: From an Ideation to Operation*, Kluwer Arbitration Blog (10 Dec. 2012), available at <http://kluwerarbitrationblog.com/blog/2012/12/10/the-international-arbitrator-information-project-from-an-ideation-to-operation/> (accessed 6 Apr. 2018).

61 *About, supra* n. 59.

62 *Ibid.*

63 This idea is in line with the results of the GPC survey. Education in business and/or law schools and the broader business community about adjudicative and non-adjudicative dispute resolution options ranked by far first among answers to the question about the most effective way to improve parties' understanding of their dispute resolution options (64%). GPC Cumulated Data Results, *supra* n. 2.

mediator and an arbitrator. Since its inception in 2010, the ADR Moot has been conducted annually by City University of Hong Kong in association with the CIETAC, Columbia University (New York), and UNCITRAL Regional Centre for Asia and the Pacific.[64]

According to the rules of this moot, every round starts in the format of arbitration.[65] The panel of three arbitrators convenes the session. The student designated as mediator/arbitrator serves as the chairman of the panel. The other two arbitrators are the judges of that match, sitting together with the student mediator/arbitrator. At the end of the two teams' presentations during the arbitration or at the end of the allocated time for the whole arbitration process, the panel gives an opinion that the parties should go for mediation. The moot rules provide that the parties' consent to mediation is deemed to be present. In that way, the round moves to the mediation stage. The student mediator/arbitrator assumes the role of the mediator and conducts the process. This ADR Moot allows students to gain practical skills and experience in the same neutral arb-med-arb. Similar moots could be established to enable students to learn about other combinations.

9.5.2 Training in cross-cultural awareness

Gao Haiyan, the case introduced in Section 8.2.2.3.1.2, vividly illustrates the pitfalls of enforcing international arbitral awards resulting from the same neutral arb-med-arb due to cultural differences between the place of arbitration and the place of enforcement. It, thereby, highlights the need for increasing cross-cultural awareness of dispute resolution practitioners around the world.

In *Gao Haiyan*, the cultural differences surfaced when the Hong Kong Court of First Instance (CFI) and the Court of Appeal (CA) had to decide on whether the way mediation had been conducted during arbitration proceedings in mainland China created bias sufficient to refuse the enforcement of the award for being contrary to public policy.[66] While the relevant facts of the case have been presented in Section 8.2.2.3.1.2, the discussion in this section is focused on the two decisions of the Hong Kong courts on the issue of bias.

The CFI found that a meeting between Pan, Zhou, and Zeng over a private dinner on 27 March 2010 created apparent bias by the Tribunal and refused to enforce the award for being contrary to public policy.[67] According to the CFI,

64 City University of Hong Kong, The International ADR Mooting Competition, *About the Moot*, available at <www.cityu.edu.hk/slw/ADR_Moot/about.html> (accessed 14 Jan. 2018).

65 City University of Hong Kong, The International ADR Mooting Competition, *Structure of the Moot*, available at <www.cityu.edu.hk/slw/ADR_Moot/structure.html> (accessed 14 Jan. 2018).

66 This was the second issue that emerged in *Gao Haiyan* case. The first was the issue of waiver discussed in Section 8.2.2.3.1.2 *supra*.

67 *Gao Haiyan v. Keeneye Holdings Ltd* [2011] 3 HKC 157.

the events of 27 March 2010 would have caused a fair-minded observer to apprehend a real risk of bias on behalf of the Tribunal and that the Tribunal favoured the Applicants.[68]

However, about eight months later, the CA reversed the CFI judgment on appeal of the Applicants and held that the Applicants could enforce the award.[69] Although the CA determined that a clear case of waiver had been established, it proceeded to consider whether the events of 27 March 2010 caused concerns of bias sufficient to give rise to the issue of public policy. The CA noted on this point:

> With respect, although one might share the learned Judge's unease about the way in which the mediation was conducted because mediation is normally conducted differently in Hong Kong, whether that would give rise to an apprehension of apparent bias, may depend also on an understanding of how mediation is normally conducted in the place where it was conducted. In this context, I believe due weight must be given to the decision of the Xi'an Court refusing to set aside the Award.[70]

Thereby, the CA demonstrated greater respect for cultural differences and a sense of comity with the Chinese arbitrators and courts, which the CA regarded as being in a better position to detect any bias in the process than the Hong Kong courts.[71] Notably, different judges in Hong Kong took starkly contrasting positions in relation to the same set of facts and issues.[72] Although the questions that the judges had to deal with probably did not have straightforward answers, the CA appreciated the cross-cultural nuances of practices in mainland China, which contrasted with the CFI's position heavily coloured by a common-law interpretation of the events.[73] Yeoh and Ang commend the CA approach for placing facts in the appropriate cultural context, which allowed consideration of the parties' expectations and the standards subscribed to when they agreed to arbitration in mainland China.[74]

The differences in practice of mediation in mainland China and Hong Kong that surfaced in *Gao Haiyan* are an example of a broader dichotomy between the practice of mediation in Asian and Arabic countries and the West. While, in the former, mediation is claimed to be intuitive and informal, in the latter, it seems to

68 *Ibid*, at ¶¶ 53–54.

69 *Gao Haiyan v. Keeneye Holdings Ltd* [2012] 1 HKRLD 627 (CA).

70 *Ibid*, at ¶ 102.

71 Paul E. Mason, *Follow-Up Note to 'The Arbitrator as Mediator, and Mediator as Arbitrator' (2011), J. Int. Arb. 6, 541 et seq.*, 29(2) J. Int'l. Arb. 225, 226 (2012).

72 Zhuang-Hui Wu, *Enforcement of an Award Rendered Following Arb-Med Proceedings*, 27(1) Mealey's Int'l Arb. Report 1, 9 (2012).

73 Friven Yeoh & Desmond Ang, *Reflections on Gao Haiyan – Of 'Arb-Med', 'Waivers', Cultural Contextualisation of Public Policy Arguments*, 29(3) J. Int'l. Arb. 285, 296 (2012).

74 *Ibid*.

be cognitive and scientific and, consequently, more formal and adversarial.[75] Cheng and Kohtio delineate a fundamental difference between conceptions of mediation in China and the United States.[76] In the view of these authors, while it is common for mediators in the United States to aim at identifying the interests of the parties and assisting in reaching a settlement that meets all parties' non-negotiable interests, in China mediators tend to simply dictate a proposed settlement and threaten to issue a binding decision incorporating the proposal if parties reject it.[77] Alexander explains the differences in how one views and applies mediation in practice by the influence of national legal-political structures and cultural attitudes to conflict and dispute processing that can vary dramatically from nation to nation.[78]

The Swiss practitioner interviewed for this study emphasised the specificity of mediation practised in countries following the Germanic tradition and the importance of having clarity about the kind of mediation and combined process in each particular case. He noted,

> In Switzerland, Germany, and Austria where this [mediation by an arbitrator] is a frequent practice, mediation or conciliation is not exactly the same as the type of mediation when one speaks about a separate process because it is more or less anticipation of the outcome of the procedure ... One really has to be careful in knowing what one talks about when combining mediation and arbitration.[79]

At the same time, differences exist in the practice of mediation even within one country. For example, the US practitioner observed,

> there are significant differences in the way mediation is practised regionally, even within the United States. I think that California mediators are much more likely to be evaluative. There are also distinctions between the use of joint sessions and caucuses. There is much more emphasis on caucus in California mediation.[80]

Apart from differences in conceptions and practice of mediation around the world, we saw in Chapters 4 and 5 that differences exist in the practitioners' perception and use of the same neutral (arb)-med-arb. This was explained by

75 Jesus Almoguera, *Arbitration and Mediation Combined. The Independence and Impartiality of Arbitrators*, in *Liber Amicorum Bernardo Cremades* 101, 109 (M. A. Fernandez-Ballesteros & David Arias eds, La Ley 2010).

76 Tai-Heng Cheng & Anthony Kohtio, *Some Limits to Applying Chinese Med-Arb Internationally*, 2(1) NYSBA New York Disp. Res. Law. 95, 96 (2009).

77 *Ibid.*

78 Alexander, *supra* n. 43, at 3.

79 Practitioner from Switzerland, Interview 4.

80 Practitioner from the United States, Interview 5.

reference to the practitioners' legal culture. The literature and empirical evidence presented in Chapter 4 show that practitioners trained in the common-law tradition generally prefer involving different neutrals in the mediation and arbitration stages of the combined process. Continental European practitioners, particularly those from countries following the Germanic tradition, appear to be more open to the idea of mediation by an arbitrator but disfavour the use of caucuses in the mediation stage. Chinese and Japanese practitioners emerge as the foremost proponents of the same neutral arb-med-arb that involves the use of caucuses. The questionnaire result showing that the most frequently used combination is diff neutral (arb)-med-arb has been explained in Section 5.2.3.2.6 by the legal culture of the participants with experience in combinations who originated mostly from jurisdictions with an unfavourable attitude to mediation by arbitrators.

Since international dispute resolution involves practitioners of different legal cultures with different understandings of mediation and appropriate ways of combining mediation and arbitration, more efforts need to be directed towards improving the skills of arbitrators, mediators, dual role neutrals, and dispute resolution practitioners in general in recognising, managing, and overcoming cultural differences.

To teach future practitioners how to achieve that goal, it might be wise to start by changing university programmes.[81] Universities should focus more on international and comparative law in training law students because, even though the world is becoming increasingly globalised, the curriculum of the majority of law faculties in the world is mostly domestic. While this seems to be slowly changing, many lawyers trained in one system of law by and large see things in a domestic manner.[82] It is, however, essential for dispute resolution practitioners acting in the international arena to be open to other cultures.[83] These practitioners would benefit from a cross-cultural training focused on improving their understanding of the impact of culture on local legal practices.

The current tendency of dispute resolution practitioners to approach things in a purely domestic manner and to take a rigid stance on the same neutral (arb)-med-arb, either endorsing or disapproving of it, may be a reason why the Australian practitioner advocated for the possibilities lying between the same neutral (arb)-med-arb and diff neutral (arb)-med-arb. In particular, he said,

> The debate about arb-med or med-arb is really better conducted in the context of the continuum where at one end you have distinct processes separately conducted; on the other hand, you have some combined process

81 *Q&A with Professor Pierre Lalive*, 3(5) Global Arb. Rev. 1, 3 (2008).

82 *Ibid.*

83 *Ibid*; Horacio A. Grigera Naón & Paul E. Mason, *International Commercial Arbitration Practice: 21st Century Perspectives*, § 6.05 (LexisNexis 2010).

> like the CIETAC process. But they are two ends of the spectrum and there is so much that can be done in between.[84]

The author turns now to examine what 'can be done in between' these two ends of the spectrum.

9.5.3 Training in flexible process design

Although using the same neutral (arb)-med-arb can be effective in the resolution of disputes, it is not always the best solution.[85] Other combinations, their variations, or a stand-alone mediation or arbitration might better suit the dispute in hand.[86] In the field of international commerce, even more than in the domestic field, dispute resolution procedures need to be tailored to meet the particularities of the conflict, the type of transactions involved, as well as the legal, economic, social, and cultural backgrounds of the various participants.[87] The interview data echoed this idea. When asked about the ways to enhance the use of combinations in international commercial dispute resolution, the Belgian practitioner noted,

> I think, first, it's a matter of legal culture. It depends where you sit; it depends on the type of the dispute. It also depends on the feelings of the panel, whether the parties want to settle ... it's a combination of so many things, there is no overall pattern.[88]

The US practitioner similarly observed that,

> One should not establish cast-iron rules for dispute resolution process. One should never say never ... For me it's more a matter of education and priorities of the parties. There may be circumstances where they say the role

84 Practitioner from Australia, Interview 2.

85 Blankenship, *supra* n. 53, at 39.

86 *See, e.g.*, Kathleen Paisley reporting a case where she represented a party in a complex dispute between two major technology companies. In her view, the parties settled because the time and cost of the complex, multi-step procedure devised by one of the arbitrators were too much to be borne, and the parties may have felt better served by a stand-alone arbitration, which is what they originally agreed to. *Summary Report of the First Meeting in September 23–24, 2016 of the International Task Force on Mixed Mode Dispute Resolution: Inaugural Summit at Pepperdine University, Malibu, CA, USA*, International Mediation Institute 21 (2017), available at <www.imimediation.org/about-imi/who-are-imi/mixed-mode-task-force/> (accessed 4 Apr. 2018) [hereinafter, First Summary Report of Mixed Mode Task Force].

87 Bühring-Uhle et al., *supra* n. 40, at 247; *but see* Pappas, *supra* n. 49, at 190 (observing that propagating the notions that 'one size does not fit all' and 'flexibility and choice' as hallmarks of ADR ignores the reality that ADR processes are now the primary mechanisms for resolving legal disputes and they require careful examination).

88 Practitioner from Belgium, Interview 6.

> involving multiple hats may make perfect sense or may be a situation in which there is a close teaming between a facilitator and an evaluator.[89]

What could contribute to promoting a flexible approach to process design is broadening the ADR curricula of law schools to include, apart from a study of ADR forms and methods, courses such as 'Creative Problem Solving'. This course could educate students about the same neutral (arb)-med-arb and other combinations introduced in Chapter 2 and discussed in detail in Chapters 6 and 7, and how to design a dispute resolution process depending on the needs of a particular dispute. Similar but more advanced programmes can be developed for experienced dispute resolution practitioners. These might be particularly useful to legal counsel who draft dispute resolution clauses. Advanced programmes on 'Creative Problem Solving' will help go beyond the mindset that there is only a limited number of unalterable ADR methods available.[90]

Also, as noted by the Australian practitioner, it is important to consider what characteristics of mediation can be incorporated in arbitration. He said,

> So, my view is that debating the question of arbitration and mediation as two separate concepts that may be pushed together is a less than sensible or helpful way of analysing the topic. One is better off looking at what characteristics are involved in the process of mediation, which could sensibly be incorporated in the adjudicative process of arbitration. And what can't sensibly be incorporated.[91]

In fact, four of the six practitioners interviewed for this study reported experience with the use of mediation techniques in the arbitration process rather than the use of the discrete processes of mediation and arbitration.

Two of these four interviewees understood the combination of mediation and arbitration as the interactive and transparent conduct of the arbitration procedure, which enables parties to participate in the tribunal's growing understanding of the case and the process of finding the decision. The Swiss practitioner noted,

> In an interactive way ... you let the parties participate in your growing understanding of the case and in your process of finding your decision ... my experience and my thinking about this combination, which I will do as an arbitrator, is more a development or a form of the interactive conduct of the procedure.[92]

89 Practitioner from the United States, Interview 5.

90 Blankenship, *supra* n. 53, at 39 (referring to the saying 'if the only thing you have is a hammer, everything looks like a nail').

91 Practitioner from Australia, Interview 2.

92 Practitioner from Switzerland, Interview 4.

Comments of the Spanish practitioner were along the same lines:

> Well, my personal impression is that every arbitration tribunal should be very transparent to the parties from the very beginning ... every reasonable arbitrator nowadays has to mediate in order to put very clearly to the parties what is his way of thinking.[93]

For two other interviewees (of four with experience of the use of mediation techniques in arbitration), the combination meant the use of mediation for handling procedural matters in arbitration. The Australian practitioner said,

> In the way in which the procedural issues are handled [in arbitration] I think there is an enormous opportunity for consultative mediation between the tribunal and the parties ... In the design of arbitration processes it is very much a mediated outcome: mediated by making suggestions as to what should be done letting the parties then think about it ... Every arbitration is a mediation procedurally at least.[94]

This was echoed by the US practitioner, who noted,

> As an arbitrator, I think of my role as involving a facilitative function on procedural matters ... In that sense in a very broad way I am functioning as a mediator, although my role is ultimately as the arbitrator is adjudicator.[95]

Chapters 6, 7, and 8 discussed numerous ways to combine the discrete processes of mediation and arbitration. However, as the above comments of highly experienced dispute resolution practitioners demonstrate, there is huge potential for the use of mediation techniques in arbitration. These can assist in conducting arbitration proceedings in an interactive and transparent way by allowing parties to participate in the arbitrator's growing understanding of the case. Mediation techniques can also prove valuable in handling procedural matters in arbitration. These comments of the practitioners create avenues for further research into the kind of mediation techniques that can be incorporated into international commercial arbitration process, and the benefits and potential problems of their use. In fact, research of this nature is already being conducted.[96] The results of this future research might be useful for the proposed course on 'Creative Problem Solving'.

93 Practitioner from Spain, Interview 1.

94 Practitioner from Australia, Interview 2.

95 Practitioner from the United States, Interview 5.

96 A recent article explicitly distinguishes between the use of mediation techniques *in* the arbitration and mediation conducted *separately* from the arbitration and addresses the former. *See* Klaus Peter Berger & J. Ole Jensen, *The Arbitrator's Mandate to Facilitate Settlement*, 40 Fordham Int'l L.J. 887, 894–895 (Apr. 2017).

This course, however, can be developed already based on the results of this book. The course on 'Creative Problem Solving' could explore various combinations, benefits, and concerns associated with their use and enable students to apply their knowledge through, for example, designing the most suitable dispute resolution process for hypothetical cases. Being equipped with this knowledge, new and experienced practitioners will be more prepared to assist parties to tailor a dispute resolution process to fit their specific needs.

The benefits of adopting a flexible approach to process design are illustrated by the following three cases.

9.5.3.1 Financial advisory algorithms case

This case related to a dispute between a firm and an ex-employee over the alleged theft of financial advisory algorithms for hedge funds.[97] The process started as mediation, which resulted in the parties' agreement on the dispute resolution process: a neutral person would review the ex-employee's by-subscription-only digital platform to see where it infringed on his former employer's digital platform. The neutral here served not exactly as an arbitrator because all communications after the mediation were ex parte. The reason for these ex parte communications was that the parties did not want to share their digital platforms with one another. The neutral reviewed the platforms and directed changes as were required and confirmed to the former employer that the given directions for changes had been complied with. The parties provided informed consent to the process.

9.5.3.2 Insurer and broker case

This case involved a plaintiff suing its insurer and broker and a two-day mediation in the shadow of fully filed summary judgment motions.[98] In the plaintiff's view, both defendants were at fault and it did not matter who assumed responsibility for the claimed amount as long as someone paid. After multiple phone calls to all parties, the mediator managed to have the settlement agreement signed to resolve the plaintiff's claim for $7 million. The issue that remained was the allocation of this amount between the insurer and the broker. The mediator suggested various arbitration options for resolving this issue, which the parties supported. The parties, however, could not agree on the specifics such as the number of arbitrators, location of hearings, etc. The mediator assisted the insurer and broker in reaching an arbitration agreement to resolve their allocation dispute. He administered arbitration and helped select arbitrators and arrange other aspects of the arbitration process, but then turned over the matter to the

97 Edna Sussman reports this case, in which she acted as a dual role neutral. First Summary Report of Mixed Mode Task Force, *supra* n. 86, at 20.

98 The case is reported by Jonathan Marks, who acted as a mediator in it. *Ibid*, at 12.

arbitrators for resolution. The mediator did not talk to the arbitrators during the arbitration process.

9.5.3.3 IBM-Fujitsu case

In this case, IBM alleged that Fujitsu had used IBM programs to develop IBM-compatible operating systems software for its own mainframes.[99] IBM claimed several hundred million dollars in damages. In 1983, the parties signed a settlement agreement, which required Fujitsu to make a lump sum payment in exchange for a licence from IBM. However, this agreement was not sufficiently specific. Subsequent negotiations between the parties to arrange a more operational agreement failed, and in July 1985 IBM initiated arbitration proceedings under the rules of the American Arbitration Association.

The arbitrators experimented with the whole array of dispute resolution techniques. Early on in the procedure, lawyers and experts presented the parties' views before the arbitrators and one senior executive from each side. However, this mini-trial did not lead to a resolution of the fundamental differences. The panel suggested then that the parties try and negotiate the two major areas of disagreement (the scope of IBM's copyrights and the amount of 'external information' to be exchanged) with the two party-appointed arbitrators acting as mediators. The mediation efforts benefitted from the combined expertise of the arbitrators-turned-mediators in computer technology and dispute resolution. They employed the full arsenal of mediation techniques, including caucuses with each party. However, in order to maintain complete neutrality, they conducted all mediation activities jointly and refrained from ex parte communications between one of them and the party that had appointed him.

In February 1987, the mediation resulted in a framework 'Washington Agreement' which represented a breakthrough in the two major areas of the controversy and laid the foundation for the subsequent resolution of the entire dispute. In respect of the existing software, the parties agreed to an unspecified lump sum for IBM covering past and future program use by Fujitsu. The parties agreed further to create a Secured Facility regime under which each party would have limited access to the other's programming information in exchange for an annual access fee. The agreement also granted the panel the power to resolve all of the parties' disputes. However, the Washington Agreement was only a framework agreement. The determination of the exact amount of the paid-up licence, as well as the scope of the information covered by the Secured Facility regime, the amount of the annual compensation, and the task of compliance monitoring were

99 This case has been discussed by several authors. *See, e.g.*, Bühring-Uhle et al., *supra* n. 40, at 255–259; Toshio Sawada, *Hybrid Arb-Med: Will West and East Never Meet?* 14(2) ICC Int'l Ct. Arb. Bull. 29, 30–31 (Fall 2003); Peter (2005), *supra* n. 36, at 168–170; David C. Elliott, *Med/Arb: Fraught with Danger or Ripe with Opportunity*, 34 Alta. L. Rev. 163, 165 (1995–1996); Almoguera, *supra* n. 75, at 111–112.

left to the arbitration panel. The chairman of the tribunal resigned in May 1987. Instead of replacing him, the parties decided to reduce the panel to the two party-appointed arbitrators who were authorised to engage, in case of a disagreement, a third arbitrator to break the tie. The appointment of the arbitrators was extended for 15 years, thereby creating a standing dispute resolution panel to monitor the implementation of the Secured Facility regime and to resolve all disputes arising out of its operation.

After extensive interaction between the parties, including teams of technical experts, and the panel, which constantly gave guidelines on means to narrow the problems, the arbitrators rendered a framework for the creation of the Secured Facility. A similar approach was taken by the arbitrators for ultimately determining the licence fee. The few remaining issues were to be settled by last offer arbitration, but the parties settled before the arbitrators reached the point of having to choose a proposal.

Hence, in this case, the arbitrators managed to turn an arbitration procedure into a future-oriented problem-solving process that went to the roots of the parties' conflict.[100] The final solution contained a high degree of consensual elements and created value for the parties not only by resolving a costly dispute but also by creating the basis for a controlled technology transfer considered beneficial by both parties. The maximisation of consensus was achieved in a continuous revolving process in which facilitated negotiation alternated with limited arbitral decision making.

Several factors may have made possible this transformation from arbitration to a process involving a spectrum of dispute resolution techniques.[101] First, the amount in dispute reached several hundred million dollars, which prompted senior corporate officers on both sides, including CEOs, to participate. This involvement of CEOs, who took on the responsibility of engaging in cooperative dispute resolution, assisted in reaching a creative solution. Second, while often arbitrators lack knowledge of mediation and ADR, one of the arbitrators in this case was an ADR expert. Another arbitrator was an expert in information technology. Third, the combination of the arbitrators' expertise gave the parties confidence in the arbitrators, which allowed the arbitrators to design the dispute procedure the way they did. Fourth, the dispute related to the copyright protection of computer programs, which was a highly controversial legal field at that time. There were also differences in understanding the issue in the United States and Japan, which increased the uncertainty of the outcome in arbitration. This could have made parties even more motivated to take the resolution of the dispute in their own hands.

The *IBM-Fujitsu* case demonstrates how the ADR expertise of even one member of the arbitral tribunal may enable arbitrators to adopt a flexible approach to process design. In this and two other cases (*Financial advisory*

100 Bühring-Uhle et al., *supra* n. 40, at 258–259.
101 Peter (2005), *supra* n. 36, at 169–170.

algorithms and *Insurer and broker*), parties benefitted from the involvement of open-minded neutrals skilled to accommodate the needs of the dispute in hand. In this way, all three cases reinforce the importance of the training of international commercial dispute resolution practitioners in arbitration, mediation, and flexible process design.

9.6 Conclusion

A number of initiatives can be implemented to enhance the use of the same neutral (arb)-med-arb and other combinations in international commercial dispute resolution.

First, the use of combinations can be supported through the adoption of legislation explicitly providing for the use of combinations. It is suggested that, in countries where this has not been done yet, a general provision be incorporated that acknowledges that, if parties consent in writing, the arbitrator, a member of the arbitral tribunal, or a different neutral may use mediation or other processes to assist parties in reaching settlement. The legislative recognition of only one particular combination or one particular variation of a combination might prevent parties from considering other combination possibilities and exercising their autonomy in choosing the most suitable process. Before parties agree to any process in writing, arbitral tribunals should encourage parties to seek legal advice on the available combinations, advantages, and concerns associated with them.

It will help if parties can be directed to a set of guidelines defining the same neutral (arb)-med-arb and other combinations, explaining the advantages and concerns associated with them and specifying safeguards for their use. Developing this kind of guidelines is the second of the suggested initiatives. The CEDR Rules, CEDR Appendix 2, and this book can be of help when elaborating such guidelines. Parties could consult the guidelines with the aim of selecting the most suitable mechanism for the resolution of their dispute

Third, dispute resolution institutions need to take on a greater role in promoting the use of combinations by creating links between their arbitration and mediation services and, thereby, providing parties with greater choice of dispute resolution options. Procedures available at the CMAP, ICDR, JAMS, BIMCO, WIPO and SIAC-SIMC might inspire dispute resolution centres all over the world to revise and enhance the dispute resolution services that they currently offer.

Finally, to be truly effective, the adoption of legislation, development of international guidelines, and active promotion of combinations by dispute resolution institutions need to be accompanied by continuous efforts to build the capacity of dispute resolution practitioners.

Dispute resolution practitioners play a significant role in the use of combinations. In fact, the decision to use combinations or not, largely depends on dispute resolution practitioners' awareness of various combinations, readiness to assist parties in selecting the process that best suits their particular needs, and ability to properly and ethically administer the selected process. Also, since international dispute resolution involves participants from all over the world, arbitrators and mediators need to have skills to arrange a dispute resolution process in a way that accommodates parties from different legal cultures. It appears that currently not many dispute resolution practitioners are prepared to arrange a dispute resolution process differently from how they were trained to do it in their home jurisdiction. Instead of looking for a process that best meets the demands of each particular case, many practitioners still tend to opt for processes that they are familiar and comfortable with.

Considering the key role that dispute resolution practitioners play in the use of combinations, the author argues that the use of combinations cannot be enhanced without concerted efforts to build the capacity of dispute resolution practitioners in three areas.

First, more dispute resolution practitioners should be trained in both mediation and arbitration. While this kind of training is essential for those acting as dual role neutrals, knowledge and experience of both processes will pave the way for the wider use of combinations in general. The practical problem of finding a skilled and experienced dual role neutral can be addressed by including information on dual role neutrals in an online resource, such as Arbitrator Intelligence, that is accessible to the entire international dispute resolution community.

Second, taking into account the fact that international dispute resolution involves practitioners from different legal cultures with different understanding of mediation and appropriate ways of combining mediation and arbitration, more efforts need to be directed towards improving the skills of dispute resolution practitioners in managing cultural differences. It might be wise to start with changing university programmes so that they focus more on international and comparative law in training law students. International dispute resolution practitioners would benefit from cross-cultural training designed to improve their understanding of the impacts of culture on local legal practices and to provide guidance on how to manage cultural differences.

Third, dispute resolution practitioners should be trained in flexible process design. While the same neutral (arb)-med-arb is a viable combination, the author does not argue that it is a 'one-size-fits-all' dispute resolution process. Rather, it is one of many dispute resolution process options that, depending on the circumstances of a particular case, may or may not meet the parties' needs. Law school curricula could be broadened to include courses such as 'Creative Problem Solving'. These would educate students about various combinations and how to view, analyse, and choose a dispute resolution process depending on the kind of dispute underway. Similar but more advanced courses could be developed and offered to experienced dispute resolution practitioners. The existing combinations can be used more frequently, and new combinations may emerge if more dispute resolution practitioners adopt a flexible approach to process design and focus on helping parties to select the dispute resolution process that best suits the needs of the dispute in hand.

Bibliography

Articles and books

Abascal Zamora, José M., *Some Remarks on the UNCITRAL Model Law on International Commercial Conciliation*, in *New Horizons in International Commercial Arbitration and Beyond*, 12 ICCA Congress Series 415 (Albert Jan van den Berg ed., Kluwer Law International 2005)

Abramson, Harold I., *Protocols for International Arbitrators Who Dare to Settle Cases*, 10 Am. Rev. Int'l Arb. 1 (1999)

Aksen, Gerald, *Comments on Enforceability of Awards on the Role of Arbitrators as Settlement Facilitators*, in *New Horizons in International Commercial Arbitration and Beyond*, 12 ICCA Congress Series 565 (Albert Jan van den Berg ed., Kluwer Law International 2005)

Alexander, Nadja, *Global Trends in Mediation: Riding the Third Wave*, in *Global Trends in Mediation* 1 (Nadja Alexander ed., 2d ed., Kluwer Law International 2006)

Alexander, Nadja, *International Comparative Mediation: Legal Perspectives (Global Trends in Dispute Resolution)* (Kluwer Law International 2009)

Ali, Shahla F., *Barricades and Checkered Flags: An Empirical Examination of the Perceptions of Roadblocks and Facilitators of Settlement Among Arbitration Practitioners in East* Asia *and the West*, 19 Pac. Rim L. & Pol'y J. 243 (2010)

Almoguera, Jesus, *Arbitration and Mediation Combined. The Independence and Impartiality of Arbitrators*, in *Liber Amicorum Bernardo Cremades* 101 (M. A. Fernandez-Ballesteros & David Arias eds, La Ley 2010)

Anand, Su Yin, *The Risks of Arbitration-Mediation: Hong Kong Courts Decline to Enforce PRC Arbitral Award*, 16 (2) Arb. News (Newsletter of the International Bar Association Legal Practice Division) 40 (2011)

Andersen, Steven K., *ICDR Offers Concurrent Mediation/Arbitration Clause*, 63 Disp. Res. J. 15 (Nov. 2008–Jan. 2009)

Antaki, Nabil N., *Muslims' and Arabs' Practice of ADR*, 2 (1) NYSBA New York Disp. Res. Law. 113 (2009)

Bairstow, *The Canadian Experience*, in *Arbitration Issues for the 1980s: Proc. of the Thirty-Fourth Ann. Meeting of the Nat'l Acad. of Arb.* 92 (J. Stern & B. Dennis eds, 1982)

Baizeau, Domitille & Anne-Marie Loong, *Multi-tiered and Hybrid Arbitration Clauses*, in *Arbitration in Switzerland: The Practitioner's Guide* 1451 (Manuel Arroyo ed., Kluwer Law International 2013)

Bartel, Barry C., *Med-Arb as a Distinct Method of Dispute Resolution: History, Analysis, and Potential*, 27 Willamette L. Rev. 661 (1991)

Berger, Klaus Peter, *Integration of Mediation Elements into Arbitration: 'Hybrid' Procedures and 'Intuitive' Mediation by International Arbitrators*, 19 (3) Arb. Int'l. 387 (2003)

Berger, Klaus Peter, *International Economic Arbitration* (Kluwer Law and Taxation Publishers 1993)

Berger, Klaus Peter & J. Ole Jensen, *The Arbitrator's Mandate to Facilitate Settlement*, 40 Fordham Int'l L.J. 887 (Apr. 2017)

Blackaby, Nigel et al., *Redfern and Hunter on International Arbitration* (6th ed., Oxford University Press 2015)

Blankenship, John T., *Developing Your ADR Attitude: Med-Arb, a Template for Adaptive ADR*, 42 (11) Tennessee Bar J. 28 (2006)

Blankley, Kristen M., *Keeping a Secret from Yourself? Confidentiality When the Same Neutral Serves Both as Mediator and as Arbitrator in the Same Case*, 63 Baylor L. Rev. 317 (Spring 2011)

Böckstiegel, Karl-Heinz, *Past, Present, and Future Perspectives of Arbitration*, 25 (3) Arb. Int'l. 293 (2009)

Boo, Lawrence G. S., *Commentary on Issues Involving Confidentiality*, in *New Horizons in International Commercial Arbitration and Beyond*, 12 ICCA Congress Series 523 (Albert Jan van den Berg ed., Kluwer Law International 2005)

Born, Gary B., *International Commercial Arbitration* (2d ed., Kluwer Law International 2014)

Borris, Christian, *Final Offer Arbitration from a Civil Law Perspective*, 24 (3) J. Int'l. Arb. 307 (2007)

Brekoulakis, Stavros L. et al., *UNCITRAL Model Law, Chapter V, Article 24* [Hearings and written proceedings], in *Concise International Arbitration* 884 (Loukas A. Mistelis ed., 2d ed., Kluwer Law International 2015)

Brewer, Thomas J. & Lawrence R. Mills, *Combining Mediation & Arbitration*, 54 (4) Disp. Res. J. 32 (1999)

Brienza, Julie, *ADR Doing Two Things at Once Can Be Problematic*, 34 Trial 19 (1998)

Burr, Andrew, *Med-Arb: A Viable Hybrid Solution?* 8 Les Arbitres Internationaux 57 (2005)

Bustamante Vasconez, Ximena, *The Mediated Settlement Agreement*, 28 (3) J. Int'l. Arb. 283 (2011)

Bühring-Uhle, Christian, *Arbitration and Mediation in International Business: Designing Procedures for Effective Conflict Management* (Kluwer Law International 1996)

Bühring-Uhle, Christian et al., *Arbitration and Mediation in International Business* (2d ed., Kluwer Law International 2006)

Cairns, David J. A., *Mediating International Commercial Disputes: Differences in U.S. and European Approaches*, 60 (3) Disp. Res. J. 62 (2005)

Carter, James H., *Part I – Issues Arising from Integrated Dispute Resolution Clauses*, in *New Horizons in International Commercial Arbitration and Beyond*, 12 ICCA Congress Series 446 (Albert Jan van den Berg ed., Kluwer Law International 2005)

Casey, J. Brian, *Arbitration Law of Canada: Practice and Procedure* (JurisNet 2005)

Cheng, Tai-Heng, *International Mediation, Arbitration, and Innovation*, in *Contemporary Issues in International Arbitration and Mediation: The Fordham Papers 2010* (Arthur W. Rovine ed., Brill 2011)

Cheng, Tai-Heng & Anthony Kohtio, *Some Limits to Applying Chinese Med-Arb Internationally*, 2 (1) NYSBA New York Disp. Res. Law. 95 (2009)

Cohen, Cynthia F. & Murray F. Cohen, *Relative Satisfaction with ADR: Some Empirical Evidence*, 57 Disp. Res. J. 37 (2002)

Conlon, Donald E. et al., *Putting the Cart Before the Horse: The Benefits of Arbitrating Before Mediating*, 87 (5) J. Applied Psychol. 978 (2002)

Connerty, Anthony, *ADR as a 'Filter' Mechanism: The Use of ADR in the Context of International Disputes*, 79 (2) Arb. 120 (2013)

Costa Braga de Oliveira, Pedro Alberto, *Designing Effective Med-Ard and Arb-Med Processes in Brazil*, 2 (1) NYSBA New York Disp. Res. Law. 89 (2009)

Craig, W. Laurence et al., *International Chamber of Commerce Arbitration* (Oceana Publications Inc. 2001)

Cremades, Bernardo M., *Overcoming the Clash of Legal Cultures: The Role of Interactive Arbitration*, 14 (2) Arb. Int'l. 156 (1998)

Damaska M., *The Faces of Justice and State Authority: A Comparative Approach to the Legal Process* (Yale University Press 1986)

Davison, Michael & Timothy Hill, *Med-Arb under Scrutiny*, 6 (3) Global Arb. Rev. (2011)

Deason, Ellen E., *Combinations of Mediation and Arbitration with the Same Neutral: A Framework for Judicial Review*, 5 Y.B. On Arb. Mediati 219 (2013)

Deekshitha, Srikant & Arka Saha, *Amalgamating the Conciliatory and the Adjudicative: Hybrid Processes and Asian Arbitral Institutions*, III(1) Indian J. Arb. L. 76 (Jodhpur 2014)

De Vera, Carlos, *Arbitrating Harmony: 'Med-Arb' and the Confluence of Culture and Rule of Law in the Resolution of International Commercial Disputes in China*, 18 Colum. J. Asian L. 149 (2004)

Donahey, M. Scott, *Seeking Harmony: Is the Asian Concept of the Conciliator/Arbitrator Applicable in the West?* 50 (2) Disp. Res. J. 74 (Apr.–Jun. 1995)

Donahey, M. Scott, *The Asian Concept of Conciliator/Arbitrator: Is It Translatable to the Western World?* (on file with the ICC Documentation & Research Centre)

Drahozal, Christopher R. & Stephen J. Ware, *Why Do Businesses Use (or Not Use) Arbitration Clauses?* 25 Ohio St. J. on Disp. Res. 433 (2010)

Ehle, Bernd, *The Arbitrator as a Settlement Facilitator*, in *Walking A Thin Line – What an Arbitrator Can Do, Must Do or Must Not Do, Recent Developments and Trends* 77 (Bruylant 2010)

Elliott, David C., *Med/Arb: Fraught with Danger or Ripe with Opportunity*, 34 Alta. L. Rev. 163 (1995–1996)

Elsing, Siegfried H., *Germany as a Place for International and Domestic Arbitrations – General Overview*, in *Arbitration in Germany: The Model Law in Practice* 3 (Karl-Heinz Böckstiegel et al. eds, 2d ed., Kluwer Law International 2015)

Favalli, Daniele & Max K. Hasenclever, *The Role of Arbitrators in Settlement Proceedings*, 23 Mealey's Int'l Arb. Rep. 1 (Jul. 2008)

Fiechter, Eric W., *Mediation – Casting Issues: Can or Should the Same Person be Mediator, or Conciliator and Arbitrator?* 15 Croatian Arb. Y.B. 255 (2008)

Fiechter, Eric W., *Mediation – Timing Issues: When is the Right Time to Try Mediation: Before, During or After Arbitration or Court Proceedings?* 15 Croatian Arb. Y.B. 263 (2008)

Friedman, Lawrence M., *The Legal System: A Social Science Perspective* (Russel Sage Foundation, New York 1975)

Friel, Steven, *Arbitration in Context (Chapter 3)*, in *Arbitration in England, with Chapters on Scotland and Ireland* 31 (Julian D. M. Lew et al. eds, Kluwer Law International 2013)

Fry, Jason et al., *The Secretariat's Guide to ICC Arbitration* (International Chamber of Commerce 2012)

Fullerton, Richard, *The Ethics of Mediation-Arbitration*, 38 (5) Colorado Law. 31 (2009)

Garnett, Richard & Luke Nottage, *The 2010 Amendments to the International Arbitration Act: A New Dawn for Australia?* 7 (1) Asian Int'l. Arb. J. 29 (2011)

Gerbay, Remy, *Is the End Nigh Again: An Empirical Assessment of the 'Judicialization' of International Arbitration*, 25 (2) Am. Rev. Int'l Arb. 223 (2014)

Global Arbitration Review, *Q&A with Professor Pierre Lalive*, 3 (5) Global Arb. Rev. 1 (2008)

Glossner, Ottoarndt, *Enforcement of Conciliation Settlements*, 11 Int'l Bus. Law. 151 (1983)

Godwin, Peter, *Japanese Arbitration in the Wake of the 2004 Reforms: Time to Recognise the End of the Ragan Myth*, 21 JCAA Newsletter 1 (Nov. 2008)

Goodrich, Mark, *Arb-med: Ideal Solution or Dangerous Heresy?* 15 (1) Int'l. Arb. L. Rev. 12 (2012)

Greenbaum, Marcia L., *Process and the Professional Practitioner*, 2(3) Negotiation J. 225 (Jul. 1986)

Greenwood, Lucy, *A Window of Opportunity? Building a Short Period of Time into Arbitral Rules in order for Parties to Explore Settlement*, 27 (2) Arb. Int'l. 199 (2011)

Grierson, Jacob & Annet van Hooft, *Arbitrating under the 2012 ICC Rules* (Kluwer Law International 2012)

Grigera Naón, Horacio A. & Paul E. Mason, *International Commercial Arbitration Practice: 21st Century Perspectives* (LexisNexis 2010)

Guillemin, Jean Francois, *Reasons for Choosing Alternative Dispute Resolution*, in *ADR in Business: Practice and Issues across Countries and Cultures* vol II 13 (Arnold Ingen-Housz ed., Kluwer Law International 2011)

Harpole, Sally A., *The Combination of Conciliation with Arbitration in the People's Republic of China*, 24 (6) J. Int'l. Arb. 623 (2007)

Hill, Richard, *MED-ARB: New Coke or Swatch?* 13 (1) Arb. Int'l. 105 (1997)

Hoellering, Michael F., *Comments on the Growing Inter-Action of Arbitration and Mediation*, in *International Dispute Resolution: Towards an International Arbitration Culture*, 8 ICCA Congress Series 121 (Albert Jan van den Berg ed., Kluwer Law International 1998)

Holtzmann, Howard M. et al., *A Guide to the 2006 Amendments to the UNCITRAL Model Law on International Commercial Arbitration: Legislative History and Commentary* (Kluwer Law International 2015)

Hopt, Klaus J. & Felix Steffek eds, *Mediation: Principles and Regulation in Comparative Perspective* (Oxford University Press 2012)

Hunter, J. Martin, *Commentary on Integrated Dispute Resolution Clauses*, in *New Horizons in International Commercial Arbitration and Beyond*, 12 ICCA Congress Series 470 (Albert Jan van den Berg ed., Kluwer Law International 2005)

Hwang, Michael, *The Role of Arbitrators as Settlement Facilitators – Commentary*, in *New Horizons in International Commercial Arbitration and Beyond*, 12 ICCA Congress Series 571 (Albert Jan van den Berg ed., Kluwer Law International 2005)

Jones, Doug, *Various Non-binding (ADR) Processes*, in *New Horizons in International Commercial Arbitration and Beyond*, 12 ICCA Congress Series 367 (Albert Jan van den Berg ed., Kluwer Law International 2005)

Jordaan, Barney, *Hybrid ADR Processes in South Africa*, 2 (1) NYSBA New York Disp. Res. Law. 117 (2009)

Kagel, Sam, *Combining Mediation and Arbitration*, 96 Monthly Lab. Rev. 62 (1973)

Kagel, Sam & Bette J. Roth, *MED-ARB (Mediation-Arbitration)*, in *Alternative Dispute Resolution Practice Guide* § 37 (Sep. 2014)

Kaufmann-Kohler, Gabrielle & Victor Bonnin, *Arbitrators as Conciliators: A Statistical Study of the Relation between an Arbitrators' Role and Legal Background*, 18 (2) ICC Int'l Ct. Arb. Bull. 79 (2007)

Kaufmann-Kohler, Gabrielle & Fan Kun, *Integrating Mediation into Arbitration: Why It Works in China*, 25 (4) J. Int'l. Arb. 479 (2008)

Kichaven, Jeff, *Med-Arb Should be Dead*, 2 (1) NYSBA New York Disp. Res. Law. 80 (2009)

Kryvoi, Yaraslau & Dmitry Davydenko, *Consent Awards in International Arbitration: From Settlement to Enforcement*, 40 Brook. J. Int'l L. 827 (2014–2015)

Kun, Fan, *Arbitration in China: A Legal and Cultural Analysis* (Hart Publishing 2013)

Kun, Fan, *International Dispute Resolution Trends in Asia*, 10 (4) Transnat'l Disp. Mgmt 1 (2013)

Kun, Fan, *The New Arbitration Ordinance in Hong Kong*, 29 (6) J. Int'l. Arb. 715 (2012)

Kun, Fan, *The Risks of Apparent Bias When an Arbitrator Acts as a Mediator: Remarks on Hong Kong Court's Decision in Gao Haiyan*, 13 Y.B. Private Int'l. L. 535 (2011)

Lack, Jeremy, *Appropriate Dispute Resolution (ADR): The Spectrum of Hybrid Techniques Available to the Parties*, in *ADR in Business: Practice and Issues across Countries and Cultures* vol. II 339 (Arnold Ingen-Housz ed., Kluwer Law International 2011)

Lalive, Pierre, *The Role of Arbitrators as Settlement Facilitators – A Swiss View*, in *New Horizons in International Commercial Arbitration and Beyond*, 12 ICCA Congress Series 556 (Albert Jan van den Berg ed., Kluwer Law International 2005)

Lang, Jon, *Med-Arb – An English Perspective*, 2 (1) NYSBA New York Disp. Res. Law. 98 (2009)

Leathes, Michael et al., *Einstein's Lessons in Mediation*, Managing Intellectual Property 23 (Jul./Aug. 2006)

Leon, Barry & Alexandra Peterson, *Med-Arb in Ontario: Enforceability of Med-Arb Agreement Confirmed by Court of Appeal*, 2 (1) NYSBA New York Disp. Res. Law. 92 (2009)

Lew, Julian D. M., *Multi-Institutional Conciliation and the Reconciliation of Different Legal Cultures*, in *New Horizons in International Commercial Arbitration and Beyond*, 12 ICCA Congress Series 421 (Albert Jan van den Berg ed., Kluwer Law International 2005)

Limbury, Alan, *ADR in Australia*, in *ADR in Business: Practice and Issues across Countries and Cultures* vol II 429 (Arnold Ingen-Housz ed., Kluwer Law International 2011)

Limbury, Alan L., *Hybrid Dispute Resolution Processes – Getting the Best While Avoiding the Worst of Both Worlds?* in *CIArb's Mediation Compendium* (A. Hudson-Tyreman et al. eds, London 2009)

Limbury, Alan L., *Making Med-Arb Work*, 9 (7) ADR Bulletin 1 (2007)

Limbury, Alan L., *Making Med-Arb Work in Australia*, 2 (1) NYSBA New York Disp. Res. Law. 84 (2009)

Marriott, Arthur L., *Arbitrators and Settlement*, in *New Horizons in International Commercial Arbitration and Beyond*, 12 ICCA Congress Series 533 (Albert Jan van den Berg ed., Kluwer Law International 2005)

Mason, Paul E., *Follow-Up Note to 'The Arbitrator as Mediator, and Mediator as Arbitrator' (2011), J. Int. Arb. 6, 541 et seq.*, 29 (2) J. Int'l. Arb. 225 (2012)

Mason, Paul E., *The Arbitrator as Mediator, and Mediator as Arbitrator*, 28 (6) J. Int'l. Arb. 541 (2011)

Masood, Ahmed, *Settlement in International Arbitration: Comments on the CEDR Settlement Rules*, 76 (2) Arb. 269 (2010)

McGillicuddy, Neil B. et al., *Third Party Intervention: A Field Experiment Comparing Three Different Models*, 53 (1) J. Personality Soc. Psychol. 104 (1987)

McLaren, Richard H. & John P. Sanderson, *Innovative Dispute Resolution: The Alternative* (Carswell 1994)

Mironi, Mordehai, *From Mediation to Settlement and from Settlement to Final Offer Arbitration: An Analysis of Transnational Business Dispute Mediation*, 73 (1) Arb. 52 (2007)

Morresi, Renzo Maria, *The Use of Med-Arb-Like Mechanisms in Italy and Other European Countries*, 2 (1) NYSBA New York Disp. Res. Law. 106 (2009)

Mustill, Michael J. & Stewart C. Boyd, *Commercial Arbitration* (2d ed., Butterworths 1989)

Nakamura, Tatsuya, *Brief Empirical Study on Arb-Med in the JCAA Arbitration*, 22 JCAA Newsletter 10 (Jun. 2009)

Nappert, Sophie & Dieter Flader, *A Psychological Perspective on the Facilitation of Settlement in International Arbitration — Examining the CEDR Rules*, 2 (2) J. Int'l. Disp. Settlement 459 (2011)

Naughton, Philip, *The Role of Arbitrators and Arbitration Institutions in the Use of Alternatives for the Settlement of Disputes*, 73 (1) Arb. 31 (2007)

Newmark, Christopher, *Controlling Time and Costs in Arbitration*, in *Leading Arbitrators' Guide to International Arbitration* 81 (Lawrence W. Newman & Richard D. Hill eds, 2d ed., Juris Publishing, Inc. 2008)

Newmark, Christopher & Richard Hill, *Can a Mediated Settlement Become an Enforceable Arbitration Award?* 16 (1) Arb. Int'l. 81 (2000)

Nigmatullina, Dilyara, *The Combined Use of Mediation and Arbitration in Commercial Dispute Resolution: Results from an International Study*, 33 (1) Journal of International Arbitration 37 (2016)

Nottage, Luke, *In/formalisation and Glocalisation of International Commercial Arbitration and Investment Treaty Arbitration in Asia*, in *Formalisation and Flexibilisation in Dispute Resolution* 211 (Joachim Zekoll et al. eds, Brill 2014)

Nottage, Luke, *International Commercial Arbitration Developments in Model Law Jurisdictions: Japan Seen from Australia*, 29 JCAA Newsletter 3 (Dec. 2012)

Nottage, Luke, *International Commercial Arbitration in Australia: What's New and What's Next?* 30 (5) J. Int'l. Arb. 465 (2013)

Nottage, Luke, *Is (International Commercial) Arbitration ADR?* 21 (1) Arbit. Mediat. 83 (2002)

Nottage, Luke & Richard Garnett, *Top 20 Things to Change in or Around Australia's International Arbitration Act*, 6 (1) Asian Int'l. Arb. J. 1 (2010)

Oghigian, Haig, *Perspectives from Japan: A New Concept in Dispute* Resolution – *the Mediation-Arbitration Hybrid*, 2 (1) NYSBA New York Disp. Res. Law. 110 (2009)

Oghigian, Haig, *The Meditation/Arbitration Hybrid*, 20 (1) J. Int'l. Arb. 75 (2003)

Onyema, Emilia, *The Use of Med-Arb in International Commercial Dispute Resolution*, 12 Am. Rev. Int'l Arb. 411 (2001)

Panchu, Sriram, *Arb-Med and Med-Arb Are Well-Suited to Meeting India's ADR Needs*, 2 (1) NYSBA New York Disp. Res. Law. 103 (2009)

Pappas, Brian A., *Med-Arb and the Legalisation of Alternative Dispute Resolution*, 20 Harv. Negot. L. Rev. 157 (Spring 2015)

Peter, James T., *Med-Arb in International Arbitration*, 4 Revista de Arbitragem e Mediação 155 (2005)

Peter, James T., *Note & Comment: Med-Arb in International Arbitration*, 8 Am. Rev. Int'l Arb. 83 (1997)

Phillips, Gerald F., *Same-Neutral Med-Arb: What Does The Future Hold?* 60 Disp. Res. J. 24 (2005)

Phillips, Gerald F., *Same-Neutral Med-Arb: What Does the Future Hold?* 2 (1) NYSBA New York Disp. Res. Law. 75 (2009)

Phillips, Gerald F., *The Survey Says: Practitioners Cautiously Move Toward Accepting Same-Neutral Med-Arb, But Party Sophistication Is Mandatory*, 26 (5) Alternatives 101 (2008)

Pitkowitz, Matthias M. & Marie-Therese Richter, *May a Neutral Third Person Serve as Arbitrator and Mediator in the Same Dispute?* 4 Schieds VZ 225 (2009)

Plant, David W., *The Arbitrator as Settlement Facilitator*, 17 (1) J. Int'l. Arb. 143 (Kluwer Law International 2000)

Plant, David W., *We Must Talk Because We Can: Mediating International Intellectual Property Disputes* (International Chamber of Commerce 2008)

Plato, *Cratylus*, in IV *Plato in Twelve Volumes* 383 (Harold N. Fowler trans., Cambridge, MA: Harvard University Press, 1921)

Pouget, Sophie, *Arbitrating and Mediating Disputes, Benchmarking Arbitration and Mediation Regimes for Commercial Disputes Related to Foreign Direct Investment* (The World Bank, Policy Research Working Paper 6632, October 2013)

Pruitt, Dean G., *Process and Outcome in Community Mediation*, 11(4) Negotiation J 365 (Oct. 1995).

Rau, Alan Scott, *Integrity in Private Judging*, 38 S. Tex. L. Rev. 485 (1997)

Redfern, Alan et al., *Redfern and Hunter on International Arbitration* (5th ed., Oxford University Press 2009)

Respondek, Andreas, *Five Proposals to Further Increase the Efficiency of International Arbitration Proceedings*, 31 (4) J. Int'l. Arb. 507 (2014)

Risse, Joerg, *Ten Drastic Proposals for Saving Time and Costs in Arbitral Proceedings*, 29 (3) Arb. Int'l. 453 (2013)

Roebuck, Derek, *The Myth of Modern Mediation*, 73 (1) Arb. 105 (2007)

Rosoff, Jacob, *Hybrid Efficiency in Arbitration: Waiving Potential Conflicts for Dual Role Arbitrators in Med-Arb and Arb-Med Proceedings*, 26 (1) J. Int'l. Arb. 89 (2009)

Ross, Donna, *Med-Arb/Arb-Med: a More Efficient ADR Process or an Invitation to a Potential Ethical Disaster?* in *Contemporary Issues in International Arbitration and Mediation: The Fordham Papers 2012* 352 (Arthur W. Rovine ed., Martinus Nijhoff 2013)

Sawada, Toshio, *Hybrid Arb-Med: Will West and East Never Meet?* 14 (2) ICC Int'l Ct. Arb. Bull. 29 (Fall 2003)

Schneider, Michael E., *Combining Arbitration with Conciliation*, in *International Dispute Resolution: Towards an International Arbitration Culture*, 8 ICCA Congress Series 57 (Albert Jan van den Berg ed., Kluwer Law International 1998)

Schneider, Michael E., *Combining Arbitration with Conciliation*, 1 Transnat'l Disp. Mgmt 9 (2004)

Steele, Brette L., *Enforcing International Commercial Mediation Agreements as Arbitral Awards under the New York Convention*, 54 UCLA L. Rev. 1385 (2007)

Stipanowich, Thomas J. & J. Ryan Lamare, *Living with ADR: Evolving Perceptions and Use of Mediation, Arbitration and Conflict Management in Fortune 1000 Corporations*, 19 Harv. Negot. L. Rev. 1 (2014)

Stipanowich, Thomas J. & Zachary P. Ulrich, *Commercial Arbitration and Settlement: Empirical Insights into the Roles Arbitrators Play*, 6 Y.B. On Arb. Mediat 1 (2014)

Strong, S. I.,*Beyond International Commercial Arbitration? The Promise of International Commercial Mediation*, 45 Wash. U. J. L. & Pol'y 10 (2014)

Sussman, Edna, *Combinations and Permutations of Arbitration and Mediation: Issues and Solutions*, in *ADR in Business: Practice and Issues across Countries and Cultures* vol II 381 (Arnold Ingen-Housz ed., Kluwer Law International 2011)

Sussman, Edna, *Developing an Effective Med-Arb/ Arb-Med Process*, 2 (1) NYSBA New York Disp. Res. Law. 71 (2009)

Talbot, Peter, *Should an Arbitrator or Adjudicator Act as a Mediator in the Same Dispute?* 67 (3) Arb. 221 (Aug. 2001)

Tang, Houzhi, *Combination of Arbitration with Conciliation – Arb-Med*, in *New Horizons in International Commercial Arbitration and Beyond*, 12 ICCA Congress Series 547 (Albert Jan van den Berg ed., Kluwer Law International 2005)

Tang, Houzhi, *Is There an Expanding Culture that Favors Combining Arbitration with Conciliation or Other ADR Procedures?* in *International Dispute Resolution: Towards an International Arbitration Culture*, 8 ICCA Congress Series 101 (Albert Jan van den Berg ed., Kluwer Law International 1998)

Tarrazon, Mercedes, *Arb-Med: A Reflection a Propos of a Bolivian Experience*, 2 (1) NYSBA New York Disp. Res. Law. 87 (2009)

Tateishi, Takao, *The Role of the Two-tier 'Med/Arb' Scheme in Japanese Dispute Resolution*, 1 Asian Disp. Rev. 24 (2000)

Tercier, Pierre, *Foreword* in *ADR in Business: Practice and Issues across Countries and Cultures* vol I xxi (J. C. Goldsmith et al. eds, Kluwer Law International 2006)

Thevenin, Nancy M., *Caucusing and the Cross-Cultural Divide*, in *Contemporary Issues in International Arbitration and Mediation: The Fordham Papers 2012* 367 (Arthur W. Rovine ed., Martinus Nijhoff 2013)

Thomas, Michael, *Mediation at Work in Hong Kong*, 58 (1) Arb. 29 (1992)

Thomson, Claude, *Med-Arb – A Fresh Look* (2006) (on file with the ICC Documentation & Research Centre)

Townsend, Matthew & James Rogers, *Arbitral Procedure and Med-Arb from English and Chinese Eyes*, 7 (1) Global Arb. Rev. (2011)

Tuch, Andrew, *Dispute Resolution Update*, 6 (9) ADR Bulletin 184 (2004)

Ury, William et al., *Getting Disputes Resolved: Designing Systems to Cut the Costs of Conflict* (Jossey-Bass 1988)

Willams, David A. R. & Amokura Kawharu, *Arbitration and Dispute Resolution*, 2012 N.Z. L. Rev. 487 (2012)

Wissler, Roselle L., *Court-Connected Settlement Procedures: Mediation and Judicial Settlement Conferences*, 26 Ohio St. J. on Disp. Resol. 271 (2011)

Wistrich, Andrew J. et al., *Can Judges Ignore Inadmissible Information? The Difficulty of Deliberately Disregarding*, 153 U.Pa.L.Rev. 1251 (Mar. 2005)

Wolski, Bobette, *Arb-Med-Arb (and MSAs): A Whole Which Is Less than, not Greater than, the Sum of Its Parts?*, 6 (2) Contemp. Asia Arb. J. 249 (2013)

Wu, Zhuang-Hui, *Enforcement of an Award Rendered Following Arb-Med Proceedings*, 27 (1) Mealey's Int'l Arb. Report 1 (2012)

Ye, Ariel, *Commentary on Integrated Dispute Resolution Systems in the PRC*, in *New Horizons in International Commercial Arbitration and Beyond*, 12 ICCA Congress Series 478 (Albert Jan van den Berg ed., Kluwer Law International 2005)

Yeoh, Friven & Desmond Ang, *Reflections on Gao Haiyan – Of 'Arb-Med', 'Waivers', Cultural Contextualisation of Public Policy Arguments*, 29 (3) J. Int'l. Arb. 285 (2012)

Cases

Australia

R v. Magistrates' Court at Lilydale; Ex parte Ciccone [1973] VR 122

Re JRL; Ex parte CJL (1986) 161 CLR 342

The Duke Group Ltd (in liq) v. Alamain Investments Ltd [2003] SASC 272

Canada

Marchese v. Marchese (2007), 219 O.A.C. 257 (C.A.)

European Court of Human Rights

Nordström-Janzon v. Netherlands (ECHR 28101/95, 27 Nov. 1996)

Germany

Oberlandesgericht [OLG] [Highest Regional Court] 3 Jan. 2008, Zeitschrift Schiedsverfahren [Schiedsvz] (2008) (Ger.)

Hong Kong

Gao Haiyan v. Keeneye Holdings Ltd [2011] 3 HKC 157

Gao Haiyan v. Keeneye Holdings Ltd [2012] 1 HKRLD 627 (CA)

New Zealand

Acorn Farms Ltd v. Schnuriger [2003] 3 NZLR 121

Duncan & Davis Nurseries New Plymouth Ltd. v. Honnor Block Ltd., 14 Jun. 2005, High Court of New Zealand, HC Auckland, CIV 2005-404-2513 (2005)

Methanex Motunui v. Spellman [2004] 3 NZLR 454

Singapore

VV and anor v. VW [2008] 2 SLR(R) 929

Sweden

Soyak Int'l Constr. & Investment Inc. v. Hobér, Kraus & Melis, No. Ö 4227-06 (3 Dec. 2008) (Swedish Supreme Court)

United Kingdom

ASM Shipping Ltd of India v. TTMI Ltd of England (2006) EWCA Civ 1341 (16 Oct. 2006)
Glencot Development & Design Ltd v. Ben Barrett & Son (Contractors) Ltd (2001) EWHC Technology 15 (13 Feb. 2001)
Halsey v. Milton Keynes General NHS Trust (2004) EWCA Civ 576 (11 May 2004)
North Range Shipping Ltd v. Seatrans Shipping Corp. (2002) EWCA Civ 405 (14 Mar. 2002)
R v. Gough [1993] UKHL 1 (20 May 1993)

United States

Albtelecom SH.A v. UNIFI Communs., Inc., Case No. 16 Civ. 9001, 2017 U.S. Dist. LEXIS 82154 (S.D.N.Y. 30 May 2017)
Bowden v. Weickert, No. S-02-017, 2003 WL 21419175 (Ohio App. 6 Dist. 20 Jun. 2003)
Coffee Beanery v. WW, L.L.C., No. 07-1830, 2008 U.S. App. LEXIS 23645 (6th Cir. 14 Nov. 2008)
Finkelstein v. Smith, 326 So. 2d 39 (Fla. App. 1976)
Gaskin v. Gaskin, No. 2-06-039-CV, 2006 WL 2507319 (Tex. App. Fort Worth, 21 Sep. 2006)
John Eisendrath v. Superior Court (2003 DJDAR 5849)
Logan v. Logan, No. F051606, 2007 WL 2994640 (Cal. App. 5 Dist. 16 Oct. 2007)
Town of Clinton v. Geological Servs. Corp., No. 04-0462A, 2006 WL 3246464 (Mass. Super. 8 Nov. 2006) (Unreported Memo)
Township of Aberdeen v. Patrolmen's Benevolent Association, Local 163, 669 A.2d 291, 294 (N.J. Super. Ct. App. Div. 17 Jan. 1996)
Transocean Offshore Gulf of Guinea Vii v. Erin Energy Corp., Case No. H-17-2623 (S.D. Tex. 12 Mar. 2018)
U.S. Steel Mining Company v. Wilson Downhole Services, No. 02:00CV1758, 2006 WL 2869535 (W.D. Pa. 5 Oct. 2006)

Legislation

Australia

Commercial Arbitration Act 2012 (WA)
Commercial Arbitration Act 2010 (NSW)
Commercial Arbitration Act 2013 (Qld)
Commercial Arbitration Act 1984 (NSW)
International Arbitration Act 1974 (Cth)

Bangladesh

Arbitration Act, Act No. I of 2001

Bermuda

Bermuda International Conciliation and Arbitration Act 1993

Brazil

Lei Ordinária 9.307, de 23.09.96

Canada

Alberta International Commercial Arbitration Act, R.S.A. 2000, c. I-5
British Columbia International Commercial Arbitration Act, R.S.B.C. 1996, c. 233
Ontario Arbitration Act, S.O. 1991, c. 17

China

Arbitration Law of the People's Republic of China (1994), Zhonghua Renmin Gongheguo Falu Huibian

Croatia

Conciliation Act (Official Gazette NN 18/11, 2011)

France

Code de procédure civile (C. pr. civ.)

Germany

Zivilprozeßordnung (ZPO)

Hong Kong

Arbitration Ordinance (Cap. 609, 1 Jun. 2011), L.N. 38 of 2011

India

Arbitration and Conciliation Act, Act No. 26 of 1996

Japan

Chusai Ho [Arbitration Law] Law No. 138 of 2003

Singapore

International Arbitration Act (Ch. 143A, 31 Dec. 2002)

Uganda

Uganda Arbitration and Conciliation Act (2000)

United Kingdom

Arbitration Act 1996, c. 23

United States

Cal. Civ. Proc. Code Ann. (West 2013)
Colo. Dispute Res. Act (2014)
N.C. Gen. Stat. (2013)
New Jersey International Arbitration Mediation and Conciliation Act, Title 2A (2017)
Ohio Rev. Code (2015)
Or. Rev. Stat. Ann. (West 2015)
Tex. Civ. Prac. & Rem. Code Ann. (West 2008)
Unif. Mediation Act ss. 4, 5, 7A U.L.A. 117 (Supp. 2010)

Treaties

Convention on the Recognition and Enforcement of Foreign Arbitral Awards, 10 Jun. 1958, E/CONF.26/8/Rev.1

Directive 2008/52/EC of the European Parliament and of the Council on Certain Aspects of Mediation in Civil and Commercial Matters, 21 May 2008, OJL 136/3

UNCITRAL texts

Model Law on International Commercial Conciliation of the United Nations Commission on International Trade Law, G. A. Res. 57/18, A/RES/57/18 (2002), available at <www.uncitral.org/uncitral/en/GA/resolutions.html> (accessed 14 Jan. 2018)

Travaux préparatoires, Recognition and Enforcement of Foreign Arbitral Awards, Report by the Secretary-General, Annex I, Comments by Governments (E/2822)

Travaux préparatoires, United Nations Conference on International Commercial Arbitration, Consideration of the Draft Convention on the Recognition and Enforcement of Foreign Arbitral Awards (E/CONF.26/L.26)

Travaux préparatoires, United Nations Conference on International Commercial Arbitration, Activities of Inter-Governmental and Non-Governmental Organizations in the Field of International Commercial Arbitration, Consolidated Report by the Secretary-General (E/CONF.26/4, 26)

UNCITRAL Arbitration Rules (effective 15 Aug. 2010), available at <www.uncitral.org/pdf/english/texts/arbitration/arb-rules-revised/arb-rules-revised-2010-e.pdf> (accessed 6 Apr. 2018)

UNCITRAL Conciliation Rules (effective 23 Jul. 1980), available at <www.uncitral.org/pdf/english/texts/arbitration/conc-rules/conc-rules-e.pdf> (accessed 6 Apr. 2018)

UNCITRAL, *Guide to Enactment and Use of the UNCITRAL Model Law on International Commercial Conciliation* (2002), available at <www.uncitral.org/uncitral/en/uncitral_texts/arbitration/2002Model_conciliation.html> (accessed 14 Jan. 2018)

UNCITRAL Model Law on International Commercial Arbitration (effective 7 Jul. 2006), available at <www.uncitral.org/pdf/english/texts/arbitration/ml-arb/07-86998_Ebook.pdf> (accessed 6 Apr. 2018)

UNCITRAL Model Law on International Commercial Conciliation (effective 24 Jun. 2002), available at <www.uncitral.org/pdf/english/texts/arbitration/ml-conc/03-90953_Ebook.pdf> (accessed 6 Apr. 2018)

UNCITRAL, *New Instruments on Settlement Agreements from an UNCITRAL Working Group* (12 Feb. 2018), available at <http://uncitral.tumblr.com/post/170792413006/new-instruments-on-settlement-agreements-from-an> (accessed 10 Apr. 2018)

UNCITRAL, *UNCITRAL Notes on Organizing Arbitral Proceedings (2016)*, available at <www.uncitral.org/pdf/english/texts/arbitration/arb-notes/arb-notes-2016-e.pdf> (accessed 6 Apr. 2018)

UNCITRAL, *UNCITRAL Notes on Organizing Arbitral Proceedings (1996)*, available at <www.uncitral.org/pdf/english/texts/arbitration/arb-notes/arb-notes-e.pdf> (accessed 6 Apr. 2018)

UNCITRAL, *Planned and Possible Future Work – Part III, Proposal by the Government of the United States of America: Future Work for Working Group II (A/CN.9/822)*

(47th Session, 7–18 Jul. 2014, New York), available at <www.uncitral.org/uncitral/en/commission/sessions/47th.html> (accessed 6 Apr. 2018)

UNCITRAL, *Report of Working Group II (Arbitration and Conciliation) on the Work of its Sixty-Second Session (New York, 2–6 February 2015) (A/CN.9/832)* (11 Feb. 2015), available at <www.uncitral.org/uncitral/en/commission/working_groups/2Arbitration.html> (accessed 6 Apr. 2018)

UNCITRAL Secretariat Guide on the New York Convention, available at <http://newyorkconvention1958.org/index.php?lvl=cmspage&pageid=10&menu=617&opac_view=-1> (accessed 12 Jan. 2018)

UNCITRAL, *Settlement of Commercial Disputes: Enforceability of Settlement Agreements Resulting from International Commercial Conciliation/Mediation. Note by the Secretariat (A/CN.9/WG.II/WP.187)* (27 Nov. 2014), available at <www.uncitral.org/uncitral/en/commission/working_groups/2Arbitration.html> (accessed 6 Apr. 2018)

UNCITRAL, *Settlement of Commercial Disputes, Enforcement of Settlement Agreements Resulting from International Commercial Conciliation/Mediation. Compilation of Comments by Governments (A/CN.9/846)* (27 Mar. 2015), available at <www.uncitral.org/uncitral/en/commission/working_groups/2Arbitration.html> (accessed 6 Apr. 2018)

UNCITRAL, *Settlement of Commercial Disputes. Enforcement of Settlement Agreements Resulting from International Commercial Conciliation/Mediation. Compilation of Comments by Governments (A/CN.9/846/Add.1)* (15 Apr. 2015), available at <www.uncitral.org/uncitral/en/commission/working_groups/2Arbitration.html> (accessed 6 Apr. 2018)

UNCITRAL, *Settlement of Commercial Disputes. Enforcement of Settlement Agreements Resulting from International Commercial Conciliation/Mediation. Compilation of Comments by Governments (A/CN.9/846/Add.2)* (22 Apr. 2015), available at <www.uncitral.org/uncitral/en/commission/working_groups/2Arbitration.html> (accessed 6 Apr. 2018)

UNCITRAL, *Settlement of Commercial Disputes. Enforcement of Settlement Agreements Resulting from International Commercial Conciliation/Mediation. Compilation of Comments by Governments (A/CN.9/846/Add.3)* (4 Jun. 2015), available at <www.uncitral.org/uncitral/en/commission/working_groups/2Arbitration.html> (accessed 6 Apr. 2018)

UNCITRAL, *Settlement of Commercial Disputes. Enforcement of Settlement Agreements Resulting from International Commercial Conciliation/Mediation. Compilation of Comments by Governments (A/CN.9/846/Add.4)* (12 Jun. 2015), available at <www.uncitral.org/uncitral/en/commission/working_groups/2Arbitration.html> (accessed 6 Apr. 2018)

UNCITRAL, *Settlement of Commercial Disputes. International Commercial Conciliation: Enforceability of Settlement Agreements. Note by the Secretariat (A/CN.9/WG.II/WP.190)* (13 Jul. 2015), available at <www.uncitral.org/uncitral/en/commission/working_groups/2Arbitration.html> (accessed 6 Apr. 2018)

UNCITRAL, *Settlement of Commercial Disputes. International Commercial Mediation: Preparation of Instruments on Enforcement of International Commercial Settlement Agreements Resulting from Mediation. Note by the Secretariat (A/CN.9/WG.II/WP.205/Add.1)* (23 Nov. 2017), available at <www.uncitral.org/uncitral/en/commission/working_groups/2Arbitration.html> (accessed 6 Apr. 2018)

Rules and guidelines

Australian Centre for International Commercial Arbitration (ACICA) Arbitration Rules (effective 1 Jan. 2016), available at <http://acica.org.au/acica-services/acica-rules-2016> (accessed 6 Apr. 2018)

Beijing Arbitration Commission Arbitration Rules (effective 1 Apr. 2015), available at <www.bjac.org.cn/page/data_dl/bjac_guize_en.pdf> (accessed 6 Apr. 2018)

CEDR Rules for the Facilitation of Settlement in International Arbitration (Nov. 2009), available at <www.cedr.com/about_us/arbitration_commission/draft_rules.php> (accessed 6 Apr. 2018)

Chartered Institute of Arbitrators (CIArb), *Practice Guideline 7: Guidelines for Arbitrators on the Use of ADR Procedures*, available at <www.ciarb.org/docs/default-source/practice-guidelines-protocols-and-rules/international-arbitration-guidelines-2011/2011adrprocedures.pdf?sfvrsn=10> (accessed 14 Jan. 2018)

China International Economic and Trade Arbitration Commission (CIETAC) Arbitration Rules (effective 1 Jan. 2015), available at <www.cietac.org/index.php?m=Page&a=index&id=106&l=en> (accessed 6 Apr. 2018)

Colorado Mediators & Arbitrators Med-Arbitration Rules of Procedure (effective 1 Nov. 2013), available at <http://coma.com/rules/med-arbitration#Rule MA-1. Purpose of Med-Arbitration Proceedings> (accessed 6 Apr. 2018)

Conciliation Centre at Croatian Chamber of Economy (CCCCE) Rules of Conciliation (effective 17 Jul. 2002), available at <www.vsrh.hr/EasyWeb.asp?pcpid=286> (accessed 6 Apr. 2018)

Court of Arbitration at the Polish Chamber of Commerce (PCC) Mediation Rules (effective 1 Jan. 2015), available at <www.sakig.pl/en/arbitration/rules> (accessed 6 Apr. 2018)

German Institution of Arbitration (DIS) Arbitration Rules (effective 1 Jul. 1998), available at <www.dis-arb.de/scho/16/rules/dis-arbitration-rules-98-id10> (accessed 6 Apr. 2018)

Hong Kong International Arbitration Centre (HKIAC) Mediation Rules (effective 1 Aug. 1999), available at <www.hkiac.org/mediation/rules/hkiac-mediation-rules> (accessed 14 Jan. 2018)

International Bar Association (IBA) Guidelines on Conflicts of Interest in International Arbitration (2014), available at <www.ibanet.org/Publications/publications_IBA_guides_and_free_materials.aspx> (accessed 14 Jan. 2018)

International Bar Association (IBA) Rules of Ethics for International Arbitrators (1987), available at <www.ibanet.org/Document/Default.aspx?DocumentUid=B21F3C32-190E-4FB0-9750-5459AE4E8498> (accessed 14 Jan. 2018)

International Centre for Dispute Resolution, *Guide to Drafting International Dispute Resolution Clauses*, available at <www.icdr.org/sites/default/files/document_repository/ICDR_Guide_Drafting_Clauses.pdf> (accessed 14 Jan. 2018)

International Court of Arbitration of the International Chamber of Commerce (ICC), *Mediation Guidance Notes* (International Chamber of Commerce 2013)

International Court of Arbitration of the International Chamber of Commerce (ICC) Mediation Rules (effective 1 Jan. 2014), available at <www.iccwbo.org/products-and-services/arbitration-and-adr/mediation/rules/> (accessed 6 Apr. 2018)

International Court of Arbitration of the International Chamber of Commerce (ICC) Rules of Arbitration (effective 1 Mar. 2017), available at <https://iccwbo.org/dispute-resolution-services/arbitration/rules-of-arbitration/> (accessed 6 Apr. 2018)

JAMS, *JAMS Mediator-in-Reserve Policy for International Arbitrations*, available at <www.jamsinternational.com/mediator-in-reserve-policy-international-arbitration> (accessed 14 Jan. 2018)

Japan Commercial Arbitration Association (JCAA) International Commercial Mediation Rules (effective 1 Jan. 2009), available at <www.jcaa.or.jp/e/mediation/docs/rules.pdf> (accessed 6 Apr. 2018)

Korean Commercial Arbitration Board (KCAB) Domestic Arbitration Rules (effective 1 Sep. 2011), available at <www.kcab.or.kr/jsp/kcab_eng/law/law_03_ex.jsp> (accessed 6 Apr. 2018)

Korean Commercial Arbitration Board (KCAB) Domestic Arbitration Rules (effective 30 Nov. 2016), available at <www.kcab.or.kr/jsp/kcab_eng/law/law_03_ex.jsp> (accessed 6 Apr. 2018)

London Court of International Arbitration (LCIA) Arbitration Rules (effective 1 Oct. 2014), available at <www.lcia.org/Dispute_Resolution_Services/lcia-arbitration-rules-2014.aspx> (accessed 6 Apr. 2018)

Queensland Civil and Administrative Tribunal, *Hybrid Hearings* (effective 3 Sep. 2012), available at <www.qcat.qld.gov.au/using-qcat/practice-directions#2012> (accessed 6 Apr. 2018)

Safeguards for Arbitrators Who Use Private Meetings with Each Party as a Means of Facilitating Settlement (Final Report of the CEDR Commission on Settlement in International Arbitration, Appendix 2), available at <www.cedr.com/about_us/arbitration_commission/> (accessed 14 Jan. 2018)

Singapore International Mediation Centre, *SIAC-SIMC Arb-Med-Arb Protocol*, available at <http://simc.com.sg/siac-simc-arb-med-arb-protocol/> (accessed 14 Jan. 2018)

Society of Maritime Arbitrators (SMA) Conciliation Rules (effective 16 May 1988), available at <www.smany.org/concilliation-rules.html> (accessed 6 Apr. 2018)

Stockholm Chamber of Commerce (SCC) Mediation Rules (effective 1 Jan. 2014), available at <http://sccinstitute.com/dispute-resolution/rules/> (accessed 6 Apr. 2018)

World Intellectual Property Organization (WIPO) Mediation Rules (effective 1 Jan. 2016), available at <www.wipo.int/amc/en/mediation/rules/newrules.html#7a> (accessed 6 Apr. 2018)

Theses

Ali, Shahla, *International Arbitration and Mediation in East Asia: Examining the Role of Domestic Legal Culture and Globalization on Shaping East Asian Arbitration* (PhD thesis, University of California, 2007)

Conference papers

Bridge, Campbell, *Med-Arb and Other Hybrid Processes – One Man's Meat Is Another Man's Poison* (unpublished paper presented at APRAG 2014, 10th Anniversary Conference, Australia 2014)

Hindle, Royden, *Mixing it up: Medarb Re-visited* (unpublished paper prepared for the AMINZ Seminar 'Current Issues in Arbitration', Mar. 2014)

Lawday, Geoff, *Hybrid Dispute Resolution Processes* (unpublished paper presented at 'Mediation in a Global Village – Cross-cultural and International Aspects of Mediation and Negotiation', Germany 2009)

Reiner, Andreas, *Bridges Between Mediation and Arbitration: The Mediator as Arbitrator?/The Arbitrator as Mediator?* (unpublished paper presented at Tenth Zagreb Arbitration Conference, 2002)

Interviews

Telephone interview with Professor Bernardo Cremades (10 Mar. 2015) (on file with author)

Interview with Professor Bernard Hanotiau (London, 20 Apr. 2015) (on file with author)

Interview with Professor Doug Jones (Hong Kong, 20 Mar. 2015) (on file with author)

Interview with Mr Christopher To (Hong Kong, 21 Mar. 2015) (on file with author)

Interview with Professor Thomas J. Stipanowich (London, 19 Apr. 2015) (on file with author)

Interview with Practitioner from Switzerland (London, 20 Apr. 2015) (on file with author)

Internet sources

Alexander, Nadja, *The Race Towards a New York Convention for Cross-Border Mediated Settlement Agreements: The Fable of the Tortoise and the Hare Revisited?* Kluwer Mediation Blog (13 Jul. 2014), available at <http://kluwermediationblog.com/2014/07/13/the-race-towards-a-new-york-convention-for-cross-border-mediated-settlement-agreements-the-fable-of-the-tortoise-and-the-hare-revisited/> (accessed 6 Apr. 2018)

Altenkirch, Markus & Anindya Basarkod, *Arb-Med-Arb: What is it and how can it help the parties to solve their disputes efficiently?* Global Arbitration News (20 Nov. 2017), available at <https://globalarbitrationnews.com/arb-med-arb-what-is-it-and-how-can-it-help-the-parties-to-solve-their-disputes-efficiently/> (accessed 6 Apr. 2018)

Arbitration Institute of the Stockholm Chamber of Commerce, *Model Mediation Clause – Combined Clause*, available at <www.sccinstitute.com/dispute-resolution/model-clauses/english/> (accessed 14 Jan. 2018)

Arbitrator Intelligence, *About*, available at <www.arbitratorintelligence.org/about/> (accessed 26 Jan. 2018)

Baarsma, Barbara & Maurits Barendrecht, *Mediation 2.0,* Hiil Innovating Justice, available at <www.hiil.org/project/mediation-2-0?goback=%2Egmp_1863991%2Egde_1863991_member_123727192> (accessed 14 Jan. 2018)

BIMCO, *BIMCO Standard Dispute Resolution Clause 2016*, available at <www.bimco.org/contracts-and-clauses/bimco-clauses/dispute_resolution_clauses> (accessed 14 Jan. 2018)

Böckstiegel, Karl-Heinz, *Assumptions regarding Common Law versus Civil Law in the Practice of International Commercial Arbitration*, ICCA, available at <www.arbitration-icca.org/media/4/67308804210771/media113194214157020l-common_law_versus_civil_law_.pdf> (accessed 14 Jan. 2018)

Borrasso, Ava, *U.S. District Courts Rule Consent Awards Fall Within New York Convention*, Kluwer Arbitration Blog (6 Apr. 2018), available at <http://

arbitrationblog.kluwerarbitration.com/2018/04/06/u-s-district-courts-rule-consent-awards-fall-within-new-york-convention/> (accessed 11 Apr. 2018)

CCA/IMI/ Straus Institute International Task Force on Mixed Mode Dispute Resolution, *Memo on the Task Force and Project*, International Mediation Institute (5 Apr. 2016), available at <www.imimediation.org/about-imi/who-are-imi/mixed-mode-task-force/#about> (accessed 6 Apr. 2018)

Centre de Médiation et d'Arbitrage, *Autres modes alternatifs de règlement des conflits*, available at <www.cmap.fr/notre-offre/les-autres-modes-alternatifs-de-resolution-des-conflits/> (accessed 14 Jan. 2018)

City University of Hong Kong, The International ADR Mooting Competition, *About the Moot*, available at <www.cityu.edu.hk/slw/ADR_Moot/about.html> (accessed 14 Jan. 2018)

City University of Hong Kong, The International ADR Mooting Competition, *Structure of the Moot*, available at <www.cityu.edu.hk/slw/ADR_Moot/structure.html> (accessed 14 Jan. 2018)

D'Agostino, Justin, *Arb-Med Procedures and Enforcement in Hong Kong: The Crest of the Waiver?* Kluwer Arbitration Blog (16 Jan. 2012), available at <http://kluwerarbitrationblog.com/2012/01/16/arb-med-procedures-and-enforcement-in-hong-kong-the-crest-of-the-waiver/> (accessed 6 Apr. 2018)

D'Agostino, Justin, *Mediator-Arbitrators: The Perfect Match or No Love Lost? (A Valentine's Day Blog),* Kluwer Arbitration Blog (15 Feb. 2011), available at <http://kluwerarbitrationblog.com/blog/2011/02/15/mediator-arbitrators-the-perfect-match-or-no-love-lost-a-valentines-day-blog/> (accessed 6 Apr. 2018)

European Parliament, Directorate-General for Internal Policies, Policy Department, Citizen's Rights and Constitutional Affairs, *Rebooting the Mediation Directive: Assessing the Limited Impact of its Implementation and Proposing Measures to Increase the Number of Mediations in the EU* (2014), available at <www.adrcenterinternational.com/wp-content/uploads/2015/07/IPOL-JURI_ET2014493042_EN.pdf> (accessed 6 Apr. 2018)

Final Report of the CEDR Commission on Settlement in International Arbitration (Nov. 2009), available at <www.cedr.com/about_us/arbitration_commission/> (accessed 6 Apr. 2018)

Flake, Richard P., *MED/ARB – A Viable ADR Vehicle? Nuances of Med/Arb—A Neutral's Perspective*, CEDIRES, available at <www.cedires.com/index_bestanden/FLAKE_http-www.cbylaw.com-filebin_files_flake_rpf-AAA_Med-Arb.pdf> (accessed 14 Jan. 2018)

Georgiou, Phillip & Iain C.L. Seow, *Hong Kong Strengthens Position as Leading Jurisdiction for International Arbitration with Major Overhaul of Legislative Framework,* Lexology (22 Jul. 2011), available at <www.lexology.com/library/detail.aspx?g=24288c95-7f16-4ede-b7e7-41b1c8f8e1dc> (accessed 6 Apr. 2018)

Giaretta, Ben & Katherine McMenamin, *The Singapore International Mediation Centre*, Singapore International Mediation Centre (2 Nov. 2014), available at <http://simc.com.sg/resources-2/page/3/> (accessed 6 Apr. 2018)

Global Pound Conference Series 2016-17 Cumulated Data Results March 2016 – September 2017, Global Pound, available at <http://globalpound.org/wp-content/uploads/2017/11/2017-09-18-Final-GPC-Series-Results-Cumulated-Votes-from-the-GPC-App-Mar.-2016-Sep.-2017.pdf> (accessed 14 Jan. 2018)

Goodrich, Mark, *Arb-Med: Ideal Solution or Dangerous Heresy?* White & Case (30 Mar. 2012), available at <www.whitecase.com/publications/article/arb-med-ideal-solution-or-dangerous-heresy> (accessed 3 Apr. 2018)

Herbert Smith Freehills, *Going Global: CIETAC's New Arbitration Rules 2012*, Lexology (4 Jul. 2012), available at <www.lexology.com/library/detail.aspx?g=d7e31792-27c5-47f6-9815-859a8763f4ea> (accessed 6 Apr. 2018)

Herbert Smith Freehills, *UK: Can Adjudicators Get Involved?* Mondaq (12 Nov. 2001), available at <www.mondaq.com/x/14136/Property+Litigation/Can+Adjudicators+Get+Involved> (accessed 6 Apr. 2018)

How Users View the Proposal for a UN Convention on the Enforcement of Mediated Settlements, International Mediation Institute, available at <www.fd.unl.pt/docentes_docs/ma/MFG_MA_23458.pdf> (accessed 14 Jan. 2018)

IMI International Corporate Users ADR Survey (January-March 2013), International Mediation Institute (4 Apr. 2013), available at <www.fd.unl.pt/docentes_docs/ma/MFG_MA_23457.pdf> (accessed 6 Apr. 2018)

International Court of Arbitration of the International Chamber of Commerce, *Suggested Clauses for ICC Mediation: Clause D: Obligation to Refer Dispute to the ICC Mediation Rules, Followed by Arbitration if Required*, available at <https://iccwbo.org/publication/suggested-icc-mediation-clause-english-version//> (accessed 14 Jan. 2018)

International Institute for Conflict Prevention and Resolution, *Attitudes Toward ADR in the Asia-Pacific Region: A CPR Survey*, available at <www.cpradr.org/strategy/international-initiatives/asia/asia/_res/id=Attachments/index=0/asia-pacific-survey.pdf> (accessed 14 Jan. 2018)

International Mediation Institute, *Mixed Mode Task Force: About*, available at <www.imimediation.org/about-imi/who-are-imi/mixed-mode-task-force/#about> (accessed 14 Jan. 2018)

Jepson-Turner, Clemmie, *The Problems of Med-Arb – Should Keeneye Open Our Eyes?* Global Arb. Rev. (22 Sep. 2011), available at <http://globalarbitrationreview.com/journal/article/29833/london-problems-med-arb-keeneye-open-eyes> (accessed 6 Apr. 2018)

Kaufmann-Kohler, Gabrielle, *When Arbitrators Facilitate Settlement: Towards a Transnational Standard*, Clayton Utz, available at <www.claytonutz.com/ialecture/2007/transcript_2007.html> (accessed 14 Jan. 2018)

Kaufmann-Kohler, Gabrielle & Victor Bonnin, *Arbitrators as Conciliators: A Statistical Study of the Relation between an Arbitrator's Role and Legal Background*, ICCA, available at <www.arbitration-icca.org/media/0/12319144605970/00950003.pdf> (accessed 14 Jan. 2018)

Lau, Victor & Vanja Bulut, *Resolution of Disputes in China – What It Means for Australia*, Clayton Utz (15 Mar. 2012), available at <www.claytonutz.com/publications/edition/15_march_2012/20120315/resolution_of_disputes_in_china-what_it_means_for_australia.page> (accessed 6 Apr. 2018)

Leathes, Michael, *Dispute Resolution Mules – Preventing the Process from Being Part of the Problem*, International Mediation Institute (14 Mar. 2012), available at <www.imimediation.org/wp-content/uploads/2017/09/dispute-resolution-mules-final-.pdf > (accessed 6 Apr. 2018)

Leathes, Michael, *2020 Vision: Where in the World Will Mediation Be Within 10 Years?* International Mediation Institute (Nov. 2010), available at <https://imimediation.org/tools-and-resources/resources/reading-materials > (accessed 30 Mar. 2018)

London Court of International Arbitration, *Recommended Clauses: Mediation and Arbitration*, available at <www.lcia.org/Dispute_Resolution_Services/LCIA_Mediation_Clauses.aspx> (accessed 14 Jan. 2018)

Maia, Andrea, *Solving Complex Problems – Thinking out of the Box*, Kluwer Mediation Blog (25 Oct. 2013), available at <http://kluwermediationblog.com/2013/10/25/solving-complex-problems-thinking-out-of-the-box/> (accessed 6 Apr. 2018)

Majid, Saleh & Faris Lenzen, *Application of Islamic Law in The Middle East*, Mondaq (25 Mar. 2011), available at <www.mondaq.com/x/52976/international+trade+investment/Application+Of+Islamic+Law+In+The+Middle+East> (accessed 6 Apr. 2018)

Marriott, Arthur, *Litigate, Arbitrate, Mediate – Frustrate? Breaking the Dispute Deadlock,* Clayton Utz, available at <www.claytonutz.com/ialecture/2005/transcript_2005.html> (accessed 14 Jan. 2018)

McIlwrath, Michael, *Anti-Arbitration: 10 Things to Do Before the Arbitration Gets Underway*, Kluwer Arbitration Blog (12 Nov. 2011), available at <http://kluwerarbitrationblog.com/blog/2011/11/12/anti-arbitration-10-things-to-do-before-the-arbitration-gets-underway/> (accessed 6 Apr. 2018)

McIlwrath, Michael, *Anti-Arbitration: It's Not Hard to Mediate During Arbitral Proceedings*, Kluwer Arbitration Blog (13 Sep. 2011), available at <http://kluwerarbitrationblog.com/2011/09/13/anti-arbitration-its-not-hard-to-mediate-during-arbitral-proceedings/> (accessed 6 Apr. 2018)

McIlwrath, Michael, *UNCITRAL to Consider Proposal for Convention on Enforcement of Mediated Settlements,* Kluwer Arbitration Blog (7 Jul. 2014), available at <http://kluwerarbitrationblog.com/blog/2014/07/07/uncitral-to-consider-proposal-for-convention-on-enforcement-of-mediated-settlements/> (accessed 6 Apr. 2018)

Menon, Sundaresh, Keynote Address, *International Arbitration: The Coming of a New Age for Asia (and Elsewhere),* ICCA (ICCA 2012 Congress, Jun. 2012), available at <www.arbitration-icca.org/AV_Library/AV_Library_textformat/ICCA_2012_Singapore_Keynote_Menon.html> (accessed 6 Apr. 2018)

Michaels, Ralf, *Legal Culture*, Duke Law Scholarship Repository, available at <http://scholarship.law.duke.edu/cgi/viewcontent.cgi?article=3012&context=faculty_scholarship> (accessed 14 Jan. 2018)

Nelken, David, *Comparing Legal Cultures*, in *The Blackwell Companion to Law and Society* (Austin Sarat ed., Blackwell Publishing 2004), available at <www.blackwellreference.com/subscriber/tocnode.html?id=g9780631228967_chunk_g97806312289679> (accessed 14 Jan. 2018)

Nottage, Luke, *Arb-Med and New International Commercial Mediation Rules in Japan*, Japanese Law and the Asia-Pacific (21 Jul. 2009), available at <http://blogs.usyd.edu.au/japaneselaw/2009/07/arbmed_and_new_international_c_1.html> (accessed 6 Apr. 2018)

Nottage, Luke, *Arb-Med in Australia: The Time has Come*, Japanese Law and the Asia-Pacific (31 Oct. 2007), available at <http://blogs.usyd.edu.au/japaneselaw/ArbMed.pdf> (accessed 6 Apr. 2018)

Nottage, Luke, *Drafting Arbitration Clauses to Minimise Costs and Delays in International Commercial Arbitration: An Asia-Pacific Perspective*, Japanese Law and the Asia-Pacific (16 May 2011), available at <http://blogs.usyd.edu.au/japaneselaw/2011/05/> (accessed 6 Apr. 2018)

Oddy, Alexander et al., *Hong Kong Courts Consider the Mediation-Arbitration Procedure*, Lexology (8 Jun. 2011), available at <www.lexology.com/library/detail.aspx?g=dade4ce7-f513-411e-b9bf-57471a20133f> (accessed 6 Apr. 2018)

Oxford Dictionaries, available at <https://en.oxforddictionaries.com> (accessed 9 Jan. 2018)

Press Release: Singapore International Mediation Centre (SIMC) Announces Case Numbers for 2014/2015, Singapore International Mediation Centre (16 Mar. 2016), available at <http://simc.com.sg/press-release-singapore-international-mediation-centre-simc-announces-case-numbers-for-20142015/> (accessed 6 Apr. 2018)

Pryles, Michael, *Limits to Party Autonomy in Arbitral Procedure*, ICCA, available at <www.arbitration-icca.org/articles.html?author=Michael_Pryles&sort=author> (accessed 14 Jan. 2018)

Rewald, Roman & Kimberly Jachimek Weil, *Expanding ADR in Poland: Mediation and Arbitration Together*, Lexology, available at <http://documents.lexology.com/63de58ab-0582-410b-97aa-1c6f490e7f67.pdf> (accessed 14 Jan. 2018)

Rogers, Catherine A., *The International Arbitrator Information Project: From an Ideation to Operation*, Kluwer Arbitration Blog (10 Dec. 2012), available at <http://kluwerarbitrationblog.com/blog/2012/12/10/the-international-arbitrator-information-project-from-an-ideation-to-operation/> (accessed 6 Apr. 2018)

School of International Arbitration (Queen Mary, University of London), *2006 International Arbitration Study: Corporate Attitudes and Practices*, available at <www.arbitration.qmul.ac.uk/research/2006/> (accessed 14 Jan. 2018)

School of International Arbitration (Queen Mary, University of London), *2008 International Arbitration Study – Corporate Attitudes and Practices: Recognition and Enforcement of Foreign Awards*, available at <www.arbitration.qmul.ac.uk/research/2008/index.html> (accessed 14 Jan. 2018)

School of International Arbitration (Queen Mary, University of London), *International Arbitration Survey 2010: Choices in International Arbitration*, available at <www.arbitration.qmul.ac.uk/research/2010/index.html> (accessed 14 Jan. 2018)

School of International Arbitration (Queen Mary, University of London), *2012 International Arbitration Survey: Current and Preferred Practices in the Arbitral Process*, available at <www.arbitration.qmul.ac.uk/research/2012/index.html> (accessed 14 Jan. 2018)

School of International Arbitration (Queen Mary, University of London), *2013 International Arbitration Survey: Corporate Choices in International Arbitration: Industry Perspectives*, available at <www.arbitration.qmul.ac.uk/research/2013/index.html> (accessed 14 Jan. 2018)

School of International Arbitration (Queen Mary, University of London), *2015 International Arbitration Survey: Improvements and Innovations in International Arbitration*, available at <www.arbitration.qmul.ac.uk/research/2015/index.html> (accessed 14 Jan. 2018)

Sharp, Geoff, *The Handbrake on Global Mediation*, Kluwer Mediation Blog (31 Aug. 2012), available at <http://mediationblog.kluwerarbitration.com/2012/08/31/the-handbrake-on-global-mediation/> (accessed 6 Apr. 2018)

Singapore International Mediation Centre, *The Singapore Arb-Med-Arb Clause*, available at <http://simc.com.sg/the-singapore-arb-med-arb-clause/> (accessed 14 Jan. 2018)

Singapore International Mediation Centre, *What is Arb-Med-Arb?* available at <http://simc.com.sg/arb-med-arb/> (accessed 14 Jan. 2018)

Stipanowich, Thomas J., *What Have We Learned From The Global Pound Conferences?* Kluwer Arbitration Blog (27 Nov. 2017), available at <http://mediationblog.kluwerarbitration.com/2017/11/27/learned-global-pound-conferences/> (accessed 6 Apr. 2018)

Strong, S. I., *Use and Perception of International Commercial Mediation and Conciliation: A Preliminary Report on Issues Relating to the Proposed UNCITRAL Convention on International Commercial Mediation and Conciliation*, Social Science Research Network (17 Nov. 2014), available at <http://ssrn.com/abstract=2526302> (accessed 6 Apr. 2018)

Summary Report of the First Meeting in September 23–24, 2016 of the International Task Force on Mixed Mode Dispute Resolution: Inaugural Summit at Pepperdine University, Malibu, CA, USA, International Mediation Institute 26 (2017), available at <www.imimediation.org/about-imi/who-are-imi/mixed-mode-task-force/> (accessed 6 Apr. 2018)

U.S. Legal Forms, Inc., *Legal Definitions and Legal Terms Dictionary*, available at <http://definitions.uslegal.com/l/legal-culture/> (accessed 14 Jan. 2018)

Weisman, Martin C., *Med/Arb – A Time and Cost Effective Hybrid for Dispute Resolution,* Weisman, Young & Ruemenapp, P.C., available at <www.wysr-law.com/articles.html> (accessed 14 Jan. 2018)

Wilson, Claire, *The Arb-Med Hybrid in Hong Kong – Much Ado about Nothing?* Kluwer Mediation Blog (1 Feb. 2012), available at <http://kluwermediationblog.com/2012/02/01/the-arb-med-hybrid-in-hong-kong-much-ado-about-nothing/> (accessed 6 Apr. 2018)

Events and conferences

Arbitration Update for the New Year 2012 (event by HK45 Arbitration Group, Hong Kong 12 Jan. 2012)

Bond, Stephen (quote from Conference 26/11/09), available at <www.cedr.com/about_us/arbitration_commission/arbcomsampledirections.php> (accessed 14 Jan. 2018)

Hot Topics in International Arbitration 2011 (event by SJ Berwin, London 19 Sep. 2011)

International Arbitration: The View from England and China (event by the General Council of the Bar of England & Wales and the China Britain Law Institute, Beijing 22 Nov. 2011)

Ohara, Yoshimi, *Mediation and Adjudication: Where Asia Stands Now (Japan)*, CIArb Centennial Conference (Hong Kong, 21 Mar. 2015) (recorded and transcribed by D. Nigmatullina)

Other

Email from Albert Monichino to Dilyara Nigmatullina (31 Mar. 2014) (on file with author)

Letter to Working Group 2 Task Force Member (28 Aug. 2017) (on file with author)

Monichino, Albert, *Inquiry into Commercial Arbitration Bill 2011 (WA) – Clause 27D Mediation Clause* (unpublished submission to Legislative Council of Western Australia, 17 Oct. 2011)

Appendix 1

Definitions of combinations

Key combinations	*Most common definitions*	*Definition used in this book*
Med-arb	1 A two-step process, where mediation is the first step followed, if necessary, by arbitration as the second step to decide the issues not settled in mediation and where (a) the same neutral acts as the mediator and the arbitrator; or (b) the same or different neutrals act as the mediator and the arbitrator. 2 A two-step process that starts either with mediation or arbitration in which the same neutral acts as the mediator and the arbitrator.	The sequential use of mediation and arbitration, with the mediation phase taking place first where the same or different neutrals act as the mediator and the arbitrator.
Same neutral med-arb	The sequential use of mediation and arbitration, with the mediation phase taking place first where the same neutral acts as the mediator and the arbitrator.	The sequential use of mediation and arbitration, with the mediation phase taking place first where the same neutral acts as the mediator and the arbitrator.
Diff neutral med-arb	The sequential use of mediation and arbitration, with the mediation phase	The sequential use of mediation and

(*Continued*)

(Cont.)

Key combinations	*Most common definitions*	*Definition used in this book*
	taking place first where different neutrals act as the mediator and the arbitrator.	arbitration, with the mediation phase taking place first where different neutrals act as the mediator and the arbitrator.
Arb-med-arb	A separate mediation process in the course of an on-going arbitration where 1 mediation is conducted either by the arbitrator or by a different neutral; 2 mediation is conducted by a different neutral; or 3 mediation is conducted by the arbitrator.	A separate mediation process in the course of arbitration where mediation is conducted by the arbitrator or a different neutral.
Same neutral arb-med-arb	–	A separate mediation process in the course of arbitration where mediation is conducted by the arbitrator.
Diff neutral arb-med-arb	–	A separate mediation process in the course of arbitration where mediation is conducted by a different neutral.
Same neutral (arb)-med-arb	–	A joint reference to the same neutral med-arb and the same neutral arb-med-arb.
Diff neutral (arb)-med-arb	–	A joint reference to the diff neutral med-arb and diff neutral arb-med-arb.
Arb-med	1 A process that begins with arbitration resulting in a binding award that is sealed and kept confidential while parties proceed to the mediation phase. If parties settle in mediation, the award is	A process that begins with arbitration resulting in an award that is placed in a sealed envelope and kept confidential. Then the former arbitrator becomes the mediator. If parties do not settle in

(*Continued*)

(Cont.)

Key combinations	*Most common definitions*	*Definition used in this book*
	not disclosed; otherwise, the award is revealed and becomes binding. In arb-med (a) the same neutral acts as the arbitrator and the mediator; or (b) the same or different neutrals act as the arbitrator and the mediator. 2 A process that begins with arbitration and an attempt to mediate is made within the arbitration proceedings.	mediation, the award becomes binding; otherwise, the neutral never discloses the award.
MEDALOA	Mediation followed by last offer arbitration where each party submits a 'last offer' to the neutral who must choose one of them and where 1 the same neutral acts as the mediator and the arbitrator; 2 different neutrals act as the mediator and the arbitrator; or 3 the same or different neutrals act as the mediator and the arbitrator.	A process that starts with mediation and, if parties do not settle, then, each party submits a 'last offer' to the dual role neutral who chooses one of them.
Co-med-arb	1 Two different neutrals, the mediator and the arbitrator conduct a joint session, after which the mediator works with parties, including in caucuses, in the absence of the arbitrator. If the dispute is not settled in mediation, it goes to the arbitrator who renders an award. 2 A sequential use of mediation and arbitration with a different person acting as the arbitrator if mediation does not result in settlement.	A process where the arbitrator attends joint sessions in mediation (but does not participate in caucusing) and, if no settlement is reached in mediation, renders an award.

Appendix 2

Questionnaire on the combined use of mediation and arbitration in an international commercial context

INFORMATION REGARDING THE QUESTIONNAIRE THAT YOU ARE ABOUT TO COMPLETE

This questionnaire relates to your experience as an international commercial dispute resolution practitioner over the last five or fewer years as applicable. Its particular focus is your experience, if any, in the combined use of mediation and arbitration in international commercial dispute resolution. Experience in the combined use of mediation and arbitration, however, is ***not*** a prerequisite for participation in this study.

The questionnaire has 22 questions, and it should take you not more than 10–15 minutes to complete it.

You will remain anonymous, unless you indicate that you are interested to participate in a follow-up interview and you provide your contact information. Any contact information will be used for the purposes of research only.

Completion of this questionnaire will be considered evidence of your consent to take part in this research project.

Please note in this questionnaire

Mediation is used interchangeably with conciliation. Evaluative and facilitative styles of mediation are distinguished. A mediator adopting a facilitative style will not suggest specific options for settlement, express a view as to the merits of the dispute, or be directive on the outcome.

The neutral means either a mediator or an arbitrator in an international commercial dispute resolution process.

The combined use of mediation and arbitration refers to the actual use of the discrete ***processes*** of mediation and arbitration in combination. It includes any combination of processes in whatever order and whether conducted by the same or different neutrals.

Q1–4 PROVIDE BACKGROUND INFORMATION ABOUT YOUR INTERNATIONAL COMMERCIAL DISPUTE RESOLUTION PRACTICE	
1. What is your primary country of practice?	Country:
2. Are you qualified to practise as a lawyer?	a) yes b) no c) yes, but not currently in practice
3. Over the last five years what has been your most frequent professional role in international commercial dispute resolution?	a) counsel b) mediator c) arbitrator d) other. Please specify:
4. Over the last five years, approximately how many international commercial disputes have you been involved in as a professional?	a) 1–5 b) 6–10 c) 11–15 d) >16. Please specify the approximate amount:

Q5–19 RELATE TO YOUR PROFESSIONAL EXPERIENCE IN THE COMBINED USE OF MEDIATION AND ARBITRATION IN INTERNATIONAL COMMERCIAL DISPUTE RESOLUTION	
5. Over the last five years have you acted as a professional in any international commercial dispute resolution that involved the combined use of mediation and arbitration?	Please circle as many answers as are applicable a) yes, I have acted as a counsel b) yes, I have acted as a mediator in a dispute that involved arbitration with a different neutral c) yes, I have acted as an arbitrator in a dispute that involved mediation with a different neutral d) yes, I have acted as a mediator and an arbitrator in the same dispute e) no, I have not acted as a professional in any dispute involving the combined use of mediation and arbitration **(Go to question 20)**
6. Over the last five years, what is the approximate proportion of disputes involving the combined use of mediation and arbitration of your overall international commercial dispute resolution practice?	Please circle one answer a) not more than 10% b) not more than 20% c) not more than 30% d) not more than 50% e) not more than 75% f) all

(*Continued*)

(Cont.)

7. What triggered the combined use of mediation and arbitration?	Please circle as many answers as are applicable a) specifically tailored contractual provision b) model multi-tiered clause of an arbitration institute incorporated into parties' contract c) initiative of one or both parties d) one or both parties' counsel suggestion e) mediator's suggestion f) arbitrator's suggestion g) your suggestion. Please specify in which capacity you were acting: h) provision in the rules of an arbitration institute i) suggestion of an arbitration institute j) provision in the applicable legislation. Please specify the country of the legislation: k) combination of triggers. Please specify which ones (e.g. c & d): l) don't know m) other. Please specify:
8. If in Q7 you circled more than one answer, is there any that applied most frequently?	a) yes. Please specify by writing the letter (e.g. i): b) no
9. If in Q7 you circled a participant in the process other than you, please specify the country of origin or practice of such participant.	Trigger — Country — Don't know a party/parties a counsel/ counsel mediator arbitrator
10. When in the combined process has mediation been used?	Please circle as many answers as are applicable a) before arbitration b) after commencement of arbitration but before the hearing on the merits c) after the hearing on the merits but before issuing the award d) after issuing the award e) at the same time as arbitration f) other. Please specify:
11. If in Q10 you circled more than one answer, is there any that applied most frequently?	a) yes. Please specify by writing the letter: b) no

(*Continued*)

(Cont.)

12. Who conducted mediation in the combined process?	Please circle as many answers as are applicable a) the sole arbitrator b) a member of the arbitral tribunal c) a neutral other than a) or b)
13. If in Q12 you circled more than one answer, is there any that applied most frequently?	a) yes. Please specify by writing the letter: b) no
14. If you conducted mediation in a dispute involving the combined use of mediation and arbitration how would you best characterise your mediation style?	Please circle one answer a) facilitative b) evaluative c) not applicable d) other. Please specify:
15. Were caucuses (private meetings) used in mediation?	Please circle one answer a) always b) in the majority of cases c) in the minority of cases d) never c) don't know
16. How was the outcome of a dispute resolution process recorded?	Please circle as many answers as are applicable a) in a mediated settlement agreement b) in a consent arbitral award incorporating a mediated settlement agreement c) in a regular arbitral award d) in a court judgment e) other. Please specify:
17. If in Q16 you circled more than one answer, is there any that applied most frequently?	a) yes. Please specify by writing the letter: b) no
18. What types of disputes were resolved by using a combination of mediation and arbitration?	Please circle as many answers as are applicable a) complex commercial disputes b) specialised industry disputes. Please specify the industry: c) other. Please specify:
19. If in Q18 you circled more than one answer, is there any that applied most frequently?	a) yes. Please specify by writing the letter: b) no

(*Continued*)

(Cont.)

PLEASE ANSWER Q20–22 EVEN IF OVER THE LAST FIVE YEARS YOU HAVE NOT HAD ANY EXPERIENCE AS A PROFESSIONAL IN THE COMBINED USE OF MEDIATION AND ARBITRATION	
20. In your opinion, what are the main benefits to parties of using a combination of mediation and arbitration?	Please circle as many answers as are applicable a) faster resolution of their dispute (as compared to arbitration only) b) lower cost of resolution of their dispute (as compared to arbitration only) c) ability to preserve business relationship d) high quality of the outcome, i.e. the outcome of a dispute resolution process is more in line with parties' needs (as compared to arbitration only) e) possibility of obtaining an enforceable arbitral award f) no benefits g) other. Please specify:
21. Would you like to see more use of mediation and arbitration in combination for resolving international commercial disputes in the coming years?	a) yes b) no c) don't know Please provide a brief reason for your answer:
22. Would you be willing to participate in a follow up interview or survey?	a) yes. Please provide the following information: Name: Email address: Phone number: b) no
THANK YOU VERY MUCH FOR YOUR PARTICIPATION!	

Appendix 3
Semi-structured interview schedule

Mediation and arbitration can be combined in many different ways. They can be used in sequence, in parallel, and otherwise. If they are used in sequence it is possible for the combined process to start either with mediation or arbitration. Also, a combination of mediation and arbitration can be conducted either by the same or different neutrals.

Introductory questions

1 My first question refers to your own professional experience in the combined use of mediation and arbitration in the broad sense, which encompasses many different ways of combining these two processes. Could you please tell me about this?
2 Please tell me specifically about your own professional experience in the combined use of mediation and arbitration by the same neutral.
3 Has your attitude to the combined use of mediation and arbitration by the same neutral changed over time?

Questions on the substance of the research

1 Many articles address the benefits that the combined use of mediation and arbitration by the same neutral can offer to parties (in particular, the time- and cost-efficiency of the process). However, several empirical studies show that this process is rarely used in practice. How would you explain this phenomenon?
2 How do you deal with concerns related to the combined use of mediation and arbitration by the same neutral (in particular, those related to the use of caucuses) in your practice?
3 Do you think there is any harmonisation trend in the field of the combined use of mediation and arbitration? What about the use of a combination of mediation and arbitration by the same neutral?
4 What needs to be done, in your opinion, to enhance the use of a combination of mediation and arbitration in international commercial dispute resolution?

5 Imagine that there were an international enforcement mechanism for mediated settlement agreements. Do you think this attribute of mediation may make the combined use of mediation and arbitration less attractive to parties?

6 In your experience, what is the significance of the legal culture of counsel and neutral(s) for the way a combination of mediation and arbitration is conducted?

7 Is there anything you would like to add?

Index

www.ingramcontent.com/pod-product-compliance
Ingram Content Group UK Ltd.
Pitfield, Milton Keynes, MK11 3LW, UK
UKHW010955180926
475701UK00004B/387
* 9 7 8 0 3 6 7 5 8 9 1 1 0 *